Hinton Rowan Helper

The Three Americas Railway

An international and intercontinental enterprise, outlined in numerous formal

disquisitions and five elaborate essays

Hinton Rowan Helper

The Three Americas Railway
An international and intercontinental enterprise, outlined in numerous formal disquisitions and five elaborate essays

ISBN/EAN: 9783744752091

Printed in Europe, USA, Canada, Australia, Japan

Cover: Foto ©ninafisch / pixelio.de

More available books at **www.hansebooks.com**

THE
Three Americas Railway.

AN

INTERNATIONAL AND INTERCONTINENTAL ENTERPRISE,

OUTLINED IN

NUMEROUS FORMAL DISQUISITIONS

AND

FIVE ELABORATE ESSAYS;

ALL STRONGLY ADVOCATING FREE AND FAST AND FULL AND FRIENDLY
INTERCOMMUNICATION BETWEEN THE SIXTEEN ADJUNCTIVE
AND CONCORDANT REPUBLICS OF THE NEW WORLD.

BY

VARIOUS EARNEST AND CONFIDENT SUPPORTERS OF THE SCHEME; AMONG
WHOM ARE

HINTON ROWAN HELPER,
FRANK FREDERICK HILDER,
FREDERICK ANTHONY BEELEN,
WILLIAM WHARTON ARCHER,
FRANK DE YEAUX CARPENTER,
FRANCIS AUGUSTUS DEEKENS.

It is a greater credit to know the ways of captivating Nature, and making
her subserve our purposes, than to have learned all the intrigues of policy.
—GLANVILLE.

SAINT LOUIS:
W. S. BRYAN, PUBLISHER,
602 North Fourth Street.
NEW YORK: CHAS. T. DILLINGHAM, 678 Broadway.
SAN FRANCISCO: A. L. BANCROFT & CO., 721 Market Street.
CHICAGO: WILLARD A. SMITH, 182 and 184 Dearborn Street
NEW ORLEANS: GEORGE ELLIS, 7 Decatur Street.
1881.

PREFACE.

(See also the INTRODUCTION.)

STIMULATED by the conviction that the continental portions of the Western Hemisphere are destined to attain a lofty end, the Americans will continue to prove themselves true to the line of high endeavors.— *Count Gasparin.*

ACCEPTING it as an admitted fact that the transcendently multifarious and important considerations at stake justify us, over and over again, in determining that the projected Three Americas Railway ought to be built, must be built, and will be built, the momentous question arises, How shall this im-- mense New World undertaking be most expeditiously and prudently accomplished? Shall the work be done by a nationally and internationally incorporated private company, or by the concerted and concentrated action of the governments of an unbroken series of sixteen of the most stately republics that the wisdom and virtues of the noblest specimens of mankind have ever yet framed upon the earth? The latter view commends itself, in a very strong and special manner, to my own approbation. Nevertheless, I am quite willing, and not only willing, but even anxious and solicitous, to consider attentively every thoughtfully conflicting opinion which may be advanced upon this point. For, whether the road shall be built under the immediate direction and supervision of governmental engineers and other appointees in uniform, or whether it shall be constructed under the equally competent and meritorious forces in unofficial circles, which are so easily organizable into corps of efficient operators among the democratic masses of every well-ordered republic, is perhaps only a matter of mere theoretical or fancied importance.

With unflagging tenacity and intensity of remembrance, let the fact be constantly borne in mind that correspondence between merchants and others always seeks the safest and speediest route of transmission; and further, that trade and travel have an indestructible tendency to follow, as directly and closely as possible, in the track of the forward-hastening mailbag. The same means—the grandest of all the grand trunk railways—which will secure to us rapid and frequent communication with Central and South America, will also, very soon afterward, secure to us the bulk of the trade and travel of those naturally rich and magnificent countries. I am personally acquainted with many merchants in the Argentine Republic, Chili, and other portions of our sister continent, who, contrary to their sympathies and desires in most respects, do no business at all with the United States, because, if they write to New York, to New Orleans, or to any one of our other great commercial cities, their letters are first taken to England, to France, to Germany, or to some other European country; and thence, after many zigzag turnings and delays, if not detentions, they are dispatched a second time across the Atlantic, in more or less circuitous courses, toward their respective destinations. In this way six or seven weeks ordinarily elapse before the letters reach the persons to whom they are respectively addressed; and the same length of time, on an average, is required to return answers; so that a period of from three to four months is thus unavoidably consumed in obtaining information in relation to the price or shipment of any article of merchandise, or in reference to any other matter or thing whatever. The incalculable disadvantage

to ourselves in this discreditably imperfect postal intercourse, is almost wholly attributable to our culpable apathy,
or lack of foresight, in not establishing—as the governments and peoples of Europe long since established—lines
of steamships to the various commonwealths of South and
Central America. Yet what we have lost in that respect,—
and our losses of all kinds, from first to last, have been so
enormous as actually to defy computation,—may in great
measure be retrieved by an early construction and prudent
operation of the proposed Three Americas Railway.
Thereby only, in regard to commerce and manufactures,
can we ourselves be saved; and thereby only, in respect to
the same important interests, and otherwise, can salvation
ever be attained beyond peradventure by our fifteen con-
natural and companionable republics.

For the improvement and convenience of the commerce
of the world in general, it is especially desirable to secure, as
soon as possible, the cutting of a ship canal across one of the
three isthmuses of Central America, at Darien, at Nicaragua, or at Tehuantepec; but for the proper promotion of
our own commercial and manufacturing interests, and for a
judicious extension of those interests among the various
nationalities of Spanish America, the projected intercontinental railway may be rightly considered as absolutely indispensable. When built, the workings and influences of
this road will be found to be essentially for the mutual
benefit of all· concerned. Likewise reciprocally helpful to
each other will be the longitudinal railway itself and the
interoceanic canal; each will continually administer to the
wants of the other, in things to eat, things to drink, and
things to wear; in a thousand and one ways will the five
well-defined senses of man be whetted and pleased; and,
for all time to come, these two matchless monuments of
civil and utilitarian engineering will, by the diversified and

profitable business which they will ceaselessly stimulate within the world-wide sphere of home-life industry, act as effective repressers of the spirit of war, and successful strengtheners of the aspirations for peace.

Respecting the particular route which should be selected for the road, that question need not now be seriously discussed. Still, so far at least as the United States are concerned, I have a very decided preference for a perfectly direct track all along down the twenty-eighth degree of longitude west from Washington, corresponding to the one hundred and third degree of longitude west from Greenwich, from the southern boundary of British America to the northern frontier of Mexico. The line thus indicated, from which I would only with reluctance deviate so much as a hairbreadth, either to the right hand or to the left, but would follow with such exactitude that the roadbed, from the extreme north to the extreme south of our own republic, would be as rectilineal as the straightest street in the most quadrangular city, intersects Dakota, Nebraska, Colorado, New Mexico, and the western part of Texas. There bridging and crossing the Rio Grande, I would proceed in an equally uncurved course, that is to say, a bee-line, to the City of Mexico; thence as nearly midland as might be found most advisable, through Guatemala and the other Central American republics, to the Isthmus of Darien; thence into South America, passing eastward of the Andes, felling the forests and furrowing up the surfaces of Columbia, Ecuador, Eastern Peru, and Bolivia; and thence, in a nearly straight line, to Rosario, Buenos Ayres, and such other important points in the Argentine Republic as the present needs of postal facilities and trade and travel may demand.

What is meant to be accomplished by this effort is something of infinitely greater extent and value than an Appian

Way, an Aurelian Road, an Ostian Turnpike, a Simplon Passage, or a Macadamized Thoroughfare; something indeed of incomparably more magnitude and importance than all of the so-called Seven Wonders of the World, even when those astonishing structures are considered by the totality of their amazing merits; for, after all, how very local and circumscribed in their usefulness were the Colossus of Rhodes, the Temple of Diana at Ephesus, the Statue by Phidias of the Olympian Jove on the banks of the Alpheus, the Artificial Gardens of Babylon, the Walls of the Assyrian Cities. the Pyramids of Egypt, and the Tomb of Mausoleus! Those massive and costly fabrics, and many others scarcely less imposing and expensive, afford superabundant proofs of the fact that the ancients knew how to do, and did, an extraordinary amount of unworthy work. An almost equally deplorable lack of good judgment is discernible in the superlative labors and achievements of mediæval times Then the people, having very properly finished with the folly of erecting huge walls, pyramids, statues, towers, temples and tabernacles, began—apparently because they were incapable of devising anything better to do—to squander their talents and energies in the upbuilding of cathedrals, pagodas, monuments, mosques, monasteries, nunneries, and convents.

Modern days have kindly imparted to us more rational views. Our perceptive and reflective faculties have been greatly enlarged by experience. The present times and circumstances are propitious. Not only is our vision honored and blessed with a sight of the promised land—America at large—and all the good things thereunto pertaining, but we have actually entered upon it, and are occupying and enjoying it as an inalienable home of peace and plenty and pleasure, and also as a priceless possession in perpetuity. 'Tis well. Let us move onward with courageous hearts and unswerving purposes until we shall reach and realize, in all their fullness of glory, the happy destinies which await us. Already are we endowed with the inestimable riches of the printing press, the electric telegraph, the magnetic needle, the steam engine, the cotton gin, the sewing machine, the planing mill, the diamond drill, the friction match, the electric light, the reaper, the mower, the telescope, the telephone, the photograph, the compressed powers of explosive agents, the group of anæsthetics, and at least a thousand other aidful inventions and discoveries, which are every hour diminishing the physical burdens and discomforts of mankind, and augmenting the intellectual solaces and sweets of domestic life. Among the later acquisitions to our splendid inheritance, are the Submarine Telegraph, the Atlantic and Pacific and Oroya Railroads, the Cenis and Gothard and Hoosac and Sutro Tunnels, the Erie and Chesapeake and Schuylkill and Suez Canals, the London and Liverpool Docks, the St. Louis Bridge, and the Mississippi Jetties.

Looming up in the heirship of unexampled power and rectitude, and all aglow with benevolent purposes, the immediate future promises to us the Dover and Calais Tunnel; the drainage of the Pontine Marshes; a Ship Canal at Darien, at Nicaragua, or at Tehuantepec; a similar dike across the Corinthian Isthmus; also a deep water-way between Bordeaux and Narbonne; a much more extensive reclamation of the Low Lands of Holland from the Zuyder Zee; the flooding of the greater portion of the Desert of Sahara with the waters of the Mediterranean; and the diversion of the Nile into its ancient channels, whereby vast areas of Egyptian swamp-lands, now producing little else than bulrushes and crocodiles, will be rendered arable and fruitful to a degree unsurpassed in any other region of the globe; and, though mentioned last in this connection, perhaps the first to be prosecuted to completion, and by far the greatest of all, if not immensly more important than all the others combined, is the Three Americas Railway.

Specifically is the enterprise here proposed an earnest appeal to the plain, practical common-sense of the peoples of sixteen American republics, whose better protection from monarchical and ecclesiastical enmities and machinations, and whose own proper development and aggrandizement, are the more than ample incentives to its early consummation. In some respects, and for their own sakes especially, a conventional and peaceful reduction, by territorial enlargement, of the number of republics in Central and South America, would doubtless be very desirable. Instead of fifteen, might not three, or five, or at most seven, be quite sufficent? Madison, in one of his excellent papers in the Federalist, wherein he so clearly defines the fundamental differences which exist between republics and democracies, says substantially, and says truly, that the principles of government underlying a wisely constituted republic, rightly administered, may, by the admirable provisions for able and equable representation, be made to apply to a whole continent as easily as to a county; whereas, on the other hand, a democracy, in the strictest sense, is confined to the small circuit within which one's voice, when speaking in public, may be heard, and whose voice, having been so heard, may there and then be acted upon by the majority of listeners, voting *viva voce*, approvingly or dissentingly. It is sincerely hoped that our esteemed neighbors and friends in Spanish America may take such correct and good-natured views of these suggestions as may be most conducive to their own best interests.

Because of these frequent allusions and distinct references to republican Spanish America, while saying nothing at all in relation to monarchical Portuguese America, it may not be supposed that I have entirely forgotten bigoted and

benighted Brazil; priest-ridden and prelate-polluted Brazil;
slavery-sustaining and progress-retarding Brazil; negro-
cursed and hybrid-blasted Brazil. By no means. Baleful
and beggarly Brazil has already been one of the geographical subjects of my introspection; and besotted and be-
grimed Brazil shall again (and again and again, if necessary,) be the recipient of my earnest attention,—with an in-
ward-growing and ever-glowing purpose on my part to
elucidate certain exceedingly important facts, which, duly
considered, may be of signal service in helping to convert
the Black Empire of Alcantara-Braganza into the White
Republic of Brazil. Superstitious ecclesiasticism and dynas-
tic dictatorship have depressed Brazil down to the distress-
ful condition of a mediæval despotism. Democracy and
republicanism will ere long elevate Brazil up to a plane of
liberty and enlightenment commensurate with the highest
statehood of the nineteenth century. Toward the close of
this volume, under the chapter or section headed *Brazil's
Perfidious Forfeiture of Friendly Regard*, may be found
some of the weighty reasons why I regard macaronic and
monarchic Brazil as totally unworthy to be associated with
the noble network of American republics in the honors and
emoluments of solving successfully the mighty problems
connected with the Three Americas Railway.

Whether our co-republican neighbors and friends in
Spanish America shall peacefully and prudently determine
to aggregate themselves, under conventional proceedings or
otherwise, into fewer and grander nationalities, as, by virtue
of their animate existence in these latter days of the nineteenth century, it would seem they ought to be anxious
and able to do; or whether they shall prefer to remain members respectively of more than a dozen comparatively diminutive and discordant commonwealths, it is certain, in
either case, that they should immediately cease forever their

sanguinary strifes. In lieu of constantly struggling to obtain the mastery over each other, to the irreparable injury of both their enemies and themselves, let them, with all integrity and fidelity, enter at once into bonds of perpetual amity, and henceforth, conjointly with ourselves, seeking adjustment by arbitration of all grave international differences, seek also dominion over Nature, which has the singularly forgiving and beneficent habit of compensating every vigorous and discreet stroke upon her face with peace and plenty and pleasure. At any rate, let it be distinctly stipulated—and let the stipulation be observed with all the probity characteristic of men of the highest honor—that, in no event whatever, shall there be any more war in any one of the New World republics until after the Three Americas Railway shall have been completed and put in operation. Thenceforward, healthfully and happily busied with the diversified employments of agriculture, manufactures, commerce and other civil pursuits, all good citizens will find their private vocations so infinitely more profitable and respectable than fighting, that they will probably never again feel the slightest inclination to renew the deadly conflicts of former periods.

Yet, though the sword and the whole arsenal of firearms and other death-dealing artillery, throughout republican America, may at once be dispensed with, a lawful and intelligent exercise of the ballot should never be neglected. On this point it is well to be very positive and very persistent, within the bounds of a spirit of ready acquiescence in the will of the majority fairly expressed. Steadfastly entertaining these views, let us vote hereafter,—in the Argentine Republic as in the United States, in Chili as in Mexico, in Uruguay as in Guatemala, in Paraguay as in Honduras, in Bolivia as in Salvador, in Peru as in Nicaragua, in Ecuador as in Costa Rica, in Columbia as in Venezuela,—let us vote in the future, whether for Presidents, for Senators, for Representatives, for Governors, or for whatever other high officers of State, let us henceforth, regardless of any peculiarities of nomenclature in political parties, vote only for such able and excellent civilians as shall have previously pledged themselves in the most unequivocal manner to do everything in their power to secure, for postal and commercial purposes, for international courtesies and contingencies, and for social intercourse and other measures of mutual advantage, an early and perfect construction of the contemplated Three Americas Railway.

Of the five prize essays elicited in elucidation and support of the projected Three Americas Railway, what shall be said on this occasion? Am I pleased with the papers? Do they fill out the measure of my desires, my hopes and my expectations in this regard? I am more than pleased; I am delighted. A few weeks before the Committee of Examination and Award announced its final decision as to the relative merits of the respective disquisitions, one of its members, Mr. Greeley, did me the honor to congratulate me on the fact that I was soon to receive some of the best writings, according to his opinion, that he had ever read upon any subject whatever; and all of them together, as he thought and remarked, were so good that many citizens of a peculiarly enterprising and progressive turn of mind would be well repaid by coming, even from the remotest parts of the United States, all the way to St. Louis, simply to peruse the series, provided they could not obtain and read it without incurring that personal inconvenience. About the same time, another member of the Committee, Mr. Allen, assured me that, after all the awards should be made, there would still remain at least six or eight papers of such marked ability that he himself would like to see them published. Prof. Morgan, the third member of the Committee, stated in effect that he had discovered in the essays advocating the scheme, a fund of interest and instruction of which he had not previously formed any adequate conception. All the papers thus referred to are herewith published; and each, when consulted, will freely and frankly answer for itself. These papers I heartily commend to the careful consideration of such of my well-meaning and thougthful countrymen as may wish success to the unparalleled international improvment in special furtherance of which the documents were written.

With reference to the particular impressions which the perusal of these several essays produced on my own mind, I may say, with perfect candor, that when I first read Maj. Hilder's paper, I was so entirely gratified with it that I experienced much reluctance in taking up the next, fearing its merits might fall far below that sturdy standard of excellence. Before finishing Col. Beelen's paper, it seemed to me to be even better than Maj. Hilder's. Mr. Archer's was then perused, and I felt at least half persuaded that it was abler than Col. Beelen's. Next came Mr. Deekens', which, for the time, really impressed me as being the best of all the prose compositions. Nevertheless, I am well satisfied that the able and honorable Committee acted with good judgment in placing these successful essays in their allotted rank of merit; a verdict which I doubt not will be substantially confirmed by the public. In poetry,—Mr. Deekens, with my approbation, having substituted his Essay for his Poem,—Mr. Carpenter, a veritable son of Apollo and one of the Sacred Nine, has the field all to himself. How excellently well he and his Pegasus have occupied their time and opportunities within the precincts of Parnassus, will appear upon a dozen or so of the following pages. Nor is it in the least surprising that all these writers wrote so well; the subject itself having put them at their very best. Fairly dealt with, it is a subject that never fails to elevate and improve its votaries, whether they confine themselves exclusively within the spaces of mere thought, or whether they also employ their faculties and energies within the still more manly spheres of action.

H. R. H.

SAINT LOUIS, MISSOURI, May 17, 1881.

INTRODUCTION.

THE utility of the enterprise was so great and so obvious that all opposition proved futile.—*Macaulay.*

MR. HELPER TO CHANCELLOR ELIOT.

ST. LOUIS, *July 11, 1879.*

DR. WM. G. ELIOT,

Chancellor of Washington University, St. Louis, Mo.

DEAR SIR: Whilst you and your able corps of coadjutors of Washington University and its associate institutions of learning are accomplishing so much in the development of the intellectual, ethic and artistic interests of this broad, busy and beautiful city, I, working in a less elevated sphere, have projected an enterprise which looks confidently to the unparalleled growth and grandeur of its material greatness. For the further nurturing and final consummation of this enterprise, however, the early and earnest co-operation with me of three gentlemen, who are more or less familiar with the best methods of constructing and managing railroads, is now desirable.

An almost total stranger in St. Louis, and having come here especially for the purpose of promoting and carrying out, so far as it may be possible for me to do so, the important scheme alluded to above, I take the liberty to request of you the names of three gentlemen, such as I have thus indicated the wish to meet; gentlemen only of integrity, foresight and energy, whose largeness of mind and liberality of views will enable them to judge fairly and act wisely in regard to a project of uncommon magnitude, which involves very strong probabilities of both private gain and public advantage; a project in the inception and furtherance of which I have already, as an individual, spent much time and labor and money, and am willing and prepared to spend more.

It is only the names, as requested, and not a letter of introduction, that I seek by this note; for I am quite disposed to rely exclusively on my business itself, when explained, to introduce me fitly to the three gentlemen with whose address you may be pleased to favor me, and whose character and qualifications will, I trust, prove worthy of your best thoughts and designation in this connection.

One who, like yourself, as a constant friend and assistant, has stood steadily and manfully by St. Louis during a period of forty-five years, seeing her, in the youth and flush and pride and pomp of her prospective aggrandizement, gradually yet rapidly increase from a town of only five thousand inhabitants, to a metropolis with a population of nearly half a million, and who is well acquainted with a large number of her estimable citizens in every honorable vocation, can, I dare say, easily give me the names of just three superior local railroad men; and by doing me personally the little service thus solicited, you will also, it is hoped and believed, be doing an additional service to the great Central City of the Mississippi Valley.

Yours, most respectfully,

H. R. HELPER.

CHANCELLOR ELIOT TO MR. HELPER.

WASHINGTON UNIVERSITY, ST. LOUIS, *July 12, 1879.*
H. R. HELPER, ESQ.,

DEAR SIR: In compliance with your request, I give, in the inclosed list, the names of several gentlemen, who are, in every respect, well qualified to aid you in any enterprise undertaken for the public good. If needful, many others can be found; but I confidently hope that those now named will cheerfully consent to co-operate with you in your great work, and am sure that no better selection could possibly be made. Wishing to you and them all manner of success, and thanking you for the opportunity of rendering this service,

I have the honor to remain, very respectfully, yours,

W. G. ELIOT.

MR. HELPER TO BANK PRESIDENT BURNHAM.

ST. LOUIS, *July 18, 1879.*
CYRUS B. BURNHAM, ESQ.,
President of the Bank of Commerce, St. Louis, Missouri.

DEAR SIR: Of the money which you now hold in deposit to my credit, I desire to place in the hands of a local committee of three gentlemen of sterling integrity and clear-headedness, an obligation for the sum of five thousand dollars, payable to their joint order, or to the order of their chairman, on the first day of December of next year, 1880, to be then expended by them in obtaining, severally, five of the best attainable essays in English, three in prose and two in poetry, in advocacy of the early construction of a longitu-

I

dinal midland double-track steel railway through North and Central and South America, from a point on or near the western shore of Hudson Bay to such part of the northern bank of the Strait of Magellan as may be measurably equidistant between the Atlantic and Pacific Oceans.

To this end,—and I trust that the object is one which you and all eminently worthy and progressive Americans may be pleased to approve and promote,—I have to request that you will, to-day or to-morrow, issue to my order, payable, as already mentioned, on the first day of December of next year, 1880, a certificate of deposit, a note, or such other form of indebtedness binding on your admirably and excellently managed bank as you yourself may deem most convenient and proper, and which it is my purpose to use only in the manner indicated above, as will soon be more minutely and elaborately explained in a printed volume, the manuscript of which will be ready for publication a few weeks hence. Yet, until the time of the actual forthcoming of the book from the press, I indulge the hope that you will so far befriend both the enterprise and its projector as to say nothing whatever on the subject, to any person whomsoever, excepting only, at your own option, to your discreet and estimable Cashier, Mr. Van Blarcom.

Yours, most respectfully,

H. R. HELPER.

BANK PRESIDENT BURNHAM TO MR. HELPER.

BANK OF COMMERCE, ST. LOUIS, *July 19, 1879.*

H. R. HELPER, ESQ.,

DEAR SIR: As requested in your letter of yesterday, I herewith inclose to your order a certificate of deposit in this bank for five thousand dollars, payable on the first day of December, 1880; which certificate can be used for the purpose and in the manner designed by you. The enterprise outlined in your letter is of such magnificent conception, and also of such grand proportions, that it cannot, when once your plans shall be made public, fail to attract the attention and critical examination of all thoughtful and practical Americans; and I trust that the feasibility of your projected improvements may be demonstrated by substantial completion within a reasonable period of time.

I am, very respectfully, yours,

C. B. BURNHAM.

MR. HELPER TO A COMMITTEE OF THREE.

ST. LOUIS, *July 25, 1879.*

TO THE HON. THOMAS ALLEN,
President of the Iron Mountain and Southern Railway;
CARLOS S. GREELEY, ESQ.,
Receiver of the Kansas Pacific Railway; and
DR. WM. T. HARRIS,
Superintendent of Public Instruction,

GENTLEMEN: The occasion of my presuming to address to you this communication is what I have myself long regarded as a perfectly practical enterprise, of unequaled magnitude and transcendent importance, to which, through your own able and honorable selves, as a committee of three men, I now desire to enlist at once the attention and active co-operation of the multitudinous peoples of three Americas. The object thus aimed at is nothing less than the earliest possible construction of a longitudinal midland double-track steel railway, from a point high north in North America, running more or less southwardly through Mexico and Central America, to a point far south in South America ; looking ultimately to such necessary and gradual extensions at either end, from time to time, as will eventually place Behring Strait and Cape Horn, and all the intermediate localities, in uninterrupted and continuous overland communication by steam and by telegraph.

My views on this subject will appear somewhat elaborately in a book, not wholly devoted to this scheme, however, which I intend to publish in the course of the next two or three months; * and in order to prove conclusively my own earnestness and confidence in the matter, I herewith inclose a certificate of deposit for five thousand dollars in the Bank of Commerce of St. Louis, payable to your joint order, or to the order of any two of you, on the first day of December of next year, 1880; the said money to be then expended by you in obtaining five of the most convincing and meritorious essays which may be offered meanwhile, three in prose and two in poetry, in truthful and vigorous and effective advocacy of the undertaking.

Your particular names have been cordially and emphatically recommended as representing three gentlemen whose unquestioned probity, public spirit, mental capacity, and financial responsibility are all that could be reasonably wished or expected in such a council of safety and critical judgment and award as I am now seeking; and I am therefore emboldened to express the sincere hope and request that

---

* The book here alluded to, entitled "Oddments of Andean Diplomacy," has since been published by Mr. Wm. S. Bryan, No. 602 North Fourth street, St. Louis, Missouri; the same Publisher whose imprint appears on the title-page of this volume. That book contains nearly five hundred pages, and is largely devoted to a history of the claims of certain citizens of the United States against the governments respectively of Peru, Bolivia and Brazil.

you may all be pleased to give your consent to act together as a potent and permanent committee in this connection. Should you all consent accordingly, please consider yourselves as at once constituted into such a committee, for the purpose specifically mentioned above; and retaining to yourselves the certificate of deposit, already endorsed to your order, advise me of your acceptance of the trust, and also of your readiness to receive and adjudge whatever manuscripts may be submitted for your perusal and approbation. Also be kind enough to designate immediately one of yourselves as the Chairman of your committee, giving his exact postal address, and stating that all essays and communications bearing upon this project, and being prepaid, should be sent to him by express or by mail, wholly at the expense and risk of the sender.

For the proper information and guidance of all concerned, I propose to publish, as an essential part of my book itself, so far as it treats of The Three Americas Intercontinental Railway, both this communication and your reply, in orderly juxtaposition. In making the certificate of deposit payable to your joint order, or to the order of any two of you, I have very plainly indicated my wish that, in the absence at any time, from whatever cause, of any one of you, the other two shall constitute a competent and legal quorum, whose proceedings shall be as absolutely valid and final as if all three of you had acted in concert; and whether any one of your committee shall ever be absent or not, when the other two shall meet, it is my sense of right and propriety that the expressed opinions and predilections of the majority of two out of three shall always be recognized as the governing voice, and govern accordingly I trust, however, that the peerless enterprise itself may never suffer for the lack of the triple wisdom and power which all three of you, acting harmoniously together, will

be able to bring to it in any particular situation or contingency.

It is my desire, and I make it a condition-accordingly,
that all the writings of whatever nature, without a single
exception, which may be offered for prizes in this literary
and patriotic contest, shall be conveyed into your hands not
later than the first day of October of next year, 1880 ; and
you may now, if you like, completely release yourselves in
advance from the labor of examining any composition, under any circumstances, which may reach you after that date.
Two months subsequently, that is to say, on the first day of
December following, you will please make publication of
the names of the successful competitors, and on that very
same day, or just as soon thereafter as you may find it convenient to do so, you will please pay them, by means of cer-
tified checks on the Bank of Commerce, of this city, in
sums respectively, without interest, as follows :

For the best treatise in prose,   -   -   - $1,300
For the second best treatise in prose,   - -   1,200
For the third best treatise in prose,   - -   1,000
For the best effort in poetry, -   -   -   -   1,000
For the next best effort in poetry,   - -   500
_____

Total,   -   -   -   •   -   - $5,000

Other conditions which I make absolutely, and to which
I would here respectfully and especially invite the attention
of all the competitors for any one of the proffered prizes,
are these : No essay in prose must contain more than one
hundred pages of closely written cap paper, nor less than
sixty-six ; and neither of the two poems provided for must
contain more than five hundred lines, nor less than three
hundred and thirty-three. All the writings in the hands of
your committee, to whose authors prizes shall be awarded,
are at once to become the sole and exclusive property of

myself individually, and will be immediately published altogether in one volume, with any such additions, abridg-
ments or emendations as I myself may deem it prudent to
make. All essays which fail to receive prizes may be reclaimed by their respective authors on transmitting to the
chairman of your committee the small amount of money
that will defray the usual expenses of expressage or postage. It might be best for the various competitors respectively to do this at the very time of submitting their writings
for the examination and adjudgment of your committee.
This is a point which they themselves will settle, each for
himself, at his own option. Every author should keep a
press copy or other copy of his composition; and such
extra copy may, at any time, be demanded by your committee.

The several prizes thus offered may be striven for and
achieved by emulous citizens anywhere resident within the
universal Republic of Letters, which, like one of the grandest and most precious parts that compose it, the Republic
of the United States of America, is, in all things, character-
ized by fairness and justice and liberality. It is only required that all the papers which may be submitted for examination and award, shall be so written or translated as to
appear legibly in the English language.

Doubting not that your committee will be honored with
many very interesting and valuable contributions in competition, neither do I permit myself to doubt in the least that
you will constantly exercise such diligence and discretion as
will result in the strictest and fullest justice, alike to the
special object in view and to the various contestants for
prizes. It may be well supposed that the writers who will
succeed in winning both reputation and remuneration in
this respect are probably those who will detach themselves
most completely from every species of flippancy and

frivolity, from everything like superficiality and insincerity, and dive down deep into irrefragable and imperishable facts and arguments, and who will then, on the one hand at least, on the side of poesy, elevate themselves to the loftiest heights of sublime ideas and ennobling sentiments and expressions, whereby they may rightfully and triumphantly captivate the head, fascinate the heart, and enrapture the soul.

It is hoped that such an intense earnestness and enthusiasm may be awakened throughout all the countries from Alaska to Patagonia, inclusive, as will lead to the granting of all the requisite governmental guarantees and privileges and charters, by or before the 14th of October, 1882; so that the vast enterprise may be actually begun not later than that day; and that at least one hundred and fifty thousand strong-armed and cheerful-hearted laborers may soon afterward be given work on the various sections of the line, and, by fair wages and just treatment, induced to continue their wealth-creating and civilizing exertions, without any unusual interruption, until the whole undertaking, in its longest and broadest and best conceptions, shall be substantially and gloriously finished for all future ages. Seven years at most ought to suffice for the completion of this grandest and best of all the grand and good highways of the New World. The lapse of that period will find us facing the 14th of October, 1889. Three years later will take us to the four hundreth anniversary of the discovery of America. Let us be prepared to mark and honor that anniversary—a veritable index to one of the most conspicuous and momentous epochs in human affairs—let us welcome and signalize that superlative anniversary in St. Louis, by holding here, at that time, the largest and most splendid and imposing World's Fair that has ever been held on the earth; an exhibition at which shall be especially and fully represented the people, the products, the fauna, the flora, and the minerals of every American nation between the Arctic and Antarctic Seas and the Atlantic and Pacific Oceans.

That St. Louis, already the most prosperous and progressive city in the great Valley of the Mississippi, the very heart and center of the continent of North America, for railroading and steamboating, and for travel and trade and manufactures and business of almost every kind, and probably destined, within the next hundred years, to outnumber in inhabitants the combined population of New York and Philadelphia—that this wonderfully thrifty and expanding metropolis, so unmistakably betokening for itself a surpassing and transcendent future, is now, and will continue to be, the fittest possible place for such a matchlessly magnificent exhibition as I have here suggested, may be further and more fully inferred from the following pointed opinions expressed, on different occasions, by half a dozen uncommonly foreseeing and discerning men of great national renown. Nor, in the light of the astonishing acquisitions and tendencies of to-day, is it at all unreasonable to believe that the year 1979 will find St. Louis a far more numerously inhabited city than either London or Paris, if indeed it shall not then, or soon afterward, be even more populous and thrifty and progressive than both of those leading European capitals considered as one.

On the 4th of February, 1870, my old friend Horace Greeley, one of the ablest and truest and best men I have ever known, writing from the office of his Tribune, in New York, to L. U. Reavis, Esq., at St. Louis, said: " I have twice seen St. Louis in the middle of winter. Nature made her the focus of a vast region, embodying a vast area of the most fertile soil on the globe. Man will soon accomplish her destiny by rendering her the seat of an immense industry, the home of a far-reaching, ever-expanding commerce. Her gait is not so rapid as that of some of her Western sisters; but she advances steadily and surely to her predestined station of first inland city on the globe."

In the course of a letter written at Boston, under date of July 24, 1863, and addressed to Dr. Wm. G. Eliot, Chancellor of Washington University in St. Louis, Edward Everett, whose name is eminently worthy to be held in love and veneration by every American citizen, said: "The future is, of course, veiled in darkness; but when I consider your central position and your means of communication in every direction, nothing seems to me more probable than that, by the end of this century, St. Louis will be the metropolis of the Union."

Replying under date of July 16, 1875, to a letter from L. U. Reavis, Esq.,—himself an indefatigable and excellent worker in the interest of a great and growing city, a gentleman with whom I regret that I have not yet had an opportunity to become acquainted—Gen. Wm. T. Sherman said: "I have every faith in the future of St. Louis, and have in fact shown my sincerity by making it my home, and the future home of my family."

Charles Sumner, to whom the vigorous and unlimited growth of the West was always a matter of wonder and admiration, wrote as follows: "St. Louis alone would be an all-sufficient theme; for who can donbt that this prosperous metropolis is destined to be one of the mighty centers of our mighty republic?"

In his usually frank and glowing style, James Parton, the distinguished author, speaks thus: "Fair St. Louis, the future capital of the United States, and of the civilization of the Western Continent."

While delivering a speech in St. Louis, a few years since, Gen. Benjamin F. Butler said: * * * "I also remem-

ber that I am now in the city of St. Louis, destined erelong
to be the greatest city on the continent; the greatest central point between the East and the West, at once destined
to be the entrepot and depot of all the internal commerce
of the greatest and most prosperous country the world has
ever seen. * * * The next quarter of a century shall
see a larger population west of the Mississippi than the last
quarter of a century saw east of the Mississippi; and the
city of St. Louis, from its central location, and through the
vigor, the energy, the industry and the enterprise of its inhabitants, shall become the very first city of the United
States of America, now and hereafter destined to be the
greatest republican nation of the world."*

---

* These high and glowing testimonies to the superior natural advantages of St. Louis are well merited; but for even the best communities
Nature will do only so much—and no more; communities themselves
must do something. In the incomparable advantages which she conferred upon portions of Chesapeake Bay, Nature offered to Virginia
the principal seat of maritime commercial greatness in the New World;
but in consequence of the deleterious presence of Africans and African
slavery south of the Susquehanna, those advantages were completely
neutralized in the interest of exclusively European-peopled New York.
The last census, the census of 1880, shows plainly enough, that white
Chicago, like Boston, New York, Philadelphia, and other great and
glorious white cities of the North, is, as a matter of course, leaving
black and bi-colored St. Louis in the lurch. So, in the main, it has always been, and so it will ever be. The elements of brainless inertia
and darkness which make up Abomey and Timbuctoo, are very different from those of intellectual energy and light which compose London
and Paris. St. Louis, constantly preyed upon and pressed downward
by twenty thousand deadweights from Congo and Guinea,—when only
one such direful drawback would be precisely one too many,—can
never cope with any community made up exclusively, or almost
exclusively, by fair-faced demigods of the Aryan race. The
crow is a bird, but it is not an eagle; the mosquito is an
insect, but it is not a butterfly; the stickleback is a fish, but
it is not a salmon; and the ass is a beast of burden, but it is not

Not one of the foregoing opinions—four of which, significantly enough, are from far-sighted and far-famed New
Englanders—had ever come to my knowledge prior to my
arrival in St. Louis for the first time, only a few months
since. My attraction to the city was solely by its geographical position. A mere glance at the map was sufficient to
convince me that it was the most central and convenient
point in the United States from which I could operate, under a combination of really propitious circumstances, in
the initiation and furtherance of my gigantic scheme. For
a very brief period the city of Mexico, as a sort of imperfectly discerned yet friendly rival to St. Louis, laid passable
claim to my attention in this regard ; but the instability of
the government of the Mexican Republic, and the comparatively inadequate resources, in both men and means,
there existing for the organization of ample physical and
financial forces for the prosecution and accomplishment
of any great civil or secular undertaking, induced me, with
scarcely one serious thought to the contrary, to give St. Louis
the preference. Yet, if the unrivaled intercontinental railway here proposed shall be built according to the general

---

a horse. The dogwood is a tree, but it is not an oak; the night-
shade is a plant, but it is not a rosebush ; the garlic is a vegetable, a
bulbous root, but it is not an onion ; the crab is a fruit, an apple, but
it is not a pippin; and the thistle-blossom is a flower, but it is not a
tulip. Metals, like the stars, differ from each other in the glory of
their bulk and luster. In the very nature of things, lead can never be
burnished so bright, nor be rendered so valuable, as silver; nor does copper possess either the fineness or the tensibility of gold. Beauteous
and lovely Chicago is, with all meetness and good fortune, the daugh-
ter of purely white parents; who, besides, were always as free and
brave and worthy as they were white. I offer to her all that remain
unpledged of both my hand and my heart ; her resplendent virtues having challenged and received my unfeigned admiration.

                                                        H. R. H.

plans and specifications outlined in my book, it may be conceded as certain that the City of Mexico, and the whole Republic of Mexico, as also all the chief cities and republics through which the road will pass, will, with peace and good government firmly established and maintained among them, soon assume proportions of population, prosperity and progress hitherto but barely contemplated even by their most sanguine supporters.

Well conducted and wisely managed, and fully protected by national and international compacts, from the dangers of undue interference by revolutionary factions, this road of roads, this great Northern and Southern backbone, from which Eastern and Western ribs will eventually radiate by scores and by hundreds, conveying an exuberance of new life and energy and hope and blessing to tens of millions of happy human beings, ought in time to be worth three thousand millions of dollars to North America, the same amount to South America, and fifteen hundred millions, more or less, to Mexico and Central America. Of these vast valuations and earnings, St. Louis and other portions of Missouri ought to be the recipients, from first to last, of one hundred millions or more; but these mere pecuniary estimates are meditative of only a material part of the advantages which may fairly be expected to flow from the colossal enterprise after it shall have been perfected. Every intellectual, moral, social, civil, political and industrial interest of mankind will be advanced; and, as an inevitable and delightful result of the æsthetic culture which will prevail, the most simple and unaffected amenities, elegancies, refinements and purities of life will everywhere increase and abound.

Such, gentlemen, are some of the herculean, yet wholesome and pleasurable tasks to the completion of which your valuable services are now craved and solicited.

Whether, by the methods here mentioned, it is in your power to contribute in any degree to the general well-being of the United States, and of the three Americas at large, I must now leave entirely to your own judgment and decision; only yet stopping long enough to repeat once more my respectful request, that you, all three of you, will kindly consent to use and expend the five thousand dollars herewith inclosed, in the manner explained above. Though you and I may plant and sow, and others, reaping the harvest with gladness and hilarity, may enjoy the fruits of our labors, yet who knows but that, in this very way, certain of our special duties may be best performed? Next will come an opportunity for the beneficiaries themselves, or for one or more of them, if so disposed, to do something of the kind, something of far greater importance, perhaps; and by constant and judicious action upon the principle thus recognized, our world, in the very nature of things—a world in itself not half so bad as many pessimists proclaim it—can never cease to grow brighter and better and more felicit-ous'y inhabitable for all diligent and right-doing people.

I am, gentlemen,

With sincere regard,

Yours, very truly,

H. R. HELPER.

THE COMMITTEE OF THREE TO MR. HELPER.

St. Louis, *September 25, 1879.*

H. R. Helper, Esq.

Dear Sir: Having returned to St. Louis from our respective summer resorts, we have the pleasure to acknowledge receipt of your communication of the 25th of July, inclosing to our joint order, or to the order of any two of us, a certificate of deposit for five thousand dollars, in the Bank of Commerce of this city, payable on the first day of December of next year, and which you request us to expend in a manner minutely explained by you, for the purpose of procuring five persuasive and convincing essays in advocacy of the early construction of a double-track longitudinal steel railway through North and Central and South America.

You have further paid us the compliment of nominating us a Three Americas Railway Committee, with full powers to the end proposed, and have requested us to name one of ourselves as the Chairman of our committee, to whom all competitive manuscripts may be sent for perusal and adjudgment.

We have maturely considered the substantial and business-like contents and bearing of your communication; and holding in view the gigantic and important objects sought to be accomplished, we scarcely feel ourselves at liberty to refuse to perform the service which you have so politely requested us to render in this connection. We therefore, in behalf of the grand enterprise itself, unreservedly accept the commission which you have given us; and hoping thereby to be able to contribute to the general good and advancement of our own and the adjoining continent, we shall cheerfully and gratuitously perform all the duties, as we understand them, which this acceptance implies. All writings which may be submitted to us, in competition for prizes as provided for by you, should be prepaid by mail or by express, and addressed to our Chairman as follows:

HON. THOMAS ALLEN,
President of the Iron Mountain and Southern Railway,
No. 1. North Fifth Street,
St. Louis,
Missouri.

It now only remains for us to give expression to our ardent hopes, braced by a high degree of confidence, that your dearest aims and expectations in this regard may be realized in all their magnitude and grandeur, within the time specifically mentioned by you—namely, the 14th of October, 1892, which, as you yourself have reminded us, will be the four hundredth anniversary of the discovery of America.

Yours, very respectfully,

WM. T. HARRIS.
CARLOS S. GREELEY.
THOMAS ALLEN.

RESIGNATION OF DR. HARRIS.

CONCORD, MASS., *August 12, 1880.*
HINTON R. HELPER, ESQ., *St. Louis, Mo.*

DEAR SIR: Up to this time I had constantly hoped to be of service in the Three Americas Railway Committee, on which you did me the honor to appoint me. To-day, however, I am greatly concerned with the thought that it will probably not be convenient for me to return from Europe soon enough to assist in the examination of the competitive papers, if they must be read and decided upon prior to the opening of the ensuing year. Therefore I write this to express my regret that my return to St. Louis, in January next, as now contemplated, will be too late for me to serve efficiently as a member of the committee.

Under these circumstances, it seems necessary and proper for me to resign. Though this action on my part, at this late date, may appear, and does appear, somewhat unfair to you and the cause, yet I am quite unable to perceive how to avoid it. Nevertheless, while I am compelled by my circumstances to write this letter of resignation, I am hopeful that it may not in any way interfere with the important ends you have in view. Assuring you of my hearty sympathy with your noble schemes, and acknowledging the gratification I have felt in being permitted to be associated with yourself and the two gentlemen who have served with me on the committee, in this enterprise, I am,

Yours, very respectfully,

WM. T. HARRIS.

MR. HELPER'S REPLY TO DR. HARRIS.

St. Louis, August 16, 1880.

Dr. Wm. T. Harris, *Concord, Mass.*

Dear Sir: Your letter of the 12th instant, resigning your position as one of the three members of the Three Americas Railway Committee, was received this morning; and I avail myself of this early opportunity to express my sincere regret that any circumstances, whether of prolonged and indefinite absence from St. Louis, or of whatever other nature, should have arisen in such way as to lead you irrevocably to this determination.

I fear it will not be an easy task for me to find another gentleman who will fill your place so well as you have filled it yourself. On this particular subject, however, I shall soon seek the counsel and advice of the other members of the Committee, Mr. Allen and Mr. Greeley, and hope, by their joint suggestion, to be able to appoint in your stead the best possible substitute. Perhaps you yourself might mention the name of one who would herein be your worthy successor.

. May your trip to Europe be one of both pleasure and improvement; and may you soon return to St. Louis deeply imbued, or rather reinvigorated, with the true principles of Education and Philosophy.

Yours, very truly,
H. R. HELPER.

APPOINTMENT OF PROF. MORGAN AS DR. HARRIS' SUCCESSOR.

St. Louis, August 27, 1880.

PROF. HORACE H. MORGAN,

Principal of the Saint Louis High School.

DEAR SIR: Dr. Wm. T. Harris, one of three members of the Three Americas Railway Committee, having gone to Europe, where he will travel and sojourn during the whole period of time that his services here, as a committeeman, would be especially needed, that is to say, during the next two or three months, or more, I have the honor to request that you will be so obliging as to permit me to substitute your name in place of his, and thereby re-perfect the complement of the said Committee.

Inclosed herewith, and bearing on the general subject of the proposed international and intercontinental railway, are several manuscript documents and printed papers, among which you will find a very polite letter of resignation from Dr. Harris himself.   You are at full liberty to retain for yourself all the printed matter, and you will please do so, with my compliments; but at the same time I would thank you to return to me the written documents.

The Hon. Thomas Allen, Chairman,   and Carlos S. Greeley, Esq., are the two able and worthy gentlemen with whom I should be glad to have you associated in this earnest effort for the development of more extensive and mutually advantageous interests, postal, commercial and social, with our many millions of neighbors and friends in Spanish America. Should you accept the position thus tendered,—as I sincerely hope you may consent to do,— you will please consider yourself invested at once with all the privileges, rights and powers which belonged to Dr. Harris anterior to the date of his resignation.

In conclusion, heartily congratulating you on the daring and distinguished honor of your having, as " a transmississippian competitor," (so designated by a merry Massachusetts critic,) but recently won for yourself a famous literary prize in the Athens of New England, in brain-abounding Boston itself,

I am, dear Sir,

Most respectfully yours,

H. R. HELPER.

PROF. MORGAN'S ACCEPTANCE.

St. Louis, *August 28, 1880.*

Hinton R. Helper, Esq.

Dear Sir: Giving immediate attention to your letter of yesterday, I have to inform you that, while I cannot doubt but that you might easily find, as Dr. Harris' successor, some one more worthy than myself, yet, as you intimate that your letter to me was occasioned by the suggestions of the other members of the Three Americas Railway Committee, I do not feel at liberty to oppose any feeling of unfitness on my own part to the preferences of gentlemen so well and favorably known as Mr. Allen and Mr. Greeley.

I therefore accept your invitation, and will take pleasure in rendering all possible services as a member of your committee of examination and award.

I remain, very respectfully,

Your obedient servant,

HORACE H. MORGAN.

AWARD OF PREMIUMS FOR FIVE ESSAYS.

REPORT FROM THE COMMITTEE TO MR. HELPER.

ST. LOUIS, *January 8, 1881.*

HINTON R. HELPER, ESQ.

DEAR SIR: In compliance with the request which you made of us, on the 25th of July, 1879, and to which, as a Committee, we acceded on the 25th of September following, we now have the honor to report the completion of the somewhat fatiguing and responsible but peculiar and interesting labors which your partiality imposed upon us. Forty-nine competitive essays and poems, written by forty-seven contestants for prizes, all ardently advocating the construction of the projected Three Americas Railway, were formally submitted for our examination and judgment; and from these forty-nine articles, after devoting to their contents a great amount of care and consideration, we have selected five, which we regard as superior to any of the others. Exercising the privileges and powers which you were pleased to confer upon us, we have, this day, awarded prizes and executed checks on the bank, to be forwarded to the several parties for the sums indicated, to wit:

1. Frank Frederick Hilder, St. Louis, Mo., Prose,   -   - $1,300
2. Frederick Anthony Beelen, Cortland on-Hudson, N. Y., Prose, 1,200
3. William Wharton Archer, Richmond, Va., Prose,   - - - 1,000
4. Frank DeYeaux Carpenter, Washington, D. C., Poetry, - 1,000
5. Francis Augustus Deekens, Norwich, Ontario, Canada, Poetry, 500

      Total,   -   -   -   - $5,000

With this report you will receive the five papers above mentioned. Conformably to your wishes, all the other papers will be immediately returned to their respective authors. Many of the forty-four competitive essays and poems which failed to impress us as being quite equal, in the force and excellence of their composition, to any one of the five herewith dispatched to you, are nevertheless very ably written ; and in some of them are ingeniously adduced numerous facts, arguments and suggestions, which, if judiciously published, would, we doubt not, aid very materially in carrying to the minds of hosts of able and good men, throughout all the Americas, a profound conviction of the vast importance of the unrivaled railway thus contemplated. We incline to the opinion that there are but few, if any, clear-headed thinkers, in this or any other country, who will arise from a careful perusal of the five successful papers which you have thus elicited, without giving a hearty assent to the general correctness of your own views in relation to this stupendous enterprise. It affords us great pleasure, therefore, to extend our warmest congratulations to yourself and the five successful competitors, who, by your liberal provision, have won honors and prizes, in being so earnestly and auspiciously engaged in the inauguration and prosecution of a work which promises such boundless benefits. We beg to add that we have been not only much interested, but greatly edified, in the perusal of the various papers submitted, and more deeply impressed than ever before with the great resources and inviting fields of Mexico, Central and South America.

Very respectfully, yours,

THOMAS ALLEN,
CARLOS S. GREELEY,
HORACE H. MORGAN.

———

MR. HELPER'S REPLY TO THE COMMITTEE.

ST. LOUIS, *January 10, 1881.*

HON. THOMAS ALLEN, *Chairman;*
CARLOS S. GREELEY, ESQ.; and
PROF. HORACE H. MORGAN;
   Constituting the Three Americas Railway Committee.

GENTLEMEN: The Report with which you have honored me, under date of the 8th instant, detailing all the necessary particulars of your award of prizes for three of the best attainable essays in prose, and two poems, on the subject of a longitudinal railway through the three Americas, has been received, and with it the five prize-papers themselves; for all of which I beg leave to tender to you my most thankful acknowledgments. I am well aware that your labors in this respect, so cheerfully and gratuitously rendered, have been rather wearisome. Yet, after much solicitude and consideration on my own part, it seemed to me that an invitation to you to take upon yourselves this very task, was the fairest and fittest means I could conveniently devise for the right accomplishment of the important object held in view; and it was only because I had myself devoted to the enterprise a great deal of time, labor and money, that I felt justified in requesting of you the special committee-work which you have so efficiently and satisfactorily performed.   Not only are both the 'successful and unsuccessful competitors richly entitled to praise in this contest; but you also, as a Committee, whose labors, though exceedingly difficult and trying, have yet been discharged with great assiduity and fidelity, are well worthy of encomium.   A friend in Ohio, from whom I received a letter, in the early part of last month, incidentally expressed the following opinion in regard to yourselves, and I heartily subscribe to the correctness of his sentiment: "I should think that the Committee of Examination and Award would be likely to conclude that they themselves will deserve all that prize money, and more perhaps, before they finish reading and weighing all those manuscripts."

As regards the genius and ability which may be displayed in any one or all of the five essays for which you have awarded premiums, I, as yet, of myself, know nothing, not having, up to the present moment, taken sufficient time to examine so much as the whole of a single page.   To-morrow morning, however, I shall begin a very thorough perusal of all the prize papers, not doubting that they will be found quite as satisfactory as I had anticipated or expected; for I feel perfectly convinced that the subject itself is infinitely superior to any treatment that the most gifted mortal may have bestowed upon it.   Were the first named of the worthy trio whom I have the honor of addressing a Bacon, the second a Burke, and the third a Shakspeare, and the mighty mental powers of all three were combined in one philosopher, in one statesman, or in one poet, yet would even that thrice-potent intellectual giant be too feeble to do even more than a mere fraction of justice to the triple considerations of possibilities and probabilities and certainties comprised in the scheme of constructing a grand longitudinal railway through the republics of North and Central and South America.   Further and finally, permit me

to assure you that I fully appreciate the friendly words of
encouragement contained in your Report, and that I sincerely hope you and I may all continue in life and health
long enough to participate in the festivities of the celebration of the completion of the Three Americas Railway; an
international and intercontinental improvement so largely
conceived in the interest of the whole Western Hemisphere.

Yours, very truly,

H. R. HELPER.

A WORD OF COMMENDATION AND ENCOUR-
AGEMENT FROM MR. HELPER FOR THE
FORTY-TWO THREE AMERICAS RAILWAY ES-
SAYISTS WHO HAVE NOT RECEIVED PRIZES.

St. Louis, Missouri, *January 10, 1881.*

My Friends: Though it may not be said that you have
won the victory, yet you have fought bravely and judiciously; and most of you are worthy of high praise. Triumph in other battles might be less honorable and less glorious than defeat in this; for, at the very worst, you have
yielded only to a temporary repulse. The principal object
at which you and I have been aiming, with all our might
and main, will, in due time, be skillfully encompassed and
accomplished. The Three Americas Railway will soon be
generally and justly regarded as an indispensable means to
the consummation of the predestined aggrandizement and
solidification of the interests of sixteen adjunctive republics; and it will be built accordingly, orderly and quickly,
under the indomitable energies so characteristic of the patriotic and powerful peoples who have evinced the requisite

wisdom and courage to free themselves from the trammels of ecclesiastical and monarchical misgovernment.

Your respective papers, valuable but unprized, are still your own property, and will be immediately returned to you, in strict compliance with your special desires and directions. Some of you have very kindly and generously offered to present your manuscripts to me; and most of you have honored me with an expression of the hope that I may, in any event, find ample time and inclination to read your writings before they shall be sent back to you. Greatly to my regret, however, for the next three or four months at least, I shall be much too busy to do myself the pleasure and the benefit of perusing any of your disquisitions; and for this reason I have requested the polite and accommodating Chairman of the Committee, (who, like the Committee in general, has already been excessively taxed with labor and loss of time in this undertaking,) to return to you at once, at my expense,—provided any of you forgot to make the necessary provision for that contingency,—all the unaccepted manuscripts found in his charge after making awards of prizes for the five superior papers for which I had formally stipulated.

How you, or any of you, may best be able to utilize your writings for your own behoof, is a problem which I need not attempt to solve,—you yourselves being the more competent judges on that point. Several among you have intimated a determination to publish their compositions on their own account; some in books, some in pamphlets, some in magazines, and some in newspapers; while others have informed me that, failing to receive a prize, they will, with slight modification of style, change their lucubrations into lectures. Whatever course you may be pleased to adopt in respect to any of these considerations, or otherwise, will not fail to be accompanied with my warmest wishes for your highest welfare.

Yours, very truly,
H. R. HELPER.

NOTE.—Five other letters written by me, to the five successful competitors respectively, will appear in the book which will contain all the prize essays and other pertinent papers in print, and which will probably be published within the next sixty days. Among the forty-seven competitors, ten are residents of Missouri, seven of New York, four of Illinois, four of Canada, three of Pennsylvania, three of Ohio, two of Massachusetts, two of Washington City, two of North Carolina, two of Indiana, two of Kansas, two of Nebraska, one of New Hampshire, one of Virginia, one of Washington Territory, and one of Australia. Thirty-six of the competitors were gentlemen, and eleven ladies. No lady has won a prize; though, judging from the brilliant letters of at least three of the fair contestants, I incline to the opinion that *their* essays—like forty odd others, unseen by myself—must have been good. It will be borne in mind, however, that the committee, in looking for good manuscripts, had an eye, at the same time, to those that were better, and still to others that might be the best of all. Particularly on account of these daring and deserving heroines, I am already beginning to experience a tinge of regret, that I did not permit myself to be a member of the committee; for, if I possess even a single characteristic of superiority over any one of the three able and excellent gentlemen who, in general, acted so well and so admirably as committee-men, it is undoubtedly that of my gallantry,—my respectful and perfect devotion to the divinities of love and beauty. Yet it is a question, nevertheless, whether railroads and railroading may not require a sort of outdoor roughness and robustness of thought, expression and action not possible to the gentle-natured goddesses of our hearts and households.

H. R. H.

DR. HARRIS TO MR. HELPER.

CONCORD, MASS., *January 31, 1881.*

HINTON R. HELPER, ESQ.

DEAR SIR: I thank you for a copy of a circular-letter, announcing the decision of the umpires in the matter of the prize Essays and Poems. It is a very successful sequel to a grand scheme. From the names that I recognize among the successful Essayists, I conclude that the enterprise will be brought before the public in your forthcoming volume in a manner that will attract wide attention from all public-spirited Americans.

With great admiration for your zeal and self-sacrifice in the cause of civilization and progress,

I am, dear Sir, yours truly,

WM. T. HARRIS.

FIRST PRIZE ESSAY.

An Effort Advocating the Unification and Promotion of all New World Systems and Interests, by means of a Longitudinal Double-Track Steel Railway through North and Central and South America; on the bases of Hinton Rowan Helper's Propositions for the Accomplishment of the Supremely Important International work thus contemplated.

BY FRANK FREDERICK HILDER,

No. 1125 Bremen Avenue, St. Louis, Missouri.)

It is from the northern continent that those of the south await their deliverance; it is by the help of the civilized men of the temperate zones, that it shall be vouchsafed to the men of tropical lands to enter into the movement of universal progress and improvement, wherein all mankind should share.—*Arnold Guyot.*

In the marvelous volume which the nineteenth century is adding to the history of the world, by far the most wonderful chapter is that which consists of the records of railroad development, which has been in all parts of the earth, but more particularly in America, little else than a succession of surprises; passing from one great achievement to another with a constructive energy and boldness of engineering talent which appears constantly to increase and expand as the requirements of civilization and commerce increase their demands. Railroads now constitute the most extensive system of commercial investments in existence; they have practically enlarged the boundaries of

human life; they have destroyed barriers and removed jealousies between neighboring countries; and they are now
gradually consolidating the nations of the world into one
vast community, binding them together by the bonds of
mutual interests. By their means, the luxuries and the civilizing influences of cities have been disseminated through
country villages and sparsely populated districts; their products transmitted in return to central markets, and, above
all, information and instruction, literature and news, the
school-house and the halls of justice have been introduced
wherever the hardy pioneer has made his home; thus circulating, like the veins and arteries of the human body, the
warm throbbing currents of the world's life through every
region which they traverse.

In no part of the world have the benefits conferred by
railroads been more apparent than in our own country;
wherever they have been constructed they have enhanced
the value of land, and have given increased value to all the
products of labor. The extraordinary progress that the
American people have made in subduing and utilizing the
rich and rude abundance with which bounteous nature has
so lavishly endowed this continent, would have been impossible without railroads; with them we have accomplished in half a century the work of ages. All the old
limitations to human effort seem to have been swept away
by a rushing flood of indomitable energy; the success of
to-day seems but to enlarge our ideas of what may be accomplished to-morrow; passing from victory to victory
until it appears impossible to conceive a boundary to the
career of progress and development on which our people
are now traveling with such enormous strides.

Fifty years ago, on September 15, 1830, the first railroad
for the conveyance of passengers was opened in England,
from Liverpool to Manchester; it being one of the benefits

for which the old world is indirectly indebted to the new. King Cotton was the power which induced the merchants of Liverpool to furnish means for the construction of this pioneer railroad, for the purpose of facilitating the transit of the fleecy bales from their wharves to the looms of Manchester. Since that time, the marvels of railroad engineering have come so rapidly upon us that they have almost ceased to excite surprise or remark. The Mississippi has been bridged, the Alps tunneled, the Andes surmounted, and even the crater of Vesuvius is now the terminus of a railroad. As the first impulse to the movement which gave railroads to the world was given by American products, so their adoption, after that first trial, has been more speedy and on a grander scale in America, than in any other country; the necessity for them on this continent was even more urgent than in England, although arising from opposite causes. Great Britain was well supplied with means of transportation; her roads were the finest in the world, and the country was traversed by numerous canals; but the demands of a rapidly extending commerce had outgrown their capacity. In this country greater distances were to be traversed; the natural obstacles, created on a much larger scale, were more difficult to overcome; and the highways, few and poorly constructed, could not subserve the wants of a rapidly increasing population, as it spread itself over the great plains of the West, ever increasing its distance from the markets left behind. The necessity for relief was so urgent, that when it came in the shape of railroads, our people availed themselves of them with such eagerness that at present more than ninety thousand miles, within the limits of the United States, carry, safely and rapidly, millions of tons of freight, and hundreds of millions of passengers. One great enterprise has succeeded another with startling rapidity, each in its turn to be met with incredulity and opposition, until success converted ridicule into applause, which gradually subsided as the public mind became accustomed to it as an affair of daily life.

When a great invention, or plan of a gigantic public work, is first announced, it is perhaps natural that it should be viewed with distrust, and treated as chimerical by the majority of mankind; the average human mind is not capable of at once grasping the conception of a mightier intellect; but before we allow ourselves to deride or ridicule an invention or project that startles us by its novelty or magnitude, it will be well to look back to contemporary records, and see how great inventions, which have become familiar to us by use, were received when first announced; not only by the masses, but also by the greatest and best trained intellects of the period. The wisest and holiest men are far from being infallible; and we should bear in mind the fact so frequently impressed upon us, by the wonderful progress made in the present century, that schemes which to-day appear to us to be wild and visionary, may in a few years become accomplished facts. When it was first proposed to use gas as an illuminating medium for streets and dwellings, it was met with the most strenuous opposition and ridicule. Sir Walter Scott, the great novelist, writing from London to a friend in Edinburg, among other items of news, remarked, " that there was a madman proposing to light the city, with what do you think? why, with smoke!" Even the gigantic intellect and liberal mind of Sir Humphry Davy, the renowned chemist, failed to grasp the idea that gas was applicable to the purpose of lighting streets and houses. The greater the invention or the grander the project, the more it will be ridiculed and resisted at the outset. When railroads were first projected in England, they met with most virulent opposition from all classes of people; pamphlets were published, and editors bribed, to revile them; after recapitulating many direful consequences that might, could, would, or should arise from their introduction, this consolation was always offered in conclusion; that the weight of the locomotive would completely prevent its moving, and that railways, if built, could never be operated by steam power.

When the effort was made to obtain from the British Parliament a charter for the construction of a railroad from Liverpool to Manchester, the matter was referred to a special committee ; and George Stephenson, the inventor, was subjected to a positive persecution. A number of lawyers conducted a cross-examination in such a manner as to confuse and perplex him, if possible. One member of the committee sarcastically asked him " in what foreign country he got such ideas ;" another declared that he was mad.

When Stephenson said he could make his locomotive travel at the rate of twenty miles an hour, members said, " This man must certainly be laboring under a delusion." One pressed him a little closer, asking, " Suppose, now, one of these engines to be going at the rate of nine or ten miles an hour, and that a cow were to stray on the line and get in the way, would not that be a very awkward circumstance ?" " Yes," replied Stephenson, in his north-country brogue, and with a sparkle of fun in his eyes, " veery awkward, sir, for the coo." The late Lord Brougham, who was employed as counsel for the railroad company, cautioned Stephenson, that if he did not modify his statements as to the possibility of locomotives traveling at the rate of twenty miles an hour, and bring his engine within reasonable speed, he would certainly ruin the whole affair, and be himself regarded as a lunatic, fit only for a madhouse. *The Quarterly Review,* the ablest English magazine, remarked, " What can be more palpably absurd and ridiculous than the project held out of locomotives traveling twice as fast as stage-coaches ! We would as soon expect the people of

England to suffer themselves to be fired off on a huge rocket as to trust themselves to the mercy of such a machine, going at such a speed. We will back old Father Thames against the railroad for any sum. We trust that Parliament, if it sanctions any railroad, will limit the speed to eight or nine miles an hour, which is as great as can be ventured on with safety." A member of the House of Commons, who has since been Prime Minister of England, (the late Earl of Derby,) urged the House in the most solemn manner to prevent this mad and extravagant speculation from being carried into effect.

In our own country, Chancellor Livingston, of New York, who had been associated with his brother-in-law, Robert Fulton, in the application of steam to navigation, could not agree with him when he proposed to apply it to locomotive engines for railroad travel; and in a letter written in the month of March, 1811, he expressed the opinion that the objections to such a scheme were insuperable.

Such a retrospect should cause us to pause and reflect, before we condemn any scheme, however vast or apparently impracticable, and to consider that projects and works which may appear to us wonderful or immense, may, to the more advanced ideas of the next generation, present themselves as insignificant, and as mere toys for children, when compared with grander undertakings which may by that time have been accomplished.

Within the past fifty years, ten millions of immigrants have landed on the shores of America. This vast tide of humanity will for years continue to roll in upon us with increasing volume, augmenting the natural growth of our population, necessitating the opening up and settlement of new territory, constantly increasing the development of our resources, and demanding a corresponding growth in the magnitude of all our industrial enterprises and public works.

3

A railroad from the Atlantic Ocean to the Pacific was for many years looked upon as a mere Utopian project; but the men of this generation have not only seen one such road completed, but three others in rapid process of construction; while our Canadian neighbors are busily engaged in pushing forward another through the pine forests and trackless prairies of the extreme north. Vast as these enterprises have appeared, as in their turn they have been conceived and brought into existence by the fertile brains and indomitable perseverance of the men who originated them, they must recede into a lower rank, and surrender their supremacy among the world's great achievements, to a still greater project, the Three Americas Railway, a steel railroad, through North, Central, and South America, extending from the British Possessions in the North, to the Argentine Republic in the South, and perhaps ultimately to the northern shores of the Straits of Magellan.

The immensity of the proposed enterprise, exceeding as it does, in magnitude and importance, any public work that has heretofore been suggested or attempted, in any part of the world, may, at a first glance, call forth those sentiments of distrust and incredulity previously alluded to, as the natural effect of so extraordinary a project, upon minds not prepared by thought and careful deliberation on such a subject, to at once receive and grasp it; but the more attentively it is considered, the more thoroughly it is examined in all its bearings, the more feasible it will appear. The difficulties which at first present themselves will diminish, and the enormous benefits which the road will confer on the nations of North, Central, and South America, become so apparent as to ensure a unanimous verdict in its favor.

In estimating the probability of the successful prosecution of such a work, the most important factor is the character of the people to whom it is submitted, and by whom it is to be carried to completion. For inventive genius, mechanical skill, boldness of design, and unflinching determination in surmounting difficulties that to more timid natures would appear insuperable, the people of the United States are unequaled. Emanating from, and constantly reinforced by, the bravest, the most energetic and adventurous members of the superlatively progressive races of mankind, the Americans represent the active elements of the present generation, and, more fully than any other nation, the concentrated knowledge and experience of the world; and they are surely and steadily advancing to their predestined place as leaders in the true progress of the human species. To such a people it may not be necessary to exhibit, as a stimulus, what other nations are planning and executing in the shape of highways, as channels for commerce and civilization, or pathways over which their armies may pass to defend their frontiers, or to make new conquests; but it may be useful to do so, as a proof that the world is thorougly awake to the necessity of improving its means of communication, and that it has outgrown the existing facilities for locomotion.

Although neither of the great railroads now contemplated by England and Russia, will be equal in magnitude and importance to the Three Americas Railway, still they are immensely in advance of any that have hitherto been suggested or attempted in the old world; and are significant indications of the coming era of gigantic public works. Russia has for years been pushing railroads toward Central Asia, and is now maturing plans for one to terminate in the mountains of Afghanistan, and will, within a few years, have a continuous line from St. Petersburg to the frontiers of the British Possessions in India. England feels that if she is to maintain her hold upon her Asiatic Empire, she

must have equal facilities for reaching it speedily.   She finds
the Suez Canal insufficient for her needs, and is preparing
to construct a railroad, either by way of Constantinople and
Asia Minor, or by the Euphrates Valley, through Persia,
to enter India by its northwestern provinces.   Although
these roads will, in fact, be built for military purposes, yet
they will also form new channels for commerce and civilization, and will take high rank among the great arteries of
trade.   Thus, even war, the great destroyer, plays well its
part in opening new and restoring old routes of commerce.
These roads will merely return the trade of India to its ancient pathway.   According to the statements of ancient
writers, the drugs, silks, precious stones, and costly fabrics
of India, were brought by caravans to the Icarus; thence
by the Oxus, and the Caspian and Black seas to Europe.

On this continent, happily, we have no schemes of conquest, nor ambitious greed of our neighbor's territory to
promote by means of the Three Americas Railway; it will
subserve no aristocratic nor kingly despotism.   By its aid,
jealousy and ignorance, nurtured by isolation, bigotry and
intolerance, will be swept away; until, from the frozen north,
through our fertile prairies and busy cities, through the gorgeous scenery of the tropics, overflowing with the products
of a teeming soil; through the rich plateaus of the Sub-Andean Republics, to the pampas and grassy plains that border upon the noble Rio de la Plata, the tides of commerce,
civilization, science and art, shall flow and mingle as freely
as the waters of the ocean, or the winds of heaven.   In the
Southern Republics, peace and prosperity will take the
place of tumult and revolution, as they learn that construction, and not destruction, should be the work of their national life.   As new and better elements shall be gradually
mingled with the aboriginal and hybrid populations, they
will rise in the standard of nations, and enjoy the inestima-

ble benefits of the bounties with which nature has so richly endowed them.

In most of the Spanish-American Republics, a large proportion of the population consists of men who have all to gain, and nothing to lose, by the tumult and disorder of an insurrection; they are always willing, and too often anxious, to fight for whatever plunder they may be able to acquire; while in general there exists only a small conservative element in the population to object to and oppose revolutions. Throughout the United States there are large numbers of prosperous and law-abiding citizens, whose interests imperatively demand that peace and order shall prevail, and who fortunately possess strength enough to enforce the adoption and maintenance of their views.

In the Republics of Central and South America, those residents of the country who are extensive land-holders, and the prosperous merchants of the cities and seaports, take no part in politics, nor in political revolutions; they consider them as especially the province of professional demagogues, and are only anxious that the disturbers should adjust their controversies as speedily as possible, in order that they themselves may be left to pursue their vocations in peace. Happily there are exceptions to this turbulent condition of things. Some of the South American Republics are more peaceable and prosperous than others. Chili is a noble example of the better class; there the population is of a higher type; their industry has produced wealth; the beneficial influence of the foreign element is very perceptible; and its government has for years been strong and respected.

The Argentine Republic has also, within the past twenty years, made enormous strides toward prosperity; there has been a great immigration, principally of Italians; and on every hand the outlook for the future appears to be very hopeful.   Guatemala, under the leadership of her present energetic and progressive President, is advancing with wonderful rapidity on a new career of prosperity, founded on a solid basis of education, culture, and wise legislation.   Mexico is, in many respects, vastly improved; foreign capital · and energy are exerting their stimulating forces; her people are awakening to a just appreciation of the magnificent domain they have inherited; the period of civil feuds and dissensions has nearly passed away; and a new era of development and prosperity has dawned upon the former dominions of the Montezumas.   A few years ago we invaded Mexico with fire and sword; and many of her beautiful cities and plains echoed with the thunder of our cannon and the tramp of our legions.   Our next invasion will be a peaceful one, bearing in our hands the olive branch, instead of weapons of war; we shall then realize the truth of that lesson, which it appears so difficult for the world to learn, that it is better to sell to our neighbors the products of our fields and factories, than to cut their throats.   It is safer, and more rational and pleasant, in dealing with our fellow men, to exchange commodities rather than bayonet thrusts and bullets.

America, stretching from the Arctic to the Antarctic Circle, covers an immense space on the terrestrial globe; but vast as it is, there is no room on it, except temporarily, for either kings or emperors.   On its broad surface, the greatest problem of all ages, the capability of man for self-government, is in process of demonstration; eventual and complete success depends on the intelligence and patriotism of its people.   The mockery of an Empire in Brazil, an Emperor and a tawdry Court reigning over a nation of slaves and savages, will pass away like mist before the rising sun, when its people shall have become sufficiently educated and enlightened to occupy an honorable place in the great family of American Republics.

No despotism, no oligarchy, no aristocratic monopoly of territory, no system of caste privilege, can long continue to exist when invaded by the civilizing power and beneficent influences of a grand intercontinental railway, destined to unite in the bonds of peace and progress more than a dozen free and flourishing nationalities. The exigencies of commerce, and the love of gain inherent in mankind, must be the levers by which this gigantic enterprise will be set in motion.

There can be no great intellectual, political or social improvement, which is not preceded by corresponding material progress. This truth has been gradually forced upon the minds of the more thoughtful portion of the inhabitants of Central and South America, by the stern logic of events, as manifested in the direful experience of the past. They have come to understand that political convulsions have not the power to regenerate their national existence; and they are now disposed to aid, by every possible and convenient means, the carrying out of important foreign enterprises among them; notwithstanding the prejudices which have been propagated by ignorant bigots and crafty demagogues. It is to the people of the United States that they now confidently look as the friendly agency by which their cherished hopes of future prosperity are to be ultimately realized. From the beginning of the world no people ever had a grander work presented, as a field for their best energies, than the Three Americas Railway; nor so magnificent a promise of reward for the successful accomplishment of any particular undertaking.

Stretching southward, from the Rio Grande to Central and South America, from the northern temperate regions through the tropics, lies a country endowed with all the wealth and beauties of Nature; with a climate and soil capable of producing all of the most valuable vegetable productions of every zone; sugar, rice, coffee, cocoa, indigo, tobacco, India-rubber, dyes, gums, medicines, and precious woods; comprising all the products which, for ages, have made the commerce of the East Indies so important to the world that it has always enriched not only the fortunate country that controlled it, but all of those besides, through whose territory it has flowed. Thoughout the Spanish American republics the most precious and valuable minerals are also found in great abundance; and all within easy reach of the two mighty oceans of the world.

Taking all its advantages into consideration, Central America is perhaps the region most favored by nature on the whole surface of the globe. It must be destined to play an important part in the world's future history, when it shall be permeated by intellect, skill, capital and enterprise; all of which will naturally follow in the pathway of the proposed longitudinal railway. Is not the control of the commerce of this magnificent territory a prize well worth striving for? An English newspaper of late date says: "A great revival in the trade of Mexico and Central America is confidently anticipated. British manufacturers and merchants will do well to make the most of the opportunity before their French, Belgian, and German rivals shall have taken the lead in the supply of those markets." It is evident from this paragraph how small a share of the trade with these countries has hitherto been transacted by merchants of the United States, when they are not mentioned as probable, nor even as possible competitors! Under any circumstances, it is almost certain that, within a few years, this condition of things will be changed; and European traders will find, in our merchants and manufacturers, very formidable rivals in all the business centres of the South. Why not stretch forth the iron hand of the Three Americas Railway, and grasp that commerce now? We must take into consideration, not only how valuable will be the import trade of the varied products of South and Central America; but the still more important results of opening new markets for our surplus manufactures and merchandise.

One of the greatest problems that at present affects our national welfare, is that of the movement and distribution of the products of labor. We must remember that it is impossible for us to create anything; we can only direct natural forces and apply them to our service. Let us do this systematically and judiciously. Modern inventions and improvements in the mechanic arts, and the continued application of new discoveries in the natural sciences, insure an ever-increasing and cheapening supply, not only of agricultural products, but also of every article necessary for the sustenance and convenience of mankind. The one thing now needful is to facilitate the distribution of those products and articles, so that the superabundance of one region may remedy the deficiency in another. Those who give the matter due consideration will readily perceive that in the United States, this question is now rapidly growing into one of paramount importance. No longer divided in sentiment or policy by the curse of slavery, these States are now firmly united, in fact as well as in name, by the bonds of common and inseparable interests; and as the effects of our late civil war are obliterated, a new era of such astonishing prosperity as the world has never seen is opening before our people; one marked result of which is the enormous increase of all our products, which are poured forth from our fields and forests, mines and manufactories, in an ever-increasing abundance, far exceeding the needs of our own people, and rendering it absolutely necessary that we should cultivate foreign commerce, and find new markets for the absorption of our augmenting surplus.

Adam Smith, in his *Wealth of Nations*, says: "According to the natural course of things, the greater part of the capital of any growing country is first directed to agriculture, afterward to manufactures, and last of all to foreign commerce." In another part of the same book, he says: "Where the products of any particular branch of industry exceed what the demand of the country requires, the surplus must be sent abroad and exchanged for something for which there is a demand at home. Without such exportation, a part of the productive labor of the country must cease, and the value of its annual products diminish."

Although written more than a century ago, these are truths that will never grow old. In the early days of our history, agriculture was the paramount interest; then gradually followed the second or manufacturing development; and now we are entering on the third stage when foreign commerce is not only increasing, but becoming an urgent necessity. Our agricultural and manufacturing capacities are now far in excess of what the country requires for home consumption. To secure the continued prosperity of our producers, to stimulate progressive industry, and insure the maintainance and increase in value of our lands, we must avail ourselves of every opportunity to obtain the control of foreign markets, for the purpose of absorbing our constantly increasing accumulation of surplus commodities.

The Three Americas Railway, by reason of its international and intercontinental character, will not only give to the people of the United States, for all time a preponderating influence in the markets of Central and South America, and over the future destiny of the whole Western Hemisphere, but it will be the spring from which will flow, for their benefit, a never-failing stream of wealth and prosperity. Having discussed in general terms the great advantages that will undoubtedly be derived from this grand international highway, the question naturally arises as to the best location for it, and what are the physical features of the various countries it will traverse? On these subjects the limits of this essay will permit only a hasty sketch. To enter into anything like full details, or complete statistics, would expand the article to the dimensions of a volume.

A careful examination of all the surrounding circumstances would appear to indicate, that the best location for the northern terminus of the road will be at a junction with the Canada Pacific Railroad, somewhere near the one hundreth degree of longitude west from Greenwich; thus securing at once transcontinental branches as feeders, with outlets on the Atlantic and Pacific Oceans. The term feeders is here used from the fact that this part of British America is separated from Minnesota and Dakota by a diplomatic line only, and not by any physical boundary; the natural course of its trade is to the United States, as commerce will always flow by natural rather than by political or artificial routes. Passing southward, the road would traverse the heart of that vast northwestern region which is destined not only to become one of the greatest grain-producing territories of the world, but also the home of millions of hardy and industrious people.

Following as nearly as possible the one hundredth degree of longitude, the road would bisect the United States on a line very nearly equidistant between the Atlantic and Pacific oceans. While indicating this as what may be the most desirable location for that portion of the road within the United States, it should be borne in mind that deviations would be necessary at times to the east or west of the line, either for the purpose of avoiding an insurmountable physical difficulty, as a matter of economy, or to secure an important advantage in travel or traffic. All such details must, as a matter of necessity, be left for future determination, as it is proposed in this essay to merely suggest, in a general manner, the route that appears most fit to be pursued. The Three Americas Railway, so located, will cross at right angles the several transcontinental railroads, reciprocating with them an immense amount of traffic, which will naturally result from the facilities offered by the grand longitudinal trunk line; branches or offshoots from which will, in course of time, reach every part of North and Central and South America where railroad communication shall be found necessary or desirable.

Crossing the frontier into Mexico, the road will enter a country which the events of the last forty years have rendered familiar to our people. The advantages which will be derived from railway communication direct from the United States to the City of Mexico have, for a considerable length of time, been so freely discussed and described, that it is unnecessary to repeat them here. The agitation of the subject has already resulted in the formation of the Mexican Central Railroad Company, which has commenced the work of building a road from the City of Mexico to the Rio Grande, a distance of 252 miles; the first section of which, from Mexico to Leon, they expect to complete about the end of 1881.

It may be here stated that, in locating the Three Americas Railway, some shorter roads, or sections of roads, may be found, such as the Mexican Central, already built, or in course of construction, which might, with advantage to all concerned, be utilized as a part of the great highway; but this subject, as a matter of detail, must be dismissed from present consideration; leaving all such projects of consolidation or amalgamation to those who may be invested with the executive power of carrying into effect the plans of the promoters of this colossal enterprise.

Topographically, Mexico presents the same general features which are found to extend southward through the whole of Central America. Stretching inland, from the Gulf coast, is a broad tract of alluvial country, covered for the most part with forests nourished by frequent rains, where marshes and lagoons abound, sweltering under a fierce sun, engendering miasmatic vapors, and rendering the climate, in this particular locality, more or less insalubrious. Between the low country and the great mountain chain of the Cordilleras, which, throughout Central and South America, runs much nearer to the Pacific Ocean, the surface is raised into a high table-land, a great elevated plain, where the rains are comparatively light, the country open, and the climate relatively cool and healthful. There may be found, in the greatest abundance, every natural production necessary for the welfare and happiness of mankind; a fertile and beautiful land, capable of supporting an immense and prosperous population.

The slope between the Cordilleras and the Pacific Ocean, while generally dryer and hotter than the central plateau, is, from the greater purity of its atmosphere, far more healthful than the country bordering on the Atlantic, and better fitted to become the seat of a highly civilized and thrifty people. This great central plateau, with its glorious climate and manifold advantages, is clearly indicated by nature as the country best adapted for the location of the grand intercontinental railway. Throughout its whole extent northern laborers can work, at all seasons of the year, with equal facility, and with less danger from unavoidable exposure, than in the United States. Should it be considered necessary or more satisfactory to employ laborers from the United States in the construction of the railway, this fact will form a very important item in the cost of the work. The mild and equable climate will permit operations to be carried on at all seasons; the requisite shelter for the workmen will be inexpensive; and no such fearful waste of life and money will be incurred as was caused by the construction of the Panama Railroad through the swamps and forests of the Atlantic slope. Food, fuel, timber for bridges and ties, and other indispensable materials, can be readily obtained; in fact all the conditions amply exist to facilitate the progress of the work, and reduce its cost to a minimum.

As we pass through Mexico to its southern boundary, the great central plain rises to a higher elevation, reaching its highest limit in the northern part of the adjoining Republic of Guatemala, forming what is called by the natives "*Los Altos,*" (The Highlands,) where the average temperature is lower than in any other part of the country. On these highlands snow sometimes falls; but it soon disappears, as the thermometer seldom remains at the freezing point for any considerable length of time.

Guatemala, though one of the richest and most prosperous of the Central American Republics, suffers for want of good harbors; particularly on the Pacific coast, on which side the bulk of its population is located. San José, its principal port, is an open roadstead, without proper protection for vessels; it is, however, rising rapidly into importance, and is the terminus of Guatemala's first railroad, which runs inland to the flourishing city of Escuintla, about thirty miles distant. This road has been recently completed and opened for traffic, amid great rejoicings; an event which marks a new era in the history of Guatemala. With a beautiful climate, and a soil suitable for raising every variety of agricultural and animal product, from the wheat and wool of Los Altos to the cochineal, cocoa, coffee, cotton, sugar, and indigo of the lower country, nothing but the lack of good roads has prevented the profitable development of its great resources. With the

Three Americas Railway traversing its center, and opening up a route to the markets of the world, Guatemala will soon become a magnificent country.

The adjoining Republic of San Salvador lies entirely on the Pacific Ocean, with a coast line of about 160 miles. It is the smallest of the Central American republics; but it has relatively the largest population and the most extensive commerce. It abounds in agricultural and mineral riches, and particularly in vast beds of lignite, or brown coal, from which, even independently of its forests, ample supplies of fuel may be obtained. One of its chief advantages lies, however, in the share it possesses of the commodious and beautiful Bay of Fonseca. This magnificent bay is the finest harbor on the entire Pacific coast of America. It is sixty miles in length, and thirty in average width, perfectly protected, and capable of sheltering all the navies of the world. It contains several large islands, affording facilities for inner ports; while its shores present sites admirably adapted for cities and towns, and also for commercial and manufacturing establishments of every kind. The three republics of San Salvador, Honduras, and Nicaragua, touch upon the shores of this splendid bay; although Honduras has the largest frontage. It is the natural outlet of all those republics, and here their respective principal seaports are located. Captain M. T. de Lepelier, of the French Navy, thus describes it, in a report to his governnent in 1854: " Studded with beautiful islands, this vast and magnificent bay, which stretches into the land between the points of Candadilla and Cosequina, and generally known as the Bay of Fonseca, has no rival on the entire coast of the Pacific, whether as regards its extent, its security, its beauty, or its naval and commercial position." E. G. Squier, in his work on Central America, says, in alluding to this bay: "It seems to have been marked out by the Creator as the ulti-

mate center of the commerce of the Pacific. Salubrious,
surrounded by a country of illimitable agricultural resources, and with rich and inexhaustible coal, gold, and silver
mines inland; abounding in fine fish, including excellent
oysters; in short, possessing all the necessaries for sustain-
ing a large and prosperous population, the Bay of Fonseca
is unrivaled in its adaptation for the terminus of a great
railroad."

Whether the Three Americas Railway can be so located
as to touch the shores of this grand harbor, or whether it
will be necessary to communicate with it by one or more
branch lines, the fact is evident that it will form one of the
most important points on its route through the Central
American Republics. Even the dullest and most unim-
aginative mind cannot fail to look, with something akin to
enthusiasm, on the prospect afforded by the idea of what
this magnificent natural ship-home may become, when it
shall be fitly transformed by commercial and constructive
genius. Its waters whitened with the sails of ships, its
shores the sites of busy trade-centers, over whose wharves
would ebb and flow the waves of commerce; while the
great intercontinental railway would form the channel
through which would pass the exports and imports of a vast
region, so favored in every respect by nature that it requires
only the opening of means of communication with the
interior to attract to it a large and vigorous immigration,
with its helpful accompaniments of capital, industry and enterprise.

Honduras, when opened to North American energy, by
means of the Three Americas Railway, will become an immense field for mining operations. There is scarcely a
stream on the eastern slope of the Cordilleras that does not
carry down and deposit in its sands, gold, in greater or less
quantities. Some of their shores are as rich as the famous

placer diggings of California. In the interior of this republic are many silver mines, well known to be unsurpassed in
the abundance and richness of their ores; but they have
suffered so much by the disturbances resulting from the
civil wars and political convulsions which have distracted
Central America, that many of them have been abandoned,
and have fallen into decay. As yet, there is a lack of
both capital and energy requisite to restore them to even
their former imperfect condition. In first opening these
mines, there was an entire absence of system, and apparently a deficiency of the knowledge and skill necessary
to establish one. Suitable appliances were not used anywhere in working the mines; and there were no roads fit
for the transportation of heavy machinery.

Along many of the rugged paths which are used as roads
from the sea-ports to the interior, may be seen scattered
fragments of ponderous and expensive machinery, which
men, with more zeal than judgment, have endeavored to
transport for the purpose of working the mines, but which
have been abandoned in despair. The advent of the Three
Americas Railway would convert this repulsive scene of
neglect and decay, into a busy panorama of industry, and
contribute to the world's treasury an immense influx of
wealth. How great that wealth would be, can be estimated
from the fact that, in spite of all disadvantages and lack of
knowledge in working the mines, and in treating the
ores, during the Spanish rule as much as $3,000,000 was
annually produced and exported, in the shape of bullion,
from only the northern part of Honduras.

Passing southward into the Republic of Nicaragua, the
topographical features of the country are found to be very
remarkable and interesting, from the fact that to them is
due the great amount of notice now attracted to this region
from the world at large, in consequence of the facilities

4

they present for the construction of a Ship Canal between
the Atlantic and Pacific oceans. The northern part of the
republic is a continuation of the high plateau of Honduras.
Southward of the elevated district the country falls rapidly
until it forms a great basin, or valley, about three hundred
miles in length, and one hundred and fifty in width; in
which are spread out the lakes of Nicaragua and Managua;
both being magnificent sheets of water; the former upward of one hundred miles in length by forty wide, and the
latter fifty miles by forty. Both are navigable over their
entire surface. The latter approaches, at the nearest point,
to within twenty-five miles of the Pacific Ocean. From the
Bay of Fonseca to the northern point of this lake, the
Three Americas Railway will form an admirable connection, with but a very slight divergence from its direct course.
Here will be found a very important link in a route for interoceanic commerce.

Costa Rica, the next Republic in the pathway of our proposed road, is the most southern of the Central American
Republics, and, with the exception of San Salvador, the
smallest in size. The great mountain chain of the Cordilleras traverses very nearly the center of the State. From
the apexes of these mountains the country does not recede,
as in other parts of Central America, in gradual slopes, but
by a succession of terraces, which vary in climate and productions, as they differ in altitude. The plateau or terrace,
varying from 3,000 to 5,000 feet in height, (called by the
natives, " *tierras templadas*,") which is favored with a genial
climate and a fruitful soil, is best adapted for the Three
Americas Railway. The coasts of this Republic are in-
dented with several fine bays, particularly on the Pacific
side; one of which, the Gulf of Nicoya, extends nearly
sixty miles inland. Upon one of its shores is situated
Punta Arenas, the principal port of the republic, and one

which will doubtless become an important commercial point when the great want, common to all the Central American Republics, railroads as a means of communication, shall have been supplied.

Crossing the southern boundary of Costa Rica, the Three Americas Railway will enter the northwestern part of the Republic of Columbia, a short distance to the north of the Isthmus of Panama ; at which point the shores of the two oceans approach to within less than fifty miles of each other. The Three Americas Railway will here cross the Panama Railroad, and will have the benefit, through its means, of outlets to the Atlantic and Pacific, and will doubtless reciprocate with it a very large trade. In fact, this facility of communication with both oceans, forms one of the most important features in calculating the success to be achieved by the Three Americas Railway.

At several points the shores of the Atlantic and Pacific approach each other so closely as to render communication, by branch roads, a comparatively easy matter; while such connections will be of enormous benefit, not only to the great railway itself, but also and equally to the several countries through which it will pass. At the Isthmus of Tehuantepec, the Gulf of Mexico approaches to within two hundred miles of the Pacific Ocean. Farther south, the Bay of Honduras narrows the continent to less than one hundred and fifty miles ; and this space is marked by a complete interruption of the mountain chain, being traversed from ocean to ocean by a broad valley, affording an admirable location for a railroad.

In passing from the Republic of Costa Rica to the Isthmus of Panama, there is a great change of level. The railway will descend from an altitude of about three thousand feet, on the " tierra templada," to less than three hundred feet, at the point where it will cross the Panama Railroad.

In passing through the Isthmus into the continental portion
of the Republic of Columbia, our railway will again have to
ascend to a height of over three thousand feet.   These
steep grades, combined with the fact that throughout the
Columbian States of Veragua and Panama, in which are
comprised the entire territory of the Isthmus of Panama, the
country is rough and broken and overgrown with dense
tropical forests, will render this part of the road one of the
most expensive and difficult to construct.

The outlay and impediments here dreaded will arise, not
only from the natural obstructions already mentioned, but
also from the peculiar climate of the isthmus, rendering the
work there more unhealthy; although in a decidedly less
degree than was experienced in the construction of the
Panama Railroad, as the Three Americas Railway will pass
through the midland portion of the country, where it attains
the greatest altitude, and will thus avoid the malarious
swamps which fringe the coasts of both oceans.   The surmounting of these obstacles is merely a matter of expense,
and they will cause no hindrance to the progress of the
work, that cannot be overcome by a liberal expenditure of
money.   This is the only section of the vast highway, in its
entire length, from north to south, where similar difficulties
will have to be overcome.   It may be well to note this fact,
for it is very remarkable.   There is probably no corresponding extent of the earth's surface, where a road of so
many thousands of miles in length can pass, and encounter
so few excessive variations of climate, so few physical
obstructions, or find such a universally healthful and fertile
country.

In traversing the Republics of Columbia and Ecuador, it
will be found that the equatorial Andes are divided into
two longitudinal ranges, called respectively the Eastern and
Western Cordilleras.   The Three Americas Railway must

pass to the eastward of the western range, and on the high tableland lying between the two; gradually rising in altitude until the highest point shall be reached in the Valley of Quito, in Ecuador. This plateau is two hundred miles in length by fifty in breadth; it is a country so bountifully endowed by nature that, when opened to the world by railway communication, it will become a pleasure-resort and sanitarium for the whole human family.

Prof. Orton, a recent American traveler, thus describes it: "The climate is perfect. Fair Italy, with her classic prestige and ready access, will long be the land of promise to travellers in search of health; but if ever the ancients had reached this Arcadian valley, they would have located here the Elysian Fields. No torrid heat enervates the inhabitant of this favored spot; no icy breezes send him shivering to the fire; nobody is sunstruck, nobody's buds are nipped by the frost. Stoves and chimneys, starvation and epidemics are unknown. It is never Spring, Summer. nor Autumn, but each day is a combination of all of them. The mean annual temperature is 58°, the same as Madrid, or the month of May in Paris. The average range, in twenty-four hours, is 10°. The extremes of the year are 45° and 70°; and this in a country lying directly under the equator. Yellow fever, Cholera and Consumption are unknown. More coughing may be heard at a single service, in a New England meeting-house, than in the whole city of Quito in six months."

Velasco describes Ecuador as the "noblest portion of the New World." It has unsurpassed capabilities. Embracing within its limits elevations and depressions marking the highest and the lowest levels of the earth's surface, it presents every grade of climate. Along the coast one finds perpetual summer; on the great central plateau eternal spring; and among the Andean summits everlasting winter.

Bad as are the roads and other lines of communication in
Central America, it is in Columbia and Ecuador that we
come in contact with the very worst.   Only by toilsome
journeys on muleback, along rugged and dangerous paths,
can either passengers or freights now be conveyed between
the interior and the coast.   As an illustration of how this
militates   against   the   development   of   the   resources
of   the   country,   no   more   striking   example   need   be
given than in the manner of working the Cinchona forests,
which produce the so-called Peruvian Bark, from which Quinine is manufactured.   This is one of the most valuable
productions of Ecuador; but the great disadvantage connected with the trade is the difficulty and expense of transporting the bark to the coast for shipment.   The bark is
packed in small bales, which, because of the lack of roads,
have to be carried on the backs of Indians, over distances
covering sometimes hundreds of miles, until a receiving
warehouse is reached ; whence it is transported on mule-
back to the nearest shipping-place.   This is but one of
numberless instances which could be enumerated, of the
drawbacks and difficulties encountered throughout Central
and South America, on account of the absence of roads ;
but so many such cases have already been cited, that the
subject is becoming wearisome from repetition.

   The whole matter may be summed up in the assertion
that, from the locality where the Three Americas Railway
will cross the southern boundary of the United States, to its
southern terminus in the Argentine Republic, the greatest
public necessity is the railroad as a means of internal communication.   In this age, without the railroad, no real progress or advancement is possible ; with it, there is hardly a
limit to be set to the possibilities of improvement.   Under
facilities offered by the proposed road, the fairest and most
fertile portions of the globe's surface will be thrown open

to commerce, and consequently to civilization. Its steel bands will be more potent than the rod of Moses; for when the rock of isolation shall be struck by them, a gushing stream will pour forth in response that will irrigate the world with a flood of wealth.

In passing from Ecuador into the territory of the Republic of Peru, the route of the Three Americas Railway must be located to the eastward of both of the great mountain ranges, not only because it will by so doing avoid great engineering difficulties, but also because the Pacific coast presents no inducements for a railroad sufficient to repay the cost of constructing so many miles. Throughout the whole length of Peru, from Guyaquil southward, the mountains run nearly parallel with the coast, at a short distance from the shore. Even where the mountains recede the farthest from tide-water, they project great spurs down toward the sea; leaving only a narrow and frequently interrupted strip of comparatively level land, which, for the most part, is a sandy desert, lifeless and repulsive; occasionally intersected by fertile valleys, through which rivers and mountain brooks find their way into the ocean, but generally presenting the aspect and reality of an extensive waste, useless for culture, and unfit for habitation.

The eastern slope of the Andes presents a picture entirely opposite to the desolate west-coast country. Here the mountains gradually subside into a magnificent plain, combining wonderful beauty with amazing fertility; an immense plain splendidly timbered, and capable of yielding, from its rich soil, an unusually large reward to the cultivator, and of supporting, in abundance and luxury, an almost innumerable population. It is watered by hundreds of rivers and smaller streams, fed by the perennial springs and eternal snows of the mountains, which, flowing eastward, serve to swell the mighty Amazon, the Orinoco, and the

Plate. From the Atlantic Ocean steamers may pass up the Amazon, by its Peruvian tributaries, to the very feet of the Andes. The whole sub-Andean plain is a vast treasury of undeveloped wealth. It was the coveted summer-land of the Incas, who looked down upon it from their mountain fastnesses with longing eyes, but were never able to conquer a permanent foot-hold from the free and brave tribes who inhabited it. The locomotive will be its conqueror. Under the rule of the iron-horse, the whole region will be awakened to a most marvelous prosperity. The Three Americas Railway will put it in communication with all the countries north and south. Steam navigation will bear its more bulky products to the Atlantic; and through the passes of the Andes the admirable system of Peruvian railroads will be rapidly pushed forward, to connect with the great intercontinental highway.

The Peruvian Government has found on its coasts prodigious mines of wealth in the deposits of guano and nitrate of soda: the proceeds of which have been wisely used to build railroads between the seaports and the interior; engineered with unsurpassed energy and talent, over some of the most rugged and apparently inaccessible passes, into the very heart of the Andes. These roads, although they are at present unremunerative, will in the future furnish a good return for the $150,000,000 invested in them, and will render Peru prosperous when the deposits of guano and nitrate of soda shall have been exhausted. To this desirable consummation nothing will contribute more largely than early and perfect connection with the Three Americas Railway, as the great artery of American commerce. The present disastrous war with Chili is rapidly exhausting the resources of Peru and Bolivia; but when that sanguinary struggle shall have ended, the boundless mineral wealth of the land of the Incas, including the most celebrated silver mines in the world, gold, tin, and copper; the surprising deposits of guano and nitrate of soda; the wool of the Alpaca and the Vicuna, and the other animal, agricultural and natural productions, combined with unrestricted railroad communication with the whole continent, cannot fail to render Peru rich and prosperous.

Bolivia, through which republic the road will pass, when it crosses the Peruvian frontier, is as rich as Peru in most of its natural productions; but it is still more in need of the facilities for trade and travel which the Three Americas Railway will supply; as Arica, in Peru, is the only port fairly available to her for the exportation and importation of merchandise; a fact which adds enormously to the cost of all articles of foreign production consumed in Bolivia; particularly as the Peruvian government levies customs duties on them, and in addition there is the cost of transportation on muleback across the Andes. As an instance of the extraordinary outlay entailed upon the people of Bolivia by this state of affairs, tin, found in the Andes of Peru, close to the Bolivian frontiers, is shipped around Cape Horn to the United States or England; manufactured there into tin plates; reshipped, and after doubling the Cape a second time, returns past the mouth of the mine from which it was dug, and is sold to the inhabitants of Bolivia for the manufacture of the commonest household utensils.

Attempts have been made by Bolivian merchants to open up a route for their goods by way of the Madeira and Mamore rivers, and the Amazon, to the Atlantic; but they have not hitherto proved successful because of the great expense and time necessarily consumed in transferring the goods on muleback around the rapids of the Madeira, a distance of between one and two hundred miles, over a very rough country. A railroad has been projected around the falls; if built, it will prove a valuable adjunct in opening Bolivia to the commerce of the world; yet the benefits will be insignificant when compared with those to be derived from the Three Americas Railway, which will connect the head-waters of the whole gigantic system of South American rivers, carrying to their banks for shipment the various products of all the vast tract of country adjacent, and receiving and distributing the merchandise of América and Europe, which steamers will carry from the Atlantic ports.

The geographical position of the United States, and the currents of the ocean which flow from the mouth of the Amazon to our shores, will ensure to American merchants the greater portion of this immense commerce, the magnitude of which can scarcely be estimated, when all the vast regions of the interior of South America shall take the important place in the commercial brotherhood of the world for which nature has so bountifully prepared them. Many parts of Bolivia will prove quite as rich in the precious metals as Peru; in fact American travelers have expressed the opinion that the whole country traversed by the rivers issuing from the slope of the Eastern Cordilleras, from Santa Cruz in Bolivia, to the mouth of the Ucayli in Peru, is an immense gold and silver region; gold being found in the flats near the rivers, and silver in the mountains. La Paz, the capital of Bolivia, has become an important commercial center, even under the present unfavorable conditions. With the facilities which the Three Americas Railway will afford this city, it will rapidly develop into a great commercial emporium, and become the distributing point for an immense section of country.

After traversing the high table-lands of Bolivia, our railway will enter the territory of the Argentine Republic and cross its wide pampas, or grassy prairie lands, toward its terminus at some point on the Parana or the River Plate. From a careful consideration of its geographical position and other advantages, it would appear that the best and most appropriate location for a terminus would be at Rosario, on the River Parana, a tributary of the Plate; a city of growing commercial importance, being the second port of the Argentine Republic, and connected with Buenos Ayres by lines of steamboats. It may in all probability be deemed judicious, at some time in the near future, to extend the road beyond this point; but there is no doubt that it now affords an admirable location for a temporary terminus for the great intercontinental highway, and an excellent outlet for the deep and broad stream of travel and commerce that will continuously flow over its track.

Because of the vast distance to be traversed, and the innumerable advantages that suggest themselves as likely to be derived from our gigantic railway, as its course has been traced, from its starting point in the north to its destination in the south, it has been impossible to do more than present the barest and most meager outlines of the physical features which its route will present, or the tremendous revolutions it will bring about in the commercial, moral and political future, of every country through which it will pass. Still, enough has been shown to awaken in the mind a boundless enthusiasm, as it endeavors to realize the magnificence of the conception, and the mighty influence it will exercise in the affairs not only of the two continents of America, but also of the whole world. Honored and happy ought the man to be who shall succeed in presenting to the people of the United States, as concisely as possible, the most prominent features and advantages of this proposed longitudinal railway through the three Americas; it being in fact the grandest project that has ever yet been suggested as an international and intercontinental work.

The enormous proportions of the contemplated railway, and the immense interests it will control, may perhaps excite in some minds a doubt as to the policy of creating so vast a corporation. There is in this country much diversity of opinion and suspicion in regard to railroad companies, as factors in our politics; and honest but ill-founded fears are entertained concerning the influences they may exert upon our institutions through their prodigious aggregations of capital, as well as from the monopoly controlling the great arteries of communication which they have acquired. Jealousy of huge corporations has in fact become a cardinal article, not only in American political doctrine, but also in that of several European countries.

A few years since, Sir Henry Tyler, in the Report of the Board of Trade of Great Britain, stated that the time was near at hand when, "The State must control the railroads, or the railroads would control the State." Since that time, the formation of gigantic corporations in England, by the consolidation and amalgamation of railroad companies, has proceeded even more rapidly and extensively. Consequently nearly the whole railroad system of England is now under the absolute control of a few great companies. The result, so far from having been detrimental to the community, has proved not only beneficial to the stockholders, but also, in a far greater degree, to the public. A Parliamentary Committee, appointed in 1872, to investigate this subject, was induced, by the evidence submitted to it, to report that, "The growth of corporations had not brought with it the evils generally anticipated."

The fact is, railroads have outlived the first epoch in their history; that of inception and construction, and have entered confidently upon the era of maturity and consolidation. England, with her smaller mileage and greater abundance of capital, has solved the problem much more rapidly than America. As exemplifying the result, no better embodiment of facts can be presented than the following extract from the report of the beforementioned Parliamentary Committee of 1872: "The North Eastern Railway is composed of thirty-seven lines, several of which formerly competed with each other. Before the amalgamation, they had, generally speaking, high rates and fares, and low dividends. The system is now the most complete monopoly in the United Kingdom; from the Tyne to the Humber, with one local exception, it has the country to itself; and it has the lowest fares and highest dividends of any large English railway. It has had little or no litigation with other companies; while complaints have been heard from Lancashire and Yorkshire, where there are so-called competing lines, no witness has appeared to complain of the North Eastern; and the general feeling in the district it serves appears favorable to its management." Such testimony is the best possible argument that can be presented in favor of the formation of great companies, with absolute control over all the lines of transportation in the territory they traverse; powerful enough to render reckless and ruinous competition impossible, and controlling sufficient capital to enable them to provide ample service and accommodation for the public.

In our own country, the construction of railroads has proceeded in accordance with the requirements of, and under authority derived from, the various States in which they are located, entirely free from everything like National or State supervision, without the remotest trace of a general or symmetrical system, and perfectly independent of each other. The construction of railroads has been thrown open to the public as freely as any other commercial or money-making enterprise. With few exceptions, therefore, the great trunk lines connecting the prominent cities have been created by the consolidation of numerous short tracks into continuous roads under a single management, to the obvious advantage of all concerned. Railroads can never demonstrate the full extent of their usefulness to the public, or prove fairly remunerative to their owners, when operated as short lines, under separate managements, and with interests not only generally divergent, but often directly conflicting. So far as consolidation has progressed in the United States, the result has proved entirely satisfactory; the greatest amalgamated lines, which have encountered the severest censure, and have been the most reviled as gigantic monopolies, such as the New York Central, the Pennsylvania, the Baltimore and Ohio, the Louisville and Nashville, the Iron Mountain, and the Wabash, so far from using their power extortionately, have performed the largest amount of work for the public, at the lowest safely-running rates.

Politicians and demagogues may endeavor to manufacture capital out of their blantant hostility to great corporations; but in the natural course of events, such corporations must not only exist but increase in magnitude with the growth of the country and with the development of the interests they subserve. Great and beneficial as has been the work accomplished by the existing railroad corporations of the United States, it will be dwarfed by comparison with the illimitable results that will accrue from the completion of the Three Americas Railway, with its huge trunk line, forming a spinal column of communication through all the vast length of the two continents of the New World; exerting its propitious influences for the prosperity and welfare of its inhabitants; sweeping away prejudices and misconceptions; and practically uniting its diverse races into a homogeneous community, with common interests and a common destiny.

In considering the question of the construction of a work of such immense proportions as the one now proposed, the financial aspect is the most important part of the subject. What will it cost? How can the money be provided to pay for it ? Have our people so prospered as to attain to a financial condition which will enable them to undertake such a gigantic enterprise ? To the first of these questions the answer must of necessity be vague and indefinite. In regard to so great a work, extending through thousands of miles of country, much of which is as yet only imperfectly explored, no exact estimate of the cost can be made. Even after the route shall have been surveyed, and during all the time of the inaccessibility of the important data which a careful and thorough survey would give, a reliable estimate of the cost of the entire road is scarcely possible. Assuming, however, that only a single-track road is to be built at first, leaving the question of a double-track to depend on the financial returns of the single-track road, the cost of its construction will probably not be less than $300,000,000. This is a vast sum of money ; but it is really small in comparison with the grand results that will be achieved by the building of the road, and in contrast with the resources of the principal nation that will undertake it.

Never before has the Republic of the United States of America been in so sound a financial condition as it is at present ; nor has it ever before been blessed with such a brilliant prospect in its immediate future. Its credit was never better, if ever before so good, in the money markets of the world. At no time hitherto has its income been so abundant and increasing, obtainable with so little difficulty, nor the burden of national taxation so easily borne by its people. Even the enormous public debt, entailed upon the nation by the late civil war, is a drawback of but slight inconvenience. The world furnishes no record of any similar instance, where so large a portion of an immense national debt has been paid off within so short a time, by using only the surplus revenues. Since the 31st of August, 1865, the date on which the debt had reached its maximum, a reduction of more than $650,000,000 has been effected. If the present rate of reduction were to be maintained, the whole existing indebtedness would be liquidated in less than twenty-five years.

When we remember that our population is increasing with great rapidity, that our resources are being correspondingly developed, and that each repayment of debt, by diminishing the charge for interest, makes a future reduction easier, there is reason to expect that the progress of redemption hereafter will not be less rapid than it has been heretofore. Some unforeseen contingency may of course arise to check us in our work of financial reform and progress, but if it shall continue to be successfully prosecuted, the United States, free from debt, and not oppressed with enormous military and naval expenditures, will certainly soon have an immense advantage in industrial competition with the overburdened nations of Europe. As an evidence of the wonderful prosperity of the country, the following statistics of the past year present an array of figures which speak more eloquently than words :

The public income of 1880 was - - -	$333,526,610
" " 1879 " - - -	273,827,184
Increase, - - - -	$ 59,699,426
Income of 1880 as above stated, - - -	$333,526,610
Expenditures, " " - - - -	267,642,987
Surplus, - - -	$ 65,883,653
Interest on public debt 1879, - - -	$105,327,949
" " 1880, - - -	95,757,575
Decrease of interest, - -	$9,570,374
Exports for the year ending June 30, 1880, - -	$835,793,924
Imports " " " - -	667,885,566
Balance of exports over imports, -	$167,908,359

With such a magnificent exhibit, it cannot be truthfully asserted that the nation is not in a financial condition to undertake any great enterprise which, like the proposed Three Americas Railway, may be deemed of transcendent public importance, nor that the national credit is not sufficiently good to obtain any amount of capital that may be required. It will not, however, be necessary to call on the government or people of the United States to provide, from the public treasury, any part of the capital required to build the Three Americas Railway. If Congress will guarantee five per cent. interest, every dollar can be obtained just as soon as it shall be wanted.

Capital in England is, at present, over-abundant; and good opportunities for investment are scarce. A London financial·newspaper, *The Spectator,* of July 24, 1880, says: "Can nobody suggest a stiff bit of work for English capitalists to do? They are standing idle in heaps, and they do not like it at all. According to the *Statist* of the 17th instant, a sum of money estimated at £200,000,000, is lying waiting for the profitable investment it is so difficult to find." Can it be doubted for an instant, that a guarantee of five per cent. interest by the government of the United States would unlock this marvelous store of treasure, equal to $1,000,000,000, and make at least a portion of it available for constructing this unrivaled international and intercontinental railway, even supposing that, for any reason, our own capitalists should hold aloof from taking an active part in it?

What better work could possibly be done by the government of the United States, than the giving of this guarantee? For argument's sake, let us suppose that, for a few years, the government might be called upon to pay the whole of the interest on $300,000,000, (but this is by no means probable,) the total expenditure would be only $15,000,000 per annum; a sum that sinks into absolute insignificance when compared with the enormous benefits which would certainly be conferred on the country by the building of the

5

great Longitudinal Line.   Without doubt some very material aid, in the form of land grants or guarantees of interest,
could be secured from the various countries through which,
and near which, the road will pass; but if the United States
alone were to assume the whole responsibility, the public
treasury would be amply repaid for any and every outlay it
might be called on to make, by the enlarged income it would
derive from the increased prosperity of the nation.

Within a few years after its completion, the railway would
not only be able to pay the interest on its capital, but also
to release the government entirely from its obligations as
guarantor.   In adopting this course, the United States would
only be following the example set by Great Britain in dealing with the railroads in her East Indian territory,.on whose
capital the British government has guaranteed five per cent.
interest.   Down to March 31, 1879, the amount raised as
capital, and debenture stock, for East Indian railroads, was
about £98,000,000, equal to nearly $500,000,000, involv-
ing an annual charge for interest of £4,900,000, equivalent
to $24,500,000.   Many of the roads are earning sums con-
siderably in excess of guaranteed interest; but this is reduced in average by smaller earnings from new and unfinished roads, and also from some which have been avowedly
constructed more for political and military ends than for
commercial purposes.   Notwithstanding these drawbacks,
in 1878 the net earnings were £5,000,000, equal to $25,-
000,000, thus enabling the roads to pay more than the guaranteed interest without aid from the government.

If the British government and people consider it a safe
and wise policy to incur the responsibility of guaranteeing
this vast sum, to encourage the building of railroads in a
dependency separated from England by half the world's
space, how much more eagerly should the government and
people of the United States, and the governments and peo-

ples of all the other American nationalities, grasp the opportunity of conferring such an inestimable benefit upon their respective countries as the Three Americas Railway would undoubtedly prove to be ! No more efficient means could possibly be devised to enforce and perfect the principles of the Monroe doctrine. America for Americans, would be something more than a mere political war-cry ; it would be an accomplished fact. As has already been beautifully suggested by the poet Canonge, the Three America's Railway, like a giant stretching his huge length all adown the continent, his head covered with northern snows, and his feet bathed in the rivers of the south, would represent the power and excellence of popular institutions, and would forever render foreign occupation of any portion of American territory (as in the case of Mexico a few years since) an utter impossibility.

In whatever light we view this stupendous enterprise, it discloses, in every aspect, such a boundless prospect of magnificent results, that even the recapitulation of them seems like an introduction into their details of the gorgeous imagery of an oriental romance ; but here we have another verification of the fact that truth is sometimes stranger than fiction. Our thoughts and labors are with a purely practical business project. No prophetic foresight nor vivid imagination can at all times picture fully the rich results that repay the bold enterprises and masterly conceptions of commercial genius. In this instance, the grandeur of the reward will be commensurate with the magnificent proportions of the work, which, when completed, will constitute the grandest monument of American energy and enterprise that it is possible to erect. It will immortalize the name of Hinton Rowan Helper as the originator of a scheme of international and intercontinental polity and intercourse, which will form the crowning glory of the United States, and lead to the grandest achievable victory of civilization throughout the whole Western Hemisphere. Let the people of the United States, and the other peoples of America, reward him in the manner that will be most grateful to him, by such earnest and efficient co-operation with him as will herein assure success, in manfully pressing this matchless enterprise to a speedy and perfect consummation.

SECOND PRIZE ESSAY.

(IN EPISTOLARY FORM.)

DELIBERATIONS AND AFFIRMATIONS RESPECTING THE PRO-
POSED THREE AMERICAS RAILWAY, IN RESPONSE TO MR.
HELPER'S SPECIAL OVERTURES AND PROMPTINGS ON THE
SUBJECT.

BY FREDERICK ANTHONY BEELEN,

(Cortlandt-on-the-Hudson, New York.)

OF all the mighty powers that are so rapidly changing the face of the
world, the railroad takes pre-eminence as an educator and civilizer.
This mighty interest is absorbing the largest capitalists, the most active
minds, and the most gifted projectors of our time.—*Josiah Quincy.*

CORTLANDT-ON-THE-HUDSON, NEW YORK,
September 15, 1880.

HON. THOMAS ALLEN,
CARLOS S. GREELEY, ESQ., and
DR. WILLIAM T. HARRIS:

GENTLEMEN:—"The object aimed at" by Mr. Helper,
to quote from his communication to you, under date of July
25, 1879, "is nothing less than the earliest possible construction of a longitudinal midland double-track steel railway, from a point high north in North America, running
more or less southwardly, through Mexico and Central

America, to a point far south in South America; looking ultimately to such necessary and gradual extensions, at either end, from time to time, as will eventually place Behring Strait and Cape Horn, and all the intermediate localities, in uninterrupted and continuous communication by steam and by telegraph."

A celebrated French author has said: " *Malheureux celui qui est en avant de son siècle,*" ("Unhappy he who is in advance of his age,") and although, in the history of science, politics, and the ordinary management of the world's conduct, we may find teeming evidence of this truism, we need go little farther back than our own time to prove it almost an axiom.

Franklin was stigmatized as an atheist, because he made "an impious attempt to control the artillery of Heaven." In 1807, the Battery at New York, and the banks of the Hudson, were lined with a jeering crowd, who had come to see "Fulton's Folly." Stephenson was ridiculed by a Parliamentary Committee, while the rich landed proprietors of England were with difficulty persuaded that his locomotive would not endanger the safety of their cattle. Lardner, the great scientist of his day and country, demonstrated mathematically the impossibility of trans-ocean steam-navigation, A pittance was doled out to the "madman" Morse, by an incredulous Congress of his countrymen. De Lesseps' name was a byword, because he would realize the dream of Egypt's better days; and it is almost so again, because he offers to open to the commerce of the nations what Sir Walter Raleigh told his Queen, three centuries ago, were "the world's gates." Yet, despite of all, the lightning has been taught to kiss its leading strings; the splash of the propeller is on every sea and river; the snort of the Ironhorse may be heard high up on the Andes and among the pyramids; the ocean is a highway, where leviathans jostle each other; the girdle of Ariel is "around the earth"; Suez has made the once wonderful voyage to India a holiday trip; and whether De Lesseps, or Menocal, or Eads, gives to us the keys of the Isthmus, none the less is the great fact patent to the world that Darien, Nicaragua, or Tehuantepec, will soon be a pathway of the nations.

Fables of yesterday are facts of to-day; dreams are realities. Edison tells us, in a breath, of conversing *viva voce* across the ocean; of annihilating darkness; of a three-days' aerial voyage to Europe; hints at, if not the Philosopher's Stone, an almost Midas touch; and scientists credit him, while Patent Offices give their sanction to his marvelous daring. Your own lion-hearted Eads satisfies, with the audacity of genius, the engineering world; and, what is more to the purpose, a Committee of Congress is at last considering with practical earnestness the feasibility of making a portage of Central America. England and France are soon to be united by rail; steam, the wonder of only half a century, is to be a thing of the past; while we are invited to believe that perpetual motion and the quadrature of the circle are among the possibilities.

Must the author of our project, then, trust only to posterity to give him credence? Is he to be numbered among those "unhappy men who are in advance of their age," and expect too much from their cotemporaries? It is proposed to open up to the commerce of our country the untold wealth of a continent, sister to our own, but almost unknown to us; to pour into the laps of our present and future millions the riches of other zones which even now rival India, and which, comparatively unknown as they are, are not so much so as were, a quarter of a century ago, Nevada or Colorado. Is our projected railway a little more problematical than any one of the other great schemes I have named?

This enterprise must be studied by itself. Its newness

should not be a bar to its careful consideration ; although
its novelty and its magnitude may deter many from investi-
gating it.   The majority of railroad men, with the light of
their experience, may regard it as somewhat premature,
while honestly acknowledging its practicability.   Others
will, for a time, look upon it as too hopelessly gigantic to
be undertaken in this age.   But let us study it in detail,
master its magnificent alphabet, become familiar with its
individual parts, and then the only wonder that will remain
to us, and that not unmingled with regret, will be that we
ourselves were not its originators..

Mr. Helper knows well, from long residence among them,
the peoples of Central and South America.   His proposition, while at first startling, soon ceases to be so, and is far-
seeing and comprehensive, exhibiting broad and truly cos-
mopolitan views, such as could emanate only from a reflective mind familiar with the present status and the national
needs of the two great sections of Spanish America, and
with the means most likely to elevate and improve their
condition, while uniting them with us by bonds of mutual
interest ; for merely sentimental considerations, while they
may be interesting, and in many ways commendable and
beautiful, cannot of themselves constitute a lasting bond
of union between different adjoining nations.

Nature, or the invariable custom of centuries, has ordained that the habits, manners and employments of different peoples should bear a distinct relation to the geographical, topographical and climatic conditions of the countries
they inhabit.   Through these, in a great measure, though
not wholly, national characteristics have arisen.   This general remark applies, in many cases, even to minor districts
of the same country.   Even in the comparatively small region of England a great diversity of habits and customs,
and even of peculiarities of thought and language, are found

in the different counties, whether maritime or inland, commercial or manufacturing, pastoral or agricultural. Without pursuing further this parallelism, we may apply it, in a general way, to the study of the grand proposition for uniting, by an intercontinental railway, the three principal geographical divisions of North, Central and South America.

Among the first and most important things to be considered, are the extent and kind of populations, the characteristics and the present and future capabilities of the respective peoples, whom it is thus proposed to unite more closely by that wonderful modern civilizer and peacemaker, the railway. There has been a certain sort of partial, indefinite acquaintanceship, nothing more, between all the different nations of the three Americas, brought about by years of commercial transactions of an exceedingly limited character, carried on by ocean vessels, under sail, trading between them. Of late years this has been somewhat facilitated by steamships, both on the Atlantic and Pacific coasts. During the whole of the century which has witnessed the birth and growth of our own country, all of the nations of Central and South America have maintained much more intimate relations with the older countries of Europe than with the United States; owing, in a great measure, to the fact that, long before we became a commercial power, Europeans saw the advantages of a closer relationship, and laid the foundations of the immense trade now existing; and which, only in latter years, we have even pretended to dispute with them. The smallness of our merchant marine, made smaller by our late war and the continuance of our odious navigation laws, while it is another cause, precludes us from any hope of a successful competition with the European merchant by sea, and leaves us the single but unquestionable alternative of wresting from him, by intercontinental commerce, the scepter he has held so long, and, it may be added, so despotically.

In corroboration of what has here been advanced, I may quote Mr. Nimmo, Chief of the Bureau of Statistics at Washington, who, in a late pamphlet, " The Proposed Interoceanic Canal in its Commercial Aspects," assures us that we have but twenty-four vessels in the Chilian trade, against three hundred and seventy-two going between Chilian and European ports. I may add, from my own knowledge, that not one of our twenty-four is a steam-going vessel; while among the others, those under European flags, are many and magnificent ocean steamers. What is 'here said of Chili in general is equally true of any Spanish American port. Any American who has voyaged on the southern seas, whether the Pacific or the Atlantic, will remember his delight at seeing a vessel in the distance, and then his almost invariable disappointment, when, on nearer approach, some other flag than that of the United States floated from her peak. It was often sneeringly asked, in times fortunately gone by, " Who reads an American book ?" and, unless restrictions on our commerce become fewer, it may soon be asked, at least in South American waters, " Who sees an American ship ?"

All of the South American nations, excepting only Brazil, are descendants of the Spaniards; while Mexico and Central America are occupied by descendants of Spaniards and those of the Indian aborigines, which latter have universally adopted the language, religion and customs of their conquerors. It is a notable fact, that all the countries which bound Brazil, and which we will treat of separately hereafter, as they come within the scope of our proposed railway route, namely, the Argentine Republic, Uruguay, Paraguay, Chili, Bolivia, Peru, Ecuador, the United States of Columbia, Venezuela, and Dutch and British and French Guiana, are now Spanish; while Brazil, covering a territory as large as the United States, (being over three millions of square miles, and embracing nearly half a continent,) is wholly and exclusively Portuguese, in its language and its institutions; though these latter have been considerably modified during the last quarter of a century, under the influence of liberal institutions, administered by an enlightened chief magistrate.

All of these countries, excepting Brazil and Guiana, are under republican forms of government. Many of their governments are far from being stable, owing, in large measure, to the ingnorance of the great bulk of their populations; which only a long time and favoring circumstances can remedy. Nor can there be a doubt that this condition of things must retard their advancement among the nations. So long as a few bold and unscrupulous men can wield a nation's destiny, it is folly to call it free. But among them are States which, for purity of administration, a high sense of national honor, energy of character, and a just pride in their own worth, have nothing to envy in older nations.

Common human slavery has long been unknown in the Spanish American Republics; but the masses of the people have not yet been brought under the ameliorating influences of a proper education, and do not know, or do not appreciate, the value of free government. Until they have learned this much they must continue to be the real slaves of their arbitrary and practically self-constituted masters. Brazil,—with which country the Three Americas Railway will necessarily have a close relationship, in the event of the adoption of one of the routes I shall trace,—Brazil, with an imperial and constitutional government, though still containing millions of grossly ignorant human beings, and more than a million in actual slavery, is making every effort to throw off her terrible incubus. Brazil, too, is destined to become a Republic; and very probably, like some of her Spanish American neighbors, she will become so before her masses are well prepared for self-government. The world may then witness revolutionary contentions of political factions on even a larger scale than has yet been seen in any of those Republics. Ultimately, when the different peoples of Brazil shall know enough, they will all become free ; and humanity will have great reason to exult, when that day arrives, that not one human slave will be held on the Western Hemisphere, from Behring Strait to the shores of Magellan.

Meanwhile, it has seemed to me of paramount importance, to call your attention to the present and near future status of the several countries between the United States and Patagonia; as this is a necessary part of the study of plans for carrying into effect the proposed intercontinental railway ; and, if I speak somewhat authoritatively concerning them, it is because I have lived long in Central and South America, and may be presumed to have a just appreciation of them. It must be clear, then, to those who are at all familiar with the past history and present condition of the great majority of the countries under consideration, that, with only the present ocean-route avenues connecting them, to a limited extent, commercially along their coasts, and scarcely at all socially, long cycles of years must roll around without essentially changing the characteristics of the different peoples, or materially assimilating them with each other, and infinitely less with the United States, unless some new and very powerful factor, such as the proposed intercontinental railway, shall be introduced.

The marvelous effects of railways in energizing a people, and in developing and giving value to regions previously regarded as almost worthless, is now so well understood that capital generally stands ready to embark upon slight provocation, in such undertakings, in the expectation of similar favorable results. This has been shown, and at a very early date, in several Spanish American States. Thirty years ago the first railway enterprise was inaugurated in South America, in that wonderfully progressive Republic, Chili, by two Americans, William Wheelwright, of Massachusetts, and William G. Morehead, of Philadelphia. The first termini were Caldera, on the Pacific coast, and Copiapo, in the interior. The eastern terminus is now Chanarcillo, far up in the mountain region. While this enterprise was the beginning of Chili's prosperity, it has paid enormous dividends to its projectors. Gradually since then many others have been constructed in Chili, Peru, Brazil, and the Argentine Republic; all of which, designed to improve and accommodate the particular regions through which they have been constructed, have, with perhaps the exception of the Oroya, in Peru, proved very lucrative investments; and, although these railroads were not planned nor located in view of a future longitudinal Three Americas Railway, as now proposed by Mr. Helper, yet, in the event of the construction of such intercontinental main trunk-line, many of them must necessarily connect with it, and contribute greatly to its general business, at the same time increasing vastly their own traffic.

Late years have wrought vast changes in Spanish American enterprise, changes hardly to have been expected when we take into consideration the education of these peoples, under the colonial system of Spain, the never sufficiently well appreciated difficulties under which they have so long labored; difficulties not of their own creating, for they were the sins of the fathers visited upon their children; and the almost consequent tendency to retrograde rather than advance. All this has changed, and every opportunity to improve their condition is now eagerly embraced, while no offered helping-hand toward progress is ever refused.

Some of the Spanish American Republics are naturally

as far in advance of their sister states as their resources and advantages have been greater, but all feel that the spirit of the century is upon them. Some have been more than lavish in their railway expenditures; though it must be admitted that nowhere in the world can greater triumphs of civil engineering be seen than in some parts of Spanish America. Few roads can surpass the great one from Vera Cruz to the city of Mexico; while the Oroya road, winding away up among the ice-covered Andes of Peru, has no equal. It may, therefore, safely be predicted that there is not one of the South American Republics which will not earnestly co-operate in the furtherance of a project so eminently calculated to advance their almost every interest as is the Three Americas Railway. They will soon see that the construction of such a line through their territories will confer great and lasting benefits upon each one of them; that, even as nationalities of the same origin, they would be united as never heretofore; that it would be the nucleus around which would cluster a never-ending series of internal improvements, which would contribute eventually to the establishment of new and more improved industries, and to the development of resources, which, without the help of this modern right-hand of civilization, would forever remain dormant.

It would be unjust, in appreciating the more or less successful future of such a railway as the Three Americas, to do so by a comparison of the present condition of the interior of South America; the total absence there of everything, almost, which we consider necessaries of life; the ignorance of the masses; and the utter lack of all stimulus toward ameliorating their condition; in contrast with the status of nations, like England or our own, in the enjoyment of every blessing which flows from a civilization of the highest order; a knowledge of the arts; and the possession

and adaptation of all the means which science and the myr-
iad appliances the inventive age it is our privilege to live
in, has given us. Let us, rather, ask ourselves, not what we
would be without these distinctive characteristics, but what
we were in the near past, before we possessed them ; and
then let us imagine those same facilities given to the people
of Spanish America (a people with a name and a past as
proud as our own, and with a record equally great,)
and you may no longer doubt that, with such advantages,
and similarly blessed as ourselves, the southern portion of
our continent will become, and rapidly too, as much a
wonder to the world, and as widely opened an asylum
for the nations of Europe, as is our own.

A moment's retrospect at our own and England's past
may make us more forbearing toward our less fortunate
neighbors. I say England's, for whatever of advancement
she may have had, was soon equally ours ; and seeing
what she was, what occasioned the change, and reasoning
from effect back to cause, may promise well for the future
of our project. An English writer, Robert Mackenzie, the
able Editor of *The Nineteenth Century*, says :—" Until long
after the middle of the eighteenth century, commerce was
strangled by the impossibility of conveying goods from one
part of the country to another. They were almost without
roads at home. *It cost forty shillings* * *to transport a ton
of coal from Liverpool to Manchester*. The food of London was for the most part carried on pack-horses. *Often
the large towns endured famine, while the farmers at no
great distance could find no market for their meat and grain.*
Communication between London and Glasgow was maintained by a stage-coach, which undertook this great enterprise only once in a month, and accomplished it in twelve

* Ten dollars.

or fourteen days. The seclusion resulting from the absence of roads, rendered it necessary that every little community, in some measure every family, should produce all that it required to consume. The peasant raised his own food. He grew his own flax and wool; his wife or daughters spun it, and a neighbor wove it into cloth. Commerce was impossible until men could find the means of transporting commodities from the place where they were produced to the place where there were people willing to make use of them." Now we have only to substitute Spanish America for England, in the above quotation, and every syllable is exactly applicable to the interior, an interior which commences very near the coast of all South and Central America.

It is unnecessary to my purpose to go back so far in our own history. There are those on your Committee who have seen, and that only the third of a century ago, their own fellow citizens of that time, the Aulls and the McCrums, the Chouteaus, and the Valles, and others, of that noble army of St. Louis pioneers, going to the East once a year, (it was too serious a journey to undertake oftener,) to purchase their goods. Probably they have seen, as I have, coming into Pittsburg, those mammoth wagons, looking like ships on wheels, laden with goods which, bought in Philadelphia, had been on their toilsome and winding way from that city over the Alleghanies for fifteen days, and which, if the Ohio river happened not to be frozen over or dried up, as was said of it once in Congress, were fortunate in reaching St. Louis in fifteen more. *Thirty days from Philadelphia to St. Louis !* This was in our own country, not forty years ago; in a country where the rivers were frozen over for months; and where, in our Western towns, cities now, the mail came in, when it came at all, once a week, in a stage-coach, bringing not unfrequently a single passenger; in a country which only the toil of years and the sweat of man's brow could reclaim from the primitive wilderness, and his rifle defend from the dispossessed savage. Had there been nothing more, would St. Louis be to-day the great emporium she is? But there was more. The railroad came, and the rest of your history is as a tale of the Thousand and One Nights. To bring that change down to statistics, allow me to quote from a speech of Consul-General Walker, at a recent banquet in Paris:

"In 1870, the cost of transporting merchandise between the Western and Eastern States, was a cent and a half to two cents a ton a mile. I well remember a conversation I had, at that time, with Mr. Wm. B. Ogden, of Chicago, one of the modest railway kings of that primitive period. In a vein of sanguine prophecy Mr. Ogden exclaimed to me: 'Mr. Walker, you will live to see freight brought from Chicago to New York at a cent a ton a mile!' 'Perhaps so,' I replied, 'but I fear this result will not be reached in my time.' *In 1877 or 1878, the cost had fallen to three-eights of a cent a ton a mile!* The effect of this reduction in the cost of transportation is precisely as though the inexhaustible grain fields and pastures on the west side of the Mississippi had been moved bodily eastward to the longitude of Ohio and the lake region of New York." While General Walker was saying this, Mr. Edward Atkinson, the great statistician, was publishing, in London, that: "The movement of one year's subsistence of grain and meat for an adult working man, a distance of one thousand miles, is equal to a dollar and twenty-five cents, or five shillings, which sum is equal to one day's wages of a common workman, or half the daily wages of a good carpenter or mason. *Half of one day's wages, one thousand miles, and the movement of one year's subsistence, are synonymous terms! One day's pay places the mechanic of Massachusetts next*

6

door to the Western prairie a thousand miles away!" These
are facts, facts patent to all, facts to be repeated wherever
and whenever a railway system is projected to penetrate a
new and rich country.

Why not, then, carry the railway into South America, and
thereby regenerate a Continent? Is Spanish America less
inviting now than Missouri and the wild West were then?
Are the Orinoco, the Amazon, La Plata and Parana less
able to bear your mammoth barges than the Missouri and
the Mississippi? Are South America's inexhaustible forests of lignum-vita, mahogany, logwood, ebony, caoutchouc,
and rosewood, not well worth exploring? Are her silver,
gold, coal, diamond and emera'd mines, and the measureless beds of nitrate of soda, less alluring than the Californias,
which have already brought two railways across a continent?
Can there be found on earth a soil richer or more yielding,
to tempt the agriculturist?

Another inducement, and no trifling one, in connection
with our subject, is the character of the native of South
America. When I use the word "native," I mean that class
of the population which is a cross-breed, as well as the Indian. They are called "peons" in Mexico and elsewhere.
It is this class that does all the labor. When properly
treated, and their wants are extremely limited, they wi'l
work well, and are faithful. I have frequently heard Mr.
Henry Meiggs, who built several very important railways in
Chili and Peru, say that he preferred them, as laborers, to
any in the world; not only because they work well, but on
account of their very docile and tractable character. This
is no unimportant matter in new countries and in climates
which are naturally trying to foreigners; and it exclud s
the necessity of importing from the United States, or from
China, laborers who would require double the care, and
exact treble the wages, that would amply satisfy the native
workman.

I have said that the governments of Spanish America were republican, at least in form; and yet I have just implied a very marked distinction between the " natives" and the inhabitants of pure Spanish descent.   This would seem a contradiction, and the more especially so under constitutions which declare all men to be free and equal.   The same anomaly was · and is sufficiently familiar to ourselves, and it will probably remain so during long years, despite any and all legislative enactments.   The " Cholo," in Peru, the " Cuico," in Bolivia, the " Huaso," in Chili, and the " Gaucho," in the Argentine Republic,—for by these several names they are known,—while equal in the eye of the law to their more fortunate fellow citizen, and permitted by the latter to fight his battles, are as far removed from him, and by as impassable a social barrier, as are from each other the distinctive castes of India.   While the so-called " Caballero," (gentleman) or he of pure white blood, can never, no matter how poor or degraded he may become, be other than a " Caballero," it sometimes happens, under extraordinary circumstances, that the other may rise to the privileged order.   But this is the exception, and is quite as unfrequent as for a commoner in Great Britain to reach the Peerage.   There have been brilliant exceptions, as Carrera in Guatemala, Juarez in Mexico, and Paez in Venezuela.   The difference, however, does not end here.   It would be derogatory to the social status of the Spaniard to do any menial, subordinate or remunerative (except brain) work; and hence I have said that all the labor of these countries is performed by the native, or inferior classes.   Education alone can modify this condition of things; and it is already doing so to a considerable extent in Chili, in the Argentine Republic, and in the United States of Columbia, in which countries much attention is now given to the instruction of the masses; and where common schools are beginning to become the order of the day.

I have not hesitated in extending the foregoing observations concerning the character and general condition of the countries, peoples and governments with which the promoters of the great intercontinental railway must enter into such close and intimate relations. It has been with the well-considered purpose of making you as familiar with them as the limits of this paper would permit; thus enabling you better to judge whether the distant parties to be benefitted were to be obstacles in your primary surveys and ultimate construction of the proposed railway, or rather your efficient coadjutors. A complete knowledge of the peoples, their customs, ambitions, greater or less spirit of enterprise, physical condition, their systems of government, ability to co-operate with those who may have the direction of this gigantic scheme, and the probable honorableness with which they may carry out their pacted word or more serious contracts, involving the very life of the enterprise,—all these must necessarily be as unquestionably interesting as a knowledge of the physical character of the countries in which the rails are to be laid. Even more so, for while there can hardly be found a natural obstacle which engineering skill may not easily overcome, it would require superhuman power to modify at once the character of a nation.

It will be by no means a difficult matter for us, on entering Spanish America, to choose our route. In Central America there can be but one, while in South America there are two possible ones. When the necessary and proper negotiations with the several governments shall have been perfected, it will then be simply a question to be decided by the surveys. Not so in the United States. Mr. Helper's proposition does not look to any immediate construction of the entire Three Americas Railway, from Behring Strait to Cape Horn, as is erroneously supposed by those giddy-headed individuals who have flippantly commented upon it, but from a starting "point high north in North America to a point far south in South America, looking ultimately to such necessary and gradual extensions, at either end, from time to time, as will eventually place Behring Strait and Cape Horn, and all the intermediate localities, in uninterrupted and continuous communication by steam and by telegraph." It would seem folly in me, writing to Western railroad men, or to a general public conversant with all our routes, to discuss, unless in a general way, the particular line to be adopted for the Three Americas Railway while traversing our own country.

Let us consider, then, only briefly, the plan of a new and independent track, beginning at some central point in one of our most northern States, or in Canada, and running in a general southerly direction to a convenient place of crossing the Rio Grande, the northern boundary of Mexico. On some accounts it might be desirable to have such a new line upon different ground from any now under charter for other railways; but this proposition is at once met by the fact that the best ground may already be occupied; that the north and south roads, two or three of which have been constructed at great cost, have created and secured a large local business, which now sustains them; and that a proposed additional parallel line would be a rival instead of a coadjutor.

These and other considerations would probably not only prevent such roads from co-operating with, but would lead them to oppose, such new line. It will therefore be advisable to ascertain whether the project of a new and independent line, so far as our own country is to be gone over, possesses such paramount advantages as to insure its success in the face of all opposing lines. Experience has shown, in some cases, that where a single railroad, through a given region, would have been a success, the construction of two lines has rendered both unprofitable. The plan of selecting some finished line or lines, as part of the Three Americas Railway, would at once enlist those companies as active friends of the proposed system.

No single line can directly accommodate more than a limited zone through which it passes; and in the wide area between the Atlantic and Pacific oceans, embracing, between New York and San Francisco, forty-nine degrees of longitude and thirty-three hundred miles of railroad, there is room for numerous north and south lines. In fact, there are already running, between the Atlantic coast and the Mississippi River, seven railroads which may be regarded as north and south lines, or closely approximating thereto. There is another, passing through St. Louis, on the west side of the river, running to Little Rock and Austin, on its way to the Rio Grande, which it will soon reach at the city of Rio Grande; another, passing through Kansas City, running down toward the same point; another, passing through Denver, in Colorado, probably intended to strike the Mexican territory farther west; another, passing through Salt Lake City; and still another, on the Pacific coast, passing through San Francisco.

There is no doubt that all of these roads will connect with the line or lines crossing the Rio Grande, either directly or indirectly, and ultimately, as I have indicated, extending to the City of Mexico. From St. Louis, and from Kansas City northward, there are finished lines, with only a short uncompleted link in the State of Minnesota, crossing the Northern Pacific Railroad, and reaching to and beyond the northern boundary of the United States, extending into Manitoba, in Canada, and connecting with the Canada Pacific Railway at Fort Garry, on the Red River of the North, and really only three hundred miles distant from Mr. Helper's suggested terminus on Hudson Bay. This general north and south line, from Fort Garry to the Rio Grande, comprising about two thousand miles of railway, is perhaps as nearly central, with respect to the future population and industries of the country, as any single line can well be. Between St. Louis and the northern boundary of the United States, this route is already crossed by thirteen east and west railways, each of which must be a feeder to the great north and south line as well as a recipient of the traffic brought to it by that line.

A proper organization of prominent and experienced rail-road-men, interested in one or more of these north and south lines, would seem to be the most proper means of securing the best route for all that part of the Three Americas Railway across the territory of the United States, and as far north as Fort Garry, in Manitoba, in the British possessions. Under good management, there can be no doubt that the local business along the entire distance would soon yield a highly remunerative income. All this seems like romance, when we consider that the railway system, which was only fairly begun in 1828, was a quarter of a century reaching the Mississippi River; and that the project of constructing a railway beyond that to the Pacific ocean was discussed during a period of thirty years before it was finally achieved. It was at first ridiculed by the majority of mankind. Even as late as 1853, when the government ordered the surveys of three distinct routes across the continent, the people generally regarded it as chimerical, and the cost of the surveys as waste of public money. Time has shown that it was one of the best and most productive investments ever made by the people of the United States; and yet all that the government under-took, through the two chartered corporations,—the Union Pacific and the Central Pacific Railroad companies,—was to open a railway from the Missouri River, at Omaha, to the Pacific Ocean, a distance of only nineteen hundred miles.

Quite recently capital, it is stated, has been raised to prosecute the long contemplated railway from the Rio Grande, our boundary line with Mexico, to the City of Mexico. Not many years are likely to elapse ere this first link in the chain will be completed; there will then be practically a continuous line or lines of railroads all the way from near Hudson Bay to the southern boundary of the United States, and thence to the capital of Mexico. The distance between the two latter points is about eight hundred miles.

No grant has been given by Mexico, as yet, to any corporation for the construction of this road; and there is no reason why the promoters of the Three Americas Railway should not receive it in preference to any other company, inasmuch as its intention is to prolong the road, in a direct line, from the capital to the boundary with Guatemala, a distance of five hundred miles further south, and thence onward, far south into South America. The most powerful incentive that could be presented to the government and people of Mexico, to induce their favorable action, would be the statement that the construction of the Three Americas Railway had been definitely settled and well provided for through their entire country and Central America; while the strongest argument with the governments of South America will be the assurance that its construction had been secured through Central America and Mexico.

It might seem a waste of time were I to enter into any arguments, or adduce any statistics, to prove to you the immense advantages which would probably result from an independent line through our own territory, from a point high north to our boundary line with Mexico, to he continued to the capital of that country; and thence, having the grant through Mexico, moving forward to the boundary of Guatemala, and beyond, under other requisite and appropriate grants, through all the Central American Republics. Thus we may see ourselves gradually led on until we shall reach a terminal point "far south in South America." Nor need I here dwell upon the present of Kansas, or the great future of Colorado and New Mexico, through which, as we have seen, almost to the Rio Grande, there is now a nearly completed railway.

Yet I am strongly tempted, in view of the fact that our route will lie through new countries, to pause a moment, near the border-line of our own country, and take a brief retrospect, and thus answer the constantly recurring question: "What is the use of carrying a railway into those new and sparsely-settled territories?" I need not recall to you the remark of General Sherman, in 1865, that he would not buy a railroad ticket for San Francisco for his youngest grand-child." He went there four years later in a Pullman car! But I may ask you to remember the recital of Josiah Gregg, the amiable author of *The Commerce of the Prairies*, (1845,) and whom many of you in St. Louis knew well, —to remember his long adventurous travels across the then wilderness between your State and Santa Fé, occupying weeks upon weeks of toil and exposure, outlay and danger, and then, by way of contrast, to read in a correspondence, of July last, that "the railroad which first entered the territory of New Mexico, but little more than a year ago, has been built with surprising rapidity, so that Las Vegas, Santa Fé and Albuquerque are now within about four days' travel from New York." Let us remember too that, in constructing this New Mexican road, two ranges of mountains have been crossed, the Raton and the Santa Fé, the pass over the former being about 8,000 feet high, and that over the latter 7,400 feet; to reach which altitudes the track had to be laid on a grade of 186 feet to the mile, the steepest that has ever been attained and adopted by any standard-guage railway in the world. Finally, as a conclusion on this subject, I shall quote from the report of a distinquished scientist, who has just returned from New Mexico:

" The wonderful rapidity with which the great railroad lines are being extended over our Western Territories is one of the amazing marvels of the century. It used to be supposed that a country must be settled before it could support a railway ; and those who projected new lines followed the great routes, which internal commerce had already established for itself, and whose facilities it had already outgrown. The railway is now the pioneer of civilization. It pushes out into countries that are almost destitute of population, and which have not felt the stimulating influence of outside capital, following close upon the heels of the Government exploring expeditions, whose reports and descriptions of scenery read almost like the exaggerated fictions of Jules Verne. The man who invests his money in a railroad project to-day, does so not because he believes the trade of the country through which it is to pass is already sufficient to support the road, but because he expects the enterprise to stimulate travel and trade, and to create business for itself. With this object in view, these ever-pulsating arteries of commerce are boldly pushed out into the deserts and mountains, and constructed over hundreds of miles of country in which the population, if it were to abandon every other industry, would not be sufficient to furnish the labor necessary to do the grading."

These facts are too self-evident to require any further enlargement upon them ; and as the great ambition of our projector is the establishment of a route through Spanish America, now that we have already seen, with our mental vision, a continuous line of north and south railway nearly two thousand miles long,—from Lake Manitoba to the borders of Mexico,—let us at once enter that territory. Mexico is the only one of the Spanish American Republics that is not entirely unknown to a great majority of our people; but even of her something may be said as we cross her boundary.

Mexico will be the first to welcome us and give a helping hand to our great project. She knows well that all schemes of annexation on our part are at an end, and that we have at last come to recognize the fact that our present territorial limits are large enough to contain our own future millions, and still afford an asylum for the overworked and underfed multitudes of other lands. The experience cf 1867 has convinced her that if our armed forces should ever again enter her territory, it will be to defend our well-loved principle of non-interference on this continent, and not as enemies. Her motto is no longer as once, and with much reason, " *Timeo Danaos et dona ferentes.*" (" I fear the Greeks, even when they offer presents.") She has proved that she knows how to appreciate those who come with imperial crowns. She has also shown that when committees, representative of the great commercial interests of the Mississippi Valley approach her, as last year from St. Louis and Chicago, with agricultural, mining and railway machinery, tendered by the right hand of fellowship, she is ready to welcome them as friends and as teachers. Her area of 760,000 square miles, while her population is hardly ten millions, of whom more than half are Indians and half-breeds, can give ample room to fifty millions more. Her peculiar geographical position, bounded on the east by a great gulf, and on the west by a vast ocean, gives her unusually desirable commercial advantages, as yet but little appreciated. Her soil, generally fertile, and her varied climate enable her to produce all the delicious fruits and spicy luxuries of the tropics, and likewise most of the cereals of colder countries ; while her forests abound in the richest ornamental, cabinet and dyewoods.   Her mines of gold, silver, iron, copper, lead, tin, and quicksilver are proverbial for their richness, and, as yet, have scarcely been explored. All the mining region that has made the United States the greatest gold and silver producing country in the world was once Mexican territory.   Mexico's greatest drawback, in the working of her mines, is the heavy cost of transporting the bullion from the mines to the coast; and if sent to the mint, whether of London, of Philadelphia, or of the City of Mexico, the cost of transportation, and that of coining and commission, leave little margin for the successful miner.

Our exports to and our imports from Mexico are only about a hundredth part of what, with increased facilities, they would be ; the former having been, in 1879, $15,000,-000; while the latter were less than $7,000,000.   At immensely remunerative prices, in connection with the reduced freight of railway carriage, our domestics, bleached and unbleached, and our calicoes, would not find, even in China itself, a better market than Mexico, owing to the preponderating numbers of the poorer or peon class, whose dress consists chiefly of such goods.   This is not the place to enter more lengthily into statistical details.   It is sufficient to say that, as Mexico has no manufactures, there is scarcely an article we produce that would not find ready sale, but which we cannot send there now, simply for want of the means of transportation.   There are already in the country some seven hundred miles of railway and eight thousand miles of lines of telegraph.   The freight and passenger tariff, from the City of Mexico to Vera Cruz, on the railway constructed by the English engineer Lloyd, with English capital, is simply enormous ; it is prohibitive to the introduction there of much we could send them, by way of

New Orleans, the only way of sending there anything at all.

With our Three Americas Railway in operation, Mexico would soon become our best and nearest customer; while increased intercourse between us would doubtless make us better friends forever. That the road would vastly ameliorate her moral status, need hardly be argued. It will be, however, in Mexico, as in Texas years ago, and in Spanish America everywhere, not so much the people, and much less the government, that will oppose our closer relationship, as the British merchant, who naturally sees in the near future that with such a road as we now propose, the rich commercial advantages he has so long enjoyed in the absence of competition, will escape from his grasp. We have learned to rival him with success on other commercial fields; why not also in Mexico? General Grant, in a letter to General Romero, of the Mexican Cabinet, writes as follows, under date of April 13, 1880: " Mexico could send to the United States, each year, $200,000,000 of her products, tropical and semi-tropical, and could produce besides the same quantity for other markets. Moreover, the income of the Republic would augment from sixteen to eighty millions at least." And this with only one railway; that from her principal seaport to her capital. What excellent results might not follow from railroad communication through her entire territory?

Close to the sixteenth parallel of north latitude we enter what was, from 1525 to 1821, the Kingdom of Guatemala, afterward, until 1829, the Confederated States of Central America; then the five Republics of Central America; being, all the while, the second division of the three Americas. Theirs has been, from the very first, a hard struggle to maintain even a semblance of real republicanism. The pernicious legacy left them by Spain, as to all her colonies, of every vice and not a single estimable moral quality, other

than indomitable courage, together with the incessant quarrels of nearly half a century, instigated by and in the interests of first the several successful revolutionary chiefs, who
achieved their independence, and afterward of their successors, had, until a few years since, brought them to the very
lowest ebb as nations; while their intestine wars made them
the shuttlecock of every daring adventurer, and one of
them, in 1855, the mark of even filibustering greed. Yet,
through all this, without ever finding a generous friend or a
pitying foe, they have bravely struggled for better things.
They have become more stable, and consequently more respected among the nations; while, from their peculiar geographical position, and from the needs of the commercial
world, they now find themselves in the enviable situation of
being able to dictate to the promoters of the two grandest
projects of the century,—the Interoceanic Canal, or Ship
Railway, and the Intercontinental Railway of the Three
Americas,—the terms upon which they may enter and cross
their territories.

The imports of all the Central American States, in 1879,
were under $12,000,000; while their exports were $18,000,-
000; and of these Great Britain enjoyed, as usual, the lion's
share, although at treble the distance of our own markets,
with much inferior qualities of merchandise to give in return, and at prices that would gladden the hearts of our
producers and manufacturers. All this, too, simply because
she has lines of steamers direct to several ports, and which
—at least in the case of the line running to the Gulf-of-
Mexico-port of Guatemala—have no port or other charges
to pay. We have only the line from Panama to San Francisco, which touches bimonthly at one port in Costa Rica,
one in Salvador, and one in Guatemala. California, not
being as yet a skilled-labor State, has little to send in the
way of manufactures; and exports, by way of the Isthmus,

are burdened by very serious railroad charges before reaching transhipment at Aspinwall.

Guatemala, the most northerly of these States, has an area of 40,700 square miles, a population of 1,000,000, and lies between latitude 13° 45' and 18° 10'. The climate on the coasts of Guatemala is unhealthy and trying to foreigners, while the interior higher country is extremely temperate and salubrious. The country is well watered and very fertile. There would be no end to the productive capacity of this little Republic, were there any stimulus for it. Her lower classes are somewhat, though not much, in advance of those of her sister Republics; while the distinguished talents of many of her statesmen have been amply acknowledged both in this country and Europe. She was one of the first to writhe under and finally throw off that incubus of many of these commonwealths, clerical dominion in State and social relations; and now she awaits only a greater facility of intercourse with the outer world to make her commercial position commensurate with her great natural advantages. Her commerce, carried on chiefly through her only port, on the Gulf of Mexico, consists of $4,200,000 exports, and about $3,000,090 of imports. The latter comprise an infinity of articles, received mostly from Great Britain; while the former are coffee, cochineal and indigo,—these all being of superior quality,—sarsaparilla, tobacco, mahogany and dyewoods. The excellent harbor on the Gulf side, already mentioned, with others on the Pacific, would give great facilities to our railroad constructors for the debarkation of plant; while her vast forests will furnish, for centuries, at the mere cost of cutting, all the necessary timber. The character of the natives is docile. All the agricultural labor is performed by them, and they are strong and sinewy.

The route which I suggest through Guatemala would be

from a point east of the coast-range of mountains, thirty miles from the Pacific, and thence in a direct line to the City of Guatemala, the capital. From the capital to the coast a railway is now under contract, and the first section is already built. From the capital to the northern border of Salvador the distance is thirty miles, while to the boundary line of Honduras it is sixty. The mountainous nature of the country to the southeast of the capital will incline the line toward the Pacific coast, where no very high grades will be required.

- We come now to the Republics of Salvador and Honduras, lying side by side;   the latter having three hundred and fifty miles of coast on the Gulf of Mexico, and an excellent harbor on the Pacific. in the Gulf of Fonseca. Salvador lies wholly on the Pacific, and transacts her foreign commerce principally through the excellent port of La Union on the Gulf of Fonseca. It was from this same gulf to a point opposite the island of Roatan, in the Gulf of Mexico, that, in 1854, it was proposed to construct either a canal or a railway, or both; and grants were readily given for that purpose by Honduras. I would, with the best intentions, however, avoid Honduras completely, leaving her untouched by our line; not alone from the very mountainous chraracter of the country and its rather sparse population, but because the route through Salvador will be a direct one, over a comparativly easy grade, and from the further fact of there being on it three very important towns, —the capital, San Salvador, to the westward, and San Miguel and La Union, to the southeast. San Miguel is the city where are annually held the great Central American Fairs, to which congregate merchants from all parts of the neighboring Republics. Immediately opposite La Union is Estero Real, a small river of Nicaragua which empties into the Gulf of Fonseca. It will thus be observed that the three Republics, Nicaragua, Honduras, and Salvador, have each a harbor on this accommodating and commdious gulf. Our route will be, then, for one hundred and eighty miles, through Salvador, which, with a population of 600,-000, and an area of only 7,500 square miles, has an element of thriving and industrious people, and is deservedly one of the most respected of the Central American Republics. Her admirable harbor may be found of very great use in future operations. The imports of Salvador, in 1879, were nearly $5,000,000 while the exports reached only $2,250,000.

Making La Union the terminus in Salvador, a great outlay may be saved by portage from the port to the mouth of the small river directly opposite and fifty miles distant. This will be the only way of avoiding entering the Republic of Honduras, which, though with a population of only 350,000, mostly natives, is not to be lightly thought of in connection with our road. Her mineral wealth is immense, and consists of gold, silver, platinum, zink, copper, antimony, tin, opal, amethyst, and coal mines ; all of which may be said to be virgin; while her forest and fruit and vegetable sources of wealth exceed those of the adjoining Republics. Every possible advantage would be given by Honduras, whose government has always been intelligently desirous of facilitating any enterprise tending to better the condition of her people. But supposing the route I have proposed be adopted, the capital of Honduras, Comayagua, would be distant only sixty-five miles from the main line, at La Union. A railroad has already been projected, if not in course of actual construction, between the capital and the Gulf of Fonseca.

Next we come to the largest and most important of the Central American Republics—Nicaragua. There is no choice of routes here. Starting from the mouth of the

7

Estero Real, and continuing in a direct line to the city of
Leon; thence southwardly, coasting the lake of Managua,
on the west side, to the capital, Managua; thence to
Granada, on the beautiful lake of Nicaragua; thence along
the western shore of this lake to its extreme southern limit,
at the point where it empties into the San Juan river, our
route will lie southwardly to San Jose, the capital of Costa
Rica; the entire line, since entering Central America, being
seven hundred miles. In all this distance there is not a
single engineering difficulty to be overcome. The streams
met with, it is true, are mountain torrents; but they are
easily bridged. There are no very heavy grades; and the
principal obstacles will be the immense trees which cover
nearly the entire route. These must be felled.

More than once, while traveling on mule-back over the
very track above traced, I have figured to myself the
wondrous development a railway would give to this beautiful country. I have suggested the western shore of the
great lake, as it is low, while over the eastern shore tower
the mighty mountains of Segovia, teeming with mineral
wealth, which awaits only some other means of transportation than mules' backs or men's shoulders, to make it rival
California;. while the day will come when the shores of the
lovely and picturesque lake of Nicaragua will be dotted with
villas and villages. The lake is 120 miles long and 50
wide, and of sufficient depth for vessels of any size. The
climate everywhere is salubrious. Mr. Blanchette, of the
Nicaragua Canal scheme, attributes the healthy climate to
the trade-winds, which he says "are so strong on the lake
as to make it as rough as the British Channel."

Nicaragua, although the largest of the Central American
Republics, with an area of 59,000 squares miles, has only
about 300,000 inhabitants. These are mostly aborigines.
Its coast-length on the Atlantic is 280 miles, while on the

Pacific it is only 160. Both imports and exports are exceedingly disproportionate to the untold resources of the country, being together not more than $3,000,000. Nicaragua has, however, had but little time to develop those resources. What with her eternal quarreling with her sister States, her Mosquito Question with England, which was definitely settled only in 1860, and now again the rivalry between herself and Costa Rica, for the possession of the Interoceanic Canal, she has indeed had her hands full.

For a great many years it has been contemplated to construct a Ship Canal across the Isthmus; though the precise route and plan are still under discussion. My own opinion, notwithstanding the fact that it is without the slightest scientific value, and only from cursory observation of the several proposed routes, is that Nicaragua will be selected. The opening of such a canal would at once revolutionize the currents of commerce from the American ports on both sides of the continent, and also from Europe, Asia and Australia.

I would willingly dwell on the splendid future of a country in whose very heart, on the beautiful shores of her great lake, are to meet two such gigantic enterprises as the Intercontinental Railway and the Interoceanic Canal. I can only stop, however, to remark that, with our completed Longitudinal Line connecting with either terminus of such canal, (and I can conceive of no other termini than San Juan del Norte on the Atlantic and San Juan del Sur on the Pacific,) the Republics of Central America, northward and southward of such interoceanic water-way, may send their products by rail either to the one or the other to be shipped on ocean vessels, and thus avoid paying the enormous toll charges of the canal. All these Republics are admirably adapted to the cultivation of sugar, coffee and cotton, and only require better facilities for transportation. It will be cheaper for our own planters to send cotton by rail to the western terminus of the canal, for shipment to China and Japan, than by way of New Orleans, and then pay toll on the canal.   That both these countries of the East will soon need such supply, Admiral Ammen, in a late paper, thus assures us: " Years ago one of our eminent men said to me that erelong our production of cotton would, as a raw material, supply the looms of China and Japan, and that, in his belief, more cotton would find its way there through the canal than the then entire product of our country.   Present aspects point significantly to the verification of this prediction.   In China and Japan improved machinery for making cotton cloths are now at work, and the cotton supply can best come from us."

Nicaragua is densely wooded ; logwood, mahogany, Brazil-wood, ebony, and cedar abound ; while she is especially rich in medicinal plants.   Ipecachuana, aloes, copaiba, copal, ginger, sarsaparilla, colocynth, and innumerable others are found; but the careless manner in which they are gathered, and the little attention that is paid to them, would almost make a pharmacist's heart bleed.   Nicaragua has given sufficient evidence of her public spirit, and of her partiality for American enterprise, to satisfy the Directors of our road that they will have little difficulty in obtaining from her government all reasonable grants of land along the route, and whatever other rightful and necessary guarantees they may require.   I know of no country in all Spanish America whose future seems more brilliant than that of Nicaragua.

Costa Rica is the last Republic in this second division of the three Americas, but by no means the least.   She has always evinced a much greater spirit of enterprise than is usually characteristic of the Spanish American.   Nothing evidences this more than the railroads she is now building, and, above all, the stimulus her legislation has given to the cultivation and export of coffee. Thirty years ago scarcely a bag of coffee left her ports, whereas now her export of that article amounts annually to many thousands of bags. Here again I may quote Admiral Ammen, who says: "The growth of valuable products on the west coast of Mexico and Central America, especially of coffee of superior quality, a few years ago, was a few thousand sacks yearly; now it amounts to hundreds of thousands, and with a continued demand, it will doubtless soon amount to millions of sacks." The route through Costa Rica must be almsst equi-distant from either ocean; but it will pass through much well-cultivated country, among an energetic people, in whom the white element prevails more largely than among any other in Central America, and one that naturally understands and appreciates thoroughly the meaning of the word Progress. Should the road be constructed in sections, Chiriqui Lagoon, of which we have heard so much lately, as a prospective United States Naval Depot, will afford a most excellent harbor for receiving plant.

Costa Rica is equally as rich as her sister Republics in mineral and forest wealth; while her imports and exports, which together, last year, amounted in value to nearly ten millions of dollars, prove what a wonderful future is in store for these countries, once they have the means of transporting their produce easily to market, and are given the example what energy, aided by science, can accomplish for them. The area of Costa Rica is 22,000 square miles, while her population is only 350,000. Her coast-line on the Pacific is three hundred miles; while a splendid harbor on the Gulf of Nicoya will be of great future value to the railway.

From San José, the capital of Costa Rica, to the Bay of Guyaquil, a distance by land of more than a thousand miles, with little intervening of civilization, except the Isthmus of Panama and its railroad, I can say but little; for very little is known, other than that it is a region rich in mineral resources, and clothed with vast and valuable forests. There are a few towns, David, Santiago, and others; but the largest of them are of but slight importance. From Punta Arenas, on the Gulf of Nicoya, in Costa Rica, to the port of Tumbez, the extreme northern point of Peru, on the southern shore of the Gulf of Guayaquil, (and but a short distance from the prosperous city and commercial port of the same name in Ecuador,) is a distance, in a direct line, through the Bay of Panama, of 780 miles.

The duty will devolve on engineers and surveyors to judge whether it will be more available, for the present, to have the Central American terminus at Punta Arenas, and cross the Bay of Panama in steamers, or lay the road through Veragua, and so on to the line of the Panama Railroad; thence southwardly through the United States of Columbia, and through Ecuador, to Guayaquil. While this part of the road is being constructed, recourse may be had to the very easy expedient I propose. Or, it might be found preferable to make the temporary terminus at Chiriqui Lagoon, and thence in steamers, five hundred miles to Barranquilla, at the mouth of the Magdalena River, in the United States of Columbia. From this point the course of that river might be followed almost directly southwardly to within thirty miles of Bogota, a distance from the Caribbean Sea of four hundred miles. It will be observed that by adopting the former of these plans, we eliminate from the future labors of the Directory of the Three Americas Railway, the negotiations for right of way, and for other desirable concessions, with the governments of the United States of Columbia and Ecuador; while all the commerce of the latter Republic, now finding an outlet at Guayaquil, will be within one hundred and twenty miles of easy water-carriage to Tumbez, the temporary northern terminus of the road in South America.

South of the Isthmus there are two general main trunk-routes, which may now be considered. The most westerly will remain west of the Andes and be indeed a coast-line route, running through the United States of Columbia, Ecuador, Peru, Bolivia and Chili. It would necessarily continue as a coast-line so long as it should be kept on the west side of the Andes, because that vast continental back-bone is parallel with, and not far from, the coast, all the way down to the Rabudor River, in latitude 45°, where Chili, fronting on the Pacific, joins Patagonia on the east. It is probable, however, that circumstances will call for a route to cross the Andes a long way north of this point, at or near Copiapo, in latitude 27° 30', and thus connect with the railway recently projected to unite Chili with the Argentine Republic; a large portion of which is already constructed. Telegraphic communication has long since been established along the already surveyed route. The average elevation of the Andes is here 20,000 feet above the sea; but fortunately nature has provided for the exigencies of the commercial future. Near Copiapo is an easy pass through the Andes, and through which cattle are driven from the pampas of the Argentine Republic into Chili during nearly the entire year. Were it not for this and similar passes, of comparatively easy grade, all hope might be abandoned of an Argentine-Chili transcontinental railway, or of making by this route the Three Americas Longitudinal Railway of any utility to the trans-Andean countries of Brazil, Uraguay and the Argentine Republic. But, before further considering this west-coast line, I wish to go over the second or middle route, directly through the heart of South America, equi-distant from either ocean.

In order to pass through the interior of South America
and furnish railway accommodation to a vast region very
little settled, and even but partially explored, the route
would have to run from the Isthmus through the United
States of Columbia, getting eastward of the Andes and all
parallel mountain ranges along the extreme head-waters of
the Cauca, the Magdalena and the Orinoco rivers, over in
the neighborhood of the sources of the Rio Negro and Rio
Japura, important confluents of the River Amazon ; taking
in its course the cities of Barinas, in the rich Province of
that name, in Venezuela, Merida and Nutrias, near the
head of navigation of the Apure, a branch of the Orinoco ;
then deflecting slightly to the southwest, through a rich and
well settled country, to Bogota, the capital of Columbia.
Bogota is within thirty-five miles of the head of navigation
on the river Meta, another large tributary of the Orinoco.
Here the railway would have the carriage of all the freight
and passengers who, leaving the line of Bogota, Merida, or
Nutrias, could take the steamers now running on the Apure,
Meta and Orinoco, and go either to Ciudad Bolivar, the first
port of entry on the Orinoco, or to Port of Spain, on the
British island of Trinidad, at the mouth of the Orinoco ;
and thus, by ocean steamer, to Europe or to the east coast
of South America.

I am here, again, on ground quite familiar to me. Some
years ago, I received an exclusive grant from the Vene-
zuelan government to navigate by steam the Orinoco and
its tributaries, and ascended that river and its great branch,
the Apure, as far as Nutrias, a distance of more than a
thousand miles, in the first steamer that ever turned a wheel
in the interior waters of South America. That enterprise
was then a thousand times more problematical than the one
we are considering is now. To reach the field of his labors
in South America, the writer of these lines went from the

head-waters of the Ohio, in a Mississippi steamboat, across the Gulf of Mexico, and the Caribbean Sea, and then up the rivers of Venezuela to their own head-waters. The undertaking was considered chimerical. It has changed the commerce in that rich region, and its benefits were soon appreciated. But let us return.

The route we are following, after leaving Bogota, would, for a considerable distance, be exceedingly difficult, as it would have to traverse two immense mountain ranges, between the coast and the waters of the Caqueta, a prolongation of the Japura, which discharges into the Amazon, above Egoas. This brings us in view of the large Brazilian Province of Amazonas. Thence we are to proceed, across an unexplored* and thinly settled country, to the Madeira River, below the falls of San Antonio; thence across that river, and over another unexplored region, to the source of the river Tapajos and the junction of the rivers Juruena and Arinos, which form the Tapajos; and then up the valley of the Arinos, to its springs near the Diamond District, in Matto Grosso, another large province of Brazil. The mountains here are only from three to four thousand feet high; and it is but a short distance from the waters of the Arinos, which flow into the Amazon, to those of the river San Lorenzo, which flow into the Paranahiba, the Parana, and finally into the estuary of La Plata.

The river Parana is, next to the Amazon, the greatest river in South America, draining an immense and diversified territory, a very large portion of which is but sparsely settled, and much of it yet unexplored. The line would then continue down the San Lorenzo to the Paranahiba; down that stream to the Parana, and along the right bank of the same; one prong (if two or more may be supposed,) passing through Corrientes, Santa Fe, Rosario, and Buenos Ayres, the capital of the Argentine Republic; and the other leaving the immediate valley of the Parana at Rosario, to which there is already a railroad, and passing over the pampas, through the interior of the Argentine Republic, down to the mouth of the Rio Colorado, at Anegado Bay, near the fortieth degree of south latitude. This is, of course, little else than a general outline of a route which admits of alternate lines, especially through Brazil. One of these would be by turning more to the east after passing the Diamond District, in Matto Grosso, striking the Paranahiba River some distance above its junction with the Parana, where the four Provinces of Brazil, Goyaz, Minos, Geraes, Sao Pablo and Parana, approach each other.

It may be an important question whether to continue along the Parana, where it bends westerly, or to keep on a southerly course below the Yguassu till it strikes the Rio Uruguay, and then down the valley of the Uruguay, which stream is, at first, the boundary between the Province of Rio Grande do Sul, in Brazil, and Corrientes. Afterward it is the boundary between Uruguay and Entre Rios, a Province of the Argentine Republic. At the junction of the Paranahiba with the Parana, the three Brazilian Provinces of Matto Grosso, Sao Paolo and Parana connect with Paraguay. The great river Parana is the boundary between Brazil and Paraguay, down to the mouth of the Rio Yguassu, a Brazilian tributary. Below this junction the Parana runs within the territory of the Argentine Republic, down to its mouth at the head of the estuary of La Plata. There would also be an alternate and more direct route from the head-waters of the Paraguay down that river to its junction with the Parana, a short distance above Corrientes. This route leaves the Brazilian territory in the Province of Matto Grosso, and does not re-enter Brazil below that place. In that case, the only Brazilian Provinces the line would pass through would

be Amazonas, Para, and Matto Grosso, in the far interior
of the continent; they being, for the most part, unsettled
regions.

I have given these data and routes from personal observation and knowledge of the country, or from the most
authentic and reliable sources of information; and it is
only because I feel sure of the reliability of them that I have
attempted at all to consider this important subject. Without further examination, made especially with a view to the
determination of the most desirable line for the main trunk,
no route could be judiciously decided upon. What now is
necessary to be said in regard to the contemplated route
from the Isthmus of Darien, east of the Andes, and approximately to a center-line through those parts of South America
which it is designed to accommodate?

FIRST: There have never been any surveys for railways
through this interior region. It has not been surveyed at
all. Much of it has not even been explored in such a way
as to afford reliable data for deciding upon railway routes.
In fact, it may be considered that all the explorations which
are of measurable or even of supposable value have been
confined mainly to the immediate valleys of the principal
streams, the general courses and declivities of which have
thus been approximately ascertained.

SECOND: The regions in the interior of certain parts of
Brazil, which have long been known and occupied by white
settlers, are chiefly those which contain the ordinary precious
metals and diamonds. Probably to the search for these we
are indebted, in a great degree, for our knowledge, such as
it is, of the interior of the continent. The rivers, large and
small, remain much as nature left them—so far at least as
their unfretted waters are concerned; although settlements
of various kinds have been made along many of them,
towns built, and provincial governments established.

THIRD: Excepting along the seacoast, at several points, and for a few miles back of the principal Atlantic cities of Brazil, roads for wheeled vehicles are almost unknown. Within the last twenty-five years, a few good roads have been built in some of the Atlantic Provinces of Brazil, but as a rule, the whole vast interior is without roads, and without any system even of mule-paths.   With the exceptions mentioned, Brazil is little else than a wilderness, not yet reclaimed from the Indian aborigines.   Most of the other countries in South America are equally roadless and unimproved.   .

Even with the amicable co-operation of all the governments and the peoples concerned, south of the Isthmus, the survey of this long stretch of inland territory, with a view to the construction of the great north and south trunk-line which I have shadowed forth, will be a herculean task, on account of its isolaton from civilization, the rude nature of its nomadic inhabitants, the vast tracts of dense forests without human settlements, and the known mountainous character of a large portion of the country between Bogota, in latitude 5°, and the settled parts on either side of the Parana river, covering a distance of at least 2,000 miles. It will be a tedious and difficult task under the most favorable circumstances, accompanied also with danger, unless very liberal expeditures are forthcoming for the proper supply and protection of the engineering parties.   The East-Andean route, it is true, would be through a region of country which awaits only the woodman and the miner, the botanist and the agriculturist, to develop a wealth such as the world has never yet dreamed of; a region watered not by ordinary streams but by rivers navigable for hundreds and even thousands of miles ; and where the soil is a vegetable loam many feet deep, the accumulation of centuries.   But many years, no matter what might be the volume of the immigration thitherward, would probably be required to built up the local traffic sufficient to insure a reasonable return for the vast expenditure necessary to carry through such an unknown territory the superior sort of road it is proposed the Three Americas Railway shall be.*

---

* Col. Beelen, in most matters as able as he is estimable, is here bringing forward the strongest arguments attainable in support of his position as a west-coast man. The reasons he assigns for his faith are much the same as those that were, for years and years, urged, with so much more zeal than discretion, against the Union and Central Pacific Railroads, against the Northern Pacific, against the Southern Pacific, and, more recently, against the Canada Pacific. These arguments are beginning to be quite as threadbare and impotent as the one, in the form of a prodigious bugbear, that was so long and so per-sistently advanced under the name of "The Great American Desert." It was believed that not even an Ironhorse, though requiring for his stomach neither oats nor hay, could ever survive an attempt to cross that so-called grassless and Sahara-like waste. Where is that desert now? What has become of it? Was it not a mere phantasy? It exists no longer. The transcontinental railroads have converted it into beautiful farms and hamlets and happy homes. The far-reaching Longitudinal Railway, and its various latitudinal connections, will probably soon accomplish for South and Central America even more than has yet been accomplishd for North America by the transconti-nental railroads. The grants, from different governments, of a goodly number of millions of acres of the incomparably rich public lands lying all along down the eastern slope of the Cordilleras, will help very materi-ally to build the Three Americas Railway, and will forever afterward contribute largely to its maintenance and improvement. Railroads de-light especially in being located within the limits of fertile fields and fruitful orchards and forests ; and it is only upon productive soils, or in the near neighborhood of such soils, that railroads can ever become gen-erally and lastingly successful. The west coast route will not do ; it is not sufficiently midland; in fact, it is not midland at all; and, besides its being too one-sided, it is too arid, too steep, too sterile. The Three Americas Railway must be so built as to touch and tickle, day and night, and for all time to come, not the western but the eastern toes of the Andes.

H. R. H.

I have thus thought it better, and the part of discretion, to look all difficulties, whatever they may be, squarely in the face. If they exist in fact, if they be not imaginary, but real, the projectors and patrons of the grand Longitudinal Line must either overcome them or fail in their efforts.to build this gigantic railway. But they will not fail, as I shall soon demonstrate. I turn now, with pleasure, to the western coast,—the coast that, centuries ago, was the rich land of the Incas and the ambition of the Spaniards.

The route along the Pacific coast, and generally on the west side of the Andes, is unquestionably the one that should be adopted. This route will be almost due north and south, after leaving the Isthmus of Darien and entering the State of Choco, in the United States of Columbia. The great Andean range, reaching all the way from Tierra del Fuego to the Isthmus, a distance of 4,000 miles, where it terminates, divides into two chains on leaving the territory of Ecuador, near Pasto, and leaves very few engineering difficulties to be overcome from the Gulf of San Miguel, in the State of Panama, to the borders of Ecuador. All along the coast there are excellent harbors and good roads; while there are several passes over the Andes, through which branch roads can be constructed from the interior. Along the whole route, in Columbia, the country is only sparsely settled, although there are several important towns, which would soon develop into great commercial centers and depots for the rich interior and more populous provinces, once a convenient and fixed communication were established. Bogota, the capital, would be within one hundred and thirty miles of the line, unless it were deemed advisable to deviate so far away from the coast as to include that city in the route. At all events, leaving the latitude of Bogota, no new obstacle need be apprehended until we reach Ecuador, where a high grade will be required as we ascend the elevated plateau on which is situated the capital, Quito.

Along the entire route through the United States of Columbia immense forests will be found, rich in timber for architectural and ship-building purposes, dye-woods, others valuable for ornamental and cabinet work, and many that will be available in the construction of the road. Immense beds of excellent coal are found near Bogota, and doubtless many will be discovered along the coast. The whole country is rich in minerals, abounding in platina, gold, silver, copper, lead, iron, coal and asphaltum. The emerald mines, near Bogota, have long been celebrated. Along the coast, rice, sugar, cotton, tobacco, indigo, and cocoa, are easily produced, and await only the inducement of easy transportation to increase them a thousand fold; while all the products of the temperate zone may be had from the table-lands in the interior. There are no manufactures in the country; everything being imported from England or the United States, but chiefly from England. There are immense herds of cattle roaming over the western llanos, or plains, near the head-waters of the Meta and Apure; but while of excellent quality, they have little value for want of a market.

Running almost parallel with the proposed route is the river Cauca, a branch of the Magdalena. A company has been lately formed in New York for navigating it by steamboats. The Magdalena, emptying into the Caribbean Sea, and the headwaters of which are only thirty miles from Bogota, has long since had small steamers upon it. In the Province of Antioquia, in the rich delta formed by the Magdalena and its confluent, the Cauca, there is being constructed a local railroad which promises great things for the Province, to judge from the report made in January, of this year, to the government of Bogota, by Dr. Manuel Uribe, who was sent to inspect it. Could I transcribe for you his admirable report, you would not doubt for a moment of the warm reception the enlightened government of Columbia will give to the Three Americas Railway, or in fact to any enterprise that tends to a fuller development of their immense wealth.   It would corroborate, too, what I have so much insisted upon, in the course of this communication,—the fact that most of these Spanish American Republics are only waiting to be taught how to take advantage of their great resources ; and, by multiplying them a thousand fold, and with adequate facilities for transportation, they would soon take high rank in the commercial world.

To show the feelings which animate the people of Columbia, and to prove that hatred for foreigners is not predominant, I may be permitted to quote a single passage from Dr. Uribe's report.   In speaking of the Americans and English, who are constructing the railway, he says: " I have been delighted to hear so much English spoken here; for, although Progress recognizes no particular language, yet it seems to me that English is, beyond all others, that of material advancement."   He urges the government to continue its favor, and to lend every possible helping-hand to the enterprise, as one that will open up a new and brilliant era for the Province.   If such enthusiasm can be awakened by a simple local road, in a distant Province, what may we not expect in the way of encouragement when they are tendered an immediate and facile communication, not only with the vast markets of the North, but also with their own sister States, now as far removed from them, in matters of social intercourse and business, as is the continent of Europe.

I have not within reach the statistics of the exportation of indigo and coffee from Columbia, for last year, but am aware that it amounted to many millions of pounds. Venezuela, the neighboring Republic, analogous in climate and soil, exported, in 1879, coffee to the value of $20,000,000.

There is absolutely no limit to the production of these countries; while the simple exploration of her forests and mines would be sufficient to induce the offering them every facility in the way of commerce. The entire rich valleys of the Orinoco and Apure would necessarily be feeders to the Three Americas Railway. From the government at Bogota everything may be expected in the way of land grants and general assistance. Few governments can surpass that of Columbia, in enlightened and liberal statesmanship; and the company will find in her public men earnest and efficient coadjutors. I will cheerfully give elsewhere other and more extended information concerning Columbia. Here it is well nigh impossible to be otherwise than merely cursory in my remarks.

Our route now continues southwardly through the Republic of Ecuador, for four hundred miles, if we follow the coast, and one hundred, should we deviate so as to make a station at Quito, the capital. Between the rwo ranges into which the Andes devide in Ecuador there is a beautiful valley of over three hundred miles in length and twenty in breadth, which, with the coast, will give a choice of routes. That along the coast will require little or no grading; while the one to Quito, which is much more to the interest of the company, will call for a grade probably equal to that of the Santa Fé Road, over the Raton Range, in New Mexico. The climate throughout the valley of Quito is unsurpassed in the world; it is particularly salubrious and bracing; though the neighboring mountains, excepting the great range of Asuay, which rises 15,500 feet, nowhere attain the snow line. In the valley of Quito the seasons are so equable, that they are scarcely distinguishable; the temperature varying from 60° to 67° in the day and 48° to 52° at night. On the coast the mean temperature is of course much higher, but the climate is still healthful. It will there-

8

fore be seen that, so far as the climate is concerned, nothing better can be desired by ourselves or laborers.

The area of Ecuador, including the Gallapagos islands, is 249,000 square miles, and the population 1,250,000. The exports, last year, were about $6,000,000. The products of the country are as varied as the climate. The distinguishing export of Ecuador is cocoa, from which is made chocolate; while in the forests, is found the Cinchona or Peruvian bark. With this single industry of gathering the bark of the Cinchona, and with the manufacture of hats and hammocks, the people have remained content; while their forests, rich in every ornamental wood and medicinal plant, and which alone would be wealth enough for any country, if properly utilized, remain as virgin as they were when they first came from the hands of the Creator. It requires but little gift of prophecy to foretell the future riches that must flow from the mountains of this country when once they are submitted to the competent inspection of our Californian explorers.

There are about sixty miles of railway already in Ecuador; but there is no outlet for her products, except through the river Guayaquil; near the mouth of which is the city and port of the same name. It is evident that none of her products, not even her indigo, can withstand the great cost of land carriage, and that almost without exception on muleback, from the place of growth. One of the most important results of the opening to commerce of her rich Provinces, will be the navigation of the magnificent river Amazon, which, rising in Peru, forms the main boundary between the two Republics, and become navigable long before reaching the eastern limit of Ecuador with Brazil. It is needless to dwell on the vast commercial results of such an artery of uninterrupted water communication all the way to the Atlantic. But this is only one of the innumerable sources of wealth which will be developed by an American Intercontinental Railway. Very many of the better classes of Ecuador have been educated in the United States and England, and are fully alive to the advantages which must accrue to their country generally and to themselves especially as great landed proprietors and possible producers, from such a project as the contemplated Three Americas Railway, without which they must remain passive spectators of the world's progress; while their own vast resources continue as dormant as they have been for centuries.

We now enter upon the magnificent territory of Peru, with an area of 505,000 square miles, a population of nearly 3,000,000, and a coast line of 1,300 miles along the Pacific Ocean. The distance from the ocean to the foot of the Andes, averages about fifty miles; the intervening space offering no further difficulty to the passage of the Three Americas Railway than the bridging of many small streams, along the valleys of which, extending far into the Andes, are found some of the most fertile and productive portions of the country. Innumerable towns will be found along the route, some of them of very considerable importance, promising a large local trade and passenger list, and all of them entrepots of the rich back country. There are nearly 1,800 miles of railroad in Peru, and over 1,400 miles of lines of telegraph. I have near me only statistics of the exports to the United States and Great Britain, for 1878, which amounted to $30,000,000. Those to France and Germany would greatly increase that amount. Indeed Germany, in latter years, has become a dangerous rival to Great Britain in all the Spanish American Republics.

Peru is so much better known to most of our people than is South America generally, that I fear being tiresome, should I be as minute in details concerning her as I have thus far been all along our route. There is not a river, nor stream, nor any pass of the Andes, in which gold is not found; but silver is, and has always been, her chief metallic production.   Even quicksilver is abundant in the interior; and coal is found in many parts.   Of late years, a source of great wealth has been discovered in the illimitable nitrate deposits of Tarapaca.   Nitrate having recently, to no small extent, taken the place of guano as a fertilizer, is reported in vast quantities.   Until Chili commenced to compete with her, Peru had the monopoly of this rich trade.   I may say here in passing, although not in connection with my subject, that this immensely important competition has been the almost direct cause of the war at present waging between the two Republics.

Notwithstanding the fact that more attention is given in Peru to agriculture than in any of the other tropical countries, yet both it and mining, the chief industries, are in their infancy, and are almost exclusively in the hands of the Indians.   Nearly all of the more important necessaries of life, wheat, potatoes, and cattle, are imported from Chili or from California.   What a country comprising more than half a million square miles of territory, with a genial climate, rich in all the corresponding resources of the Indies, having, besides, a vegetable and forest wealth that knows no rival even in South America, and the glittering issues of whose imperfectly worked mines were the wonder of our earliest reading, might be made to produce, and unquestionably will produce, once the appliances of science are skilfully brought to bear upon it, and a more general and rapid system of interchange shall be given it, I leave you yourselves to imagine.

From Tumbez, on the extreme northwestern coast of Peru, in our course southwardly along the Pacific, we come upon many important towns; Payta, with a railway thirty miles to Pinta, in the interior; Callao, the flourishing port of Lima, with a railroad to that capital, a city of 150,000 inhabitants, and a railway extending one hundred and sixty miles into the interior; Pisco, celebrated for its wines; Islay, with a railway all the way to Lake Titicaca, which magnificent watercourse, one hundred and twenty miles long, would complete connection between La Paz, the capital of Bolivia, and the projected Three Americas Railway along the coast; Ylo, with a railway to Moquequa; Arica, within a few hours by rail of the populous city of Tacna; Pisagua, having rail communication with the interior rich nitrate district; and lastly Iquique, with still another railroad; all these, being within a distance of less than twelve hundred miles, would seem no unpromising prospect for a company desirous of establishing a successful intercontinental railway. With this flattering exhibit, we may now enter, but only for a moment and a short distance, the Republic of Bolivia, which has not more than a hundred miles of coast, on which is found a single harbor, Cobija, on the Pacific.

Bolivia, with 500,000 square miles, has but 2,000,000 inhabitants; although, no regular census having ever been taken, it is difficult to say how correct is this estimate. The mines of the precious metals in Bolivia are supposed to be inexhaustible; while the great Silver Mountain of Potosi is proverbial. With the exception of the narrow space along her coast, her entire territory is a vast succession of mountain ranges; some of them being far above the snow line; and all of which, when even partially explored, have been found to teem with every known mineral. Cocoa, coffee, cinchona and indigo swell the list of her productions. Hitherto the government has been exceedingly unstable, and constant revolutions have impoverished the country.

In latitude 24° 20′ we enter one of the most earnest and progressive of all the Republics of Spanish America. Here, for the present, the Three Americas Railway must find its southern terminus. It will be observed, from its latitude, that Chili commences in the temperate zone, and we at last come upon a people who, from climatic influences partly, and from the necessity of providing their means of subsistence,—a necessity not very imperious in some of the other Republics.—has been energized into industrious habits. Nature has done little for Chili other than to distend her mountains with the richest copper mines on earth, and cover her deserts with inexhaustible deposits of nitrate and borax. Only by the sweat of his brow has the industrious Chilian made himself and his country the envy of one portion of Spanish America, and the pride of another.

My most reliable statistics of the exports and imports of Chili are of last year, and aggregate over $70,000,000; but it must be remembered that, for nearly two years, she has been at war with two of her neighbors, Bolivia and Peru. Her exports of copper alone were over $20,000,000. The product of the silver mines of Caracoles was, in three years, over $30,000,000. The agricultural status of the country, while immensely in advance of any other South American Republic, leaves much still to be desired. Her cereals, however, amounted, last year, to 22,000,000 bushels. Very great attention is now being given to education. Not only in Chili, for a distance of six hundred and fifty miles, should our present terminus be Valparaiso, but up even to the borders of Peru and Ecuador, the Three Americas Railway Company will have to depend on the Chilian peons for labor. They are a very hard-working and easily managed class, and have constructed, under Meiggs' contracts with Chili and Peru, more than eighty millions of dollars' worth of railways. From a population of over 2,500,000 of energetic and enterprising people, with a government but once interrupted and that for only a very short period, by revolution, since her independence, and always not only ready but really anxious to embrace any and every opportunity of ameliorating her condition, the Three Americas Railway may here confidently look for substantial aid and encouragement.

I have spoken of a distance along the Chilian coast of only 650 miles. It is because, when we reach Valparaiso, we strike the railway to Santiago, the capital, at a distance of 130 miles, and from there continue due south and parallel to the Pacific, for 350 miles, over the great line to Concepcion. This will be as far as there can be any possible inducement at present to prolong the Three Americas Railway. I have already mentioned the pass near Copiapo, as the most available through the Andes, and through which will run the railway now constructing, which will itself connect Buenos Ayres, the capital of the Argentine Republic, eight hundred and fifty miles distant on the River Plate with the Three Americas Railway on the western coast of South America. There is another pass to the west of Santiago, the capital of Chili, known as the Uspallata pass, which—though at great expense—might be made available; and then the city of Valparaiso would become the western terminus.

I have now traced the route of our railway to two possible termini; the one on the Atlantic, the other on the Pacific. It remains for those who can throw more light and bring more data to bear upon the subject, to judge between them, and to decide upon their respective merits. There is still a third possible line, along the coasts of the Gulf of Mexico and the Atlantic ocean, which I shall not stop to consider. Some day, very far in the future, perhaps, the cities along those coasts will doubtless be connected by rail; but it will be mainly to satisfy local traffic. The entire distance, in South America alone, by this extreme eastern line, would be over six thousand miles. Along this contemplated line, roads will probably be constructed, from time to time, only in short sections, as the exigencies of commerce may require. I have endeavored, throughout this somewhat lengthy communication, to be exact in all the statistics adduced by me. There is much, very much, which I have omitted, but which can be easily supplemented. In neither population nor areas can any statistics be exact, because of the very nature of the countries themselves, and from the peculiar character and methods of their inhabitants.

The population of the fifteen Spanish American Republics we have traversed, aggregating over 30,000,000, is sufficiently numerous to support a railroad through their territories. What is now particularly needed is the time and opportunity of satisfying their peoples and their governments in regard to this fact, and of impressing them with a knowledge of the vast benefits which invariably accrue from the introduction of railways. In the early days of railway projects in our own country, it was sometimes exceedingly difficult to convince the people, in comparatively sparse settlements, that they were able to aid materially in constructing a railroad, and that they would ultimately be richly repaid by the conveniences and advantages it would afford them; nor were they easily persuaded to invest their material, their labor, or their capital. Since then, however, capital has grown to such enormous proportions that it is ready to invest in any fairly promising scheme of improvement, as I have conclusively shown in my remarks on New Mexico. Such investments in the proposed Three Americas Railway must naturally depend upon what the peoples and governments of the Spanish American Republics may be willing to do by way of sanction and encouragement; and what they may be inclined to do will depend almost wholly upon just and skillful management on the part of those who will have charge of the undertaking. There being no doubt of the extent of the benefits to be derived, let the Three Americas Railway Directors' first endeavor be to convince their Spanish American neighbors of this fact, and they will soon become deeply interested in the enterprise. It might be difficult or impossible to induce the government or people of any one of the Republics of Central or South America to interest themselves actively in behalf of a local railway project, even in their own territory; but when it can be clearly shown that such improvement is also to constitute a part of the most important railway in all the world, and that it will place them themselves in immediate and continuous communication, north and south, with two great continents, the case will be essentially changed. In speaking of Mexico, I have, I trust, already adduced a very convincing argument.

Above all, let us not be mistaken in the character of the Spanish American Republics. We will have to deal with proud, sensitive, suspicious but high-minded peoples—proud of their origin, and rendered mistrustful only by the innumerable deceits which have been practiced on them by adventurous speculators; with peoples who have struggled for years to maintain the independence of their respective nationalities; but who, by virtue of their admirable steadfastness and bravery, have at last become honorably and fixedly independent, after two centuries of tutelage far more aggravating and grinding than any body politic in the history of nations has ever undergone; with peoples who, with the sudden and dazzling blaze of freedom full upon them, became blinded and unable, for many years, to do more than grope in the uncertain footsteps of those whose colonial education had been gradually leading them up to liberty before it happily became theirs. Years of faithful apprenticeship followed; and, while some of them have taken high rank among the nations, others still feel the effects of the severe ordeal through which they have passed.

It should be no surprise to us that such causes should have
produced precisely the results of which we know. Rather
might we, with reason, be surprised at the fact that even the
semblance of nationality still remains to these courageous
and worthy people. We will find them ready and pleased
to receive us,—at first somewhat timid of our advances, but
timid only until convinced of the honorableness and judi-
ciousness of our motives.

One word more, and I shall have finished my plea for
the Three Americas Railway. I remember, years ago, standing high up on a slope of the Cordilleras. The sun was
shining brightly above, while below rolled an ocean of cloud.
A moment more, and the sun claimed the mastery. The
great cloud-bank melted away; and it seemed to me the
upheaving of a new creation, as, from out that chaos, there
came mountain and valley, city and town, field and forest,
lake and river, clothed in the brilliant green and gold of
tropical gorgeousness. Gentlemen, the memory of that
hour comes back to me again, as I perceive, in the near
future, the sunlight of our country's enterprise carrying in
its train the manifold blessings of a higher civilization, the
vivifying forces and the giant powers of intelligence necessary to recreate a continent; darting the most irresistible rays
of refulgence upon those fog-banks of ignorance and superstition which have lain for ages like an incubus upon much
of that loveliest portion of God's earth, energizing it into
usefulness, and making it, really and indeed, a sister of our
own. As the heart thus rejoices in imagining the future of
that fair and virgin continent, under such ameliorating influences, I envy the mind that first dreamed of lifting it from
the semi-chaos of centuries.

THIRD PRIZE ESSAY

A MODICUM OF FACTS, ARGUMENTS AND SUGGESTIONS IN
SUPPORT OF MR. HELPER'S SCHEME FOR THE CONSTRUC-
TION OF A THREE AMERICAS LONGITUDINAL DOUBLE-
TRACK STEEL RAILWAY.

BY WILLIAM WHARTON ARCHER,

(No. 201 East Main Street, Richmond, Virginia.)

NOTHING is more natural than that a nation, after having assured
itself that an enterprise will benefit the community, should have it executed by means of a general assessment. When railways and
bridges are really needed, it is sufficient to demonstrate their necessity
to justify appropriations of the public money, public lands, or other
public property, for their construction.—*Frederic Bastiat: Political
Economy.*

IN coming to the consideration of a subject so vast as the
one now appoached, the finite mind must reel in vain attempts to grasp it in its entirety. The solitary traveller
nearing the dome of the celebrated Cathedral of St. Peter, at
Rome, pauses awed; and in silent wonder gazes upon that
supreme erection. Not a seam, not a break in the gorgeous
mass of white splendor before him; it is elevated in beauty
unsevered; and, overcome by its grandeur, his brain throbs
impotent; nor can he realize the fact that the superb temple is made up of pieces; he can only perceive the one
grand completed piece. Yet, entering that structure, and
ascending that dome, he will observe that what he viewed
as only one great stone is made up of thousands, and that it

139

is the tesselated intricacy of art which has woven them in such close-knit splendor.

Fronting the stupendous enterprise outlined in the projected Three Americas Railway, and, looking at it as a whole, reason might be overshadowed by its gigantic proportions, if it were not examined step by step, while the aggregating facts, reasoning for themselves, clinch the argument in its favor. The wealth of material, the limited space at command, together with the fact, that large questions concerning the government, commerce and morality of many peoples, are inseparably interwoven with this subject, render the more difficult any effort to do it justice. In the progress of investigation, it will be seen that two of the greatest divisions of the world are here directly concerned,—North and South America. Further still, it will be granted that what concerns these two continents directly must indirectly affect the whole civilized world.

While the progress of many parts of North America challenges historical parallel, South America, except in very circumscribed localities, has made no move forward; the mists of her future are as dense as the gloom of her past. In the wildernesses of the two great Americas the march of civilization was begun almost simultaneously; perhaps South America gained the start; and the country far beyond the Rio Grande, for the time, lagged behind, only to forge steadily to the front; not alone of the new-country rival, but in the end to stand abreast with the very staunchest of the old world nations. The causes of the failure of the one, and the success of the other, need not be precisely stated anywhere; for the remedies pointed out will manifest the source of the evils in the former, as well as delineate the road successfully followed by the latter.

It is necessary first to look at the present condition of South and Central America and Mexico. The vast region known geographically as South America, is in many places so rich in climate as to give three crops a year. Its mountain recesses hold abundant stores of gold and silver; in the beds of its rivers, diamonds and other precious stones are found; its forests contain timber enough to supply the world. Excepting Central America and Mexico, it has a network of rivers which, as affording means of irrigation and inland communication, excel those of the northern division of the continent. Here nature is most prodigal; here the willing soil takes care of everything committed to it; and yet, with an array of advantages so conspicuous, here, of all places, is where man has done nothing to reap the boundless benefits held out to him. Here a people, long lethargic, cannot even gather the annual waste of an over-exuberant country, which, to-day, is comparatively idle in the great markets of the world, and which produces raw material enough to run the whole universe of manufacturing industries Here uneducated masses rule; and civil war ends in one place only to spring up in another. Here thirty millions of people live isolated from the richest and most progressive Republic on the earth, their next door neighbor; while the startling spectacle is afforded of this population of thirty millions buying almost all their supplies from countries across the ocean; and the country which lies by its side, on the adjoining continent of America, sells it comparatively nothing, and at the same time buys more than half its produce, paying therefor the money which is passed over to English, German and French creditors. Here the people are supplicating for an outlet for their productions; are clamoring for the influx of an energetic population to aid in the devolopment of their rich possessions. Here dwell a people in a naturally magnificent country, of which less is known in the United States to-day than is known of Asia or Japan, or even of Australia; a country teeming with similar productions which are imported into our Union from continents on the other side of the world.

Such is a bird's-eye view of South and Central America and Mexico; and now the earnest, the patriotic citizens of the United States, as well as the thoughtful statesmen of the great Southern Hemisphere, are confronted by an important problem which can be put aside no longer. How can South America, Central America and Mexico be developed and gain that healthful revivication accompanying wholesome immigration; in fact, be brought into real close business-like connection with the civilized world, and their governments be placed on the firm basis which alone assures prosperity, private or public? The answer is, that these great ends can be accomplished only by the construction of "a longitudinal midland double-track steel railway, from a point high north in North America, running more or less southwardly, through Mexico and Central America, to a point far south in South America."

As has already been remarked, this enterprise, so pointedly restated in the last part of the foregoing paragraph, appears at first of dimensions too gigantic to be fully considered at once; and therefore it is incumbent to approach it step by step; and then, after it has been looked at in its different aspects, to sum up the whole, and to ask whether or not, where, in what way, it will be beneficial; and if beneficial, in what quarter should it be begun? To one who has, even to a limited extent, looked into this subject, and certainly to one who has been over the vast expanse of country through which this road will run, the bare suggestion of impracticability will be counted absurd; and it is therefore proposed to advert to this branch of the subject briefly, and not to dignify a puerile point of this nature with anything like discussion. It may well be asked in what particular is this grand scheme impracticable, and the query itself is the strongest argument in its favor, because it cannot be answered. It is a fact familiar to all acquainted with South America, that the popular idea, among those who have not seen the country, is that it is made up of a succession of Andean mountain heights, crossed at life-risk on muleback; or else that, where craggy barriers do not exist, it is covered by a succession of morasses and rivers as impassable as the perpetually white peaks of the Cordilleras. While, as a matter of course, a full corps of engineers will go through this territory and select the route of the proposed railway, yet, by looking even cursorily at the country, it may not be difficult to form a tolerably correct idea where the track should and doubtless will be located.

Starting near the fiftieth degree of north latitude, on or near the hundreth parallel of longitude west from Greenwich, and running between the hundreth parallel and the ninetieth, through a country singularly free from obstacles, to St. Louis, (which from its geographical position, will be the great center of this vast work,) thence it must go westwardly; and, skirting the Spanish Peaks, take in Santa Fé, not alone because it is the heart of the great undeveloped silver-country of the United States, but also because the elevated table-lands, which extend from Mexico into the United States, gradually slope toward the border-line, then find their lowest elevation, and then ascend, in the shape of an inclined plane, northwardly through New Mexico; for, as Humboldt himself ascertained, the country is so level that "carriages may run from Mexico to Santa Fé." Still another authority has said "a wheeled-carriage could start on the table-land, five thousand five hundred feet high, in the State of Oaxaca, a little above the Isthmus of Tehuantepec, and as far south as latitude 16° 20', and roll on without difficulty to Santa Fé, in the north, a distance of above

one thousand four hundred miles. In fact, the plateau of
Anahuac is a great central table-land, and comprises three-
fifths of the entire surface of the country. Well might the
Pacific Railroad Reports consider the situation of Mexico
"another invitation from Nature for the advance of Railways." Not only is the getting into Mexico, from the
United States, so entirely free from great barriers, but the going from the State of Oaxaca, through Central America, is
done by an ascent as gradual as that encountered in entering its borders from the United States. Throughout Central America these plateaus extend; and while, in some of
the States, they are rougher than the Mexican plains, yet,
by here keeping upon the Pacific side of the mountains,
(which will be necessary, for another reason appearing
further on,) they are found much less rugged than the Car-
ribean-sea side.

Upon the very threshold of the entrance to Columbia,
the first obstacle deserving the name presents itself; for
here the Andes are to be crossed. But this cannot be
deemed impracticable; for Peru, alone and unaided, has
achieved the more gigantic feat of crossing the range where
its height is greater; and at half-past seven o'clock every
morning the train leaves the Pacific coast for lake Titicaca,
12,800 feet above the sea; passengers on the route take
dinner at Vincamayo, the highest village in the world, at an
altitude of 14,443 feet. When the single government of
Peru courageously and successfully pushes her road on to
Bolivia in this way, it is time to lose all tolerance at the idea
of a great international work, such as the one we are now
considering, pausing at the foot of the Andes in the United
States of Columbia. When such time comes, if it ever does
come, it will be when the spirit of American enterprise is
dead, and when the energy now belonging as a rightful inheritance to the United States of America, is palsied. Any citi-

zen of our Union, with that proper pride and faith in the ability and persistence of purpose claimed for this people, would lower his head in shame at any hint that this great undertaking is impracticable. What man has done man can do, and more. What the enervated Peruvian did the vigorous native of the United States can do, and more. What a weak government has accomplished for the general welfare, a strong government, rightly administered, can certainly accomplish, and more. Therefore such herculean and praiseworthy labors as the enfeebled Republic of Peru has performed, the powerful Republic of the United States can also perform. From the neighborhood of Bogota to Encarnacion, on the southern border of the Argentine Republic, no such obstacle as that of crossing the Andes, to gain entrance to South America, will be met; for the road will be located far enough west of the Maranon to be out of the reach of its fluctuating tides, and near enough to get the benefits of the overwhelming and almost untouched commercial wealth of the valley of the Amazon.

The present condition of North and South America and their relations to each other, are so anomalous, compared with other countries on other continents, as to be without a parallel in the history of the world. That, in this age, two peoples inhabiting contiguous continents, and not five thousand miles apart, with not even a strait between them, should be so completely separated from each other; that each country should possess exactly what the other needs, the one in manufactures, the other in raw material; that South America should be commercially nearer to European markets than to those of the United States on her sister continent; that the United States should daily witness the humiliating spectacle of England and France and Germany selling to South America millions of dollars worth of their respective manufactures; while our great Union of States

9

sells the same country comparatively nothing; this is a state of affairs so unprecedented, so grave in its importance to the future of North and South America, that the time has come, in the history of each, to look into a series of circumstances, wide-spreading and deep-rooting, which, while benefitting neither, threaten the ruin of both. Without here going into details, the reason for this apprehension may be very briefly stated; as, first, so far as South America is concerned, the want of a more thorough development of the country; and, second, so far as the United States is concerned, the want of an outlet for the fabrications of numerous mills, and in fact all manufacturing industries. It is for the relief of both that a longitudinal railway is projected to run from the northern part of the territory of the one, into the southern part of the territory of the other. It is by such a far-reaching railway only that the needed relief can be had. Steamship lines cannot give it; the Darien Canal cannot give it. While perhaps offering an improvement on the present condition of affairs, yet they cannot come up to the measure of the wants of either country; in fact, it may be questioned whether the Darien Canal might not prove disastrous to the commerce of the United States with the Pacific-coast Republics.

South America is undeniably one of the richest countries in the world; and it is particularly rich in those very things in which the United States is deficient. Starting in the northern part, it may be well to look at Venezuela, of which perhaps less is known than of any of the other divisions of this very important section of the continent. Yet its soil is so fertile that, in cases of drouth, the inhabitants of Cumana have often migrated to the forests, where they find ample subsistence in succulent plants, among which are the cabbage-palms and fern roots and the nutritious fruits and nuts of various trees. In many places the climate is delightful, and so healthful that Humboldt found numerous aged and infirm missionaries, who regularly and successfully sought for health in the salubrious air of the mountains of Caripe. The principal productions of Venezuela are cacoa, coffee, sugar, indigo, cotton, tobacco, sago, dye and furniture woods, and many kinds of excellent fruits. Like most other parts of South America, it is rich in minerals, and produces gold, silver, tin, lead, iron, coal, salt, asphaltum and petroleum.

The Republic of Columbia is likewise rich in minerals and soil; and grain may be sown advantageously in any season of the year. Not the least of its valuable exports is Peruvian bark.

Ecuador, lying like a wedge between Columbia and Peru, is a country presenting every grade of climate, from the everlasting summer on the coast and in the Orient, to the perpetual winter of the Andean peaks; while eternal spring rests over the high and extensive plateau between the eastern and western Cordilleras. Properly opened to the civilized world, this must become a beautiful and magnificent country. The Napa, the Pastasa, and the Santiago, all tributaries of the Amazon, connect it with the most fertile part of South America; while the Mira, the Esmeralda, and the Guayaquil flow westwardly into the Pacific. Situated on the equinoctial line, it embraces within its limits some of the highest as well as some of the lowest dry land on the globe. Its vegetable productions are consequently varied and prolific; and the strange picture is presented of tropical and temperate and arctic fruits and flowers growing in great profusion. The Ecuadorian, looking heavenward, sees all the constellations of the firmament; and gazing earthward, he discovers every family of plants; while, from certain places, his eye can embrace an entire zone; discerning above him the barley-field and potato-patch, and below him the sugar-cane and the banana.   This country is in fact one of the garden spots of the continent.   The immense quantities of Peruvian bark and other exports from Guayaquil, bear but little proportion to the capabilities of the country; and with the Three America's Railway entering its territory, Ecuador will cease to be a bankrupt Republic.   Here the silk-worm thrives as well as in any portion of the globe; and, in competition with France and Persia, the silk of Quito gained a gold medal at the late Paris Exposition.

Peru has been styled " the France of South America;" but the comparison is scarcely a compliment to Peru; for certainly, in natural and undeveloped wealth, France is not the equal of this magnificent country, though it is now so nearly cut off from the world.   All the kinds of fruits and grains of the earth can grow luxuriantly in this soil.   Bounded on the west by the Pacific, on the east by the navigable sources of the Amazon, while through her center run huge mountains of mineral wealth yet untouched; the valleys, holding a lavish soil, and stretching toward the eastern pampas, whose fertility is only equalled by the Nile plains of Egypt; here indeed is a land of promise.   Wild sheep roam over the country in countless flocks; and were any attention given to raising and improving them, Peru would derive a very large revenue from the sale of wool.   Like her neighbors, this Republic has an abundant supply of rubber, cacoa, and cinchona, and many valuable plants.

Of the rich and wilderness-like empire of Brazil, despite the enthusiastic description of travelers, the outside world has little conception.   From the river Trombita to Rio Cura de Santarem, a perfect network of lakes and rivers encompass the mighty Amazon; and there is nowhere else in the world anything like it.   The Amazon is wider and deeper than either the Nile or the Mississippi.   It carries more water than the two together; and it has a much greater extent of navigable surface with its side channels and numerous tributaries. It extends from the Andes to the Atlantic Ocean, and drains a valley nearly as large as Europe. So many and far-reaching are its tributaries that it touches every country on the continent, except Chili and Patagonia. It is plain that Brazil was designed for the sustenance of millions. There must be some reason for this bountiful irrigation, fertility of soil, and salubrity of climate. It should not be believed that India-rubber, cacoa, coffee, and hides are the only valuable products of Brazil. In its forests there are now rotting unheeded vast quantities of rich flavored nuts and oily seeds, resins yielding the finest varnishes, plants giving the most brilliant hues, and others with fibres that would serve not only for the finest weavings, but also for the strongest ropes; and besides, it has about forty of the most indispensable drugs.

Tropical vegetation is noted for its variety and luxuriance; but no other part of the world, in the same latitude, can offer so great a number of useful plants as does the valley of the Amazon. The curana, a sort of wild pine-apple, gives a delicate and transparent flax, of a silky lustre, which is sold under the name of palha, at Rio de Janeiro. The tucum and the javary make excellent ropes, cords and nets, and are well calculated to resist moisture and rot. The piasaba and murity readily supply solid brushes, brooms, hammocks, hats, baskets and mats; while the snow-white bark of others would furnish abundant material for excellent paper. Of the extraordinary wealth of the Brazilian forests, the civilized world knows little more now than it did in 1851-2, when Lieut. Herndon, after penetrating only a short distance within their limits, was able to report as follows: "The importance to the world of settlement, cultivation and commerce, in the valley of the Amazon, cannot be overestimated. With the climates of India and of all the habitable portions of the earth piled one above the other in quick succession, tillage and good husbandry here would transfer the productions of the East to this magnificent river basin. The capacities for trade and commerce along the Amazon are inconceivably great. Its industrial future is the most dazzling ; and to the touch of steam, settlement and cultivation, this rolling inland ocean and its magnificent water-shed would start up into a display of civilizing and refining results that would strongly indicate the valley of the Amazon one of the most enchanting regions on the face of the earth."

If these great things can be truthfully said of Brazil, they, with like force, apply to Bolivia, Paraguay, the Argentine Republic, Chili and Uraguay. The banks of the river Mamore, which runs nearly through the center of Bolivia, offer the same fertility of soil and variety of production as the Madeira and Amazon country. Of this region, a gentleman of Chili, who was met by Gibbon, at Cochabamba, in Bolivia, wrote: "In the country lying on the banks of the Mamore the richest cacoa and coffee grow almost wild ; and the greater part of the former is consumed by monkeys and birds, because of the lack of means for transporting it to a market. Sugar-cane, of gigantic growth, is found everywhere, with white and yellow cotton, of a staple equal to sea-island. Several kinds of cascarilla grow in abundance ; as also sarsaparilla and gums, ornamental and other woods, and honey and wax in immense quantities. The whole country between the Mamore and the Itenez, from latitude 14° to the equator, is a gold district." Bolivia and Paraguay, being the only two entirely inland Republics of South America, are more completely cut off from the wold than any of the others.

The Argentine Republic is a country of splendid promise, and its agricultural capacities are immense. Taking into

consideration the fact that the land under cultivation is only
one to ninety of the total area of the country, and that almost the whole of it is arable, some idea may be formed of
the grand field that exists here for future development in
this respect. The soil in several of the Provinces is especially adapted to the cultivation of the cereals, fine wines,
and sugar; in fact, so far as the latter is concerned, there is
never any necessity for replanting the cane; for it is perennial. Sheep and cattle are also very important objects of
the industries of the Republic. It needs only proper development to make Chili one of the greatest wheat countries in the world; and Uruguay with its superabundant
crops of rice, maize, and wheat, and its pampas crowded
with millions of wild horses and horned cattle, requires now
only the advantages of more intimate intercourse with the
outside world in order to become a prosperous and progressive Republic.

It may well be doubted whether, on the whole face of the
globe, there is any one body of land so overflowing with
miscellaneous riches as South America; and the fact that it
is lying in comparative uselessness, in an age when American energy is rushing everywhere else—when this fact is
fairly considered, it is high time that vain regrets and repin-
ings were discarded forever, and a resolute fight opened in
the interest, not of war and carnage, but of peace and
plenty. The great German scholar and philosopher, after
he had travelled over the richest portion of the world, spoke
from the fulness of his large heart, when he mused thus
sadly on South America: "On the ocean and in the sands
of Africa, we with difficulty reconcile ourselves to the dis-
appearance of man; but here his absence, in a fertile country clothed with perpetual verdure, produces a strange and
melancholy feeling." To the political economist there can
be nothing more startling than the realization of this fact,

that, in an era when the civilized world is over-crowded with
starving and homeless multitudes, these great solitudes are
replete with riches, occupying the wild space where millions
of the human race might dwell in plenty and happiness, and
where nature annually wastes more than would support in
comfort the population of either the United States or Great
Britain.

There are now in these forests hundreds of plants, as yet
unknown to commerce, of virtues the most rare. Of those
already examined by the botanist and which contain oil for
cooking and lighting, and some of which are excellent for
the manufacture of soap, there are sixteen. Of those containing odorous oils, there are five; resins, gums and milk-
saps, fourteen; dyeing-stuffs, eight; important medicinal
plants, thirty; plants suitable for making cords and ropes,
thirty-three. Large as is this list, it does not embrace all;
nor does it include those found in Mexico and on the coast
of Brazil. There is the cacoa, which is known only in the
United States as high-priced chocolate; but in various parts
of South America it is beneficial in many other ways; not
the least of which is in affording a delightful and harmless
drink, made from the white pulp surrounding the seeds;
while from the pulp itself comes a delicious amber jelly,
which in the markets of the world would soon become more
popular than guava. Even the cacoa shells are burned,
aud from the ashes, in combination with other materials, a
powerful brown soap is prepared. Of the coffee of Brazil,
nothing need here be said, save that the best is brought to
the United States and sold as high-priced Java; while that
which has been picked over, is sold as Brazilian. The
mandioca, or tapioca of commerce, is another article of
wholesome food, which flourishes throughout the country,
both north and south; and which, as bread, is found upon
the tables of all classes of the people in Brazil. The re-

freshing and delightful drink, maté, or Paraguay tea, is another precious and profitable product of South America, especially of Paraguay and Brazil; while, among other articles
not already enumerated, there are moira pinima, moira pi-
ranga, moira coatiara, itanba, palo de sangre, massaran-
deiba, sapucaya, jacaranda, cedar, cumaru, sarsaparilla,
vanilla, copaiba, quarana, tonqua beans, nuts, farina, cotton, rice, tobacco, piasaba, rubber, pita, copal, and many
others of corresponding value.

There is no country in the world where industrious people can produce for themselves so many of the necessaries
and luxuries of life as in South America. Indian-corn, rice,
sugar, coffee, cotton, beef, poultry and pork; with oranges,
pine-apples, bananas, and a luxuriant variety of other
tropical and semi-tropical fruits, are all to be had in the
greatest abundance, and with but very little labor. Three
hours' work in the morning and three in the afternoon or
evening will produce more than twelve hours' drudgery in
North America or Europe. There are two or three hundred
different kinds of valuable timber, including the cedros
ceibas, pale woods, dark woods, and many others of less
pronounced colors; in fact, no other country in the world
can be shown where there is such an amount or such a variety
of useful and ornamental woods, as may be obtained in the
virgin forests which stand around and within the basin of the
Amazon. Over one hundred different kinds of fine-grained
and excellent wood have been cut from a piece of land less
than half a mile square. Many of these are susceptible of
high polish, and are as beautiful as the best quality of rosewood, which is itself among them.

As is South America, so are Central America and Mexico.
These more northerly regions of Spanish America, though
not quite so rich in variety of products, are still rich enough
to offer a most tempting field for commerce. Guatemala,

San Salvador, Nicaragua, Honduras and Costa Rica abound in superior timber-lands and fertile fields, where coffee, tobacco, maize, and most of the other products of South America, can be successfully cultivated. Mexico, like Ecuador, presents every variety of climate; while its gold, silver, copper, and lead, are, in many places, still almost untouched. The weight of testimony goes to prove that the richest mines of the Republic of Mexico are in her northern States, near the border. The States of Durango, Sonora, Chihuahua and Sinaloa contain numerous mines hitherto but little known, and yet holding out, whenever they have been tested, a satisfactory promise of riches far greater than anything that Mexico has yet produced. Any one who has been through Mexico need not be retold the fact that, in many places, where mines were first discovered, the Spaniards did little more than work the surface ores. When a mine became too deep for convenient ingress and egress they left it and went to another.

Such is the new though near country still shut out from the world; such is the plain and unpretending, but accurate description of an almost unknown section of the earth; such is its unbounded wealth; such is the really bright side of the picture. Yet with all its brightness, it has a sombre opposite; an opposite especially dark when looked at by an enlightened citizen of the United States. The actual condition of many of these South and Central American countries is simply lamentable. In Mexico and several of the other Republics south of her, the lack of stable governments is a menace to commercial prosperity, superinducing meanwhile the neglect of agriculture and all other peaceful pursuits; while, sadly enough, in the Empire of Brazil, it has been found that the gradual emancipation of the slaves is steadily decreasing the supply of labor in the agricultural districts. Following a deficiency of education among the

masses, is its inevitable and close accompaniment, a deplorable and depraved state of morals; while absolute government always remains in the hands of either the sharp and
restless military schemer or the ambitious politician; each
bent upon filching from a depleted exchequer all he can
grasp. There is, under the circumstances, no incentive to
the people to work; for such is the richness of the soil that
a sufficient supply of food is perennial in superabundant
luxuriance. Therefore, and unfortunately, do men live without well-directed labor.

In each of these countries there is a grievous lack of a
sufficiently large population to develop the natural resources; and, moreover, the population is composed of several races, and is not of the most industrious character. On
all sides the absence of a diligent and intelligent laboring
class is apparent. The inestimably valuable cinchona industry is receiving staggering blows; the trees, all of spontaneous production, are being destroyed because the natives
will not even exert themselves in the least to encourage their
growth. This priceless febrifuge is becoming every day
more costly; and the bark-hunter has to penetrate farther
and farther into the thicknesses of the forest to find it.
Unless it shall be better protected, it will soon disappear entirely. So too with the rubber industry. The same reckless and improvident spirit is here manifested. This valuable commodity is fast disappearing; for people who can
live on the mandioca and plantain, without labor, will not
cultivate the caoutchouc, or attempt to save it. Hence the
article grows scarcer year by year, while the demand for it
increases every day. Other disadvantages are apparent.
Valuable timbers cannot be easily obtained; for the men
thereabout are too lazy to hew the trees.

The governments of Central and South America, recog-
nizing the need of immigration, offer every inducement to

emigrants from the United States and Europe; but no enterprising man of good judgment will go to countries so
isolated, and where life and property are so insecure. The
loosely-knit provinces of Mexico are now in such condition
that their central government cannot afford the better classes
of the people adequate relief from the depredations from
which they suffer.   These countries are almost entirely cut
off from intercourse with their near neighbor, the United
States; and their principal dealings are with Europe. As a
climax and perpetuation of all these evils, there is the curse
of red-tapeism, which is a most disagreeable and disadvantageous characteristic of all the South American governments.

On a continent like South America, where nature has
been so lavish in her prodigality, there must be a constant
overflow of the elements of wealth, which should go to the
benefit of such countries as have not been so highly
favored.   There is such an overflow, an incomparably rich
overflow, but it seldom helps the northern sister in the same
hemisphere, the United States. More generally it swells
the coffers of England, France and Germany; and what
they have picked over and left is eagerly taken by the United States ; while the noisy chant of " American enterprise "
expands into a grand chorus throughout the land. This is
no rhetorical bombast.   Facts, stubborn, gloomy, disgrace-
ful facts are here.   American enterprise and English enterprise meet; and England goes from America's own continent the winner.

England has a grip upon South and Central America, and
will, if possible, hold it with her figurative bull-dog tenacity.
Is the prize worth the contention ? Figures, pointed, in-
controvertible, answer in the affirmative.   From all the South
and Central American nationalities (excepting Mexico, Chili,
and British Guiana,) the United States buys more than she

sells to them. The exports from our Union to that division of our hemisphere, last year, amounted in round numbers to only twenty-one million dollars; while we imported therefrom fifty-nine million dollars' worth of goods. England's shrewdness and energy succeeded better. She sold to these countries sixty-five million dollars' worth of her manufactures and other merchandize, and bought from them to the amount of only twelve millions. In her dealings with the commonwealths of Spanish America, which are separated from her by the Atlantic Ocean, she comes out with an annual profit of fifty-three million dollars. In the dealings of the United States with these same commonwealths, our next-door neighbors, this great Republic comes out every year with a cash balance against it of thirty-eight million dollars. Will it be denied that there is a grave cause for alarm? Will it be contended that the United States should not exert herself to prevent this annual outgoing of thirty-eight million dollars? Does England still hold her commercial supremacy throughout South America?

As far back as 1857, Brazil, as a passive power, had six different lines of steamers connecting her with England, France, Germany, Portugal, Belgium and Italy. At that time the United States had not a single line to any portion of South America; and while England was and is reaping golden harvests, the balance of trade was each year increasing against our Union. England's commerce with Brazil, since the establishment of her first line of steamers in 1850, has increased her exports more than one hundred per cent; and she is now exerting herself to the utmost to advance her interests still further in South and Central America. Irrespective of its own large trade, Brazil is looked upon by the commercial nations of Europe as the key to the commerce of all South America. For this reason, as well as the hope of increasing traffic with Brazil, there is strong competition between different nations to control its markets. Germany and France, each almost as eager as England, are endeavoring, by steam communication, and also by flattering trade inducements, to turn the commercial currents toward their respective shores.

The Consul-General of the United States at Rio de Janiero, reports thirteen foreign steamship lines calling regularly at that port. Of these six are British, three are French, two are German, one is Italian, and one is from the United States. Nor can it be truthfully denied that England now holds the vantage-ground in every Republic of South and Central America. At Rio de Janiero it will be found that, on the Rua Primeiro de Marco, the great banking and commission-house center, nearly all the business is carried on by English and German firms. The very gas with which the city is lighted is made from coal that comes from England and Wales. So too, glancing from Rio de Janeiro to Iquitos, the most thriving town on the upper Amazon, it will be seen that the government ironworks are carried on by English mechanics; while the coal for the furnaces is brought from Swansea or Cardiff. This is not all. Great Britain, jealously watching our movements, will endeavor to thwart every attempt made by our manufacturers to gain a foothold in South and Central America. In her opposition she is supported by France and Germany. In the efforts which have been made to establish a " Permanent American Exhibition " at Rio de Janeiro, the most vigorous and persistent opposition to the scheme has come from the foreign commission merchants of European birth and proclivities; nor can it be denied that, but for the fact that Count D'Eu, the son-in-law of the Emperor, and other prominent Brazilian statesmen, favored the scheme, it would have been defeated by its foreign opponents.

Two-thirds of the Brazilian rubber crop is sent from Para

to the United States. It is well known that the rubber trees are being every year neglected; and unless American energy shall be there to save them, this great product, so important to the manufacturing interests of the United States, will be allowed to dwindle away and disappear. It requires fifteen years to grow the rubber tree, and the Brazilians do not look that far ahead. England looks at least thirty years forward; and soon she will appear in the field as a powerful rival, ready to wrest from Brazil, and from the United States, the inestimably valuable trade in rubber. Not long ago, a large quantity of rubber seeds were carried to England, and there planted in the public conservatories. A few of them produced healthy plants, which were sent to India, and there transplanted along the lowlands of certain rivers. No less startling is this fact than another, namely: England's designs to monopolize the highly profitable advantages of the cinchona bark industry. Already she has planted over a million trees along the slopes of the Himalayas; and she will soon openly begin her endeavors to turn the quinine of commerce from the Andes to India. So, while Peru is, on the one hand, threatened with the loss of her cinchona interests, England will rob Brazil of her rubber industry, unless immediate steps be taken to improve and protect the important American products thus endangered. Great though Brazil's loss would be, that of the United States would be greater; for nearly all the raw rubber is now sent to this Union, where its uses, in manufactured forms, are countless. If the field of its production be changed from Brazil to India, it will never reach the United States, save in the form of fabricated articles from English manufactories.

Even in Peru, England's foothold is no less firm than it is in Brazil. All the great commercial houses there are either owned or managed by subjects of Queen Victoria. Often the chief house is established in London, or Liverpool, with branches at Lima, Callao, and other cities of the Republic; and some with branches at Valparaiso, Santiago, and other parts of Chili.   There are about two thousand British subjects in Peru, connected with commerce, steamship companies, and railroad and gas corporations. The principal foundries and machine shops are carried on by Englishmen. With such formidable obstacles to impede them, it is not at all a matter of wonder that there are only five hundred American citizens in Peru. Wherever South America is visited, it will be found that England is far ahead of the United States.   The modern Albion has a powerful link binding all of her establishments in one great commercial chain.   She gathers up the fruits of the Englishman's trading operations from every part of the coast, and thence taking them to England's markets, afterward brings back articles with which to barter again.

Such, in short, is what is being done by the Pacific Steam Navigation Company of Liverpool, with its capital stock of fourteen million seven hundred and ninety thousand dollars, and owning upward of fifty first-class steamers, from a thousand to over four thousand tons capacity. Every fifteen days a steamer leaves Liverpool, touching at French, Portuguese, Brazilian, Chilian and Bolivian ports; arriving at Callao, discharging and receiving there the products gathered by the other boats of the company from ports in Columbia, Ecuador, and Peru, north of Callao; returning to Liverpool; retouching at all the above-named countries, and freighted with the products of the fields, forests and mines of South America.   That splendid steamship line commands commercially the whole South American coast, from Panama up through the Strait of Magellan, and down to Pernambuco; a line of 113° of latitude, counting both the east and west coasts, and drawing from and supplying no less than forty-three ports.

English capitalists have completed, and are the chief
owners of the railway from Vera Cruz, the most important harbor of Mexico, to the highly elevated and beautiful
capital of the Republic. English capitalists control the interoceanic railway at Honduras; it being used now principally to transport valuable woods for shipment to Europe.
British traders are now the leaders in business at Belize,
Greytown and Port Limon. Everywhere in South and Central America one may find the Englishman, ruddy, busy and
prosperous. No American Consul has ever left the United
States who has not earnestly called the attention of his government to the increasing encroachments of foreign powers
in the Spanish-speaking Republics; no traveler has ever
gone there from our Union who, from the standpoint of his
nationality, has not been mortified by the accumulating
proofs of English energy from the sea-coasts to the Andes,
while America's products have been conspicuous only by
their absence.

France and Germany have also a strong foothold in
South and Central America; both, in fact, being more firmly
fixed there than the United States. Proof of this may be
had by looking at the cacoa trade. At present, about seven
million pounds of cacoa are exported every year, (mainly
from Para;) and nearly all of this goes to France, a little to
England, and, according to the latest returns, " none at all
was sent to the United States." Cacoa goes to France and
England, and is there made into chocolate and cocoa.
Thence much of it is exported to the United States, reaching the American consumer after paying three or four duties, and the profits of a dozen merchants, in as many different places, besides compensation to the manufacturers.
Thus our Union obtains her large supply of chocolate; an
article which, in Spanish America, is one of the cheapest of
its bountiful products; but which, when it reaches the Uni-

ted States, with its label, " best English chocolate," or " best French chocolate," is one of the most costly luxuries. This is a strange and sad commentary on the commercial condition of the United States, that, in many localities at least, an American delicacy can be procured only with an English or French label upon it.

Nearly every Republic in South and Central America is annually, zealously canvassed by agents for German firms, and with such success that their goods, in great variety, are found even in the smallest villages. With these facts fronting them, thinking men in the United States can no longer deny that the foreign elements have now the advantage over this country in South America; nor can they fail to be conscious that some measures ought at once be taken to advance the interests of the United States in that vast section. The proper development of our sister continent can come only through the United States; and the sympathies of the people of that continent are to a greater extent with the United States than with any other commonwealth on the earth.

The opinion has already been advanced, an opinion which will here bear emphatic repetition, that the only way to open up South and Central America and Mexico, and give them free outlet for their immense productions, as well as an energetic population to make those productions fully available, is by means of a longitudinal and intercontinental railway. The opinion has also been expressed that the United States can only, by availing of the advantages that such a railway would give, successfully resist the foreign elements which now hold the key to the trade of South and Central America, to the detriment of the commerce of our Union. That these questions may be better understood, it will be necessary to follow the route of the road, looking at it as solving both the great problems of distribution and civilization throughout an undeveloped continent.

The extreme southern end of the road must be at Encarnacion, situated on the southern border of the Argentine Republic, near the banks of the Rio Negro. Of course it is understood that the line will ultimately be extended through Patagonia, to the Strait of Magellan; but this extension will be gradual. The road will run through the center of the Argentine Republic, and will traverse the very heart of the richest portion of that splendid country. More than this, it will open up every part of this wonderfully fertile and advancing nationality; for in its course it will cross or touch no less than eight navigable rivers, which traverse the Republic in every direction; three of them running across the whole country, from the Andean heights to the Atlantic Ocean. At Cordova the Three Americas Railway will be tapped by the Cordova and Tucuman Railroad, which latter gives Cordova direct connection by rail with Buenos Ayres and the great Rio de La Plata. Even now Cordova is also connected by this railroad with the Province of Tucuman, which is fondly designated by Argentines as "the garden spot of the Republic." The Cordova and Tucuman Railroad traverses five hundred miles of the Republic; and, with the aid of the projected international improvement and the numerous tributaries of the magnificent rivers Parana, Salado and Vermejo, there will not be a Province of the Republic, from the Andes to the River Plate and the Atlantic Ocean, that will not be enabled to pour its riches into the cars of the great Three Americas Longitudinal Railway, and receive at their very doors the manufactured goods of the United States. Cordova is destined to be the great railroad center of the Argentine Republic. Wheelwright's railroad connects it with Rosario and the Rio de la Plata, as well as with Buenos Ayres.

The Republic of Chili will pour out its products by means of its railroad across the Andes, from Santiago and

the valley of Aconcagua to Mendoza. That enterprising
Republic is now pushing across the mountain range, and
will soon have its railroad well within the borders of the Argentine Republic, ready to tap the Three Americas Railway.   The Argentine and Chilian Transcontinental Railroad
must be continued from Mendoza to Cordova, or to a place
more directly west of Buenos Ayres, where the products of
Chili will be emptied, together with the immense commodities of the Argentine Republic.   Here too Uruguay will be
enabled to send her superabundant supplies, by the Uruguay
River, and up the Rio de la Plata, to Rosario; from which
city Wheelright's railroad will take them to Cordova.   After the Three Americas Railway shall have crossed the
northern boundary of the Argentine Republic, it will receive tribute from Paraguay, and pay its own tributes by
means of the river Pilaya, a continuation of the Pilcomayo,
which empties into the great River Paraguay, opposite
Asuncion.   By means of the Paraguay, not only will the Republic of that name have a splendid outlet for its surplus
products, but the extraordinary fertility of the soil along the
banks of the river will be at once utilized in the interests
of civilization.

In this latitude, or near it, a few hundred miles of railroad
from Rio Janeiro would place that city in connection with
our great Longitudinal Line.   The completeness with
which the whole of the southern portion of South America
may be reached by the Three Americas Railway, is now discovered.   Entering Bolivia, the mission of our road will be
found to be even grander; for here is a noble inland country, hemmed in from the world, where inexhaustible and
untouched treasures are now locked up as if they were hidden away within a region of impenetrable darkness.   The
Three Americas Railway, by running through this Republic,
from the Argentine border across navigable Mamore and

the head-waters of the Guapore, will enter a small section of western Brazil, and cross the obstacle known as the Falls of the Madeira; thus developing one of the richest portions of the globe. Here too the great international railway will have another iron feeder in the Madeira and Mamore Railroad, which, when built, will connect the upper and lower plains of the Madeira. Our railway will also receive the homage of the great Madeira, the longest and largest tributary of the mighty Amazon. This river has a length of about two thousand miles; one branch of which, the Beni, rising near lake Titicaca, drains the fertile valleys of Yungas and Apollo, rich in cinchona, chocolate, and gold; another branch, the Mamore, springs from the vicinity of Chuquisaca, within fifteen miles of the source of the Paraguay, traversing the rich territory of the Moxos; while still another branch, the Itenez, washes down the gold and diamonds of Matto Grosso. Above the Madeira Falls are the cities of Exaltacion, Trinidad, Santa Cruz, Oruro, Cochabamba, and La Paz. There is the Beni Valley, abounding in gold, silver, tin, copper, lead and mercury. Merchants will find the banks of the Mamore literally studded with vast qualities of cinchona bark, rubber, coffee, cacao, sugar, rum, vanilla, copal, wax, dyes, sarsaparilla, tobacco, farina, cotton, llama and alpaca wool, cattle, hides, horns, tallow, dried meat, tiger and deer skins, furs, feathers, hammocks and hats.

Through Bolivia, Peru will send her own riches, from the Pacific side of the Republic, across the Andes by her railroad from Mollendo to Lake Titicaca, which road must be extended latitudinally to the Longitudinal Line. Such a road, crossing Bolivia from west to east, will be no less important to the latter Republic than to Peru itself; for it will provide an outlet for Bolivia's merchantable products which lie beyond the navigable rivers. While the Mollendo and

Titicaca Railroad will give Peru one splendid outlet for her Pacific slopes, she will also be able to utilize her grand streams, the Huallaga and the Ucayli, which drain her central and northern territory. Both of these rivers empty into the waters of the Amazon some distance above the point at which the Three Americas Railway will cross it. Thus while the products of one portion of Peru will reach the great central line by rail, those of the other will come by water. The Oroyo Railroad, leaving the coast at Callao, and coming through Lima, will also connect with the Three Americas Railway. Here then is the solution of the problem of giving this rich republic of South America direct communication with the civilized world. The Ucayli is navigable for about seven hundred miles. Its basin extends to the west, at varying distances, from fifty to one hundred and thirty miles, up to the foot of the eastern Cordillera. It runs from south to north in Peru, and goes through one of the richest portions of the ancient empire of the Incas. The Huallaga flows through the republic in the same direction, but nearer the Andes. It is about half as long as the Ucayli, and runs through a fertile plain, presenting to the agriculturist the promise of a glowing future. Cotton is here gathered within six months after sowing, and rice within five months.

From the Falls of the Madeira River the Three Americas Railway will run across the extreme western end of Brazil, bridging the rivers Purus, Tefle, Jurua, Jutay and Maranon; after which it will enter and cross the eastern end of Ecuador. In its passage over Brazil, it will, in great part, secure to itself the inconceivably immense commerce of the basin of the Amazon. That wonderful river drains a surface equal to two-thirds of all Europe; and it has well been named the Mediterranean of the New World. Among the many rivers emptying into its great waters, there are six tributaries

superior to any river in Europe, outside of Russia, save the
Danube; and ten times greater than any stream on the west
slope of the Andes. Its extent of water communication is
unparalled; its tributaries, as has already been remarked,
touching every country on the continent except Chili and
Patagonia. Twelve of its tributaries are each over a
thousand miles long; and many of them are united by a
marvelous network of natural canals. The world has now
only the faintest idea of the inexhaustible natural wealth of
this teeming region; but the Three Americas Railway will
be enabled to gather and distribute it. At the point where
the road will cross the Maranon it will be widely and nobly
connected, by the Amazon, the Ucayli, and the Huallaga,
it will easily communicate with Peru and all Brazil; by the
Yavari, the Jutay, the Jurua, the Purus, and the Madeira,
with Peru and Bolivia; by the Santiago, the Pastaza, and
the Napo, with Ecuador; by the Ica and the Jasara, with
Columbia; by the Negro and Branco, with Venezuela and
the Guianas; and by the Madeira, the Tapajos, the Tocan-
tins and the Xingu with several of the interior Provinces of
Brazil.

Ecuador, whose valuable treasures are now hid from the
world by the Andes on one side and the Empire of Brazil
on the other, will be equally fortunate in her connections
with the grand American Longitudinal Railway; for the
road will cross below the point where her Piguena and her
Napo empty into the Maranon; and, after running half way
across the Republic, it will span her great water highway,
the Ica, which, rising among the Andes of Columbia, rolls
itself across the Republic of Ecuador. Our road will then run
through Columbia, whose rivers, the Guaviari, the Vichada,
the Meta, and the Magdalena, with their numerous feeders,
cross the Republic in every direction. All these rivers lie in,
or are adjacent to, the line of the Three Americas Rail-

way. It might seem, at first thought, that Venezuela and
Guiana, resting far off on the Atlantic seaboard, would be
beyond the reach of the benefits of this matchless railway;
but the superb Orinoco appears, as if it were there under a
special providence, with its far-reaching tributaries, moving
majestically across Venezuela, and having its very home
along the borders of Columbia; while the Vichada and the
Guaviari pour their waters into the great Orinoco itself. As
both the Vichada and the Guaviari will be crossed by the
Three Americas Railway, the products of Venezuela and
Guiana have only to be brought from the Orinoco into these
two rivers, and there and then be unloaded from the vessels
into the cars. It has now been seen how the proposed
Three Americas Railway will, with the aid of the grand
river systems of South America, reach and develop every
Republic of that vast area of the New World.

Leaving South America, and crossing the Isthmus of
Darien, our road will enter Central America and Mexico.
Here is a portion of our own continent which has, at
best, only the semblance and not the reality of a river
system; and were such the case in South America, the
Three Americas Railway would be of little avail toward
reaching and developing the immense resources of that
most fertile country. South America has, however, no
parallel in the grandeur and wealth of its navigable rivers.
Yet, in considering the formation of Central America, it
will be seen that the same Power which made South America,
with a breadth of three thousand two hundred miles, filled
that wide domain with a noble network of rivers; at the
same time making narrow and isthmuslike that portion of
North America which had no rivers; while, when it was
broadened into the fair proportions of Mexico, the beautiful Santiago, the stately Rio Grande, and many others,
were graciously given to the land. From Panama to the

city of Mexico the scarcity of navigable streams is especially noticeable ; but, owing to the short distance between ocean and ocean, the Longitudinal Railway will develop the resources of all this isthmian country.

It is not alone because this portion of the continent is narrow, that it is peculiarly capable of being developed under the operations of the projected railway. Upon the Pacific side the track must be laid ; for that side is far less rugged than that which borders on the Caribbean Sea. By a happy coincidence, the fact appears that the great mass of the population is on the Pacific side ; that the enterprising and progressive Republic of Salvador lies entirely on the Pacific side ; that the largest and wealthiest cities are on the Pacific side ; that the best soil for coffee is on the Pacific side ; that the spacious and splendid harbor of the Gulf of Fonseca is on the Pacific side ; that the Pacific side is the more healthy ; that while the Caribbean side is often swept by terrible hurricanes, the Pacific plateaus, deserving the designation, rest undisturbed by any such howling and vehement forces of destruction. Nature seems to have ordained that the most level pathway for our road is to be found through the richest portion of the country. The Three Americas Railway will, in its passage through Central America and Mexico, cross the Panama, the Costa Rica, the Honduras, and the Tehuantepec Interoceanic Railroads, and will, in this way, secure as freight the products of the eastern coasts ; while the San Juan River and Lake Nicaragua will aid materially in the development of the great resources of the Republic of that name. It is therefore apparent that, while Honduras, at present perhaps the least improved of the Central American Republics, will readily reach the Longitudinal Line, the grand railway itself, moving northwardly, will pass through the very heart of the richest of these countries into Mexico. Nor will it be long

before each and all of these small republics will be connected with the Three Americas Railway by means of short
lines from their Atlantic and Pacific coasts. Even now the
diminutive but busy and productive Republic of Costa
Rica is struggling bravely to complete an interoceanic railroad from Port Limon to Punta Arenas. This will eventually be one of the many feeders of the Three Americas
Railway.

Mexico is now, to a great extent, as it has always been,
commercially cut off from the rest of the world. As if by
a decree of nature herself, this rich Republic can reach the
markets of the world, advantageously, only through the
United States. She cannot do so through her own seaports; for she possesses none that are, in all respects, available. It has been seen that the general course of the high
Mexican plateaus is northwardly into the United States. It
has also been seen how these peculiar formations constitute
an almost insurmountable barrier between the coasts and the
great interior of Mexico. The report of the Mexican Committee on Mining Taxes says: "The central table-land of
our country is separated from either seacoast by rugged
mountains and deep ravines, breaking it into longitudinal
zones of different temperatures and varied productions; but
this fact almost cuts off communication between these zones
and the seacoast. The ascent from the coast to the central
table-lands is difficult." It is thus apparent that whatever
barriers nature has placed in the way of progress in Mexico
are between the coasts and the interior, and not along the
elevated table-lands themselves; for they render the building af a railway north and south, through the great interior,
comparatively easy. By another very happy coincidence, it
is apparent that this very portion of Mexico, level enough
for the passage of a railway, is that which embraces the
richest part of the country, so far as both soil and the
precious metals are concerned.

It is now an open secret that the richest mines of the Republic of Mexico are in its Northern States, near the border. Consul Ward, in his official report to the British Government, said : " The States of Durango, Sonora, Chihuahua, and Sinaloa, contain an infinity of mines hitherto but little known, but holding out, whenever they have been tried, a promise of riches superior to anything that Mexico has yet produced." Through this now remote section of the Republic, or at least near enough to these several States to develop them, the Three Americas Railway will pass. It is not alone in the inexhaustible hills of gold and silver that Mexico's riches consist. Her soil is one of the most fertile in the world ; and it should be noted that the sharpest observers of nature, the civilized native races, chose the table-lands of Mexico as the fittest place for founding their empire. These lands are capable of yielding enormous quantities of wheat, cotton, Indian corn, barley, coffee, sugar, fruits, and wines. Such is the wonderful fertility of the soil that two crops may be raised in one year in much the larger portion of the Republic. Mexico is equally rich in cattle, sheep, cochineal and silk. It is through the center of this table-land section that the Longitudinal Line will run ; and Mexico, whose rather rocky and sandy and inaccessible seacoast now measurably prevents her from sending out her crude wealth, and from freely receiving in exchange the manufactured articles she desires, will have a grand iron highway through that part of her territory in which so many of her natural productions annually rot in useless profusion.

In crossing the Mexican border, the Longitudinal Line will enter upon the grand work of developing the new and rich silver-country of the United States. After traversing the western neck of Texas, it will enter New Mexico, and running through that argentiferous Territory to Santa Fé, will then branch off in a northeasterly direction, following the Santa Fé route, and go through Kansas to Missouri and St. Louis. From St. Louis our road will run through Iowa and Minnesota to Manitoba. This would appear to be the best route for the road through the territory of the United States; but the engineers will have at least one other to consider, namely, a route through Texas to Arkansas, and thence on to St. Louis. This latter route would pass about one hundred miles west of Austin, and would be shorter than the line suggested above. The road through New Mexico will have the advantage of rendering available one of the richest gold and silver regions in the United States; the same, on account of its present comparative remoteness from the great centers, being now almost worth'ess. Arizona and New Mexico would thus be placed at once in the line of direct and rapid communication with other portions of the United States. This southwestern section of our Union has many advantages; its soil is rich, its climate delicious, its precious metals abundant.

In its passage through the United States, the Three Americas Railway will cross scores of smaller lines, and will itself bring into existence many more that will tap it at various points. As the road will not at first be extended to the Strait of Magellan, neither will it be immediately constructed through British America to Alaska and Bhering Strait; although, in coming generations, it will end there. It should, however, in its inception, reach as far north as the Saskatchawan River. It will cross the Canada Pacific, which will give it the products of both east and west British America, including the prosperous Province of Ontario. Of this region, a distinguished American statesman has recently written as follows: "North of lakes Erie and Ontario and the river St. Lawrence, east of lake Huron, south of the 45th parallel, and included mainly within the present Canadian

Province of Ontario, there is as fair a country as exists on the North American continent, nearly as large in area as New York, Pennsylvania and Ohio combined, and equal, if not superior, to these States in its agricultural capacity. It is the natural habitat on this continent of the combing-wool sheep, without a full, cheap and reliable supply of the wool of which species, the great worsted manufacturing interests of the country cannot prosper, or we should rather say, exist. It is the land where grows the finest barley, which the brewing interest of the United States must have, if it ever expects to rival Great Britain in her present annual export of over eleven million dollars' worth of malt products. It raises and grazes the finest of cattle, with qualities especially desirable to make good the deterioration of stock in other sections; and its climatic conditions, created by an almost complete encirclement of the great lakes, specially fit it to grow men."

The Saskatchawan River terminus of the Three Americas Railway, will render more available and valuable the rich fur-country; and, by tapping the Canada Pacific, our road will be indirectly connected with British Columbia and Nova Scotia. It will pass through the no less productive and desirable territory of Manitoba and the Red River Valley. The average number of bushels of wheat to the acre in Ontario is larger than the average in the wheat-growing sections of the United States, with perhaps one or two exceptions; and the average of wheat to the acre in Manitoba and the Red River Valley is even larger than the average in Ontario. Our great road, in piercing British America, will open up a country of which, in many respects, less is known than we now know of South America; which abounds in riches of a different nature, but which are equally necessary to the comfort and well-being of civilized communities. Out of a total area of 3,346,701 square miles, there are two million square miles of timbered and agricultural lands; and in the remainder, which as yet has been only partially explored, there are known to be valuable minerals, fur-bearing animals, and profitable fisheries. Connected with British Columbia by the Canada Pacific, the Three Americas Railway will bring the Aleutian Islands and their costly stores of furs of amphibious animals several thousand miles nearer to the commercial centers of the United States. The dense forests of British America will also be reached; and the superb timber of that section will be made more generally available.

It is not at all improbable that the European projectors of the Darien Ship Canal will oppose the building of a longitudinal double-track steel railway through North and Central and South America. Such a railway will of course cross the canal. That the existence and working of the railway will be detrimental to the trade of European nations with Spanish America, cannot reasonably be denied. Europe will be the loser; the United States the gainer; Spanish America itself will be the greatest gainer. One significant fact, always to be remembered, is that this railroad is now, and is forever to remain, purely an American enterprise; not American in that general, yet circumscribed acceptation of the term which makes it spring solely from the United States; but American in the broarder sense, in the right sense, which renders it the production, as it is hereafter to be the pride, of all the Americas.

The Darien Ship Canal, while it would increase the commerce of Europe with South and Central America, would be of little benefit to the United States. It would perhaps, on the other hand, but fasten the hold of transatlantic power upon South and Central America; and its existence as an unobstructed water-way, would be a menace to the commercial welfare of the United States, unless it should be well guarded by governmental guarantees. No better check can possibly be placed against any injurious influences it may threaten to exert, than the early construction through the three Americas of just such a railway as is now proposed. The Darien Canal is essentially a European enterprise. When the Interoceanic Canal Congress met at Paris, May 15, 1879, the United States Government sent, as its representatives, Rear Admiral Daniel Ammen, and Engineer Aniceto G. Menocal. The high standing and well known attainments of these two officers, and the fact that both had been conspicuous in repeated Central American canal surveys, entitled their opinions to great weight in that congress of scientific men. An equally important consideration was also the fact that they were from the continent of America, through which the ship canal is to be cut. Yet so far from having any weight or influence with that foreign body, these gentlemen were treated with official discourtesy; and no attention whatever was given to their arguments. The packed congress did the work cut out for it; that is to say, it adopted the Darien route, which, by actual figures, has been shown to be nearly fifty per cent. more costly than the route through Nicaragua. That congress, of which M. Ferdinand de Lesseps was the ruling spirit, refused even to consider the obvious claims and merits of Tehuantepec and Nicaragua.

When the fact shall be fully realized that, in comparison with Tehuantepec and Nicaragua, Darien is from one to two thousand miles farther from the Atlantic and Gulf seaports of the United States, and therefore from one to two thousand miles nearer to Europe, the reason for the selection of Darien by the European congress, and the motives which led to the snubbing of the representatives from America, will be quite apparent. M. de Lesseps and his partners are at the head of a European company, with European capital, under a European charter; and they propose to take absolute control of the canal in the interests of Europe. Several of the ablest American statesmen hold that the United States cannot prevent the building of the Darien Canal, as our government, under the law and treaties, is pledged to strict neutrality. Conceding this, then it must be admitted that the United States will be compelled, in some way, to counteract the ruinous influences of this highway controlled by European policy. There could then be no better protection to the interests of the Union than the Three Americas Railway. With such a railway, the United States can well afford to be neutral, so far as the canal is concerned.

On the other hand, suppose the Monroe doctrine be practically applied to the Darien enterprise, and as the result thereof the Tehuantepec or Nicaragua route be selected, and a canal, backed by American capital, be cut through Central America. Let that be exclusively an American enterprise, or at least let American capital be in such preponderating proportion as to control its administration. Yet, even with this advantage over Darien, the mercantile marine of the United States cannot now compete with that of England. In the first place, the United States cannot, at this time, construct steamships so cheaply as they can be built in Great Britain. Not only are England's rates of wages much less, but her ship-building yards on the Clyde, on the Tyne, and on the Mersey, are all situated in close proximity to the raw materials, the iron and the coal, required for the purpose of steamship construction. This circumstance will, for a long time to come, continue to give Great Britain an important advantage over the United States in respect to navigation by steamers. Under the present condition of things, the first cost of her steamships will invariably be less, and so the capital invested in them being less, they can of course be profitably worked at lower rates.

The late Horace Greeley said on this subject: "There are reasons for our backwardness in building and running ocean steamers, which no policy could surmount. Our labor is dearer, our facilities for the cheap production of steamships less ample, than those of Great Britain. While the ocean was navigated by sailing vessels almost exclusively, the abundance and cheapness of our timber gave us advantages which counteracted the cheap labor and metals of our European rivals; but we lost this when steam was substituted for wind as a motive power." Besides the overwhelming advantages of cheaper vessels worked at less cost, Great Britain can boast of still 'another very great gain over the United States, in her commercial relations with South America. Through habits and customs of long standing, the current of South American commerce turns to England; and there is no fact better understood than that regularly established trade-currents are hard to change. Even with superior vessels and consummate seamanship, it requires years on the part of one nation to divert the commerce of another from a set channel. Such being the case with nationalities equally matched in marine equipment, the task would be quite hopeless in the United States, which, humiliating as may be the admission, is now almost irretrievably behind England in the prime essentials of a mercantile navy.

Even admitting that our Union would secure an equal share of the advantages claimed for the Darien Canal (or any other Central American canal,) it is evident that such water-way can never accomplish the work of a great longitudinal railway. The utmost benefit urged by the supporters of the canal scheme is that it would bring the whole western coast of South America nearer to the United States. It would certainly bring the same coast much nearer to England. Yet the western coast of South America is

really very insignificant in comparison with the country
through which our railway is to run.   The territory naturally
tributary to the commerce of the Pacific coast lies between
the eastern and western Cordilleras, on the western slope of
the coast range.   This territory embraces about 427,000
square miles, and constitutes only six and one half per cent.
of the entire area of South America.   Col. George Earl.
Church, a gentleman whose long connection with important
public enterprises in South America entitles him to speak
with authority, stated, in reply to the question, What extent
of country east of the Cordilleras can be made tributary to
the Pacific coast ports by steamship communication ? " I
unhesitatingly answer very little; not exceeding four and a
half per centum ; thus leaving eighty-nine per centum of
South America to be developed from the Atlantic coast."
It is thus seen that, while steamship lines, the majority of
them being English, can, by strenuous exertions, reach only
four and a half per centum of the territory of South America, our grand longitudinal railway, in connection with latitudinal lines, will take in eighty-nine per centum of the
country; and even more; for the Pacific coast ports will
seek the quicker outlet afforded by the railway for their products.   Nor is this all.   Mexico, which, on account of its
comparatively rock-bound and inaccessible coasts, cannot
be so safely or conveniently reached by vessels going
through the canal, will always be within easy access to the
United States by means of the Three Americas Railway,
running through its interior.   Thus its rich productions will
continue, in great measure, to be locked out from European
nations.

   If American vessels can pass through the Ship Canal, so
also can English vessels.   It is plain, therefore, that our
Union, as a competitor against England for South American commerce, must resort to some other means than ships;

that South and Central America and Mexico must be reached by a route other than by water; and that barter between our Union and these continental neighbors must be largely conducted without sea-going vessels. It is here that the rival claims of railways and canals present themselves. In the commercial history of the United States, during the last quarter of the present century, there is probably no fact better established than that canal and river navigation, as means for the certain and rapid transportation of the commodities of an uncommonly · productive nation, are not to be compared with railways. It is not denied that, in their day, canals did good work toward the development of our Union; but the population of our country has now happily become too large and too full of business for such slow water-ways. Competition is too active; it requires the locomotive to keep pace with the times.

When General Washington, as commander-in-chief of the continental army, laid aside his sword, and assumed the duties of President of the United States, one of the first schemes that attracted his attention was a plan for connecting the waters of the James River, in Virginia, with the Ohio, by means of a canal. His earnest advocacy of this work resulted in the construction of the James River and Kanawha Canal. To-day a railroad runs upon the towpath of that canal; and the stream, in some places, is dried up; in others it is turned into a millrace. A still better illustration of the failure of canals to successfully compete with railroads, is seen in the case of the great Erie Canal; for here, while the canal continues in full operation, it has a railroad rival; the two important highways of commerce run side by side nearly all the way from Albany to Buffalo. What is the result? The railroad has secured more than ninety per cent. of the local traffic.

General merchandize shipped from New York City to

the towns and cities between Albany and Buffalo, is chiefly transported by rail.   During a period of twelve years, that is to say, from 1866 to 1878, the tonnage transported on the New York railroads exceeded that on the New York canals by 52,889,585 tons. · During the last ten years, there has been an almost entire diversion of the class of freight known as general merchandize, from the canals to the railroads.   In the active competition between lake navigation and railroads, the results have been similar.   In 1863 the shipments of flour from Chicago by lake constituted eighty-one per cent. of the total movement; but in 1878 only twelve per cent.   The shipments by rail, during the year 1878, were about eight times as great as those for the year 1863. Over river navigation the triumph of the railroad has been no less marked.   More than ninety per cent. of all the commerce between the West and the seaboard is now carried on over the great trunk railroads.   At least three-fourths of the commerce of St. Louis, the central city of the finest river system of the whole Union, is carried by the railroads.   It is therefore apparent that, as commercial highways, neither canal, nor lake, nor river, can bear comparison with railroads.

The United States, by reason of its favorable situation, having territorial connection with Mexico and Central and South America, has an overwhelming advantage over Great Britain and other foreign competitors for the Spanish American trade.   While our Union can readily reach all the countries of the South by rail, England cannot.   While the railway from our Union must penetrate the great undeveloped interior of Central and South America, England's vessels can only hang, here and there, around the coasts. While England will require from three to six weeks to reach the ports of South America, trains from the United States will need only from one week to ten days to go to the very heart of the Southern Continent.

In the current history of the world the time has come when America, as a whole, and not America in its divisional parts, must be considered. Europe and portions of our own New England are already over-crowded; and each succeeding year hundreds of thousands must look to the great vacant spaces on the two American continents for homes. It is important, therefore, that all the countries of the New World should be brought closer together, socially and commercially; the various sections aiding each other in the development and building up of one grand commonwealth. It is the mission of the continents of America to furnish homes for millions from Europe. From the year 1868 to 1879, immigration into the United States ranged from one hundred and thirty-eight thousand per year to four hundred and fifty-nine thousand. Last year there was an increase of thirty-nine thousand over the preceding year; and during the past twelve years the total number of immigrants coming into the United States was three million three hundred and seventy-seven thousand and ninety-four. At this rate, including the increase of the native population, almost the whole of the eastern or Atlantic portion of the United States, in the course of a few decades, will suffer like the countries of Europe from the evil of over-crowding, unless meanwhile our own great agricultural and silver regions of the Southwest and the countries of Central and South America shall be developed. Yet this development will be impossible until these divisions shall be brought into closer commercial relationship with each other. The only link which can properly unite and bind them is an intercontinental railway. That railway must be the grand longitudinal and intercontinental road here proposed.

Lord Bacon once wrote, "There be three things which make a nation great and prosperous; a fertile soil, busy workshops, and easy conveyance of men and things from

one place to another." This whole vast southern territory
has the first indispensable requisite mentioned by the erudite philosopher, a fertile soil, and it cannot be doubted that
the second, busy workshops, will follow the easy conveyance
of men and things from one place to another. A great
part of the new country through which the Three Americas
Railway is to run will be found to be wild and uncivilized;
and this brings forward a very important branch of the subject, namely, raliroads as civilizers. " The natural effect of
commerce," says Montesquieu, "is to tend to and consoli-
date peace." This remark is all the more true and forcible
when commerce is carried on by means of railroads. Nothing so unites the different parts of a country as a railroad
running through it; and when upon the line of such road
there is one place blessed with the multiform advantages
which civilization brings, all the other places upon that line
will surely reap to some extent the same ennobling benefits. When trade is carried on between two or more nations
by means of a railroad, they soon become respectfully and
goodnaturedly interdependent. While one may be interested in buying, the others may be equally interested in
selling; and so strong ties of friendship, commercial and
social, grow out of their mutual wants. Cheap and quick
means of intercommunication most effectively facilitate and
develop commercial relations. The more rapid the vehicles
of communication, the closer and more binding the fasten-
ings between the connected countries.

European ships reach most of the ports of South America as soon as those from the United States; and as Europe
began trading there first, her relations with the southern
countries are now far more intimate. Yet England's communications could not possibly be so close, (because not so
rapid,) if a railway ran from the United States to those
same countries. Therefore, with the Three Americas Rail-

way, new and important commercial ties must be formed;. and will not England, by reason of the immense separating stretch of water, then be hopelessly distant from those great southern trade-fields?

The wonderful success of railroads, as civilizing agents, has been fully demonstrated in the history of America. At first, small settlements sprang up along the line; the inhabitants, like the country itself, being rough and lawless: but every passing train contributes its element of enlightenment. The wild camp assumes a name; the disorderly mob choose a ruler, generally the best man among them; and finally law and order are educed out of confusion. But this is not all. The railroad performs a no less important mission as a distributing agent. Nature has latently implanted in mankind cravings for the productions of other soils and other climates. Civilization is rapidly developing these half-concealed longings. The staples of each particular country are obtainable in superfluity, and are infinitely more in quantity than the people amid whom they are produced have need of; while other and distant peoples are in a like situation; having a superabundance of some products and an insufficiency or a total absence of others. The desired exchanges are most readily effected by means of railroads. Increased speed of transport makes available many classes of articles which are absolutely useless if not consumed within a certain time; and the advantages of railways over ships in this respect are plainly apparent.

The problem of distribution is one that is beginning to occupy the attention of the ablest political economists in the world. In many of the States of our own Republic manufacturing facilities have been greatly increased; and many articles have been put out in excess of the demand. For these redundant goods new markets must be reached. An English economist, commenting on Mr. Gladstone's

prediction that America will be the future great commercial
nation of the world, is comforted by the thought that " when
America is fully peopled, wages for agricultural laborers will
sink to the level of those paid by the other developed
States of the world." In other words, he sees in the future
the danger of over-production in our own Union; and recog-
nizing England's present commercial hold upon Spanish
America, he does not yet perceive the possibility of any
outlet for the excessive manufactures of the United States.
Nor can there be such an outlet without a grand Three
Americas Railway. Unless such a line shall be completed,
England can safely congratulate herself that the United
States will be unable to sell abroad any considerable quantity of her manufactured articles. Mr. Victor Drummond,
of the British Legation at Washington, is also cheered at
England's prospects, as he writes home that there need be
no fears of American competition; and he too sets down
for Great Britain's rejoicing " over-production, the dangers
of the communistic and socialistic movement, probably receiving accession to its ranks from the number of people out
of work." The question of over-production is really at the
bottom of many of the evils now afflicting the United
States; and its successful solution will be a national blessing. That blessing will come in the form of the Three
Americas Railway. Look at what Europe actually does
sell in the Central and South American Republics, and at
what the United States could easily and profitably sell there
with the aid of a railway, and an eager demand is at once
created for supplying the great desideratum. While the
United States suffers from over-production, Mexico and
Central and South America, and also the wild but fertile districts of British America, groan under the equal evils of
being productive countries without produtive populations.
Railways, as distributing agents, are no less successful in

distributing labor than supplies; and therefore the same Longitudinal Line, which will help the United States by giving it an outlet for its superabundant productions, will give these other countries respectively an energetic population to develop them.

Within the last few years the gravity of the situation has forced itself upon the Government of the United States. In 1877, Secretary Evarts issued a circular-letter to the consular and diplomatic officers of the United States in Spanish America, in which he said: "It is believed that the period has now arrived when it would be wise for all the nations of this continent to consider more carefully than heretofore how they may best enlarge their trade with each other. Their geographical position and the resemblance between their political institutions facilitate the cultivation of such commerce. The United States are in a condition to supply cheaply and easily many products and manufactured articles suitable to their wants, to all, or nearly all, of the Spanish American Republics, as well as to the empire of Brazil; receiving in return natural products which can be utilized here. A favorable opportunity for the development of such trade would seem to be now offered by the prevailing stagnation of business, and depression of prices. It is desirable, of course, for the United States, that they should find markets for the export of their products and manufactures; and, on the other hand, it is advantageous to the people of these countries that they should be able to purchase at the present decreased valuation. Apart from questions of merely commercial or pecuniary advantage, the development of such trade would also have a beneficial influence upon the political condition of the Republics of this continent. It is for the interest of both North and South America that all those republican governments should have stability, peace, law and order. It is not unreasonable to believe that when the popular energy, now wasted upon schemes of revolution and military aggrandizement, shall have been turned toward more peaceful and profitable enterprises, the republican form of government, in each and all of those countries, will thereby be strengthened, and more harmonious relations will prevail between them. In view of these considerations, it is desired by the Department of State that its diplomatic and consular officers should devote attention to the question of methods by which trade with the United States can be most judiciously fostered."

Much has been said of the advantages which will probably accrue to the United States, to Mexico, to Central and South America, and also to British America from the proposed railway. Yet the benefits of the enterprise are far-reaching enough in their effects to take in all Europe, which cannot now comfortably support its immense population. With a teeming southern continent opened to the world, and connected with the great North American centers by rail, it is impossible to estimate the number of worthy but oppressed peoples from Great Britain, France, Germany, and Italy, who will hasten to seek homes in the land where want is absolutely unknown. A third of the population removed from those European countries would benefit the peoples left behind; for the land which could but scantily support all, would abundantly support the remaining two-thirds. In other words, there would be room enough in the country which was before overcrowded; and there necessary food and clothing would be cheaper because more plentiful.

Not the least among the many important considerations attaching to this stupendous enterprise is the fact that it must add very largely to the food supply of the civilized world. What is of no value in one part of the globe is often especially valuable in another. In British Columbia and Alaska which will ultimately be reached by the proposed railway, salmon is the commonest of common fish in all the rivers of the North Pacific, and is therefore considered fit only for those who can get no better food. Yet this same fish is a real delicacy in the United States and Europe. The extensive cod-banks off the Aleutian Isles, and many parts of the northern Pacific coast, will render still larger and cheaper the immense supplies of fish. These enormous catches from the Pacific waters, as well as beef from the countless herds of cattle roaming over the plains of Central and South America, can then be shipped to Europe in quantities more than sufficient to revictual the homes of starving thousands.

Great Britain herself must continue to deal extensively and directly with America. She has no other choice; for she is at present in the startling position of being able to produce only enough food to supply the wants of little more than half her inhabitants. England is the largest importing nation in the world; and although, after the construction of the Three Americas Railway, she will lose much of her export trade to South America, yet she will be forced to continue buying from that continent; especially as the railway will greatly cheapen the productions of America. Germany, France and Italy will, in like manner, discover that they can no longer sell their fabrics with profit to these South and Central American continents, as the United States will be in position to undersell them. They however, like England, will always be under the necessity of buying much of their raw material from the American continents. While satisfactorily solving the question of greater food supply in Europe, the Three Americas Railway will have a no less important bearing upon that question in the United States; for in the republics of Central and South America there is no stoppage of agricultural productions during winter; but crops may be had, and poultry raised, all the year round; while the immense herds of cattle on the vast natural pastures will furnish milk and butter in measureless quantities. Therefore the astonishing fact will be realized that, just when vegetables, milk, butter, poultry and fruits have disappeared, or are scarce, in the United States, they will come in abundance, and at a week's notice, from Central and South America.

In the very beginning of the consideration of this project, its immensity, and the difficulty of doing it justice, were subjects of remark. So manifold are the advantages in prospect, as the outgrowth of such an unparalleled railway, and so far-reaching its probable benefits, that they affect almost all interests, public and private, aid in the solution of nearly all questions affecting either of the American continents, and vitally touch the well-being of citizens of every clime and condition. An assertion so all-embracing should not be confined merely to its utterance. Facts should sustain it. Such facts have already been given, drawn from official sources; and from those facts the reasons for the assertion are evidenced. Yet to do the entire subject at least partial justice, it is right that its largest branches should be touched upon, leaving the smaller ones to assert themselves by the light of facts already educed.

FIRST.—Timber Supply: This, from being, twenty-five years ago, a mere question of convenience, has now risen to the dignity of a national problem. The demand for timber is daily increasing, as the timber itself is daily decreasing. While the population of the United States increases, within a decade, thirty-five per cent., the increase of the consumption of wood is sixty-five per cent. England alone imports wood to the value of sixty million dollars, that being three times the value of her own ligniferous products. As countries become civilized the uses of timber multiply. No hard timber is found in the United States west of the one hundredth meridian. The great Longitudinal Railway, starting within the splendid forests of hardwood in British America, will pass through the stately forests of the Amazon Valley and the Grand Chaco, bordering on the Parana River; thus rendering accessible to the world the richest varieties of lumber for construction as well as for ornamental purposes.

SECOND.—The creation of new industries: It must inevitably follow that the existence and operation of a great railway, from one end of America to the other, will rapidly develop new and important industries in the various countries of both continents. In the absence of a cheaper and better method of artificial congelation than chemistry has yet been able to discover, an extensive and profitable ice-trade could be carried on, from far north in British America, with Mexico and Central and South America. Placed in cars made for the purpose, this great luxury could be safely conveyed to the tropical countries every week; and the single item of handling and distributing it at various stations along the road, would employ the labor of thousands. This ice industry, extending through Mexico and Central and South America and the British Possessions, would be worth millions to both continents.

It has been ascertained that green tea can be successfully cultivated in portions of South America; but the indolent disposition of the present inhabitants has led them to neglect this important product. With the energetic popution which our Longitudinal Line will intersperse throughout the Spanish-speaking Republics, it may not be long before America will become the rival of Japan and China in the production of tea. There is still another article, which, as a valuable commercial commodity, will certainly be developed; and that is the maté, or Paraguay tea. When it is considered that this staple affords the principal refreshing beverage of a large majority of the Spanish Americans south of the Equator, and that millions of dollars are annually expended in the Argentine Republic, Bolivia, Peru, and Chili, in its production or use, it will readily be admitted that it must possess rare virtues. Only those who have tasted it can form a just conception of its grateful flavor and delightfully stimulating qualities. Its cheapness will, with the aid of the intercontinental railway, soon introduce it into the United States.

A gigantic fruit trade must also spring up between the tropical countries and the United States, a trade which, as it has really never heretofore existed, may be looked at in the light of a new industry. The most delicious fruits of those countries cannot now reach our Union, because their perishable nature renders them unfit for slow and uncertain transportation in ships. Mere contact with the sea seems to cause an almost immediate deterioration of their excellence. Between salt water and fine fruits there is little affinity. A fifth branch of industry, which can be easily built up, will be the important one of paper-making. The demand for paper has increased to such an extent that, within the last five years, its price has risen to an alarming degree. If there is one thing above all others in which the Valley of the Amazon is rich, it is in plants whose fibers would make the best paper. Wool, other than that which comes from the sheep, will be another and no less important item of trade. In South America the Alpaca, Guanaco, and Vicuna, furnish the best kinds of wool; and while the export of the fleeces of these animals is now but comparatively small, it might be increased a hundred fold, and thereby cheapen the present high price of woolen goods in the United States. By opening up an almost unknown territory, the

Three Americas Railway will either encourage or new-create many smaller industries; while the varied products of the different sections will be utilized and taken to the best markets by the active population which will people the teeming soil.

THIRD.—The changing, in great measure, of the current of European continental tours: It is well known that many millions of dollars are annually spent upon the continent of Europe, by tourists who go from one portion to another, engaged in sight-seeing. Year after year thousands make the same tour; thousands from the United States as well as from Europe itself. What will undoubtedly be the result when a new world shall be opened up and made readily accessible? Beginning with Mexico, this entire southern country is rich in interesting antiquities; but its ruins will by no means be the greatest attraction. The splendor of the scenery, as well as the fact that it is purely Central and South American, and unlike that of any other part of the world, must turn the tide of tourist travel toward it.

This new route will be a delightful change to those who have so often wandered over the daily-trodden paths of Europe. The lofty summit of Chimborazo towers up twice as high as Etna; and the Amazon is a giant in comparison with other streams. The scenery of the middle and southern portions of Spanish America is so entirely unlike anything that the mere European tourist has ever seen, that its very newness will greatly enhance its attractiveness. Nor can any other part of the world furnish a railway which will run through such interesting varieties of country and climate as the proposed Intercontinental Line. There would not be, to the American tourist, those annoyances which mar so frequently the pleasure of European travel, the almost continual change from car to boat, from boat to diligence, and from diligence to car again. On our Three

Americas Railway the traveller will get in the cars, and he need not leave them, except by his own volition, until he reaches his destination.   One month spent upon the line of this railway will enable the tourist to see and enjoy more than three months' roaming in Europe; and he can see beautiful and sublime pictures here, which nature nowhere else repeats.   Such is the vastness of the undeveloped territory in Central and South America, that it will require years for the world to become well acquainted with it; and therefore its exploration must be a source of almost never-failing novelty.   That thousands who now spend their winters in Italy will sojourn in Quito, Cochabamba, Santiago, and other delightful Andean cities, cannot be doubted.

FOURTH.—New Health Resorts: To no class of individuals will the railway be more beneficial than to the health-seeker.   While as yet no attention has been paid in South America to Mineral Springs, it is because that part of the world has even a richer inheritance in mountain resorts, with air purer and more life-giving than any spring that ever gushed from the earth.   This is one of Nature's priceless gifts to South America, and one of which the world in general is strangely ignorant.   Want of knowledge in this respect is the more remarkable when the fact is considered that several of these Andean sanitariums are most potent in their cures of those very diseases which mineral springs, in every part of the world, have failed to cure, and which it is not now even claimed that mineral waters can cure; such especially as those dreaded and devastating scourges, consumption, yellow fever and cholera.

Huanuco, in Peru, must become the Mecca of consumptives.   Tarma, in the same Republic, and Quito in Ecuador, are also favorite resorts.   In Huanuco it is an established fact that no cases of affection of the chest are found among the natives; on the contrary, people suffering with these diseases sojourn there for a time, and are cured. It is equally well known that consumption, yellow fever, and cholera, do not exist in Quito. Cases carried there have at once yielded to the wonderfully healing properties of the climate. The aboriginal races around this ancient territory of the Incas, have disproportionately large lungs; and certainly no better evidence of the extraordinary power of the climate in bronchial affections could be established than this fact. When the fame of these healing heights shall have extended over the world, and by a railway they are placed within the convenient reach of sufferers, thousands, not only from America, but from Europe also, will flock to them for relief. Then, within several days' travel from the United States, they can be visited without difficulty; while now the risk of the stormy passage of the Atlantic coast renders their approach by invalids well nigh impossible.

The most attractive history of the world is the history of great enterprises; but no annals have yet recorded an enterprise so grand in all its aspects, so noble in all its probable results, as may be discerned in the projected Three Americas Railway. It will be in America the second great revolutionary war, but without bloodshed. The first struggle was to secure for the people of the United States political independence; the second is to assure to the inhabitants of the two continents of America commercial freedom, and to make not only the United States, but the vast division of which it is the central part, a land wholly self-sustaining and leading the commerce of the world. It will create an open avenue through the very heart of America, a grand longitudinal street, leading from the metropolis of one continent to the great rural districts of another.

In the examination of a theme so extensive and significant, it has been necessary to delve deep into the mine of facts and figures with which it is itself replete, and which

12

argue with eloquence more sublime, and with utterance m re unmistakeable, than sentences richly wrought by the aptest rules of logic. The figures and facts thus educed have answered, in a limited manner, the questions which met the great undertaking in its incipient consideration. They have shown that the scheme is practicable, and demonstrated that the idea of impracticability finds lodgment only in narrow minds. They have answered the second question, whether or not the proposed Longitudinal Line will be beneficial, and if so, where, and in what way ? They have answered the third inquiry, If beneficial, in what quarter should the work be begun ? It has been seen from these facts and figures that North and South America are now, commercially, almost strangers to each other ; that South America is richer in those things in which the United States is deficient, and that the United States has what South America desires. It has been seen that in a region with plains surpassing the Valley of the Nile in richness, food products, in wild profusion, are perennial in growth; while the fields are full of gold, and silver gleams on the mountain sides. Therefore these facts answer the second question ; for a railway opening up such a large and fertile region will of course be beneficial; it will be beneficial by giving the manufacturing country a new field for its manufactures, and by giving, at the same time, the undeveloped country a new population for its development.

. Clearly and regretfully has it been seen that South America is deficient in stable governments ; that civil war, with all its evils, devastates the country; that there is a sad lack of education among the masses ; wherefore the intelligence and virtue requisite to render the country orderly and happy are not there; that the people, long unused to labor, are, by neglect, permitting the rapid diminution of their most valuable exports, the cinchona bark and the rubber product ;

that England, experimenting in arboriculture, is manoeuvering to raise the plants of these trees in her own India; that Great Britain, France, and Germany now control the commerce of South and Central América; that Great Britain annually sells to them sixty-five million dollars' worth, while the United States sells to them only twenty-one millions; that Great Britain buys from them only twelve millions' worth, while the United States buys from them fifty-nine millions. It has been seen that, while foreign steamship lines have, for years, connected South America with Europe, the United States, only within recent years, has had but one line; that, from long control, the foreign elements have now so strongly established the current of ocean commerce, that it cannot be easily turned by the United States. Therefore, seeing that a grand longitudinal railway running through the three Americas, would be beneficial, the inquiry as to the section in which the enterprise should be begun, must promptly receive the answer that it should be started in the United States; for our Republic, though it is only one of sixteen American Republics, is the most deeply interested in the scheme. The position and power of the United States, as the principal nationality on the continent of North America, fit it especially for the beginning of this great work.

With equal clearness has it been seen that South and Central America are ready to join in an enterprise of this nature. Peru having already spent one hundred and forty millions on her railroads, will eagerly seize this avenue of connection with the civilized world. Bolivia and Paraguay, being the two most inland republics in South America, are perhaps more vitally interested than the others. In every commonwealth of that part of the New World, the desire for communication with the outer world is dominant. South America's network of rivers is phenomenal; and, as an aqueous adjunct of our great railway, it will be of inestimable value. These rivers, after traversing every South American republic, save two, empty into the broad Amazon, at points from which their products can be easily brought to the railway ; so that they, in effect, will act as a hundred branches of the great trunk line.

Unmistakably has it been seen that the age calls for this grand central highway ; that Mexico, with a scarcity of good seaports, and lacking navigable rivers, is too nearly cut off from the civilized world ; that much of the rich silver territory of the United States is isolated and well neigh useless for want of such a railway ; that the most fertile and otherwise valuable portions of British America are locked in from the world for want of such a railway ; that an immense fur-country, of inexhaustible wealth, is almost unavailable for the want of such a railway ; and that fisheries of incalculable value can be gained with such a railway. In view of these vast advantages to all divisions of the three Americas, can there be any doubt of the immediate necessity for the Three Americas Railway ? The United States Government, after sending explorers to the Amazon, and officers to the Isthmus ; after repeatedly uttering its official praises of the naturally beautiful and productive countries south of our Union, is now called upon to act. By its words in the past, by its words recently spoken, it is pledged to the endeavor to gain communication with all those Arcadian countries. Its Secretary of State—our own Mr. Evarts—has wisely and ably urged the necessity for closer relations.

The Darien Canal, a European enterprise, controlled by European capital, cannot afford the desirable means of intercommunication. Even though it were controlled by American capital, a canal could not furnish the opportunity so much coveted ; for England's superior merchant navy could use the canal as freely as the United States ; and such canal, as has been shown, could make available only four and one-half per cent. of the territory of South America. Thus it is seen that the only means of effecting the important end in view is by the proposed railway. The necessity for immediate action is no less apparent; for each year brings hundreds of thousands of emigrants to America. In manufactures, as well as in labor, the supply is now greater than the demand; and a new and large outlet must be created, during the ensuing twenty years, or the even tenor and peace of the Republic may be endangered. That all necessary relief would soon follow the completion of this all-relieving railway, may not be doubted for a moment. A great army of workmen would be employed in carrying out the enterprise, who would afterward settle permanently in the new territory. In Ecuador, in addition to the many pursuits in which the energetic settler may profitably employ himself, there is one which must erelong assume gigantic dimensions; namely, the silk trade.

Americans are generally practical and sagacious; and the first question asked by them in relation to any enterprise offered for their consideration is, " will it pay ? " That the Three Americas Railway will be a handsomely paying undertaking to each and 'all of the nations of the New World, is already a foregone conclusion. The value of the foreign commerce of the countries lying south of the United States within the limits of Central and South America, may be safely estimated to be, at the present time, not less than five hundred and twenty-five millions of dollars; in which the United States shares to the extent of only about one hundred and twelve millions of dollars; not over one-third of which, (if the humiliating and shameful truth must be told,) is transported under the flag of the United States! Of this large commerce, it is safe to assume that the United States, after the completion of the proposed railway, could easily secure at least four hundred millions' worth annually; the profits on which, in the course of a few years, would more than reimburse our Union for its outlay in constructing the work. Europe's exports to Central and South America consist mostly of cotton goods, cotton yarn, iron, steel, machinery, woolen stuffs, linen, and linen yarn. Each of these, of excellent quality, could be readily furnished by the United States, and at cheaper rates than are now paid to foreign manufacturers for them. It may therefore be safely asserted that the United States, within one year after the projected railway shall be opened, will get not less than four hundred million dollars' worth of the existing Spanish American commerce. That lovely country, whose populations by immigration and by birth, would largely increase every year, would soon have an energetic and powerful working class, who would rapidly develop its fertile territory. Intelligently mindful of their own interests, these peoples will, of course, trade with the United States, obtaining, in exchange for their raw products, the manufactured articles which they desire. Nor is this the only new element of wealth to be created in and for the United States. There are others: The immensely valuable salmon and cod fisheries of the North Pacific will be largely shared in by the United States.

The location of the Three Americas Railway will greatly facilitate the building up all the territories of the United States on the Pacific, near Mexico, and will enable our Union to compete more directly with England, and more successfully too, for the bulk of the trade of China and Japan. Despite the fact that England has shortened her route by the Suez Canal, the Southern Pacific ports of the United States will, after a while, in competing for the trade of the East, have a decided advantage in situation. The splendid harbor of San Diego is 2,707 miles nearer Hong

Kong than Liverpool, and 6,264 miles nearer Yokohama than the same English seaport. Taking into consideration these significant facts, it may be safe to surmise that the trade of the United States, beyond that already named, will be increased at least one hundred millions of dollars more; thus aggregating an annual trade of five hundred millions of dollars, which will owe its existence to the Three-Americas Railway. This estimate is within the limits of moderation.

To South America the trade and profits of trade will, in porportion to her number of inhabitants, be even greater; for, in the first place, she will sell her immense tracts of land now lying useless. The new population, following the building of the railway, will purchase land; and if, on the continent of South America, but one-fifth of the surface shall be sold, at the low price of one dollar an acre, it will diffuse there a cash circulation of about a hundred million dollars. The very presence of an active and hardy population will at once beget a spirit of laudable competition in every department of industry and business; and the land itself, though at first bought for a mere trifle, will soon increase at least fifty per cent. in price. Not only in much greater value of lands will South America be benefitted. Instead of so many of her precious products disappearing from sheer neglect, as they now disappear, the new people will have a vital interest in fostering and increasing their growth. For cinchona and rubber, the demand is now in excess of the supply; and therefore with a larger and more improved cultivation of these products, the wealth of South America will continue to be augmented.

It is a truth beyond dispute that a railroad judiciously laid down, acts as an inducement alike to capitalists and laborers to settle in a new country; and millions of dollars now idle in Europe will seek and find profitable investment on the continents of America, so soon as our great Longitudinal Line shall be finished.   Capital is timid, and rightfully timid.   It cannot afford to incur risk in a country torn by internal dissensions.   With direct communication with the outside world, the South and Central American Republics would soon lose the petty jealousies which so frequently culminate in bloody revolution.   They would acquire larger and more ennobling interests.   An infusion of the advanced civilization and business talent of the northern continent wou'd impart to the southern continent the prosperity and dignity which characterize commercial nations.   It is a startling and terrible fact that within the last twenty-five years, the total amount of money spent in Mexico and Central and South America for the conduct of civil wars, is at least double the amount which will be necessary to construct the proposed intercontinental railway; and it cannot be reasonably doubted, that had such a railway been in operation, there would probably have been no wars.   With the sale of lands; with the opening of new trade currents; with the yearly throngs of jovial and free-spending tourists; with the gainful sale of now worthless productions; and with the advantages which will arise from numerous other interests, it is safe to assume that South and Central America and Mexico will receive an annual income of no less than three hundred millions from this grand longitudinal and international railway.

British America has been, as yet, but very imperfectly developed.   There are immense tracts in her grain-growing zone, the whole of which, cultivated and uncultivated, is estimated at one million square miles.   This extensive territory has yet to be opened up; yet, even when opened up, it can never reach the civilized world advantageously save only through the United States.   The splendid region of Ontario has already been mentioned, together with the fact

that it grows the finest barley, so important to the great
brewing interests of the United States and Canada.   With
all these interests well developed, is it not to be confidently
expected that British America and the United States will
enter into very lively competition with England in her
present annual export of over eleven million dollars' worth
of malt liquors?   Is it not quite safe to assume that British
America will derive at least five millions annually from this
source?   Furs throughout the world are high priced, because
the difficulty of obtaining them is great.   Were they more
readily procurable their sale and use would be largely increased.   Our far-reaching railway will go into the center of
the great fur-producing region, and will render the needed
facilities for their distribution throughout the United States.
It is likely that this enlarged source of profit would be worth
to British America not less than twenty millions of dollars
per annum; and the disposal and development of her lands
would probably be worth not less than fifty millions.   These
estimates are all moderate, and are based upon facts which
more than sustain the calculations.   It is designed, however, that the lowest figures, in each instance, shall be presented, because they themselves demonstrate that the
Longitudinal Line will give enormous profits to each and
all of the nationalities on both continents of America, and
also that it will avert certain grave perils with which each is
threatened.

From Canada tens of thousands are now emigrating
across the border into our own Union, because the latter
commonwealth, in consequence of its superior development, has now a manifest advantage.   It is for the interest
of Canada to stop this desertion at the earliest practicable
period; and she can do so only by making her territory
equally attractive.   Connected with her neighbor by means
of a great steel highway, she will steadily approximate
toward equality with the United States.

The Spanish-speaking Republics are not only threatened
with the destruction of several of their most valuable
products, but the dangers of civil war will continue imminent so long as those countries are so nearly locked in from
the rest of the world.   The United States cannot too soon
nor too fully realize the fact that competition in all branches
of industry is greater now than it has ever been known to
be in the past; nor can it be doubted that this is much
more likely to increase than to diminish.   All civilized nations are now earnestly seeking for new markets, and for
new fields of employment; and each is striving to discover
permanent purchasers of its products, and to secure a larger
proportion of the commerce of the world.   England, Germany, and other European nations, are looking with longing
eyes toward the inexhaustible riches of the southern continent of America.   What India is to England, Spanish
America may become to the United States; only in a much
higher and better relationship.   It yields all the productions
of India; and, with our projected railway in operation it
will be far more accessible.   It must inevitably be developed,
and the question should at once be decided whether the
United States or foreign nations are to enjoy the benefits of
this development.   A cash balance of about seventy millions
is here against us every year; and these millions are in a
manner lost, which should otherwise go to building up and
strengthening our own nationality.

Thirty years ago, Lieut. Maury said: " The Annals of
Commerce, among friendly nations, may be challenged almost in vain for another case like this, a case where the nation supplying the elaborated article and receiving in exchange raw produce, finds herself at such odds as to leave
the balance, year after year, heavily against her."   This
humiliating spectacle of American neighbors selling and
buying so largely in distant European markets, is one which

seriously affects the claims of the United States as an enterprising nation. Summed up, the great Longitudinal Line
will be worth to the two continents of America eight hundred and seventy-five millions dollars' worth of trade per
annum; and the profits on that trade will very soon cover
the cost of consummating the work.

Looking to the future, it is apparent that the Three
Americas Railway will greatly enhance the value to the
United States of the recently acquired territory of Alaska.
In time, as the country increases in population, the Longitu-
dinal Line must be extended to that distant region. Nor
can many years elapse before this will be found necessary.
The market value of the annual shipment of furs from
Alaska, by the Russian American Company, just previous to
our acquisition of the Territory, was six million dollars.
Considering this, in connection with the valuable fisheries,
it does not appear that Alaska was a bad purchase.

In view of the vast and varied interests which will accrue
to the United States from the construction of the Three
Americas Railway, and mindful of the central position of
our Union on the northern continent of the New World, it
is clearly incumbent that the enterprise should be started
here. Congress and the Cabinet at Washington should lose
no time in this matter. Provision should be made at once
for the calling together of an International Railway Congress, made up of delegates from British America, the
United States, Mexico and all the Central and South American Republics. The specific business of this Intercontinental Congress would be to deliberate on and discuss all
questions relating to the projected railway, and present a
plan for its building; afterward requesting the appointment
of a corps of engineers from the different governments;
such engineers, with the least possible delay, to make full
and perfect surveys. This American Railway Congress

would also agree upon the outlines or specifications of a bill to be passed by the various governments for promptly carrying out the great work. The action of such congress would, of course, need to be ratified respectively by the several governments themselves. In this way, the whole scheme would be judiciously and prominently brought before the American peoples; and that frank and full discussion which should precede the enactment of every important national and international measure, would be elicited.

Once well understood and rightly appreciated, the success of the enterprise will be assured. The measure needs only to be intelligently introduced into the Congresses of the United States and the other American Republics; for its preponderating essentiality will at once commend it to the earnest attention of the nations. As an undertaking of unparalleled public improvement, it is independent of party; it belongs to the whole country; equally and forever it is to be the inheritance of the two continents. It requires genuine and practical statesmanship to consider and direct it. The railway itself should be declared on neutral ground; it should be as free and open as the high seas; and neither war nor dissension should ever be allowed to prevent it from radiating its blessings over all the land. Its mission will be to protect and encourage home industry in all legitimate pursuits, and to render the three Americas wholly self-sustaining countries, amply able to supply their own wants in every respect.

The present period in the history of America, is highly auspicious. It is beautiful in the peace and prosperity which reign throughout our Union; beautiful in the trustworthy promises of teeming blessings to come with increasing civilization. Glancing back over the pages of our great Republic's history, we perceive that the leaves are powder-stained and blurred with records of occasional disaster.

The first century of our nationality was spent in the formation of a government, the settlement of political principles, the struggle over slavery, the civil war, reconstruction,
and now reconciliation. Let the next be dedicated to peace
and progress. The time is well chosen for the beginning
of this and other great enterprises. The peace which now
blesses our own Republic will, with each mile of the Three
Americas Railway, be extended to all the Republics of our
sister continent. That surpassing railway, once well constructed and in operation, will indeed make America the
New World; a world so conspicuously new and superior in
its natural riches, that its attractions to the peoples of the
Old World will be absolutely overwhelming.

This age must be the age of railways; for the world is
but a tub fast falling to pieces; each new railway is but another iron-hoop holding it together a while longer. Upon
the railway cause, from the mists of a past epoch, the voice
of the prophet sweeps in majestic benediction: "For the
spirit of the living creature is in the wheels." Upon the
vigorous and prudent extension of our railway system depends the very life of our Republic, and the welfare of the
two American continents. The railway thus projected must
become, in due time, the great aortal artery of the commerce of America. It will be the only whole and complete
railway on the globe. Facts already educed have shown
that the enterprise will be a splendidly paying one on the
common bases of railway-building; and if individuals can
make lucrative investments in such improvements, why may
not governments do the same? Higher and holier than
all, the Longitudinal Line has a mission to perform in Right
Conduct. Railways extend civilization, and civilization
tends toward the practice of pure morality.

There are periods in men's lives called turning points.
Decision in one way leads to ruin; decision in the other

way insures success.' So also are there turning points in the
life of every nation; this is the turning point in the history
of all the Republics of the New World. Is this a time, or
is this an occasion, for America to pause? No. The bright
revelation of facts already before us shows plainly the splen-
dors of a wisely assisted future. Motives broad in their patriotism must vigorously impel to action.

The scheme for the building of the Three Americas Railway has been examined; the country has been traveled;
the rich productions of the two continents, embracing every
zone, temperate, tropical and frigid, have been exhibited;
the dangers of delay have been scrutinized; and the paramount necessities of America have been portrayed. All
these considerations point to the projected Longitudinal
Line; all demand its immediate construction. Then will
the nations of America, united and strengthened as never
before, become the commercial, as well as the agricultural
and manufacturing, nations of the world; the asylums not
alone of all worthy peoples disposed to come among us, but
also the storehouses for thousands and millions from our
shores now far away.

SUBSTITUTION OF AN ESSAY FOR A POEM.

MR. DEEKENS TO MR. HELPER.

NORWICH, ONTARIO, CANADA,
March 24, 1881.

HINTON R. HELPER, ESQ., *St. Louis, Mo.*

DEAR SIR : You are aware that, among the forty-seven competitors for the five prizes so generously offered by you, for three of the best attainable essays in prose and two poems, in advocacy of your proposed Three Americas Railway,—a more than thrice worthy scheme,—I was one of two who wrote in both prose and verse ; that is to say, an entire manuscript in each style of composition. The Committee of Examination and Award sent to me a cheque for five hundred dollars for my poem—but nothing for my essay. Although I may frankly admit that such a result fell short of the measure of my ambition, yet I felt much gratification, nevertheless, in having triumphed at all in a contest wherein the odds were so greatly against me.

I am now honored with the information that the same Committee, who sent to me a prize for my poem, is of the opinion that there is probably more real merit in my prose essay than in my poem, as regards all the essential considerations connected with the great enterprise itself. The article in prose was dispatched to you a few days since ; and I now desire to request that, should you, after perusing both papers, concur in the views of the Committee, you will, in furtherance of your grand and noble project, please substi-

tute, in all respects, the prose for the poetry, at your entire
discretion, or use both, if you can conveniently find room
for them in your forthcoming volume.

Faithfully yours,
F. A. DEEKENS.

———

MR. HELPER TO MR. DEEKENS.

St. Louis, March 28, 1881.

Francis A. Deekens, Esq.,
  Norwich, Ontario, Canada.

Dear Sir: Your letter of the 24th instant, suggesting
and proposing the substitution of your essay for your poem,
came to hand this morning. Though you have received
from the Three Americas Railway Committee only one prize,
it must be to you a source of real and pardonable pride to
have secured from it, wholly unsolicited, a distinct recognition of your abilities in both departments of literature. I
have read, with very great care and interest, both your poem
and your essay; and the latter, in my judgment,—coincid-
ing with the judgment of the Committee,—is manifestly the
more meritorious for the present occasion. In fact, I regard your essay in prose as an admirable approximation to
a masterpiece in English composition, on one of the most
important and inspiring subjects that ever incited to action
an author's pen; and I heartily thank you for it, and for
the privilege of bringing it before the public in promotion
of the project now dearest to my heart.

Yours, very truly,
H. R. HELPER.

FOURTH PRIZE ESSAY.

(Substituted for the Second Prize Poem.)

———

Observations on the Prospective Advantages of a Grand Longitudinal Midland Double-Track Steel Railway, as Projected by Hinton Rowan Helper, of St. Louis, Missouri.

BY FRANCIS AUGUSTUS DEEKENS,

(Norwich, Ontario, Canada.)

In contradistinction from the brilliant but barren philosophy of the ancients, as taught by Plato and others, modern science, as we have learned it from Bacon and his successors, abounds in wisdom far more practical and preferable. This new philosophy, with which we ourselves are blessed, has lengthened life; it has mitigated pain; it has extinguished diseases; it has increased the fertility of the soil; it has given new securities to the mariner; it has furnished new arms to the warrior; it has spanned great rivers and estuaries with bridges of form and material unknown to our forefathers; it has guided the thunder-bolt innocuously from heaven to earth; it has lighted up the night with the splendor of the day; it has extended the range of the human vision; it has multiplied the power of the human muscles; it has accelerated motion; it has annihilated distance; it has facilitated intercourse, correspondence, all friendly offices, all dispatch of business; it has enabled man to descend to the depths of the sea, to soar into the air, to penetrate securely into the noxous recesses of the earth, to traverse the land in cars which whirl along without horses, and the ocean in ships which run ten knots an hour against the wind. These are but a part of its fruits, and of its first fruits. For it is a philosophy which never rests, which has never attained full growth, which is never perfect. Its law is progress. A particular point or object which yesterday was invisible is reached to day, and will be its starting-port to-morrow.—*Macaulay*

The question of establishing speedy communication between the different peoples of the two great American continents is one of such absorbing interest as to have exercised, for a considerable time, the minds of some of the

209

ablest statesmen and many of the profoundest thinkers of the day. As the present may emphatically be termed an age of progress, the merits of a project for constructing a railway which shall fully accomplish that desirable end, have been frequently discussed by certain gentlemen of expansive views and varied experience, and its absolute practicability has been confidently affirmed.

The exigencies of commerce and the restless aggressiveness of advancing civilization imperatively demand the formation of a Grand Longitudinal Highway, which, traversing the entire length of North and Central and South America, shall be the means of affording safe, speedy and profitable intercourse between the various Republics and other States representing the respective governments of this Western Hemisphere. It may be assumed that in exact proportion as the facilities for commerce and transportation southward multiply, will civilization be quickened and the white population increase in that direction, carrying the banners of progress and enlightenment in its march. The watchful eye of the progressive statesman can already detect in the hazy outline of the future a yet greater and more glorious destiny for the future of the American continents than many have hitherto conceived; when the Atlantic and Pacific oceans shall become the boundaries, to a great extent, of a universal republic of civilization and knowledge, and a powerful rival to the Old World in all the industries, arts and social refinements of life.

The creature man is no exception to the universal law which exacts from every living thing certain duties, and imposes certain responsibilities in return for the privilege of living. Progress and improvement, social and physical, commensurate with the opportunities and advantages we enjoy and the era in which we live, are among the necessary conditions of our existence; and consequently a pro-

gressive standard of moral excellence, with a proportionate
advancement in the mechanical arts and sciences, and in
all the embellishments and refinements of life, it is rightly
expected we should seek and attain. The subject is one
which appeals directly to the best thoughts and energies of
all civilized nations, and it is a question of paramount importance—in which the interests of all are identified—in
what manner they shall best contribute their quota of helpful encouragement toward the attainment of ends so desirable, and in shaping the destinies of the various peoples of
the globe.

Inasmuch as Nature is said to abhor a vacuum, we may
fairly assume, from the conditions of creation with which
we are already familiar, that she equally abhors a policy of
slothful inaction. Every created thing has its allotted task,
and every organic substance some definite end to accomplish in this wonderful microcosm of ours, as it slowly but
surely shapes and adapts itself to the final purpose for which
it was brought into existence; and even so, in regard to
ourselves, the necessity for continuous effort and exertion is
obvious and imperative, if we would preserve our frail bodies
in their normal condition of health, and protect our mental
faculties from becoming clogged or otherwise impaired.
The world is ever on the move; and the Creator, with
ceaseless vigilance, is watching night and day. The inhabitants of earth, almost as soon as they are born, are expected to exert themselves in some measure, as they are all destined to die; and at a very early age we must be recruited
into the ranks of the Grand Army of Life, and receive our
marching orders. As, therefore, we cannot possibly escape
from the duties and responsibilities imposed upon us by the
great General of the Universe, it is necessary that we should
continue to advance bravely in the front of Life's Battles,
until this our worldly campaign be brought to a close.

Under the baneful influence of torpidity and inaction, even the earth itself would speedily return to its primitive condition of chaotic deformity; for no material substance is proof against the insidious encroachments of decay. `

Although man may correctly be defined as a mere creature of circumstances, it is astounding how speedily difficulties engendered or magnified by a weak and vacillating spirit will gradually disappear before, or become subservient to, a strong and resolute will. Enthusiasm begets its counterpart in zeal by example, in the same manner that courage in the general inspires confidence in the hearts of his soldiers. Without enthusiasm and perservering courage,—the natural concomitants of success,—no worthy end can be attained, nor enduring work accomp'ished. It augurs well therefore for the success of the colossal undertaking which forms the subject of this paper, that the idea was born and nurtured in the brains of an American; and that his countrymen, in whom indomitable energy is so prominent a national characteristic, will be invited to co-operate in bringing the scheme to a glorious issue. This intercontinental enterprise, gigantic though it be, if backed by the full strength of public opinion and the unlimited resources which such opinion would command, cannot possibly fail. The generous advocacy and support of a number of great and united peoples will be a sufficient guarantee that all difficulties not absolutely insurmountable will be overcome. The well-known emulation of Americans to excel in all scientific attainments, and to be first and foremost in all that may contribute fresh laurels to the wreaths that already deck Columbia's brow, will inspire increasing confidence that any work undertaken with that object in view will not be allowed to languish for lack of the means necessary to ensure its triumphant completion.

The present, far from being a hasty or irrational plan

suggested on the impulse of the moment, is the matured and well-digested scheme of a far-seeing and public-spirited gentleman, who, inspired with the confidence of success, adopts this method of introducing it more fully to the notice of the American public. It is an undertaking which, if carried out in its integrity, will reflect infinite credit upon both his country and himself. To Mr. Hinton Rowan Helper, of St. Louis, Missouri, belongs the credit of being the originator of the unequaled and comprehensive idea of building a Grand Longitudinal Double-Track Steel Railway, which shall traverse the heart of the three Americas, like a great vertebral column, from the northern portions of North America to the southern shores of Patagonia. The conception is alike startling and magnificent in its grandeur of outline and in its bright promises of beneficial results, and is deserving of the enthusiastic reception which will doubtless be accorded it by all genuine statesmen and philanthropists, wheresoever they may reside. Grateful and stimulating to the patriotism and the *amour propre* of Americans, it has already excited, on the part of many of those acquainted with the outline of the scheme, a vast amount of sympathy and wondering speculation. For the last thirteen or fourteen years, the project has been assuming form and strength in the mind of its enthusiastic promoter, during his official residence in South America; and it is now sufficiently matured and developed to be presented to the public as a work, the entire feasibility of which he is, from personal inspection and experience, and from the nature of his investigations, fully and absolutely convinced. Both time and money have been sacrificed by Mr. Helper, with the laudable object of placing before the people of this hemisphere a plan of commercial, social and political amelioration which, at a glance, must commend itself to all; and which, for amplitude of grasp and scope of usefulness is perhaps unparalleled in history.

The initiatory difficulties inseparably connected with an undertaking of such magnitude, and which consist mainly in educating the masses and in arousing the enthusiasm of men of capital and enterprise, as regards the *bona fidès* of the undertaking and its manifold prospective advantages, are being met· with very encouraging success; and there is little doubt that it will erelong receive the enthusiastic support of the great American Republic with its fifty millions of souls. It will be readily admitted that a railroad can exercise,—especially in those countries in which the means of communication are few and insufficient,—an immense influence for good, if its powers be rightly directed; and that the establishment of a far-reaching line, such as that now proposed, would confer incalculable benefits upon millions of human beings at present in a condition of comparative social degradation, and also upon the whole civilized world, in a mercantile, moral and political sense. In addition to this, it will reflect enduring credit upon its intelligent promoters, upon the engineers and other executive officers connected with its construction, and upon the United States government in particular.

Should the untiring efforts of Mr. Helper and his able coadjutors result in stimulating the Congress of the United States to take suitable action in furtherance of the enterprise, and in enlisting the zealous co-operation of the various Republics and other States through which the new railway is destined to pass, in favor of a project so richly endowed with probable future advantages, he is confident that, by the employment of an adequate staff of capable men, the necessary charters and privileges may be obtained, and the surveys and other preliminaries completed, within a couple of years from the present date; so as to be ready to

commence the actual construction of the line at that time.
He is, moreover, sanguine that, under favorable pecuniary
auspices, and the strict observance of contracts, the whole
line,—or so much of it as it may be deemed advisable to
build for the present,—may be completed in seven years,
say by the autumn of the year 1889. As the year 1892
will usher in the four hundreth anniversary of the discovery
of America, it is proposed that a grand International Jubilee shall be held in the city of St. Louis, in commemoration of that interesting event, in a manner worthy of the
occasion, and on a scale of magnificence hitherto unequaled. On that festive occasion the Three Americas
Railway will meet with its full share of popular recognition,
and play a significant part as the chief agent by means of
which will be gathered together, within the limits of a single
city, hundreds of thousands of people representing the different nations, together with the products and manufactures
of every possible kind obtainable within the limits of either
of the two American continents. It is proposed to confer
this special honor upon the city of St. Louis, not only as a
mark of the national appreciation of the energy and enterprise of its inhabitants, but also on account of its central
position, its convenient network of rail and water-ways, and
the many social and industrial advantages to be generously
offered by its citizens. The gigantic strides which that
flourishing city has already taken in the march of civilization and commercial prosperity, in the course of only a few
short years, render it a matter of certainty that she will
speedily become not only the Metropolis of the West, but
possibly the fairest and most prosperous city of the United
States.

Not to speak too minutely of the splendid network of
railways environing the Western cities on the line of the great
rivers, and the enormous amount of capital which their con-

struction and their magnificent town-stations represent, the bridges alone which cross the Mississippi testify to the unmistakable energy and resources of the Western people; the aggregate value of those structures being set down at over twenty millions of dollars.   The city of St. Louis can boast of nearly half a million of inhabitants, and covers about 40,000 acres of ground.   It has a river frontage of eighteen miles, and contains about four hundred miles of street pavements, including the smaller highways and passages. There are in all eighteen inclosures of land laid out as public parks, of which one has an extent of nearly 1,400 acres. There are nearly 65,000 houses in the city, about 19,000 of which have been built during the last five years.   The shipments of grain in bulk from St. Louis to the Gulf, in the year 1879, were more than ninety-three times greater than in 1870.   In the latter year the receipts of cotton were 20,000 bales and upward, against 430,000 bales in the season of 1879–80.   There are additional storage and compressing facilities in course of construction, capable of handling one million bales of cotton per annum.   The movement of grain from St. Louis, by river and rail to New Orleans, is on an enormous scale.   In one week, in the month of August, 222,600 bushels of wheat were sent thither by rail, and 406,900 bushels by river.   During the same period were shipped 23,700 bushels of corn by rail, and 115,900 by river.   Such glowing statistics as these will convince even the most skeptical of the astonishing progress which characterizes the commercial growth of St. Louis.

A festival in commemoration of the opening for traffic of a Grand Trunk Railway traversing the greater portion of the length of the Western Hemisphere, would be sufficiently memorable in itself to awaken extraordinary enthusiasm.   Could the proposed *fete* be arranged to take place in connection with a great International Jubilee in honor of the immortal

Columbus, a celebration of such magnificent proportions and thrilling interest would be the event of a lifetime; an event which, once witnessed, could never be forgotten. It would be almost superfluous here to allude to the many collateral advantages certain to accrue from the general dissemination of the seeds of civilization and commercial activity over the vast area which the proposed railway will control. Not only will the present and future dwellers upon this continent derive benefit therefrom, but the world in general will participate in the harvest of profitable results which will follow as a natural consequence of its successful inauguration. By the judicious application of capital and steam, wonderful ends may be accomplished. By means of these we may span half the length of the habitable globe, and brace it together with bands of iron, strong enough to bring all its vast commercial resources into subjection. Lands, now comparatively valueless, will, by such agency, develop their latent elements of wealth and fertility; and, by practical reclamation, they can be made tributary to the revenues of the respective governments and the ever-increasing requirements of mankind; while the social, political and commercial status of those communities, will be proportionately elevated and improved.

Governments willing to expend the moneys of the people confided to their care, in progressive improvements, and for the promotion of their civil and educational advancement, will acquire greater popularity than by squandering those hard-earned millions in costly fortifications and armaments. No policy can be more suicidal to the general interest than that of embarking in oppressive and sanguinary wars, for— as is too frequently the case,—the mere gratification of an idea, or the personal antipathies of an over-ambitious statesman. The imperial share of the indemnity paid by France to Germany, in the late Franco-German war, amounted to

the modest little sum of more than one billion of dollars!
What benefit did France derive from such an enormous outlay and sacrifice of so many thousands of valuable lives?
By all accounts, that disastrous campaign was undertaken
simply *pour la gloire*, (all for glory,) as the French say,—
precipitated through the insane folly of the Emperor, Napoleon III, and his most culpable ignorance of the real
state of the military resources of his country. What is
glory, after all? A base coin, which passes current, only for
a time, in certain localities and under certain conditions,—
a passing sentiment in which fools indulge, often based upon flagrant injustice, arrant cowardice, and a perfect holo-
caust of human misery; upon the unjust acquisition of territory, the violation of treaties, the alienation of the rights
of others, and the unscrupulous oppression of the weak by
the strong.

What is called national glory is very often nothing but
national dishonor in the truest sense. There is no heroism
in outnumbering the enemy, and then winding up with massacre and spoliation. Happy those nations possessing wiser
magistrates, who, instead of squandering the lives and properties of the people in the manner indicated, strive rather to
lead them forward in the paths of virtue and progress; and
who, avoiding a policy of rapacity and extortion, encourage
the introduction of reproductive works, the harbingers alike
of peace and prosperity established upon a safe and enduring basis. How many railroads, for instance, profitable for
all time as arteries of commercial activity, might have been
constructed for the amount sacrificed in the Franco-German
war? What is the present annual cost to France of keeping up her standing army of a million and a half of men?
It is stated to be equal to one hundred and seventeen millions of dollars, or a tax of twenty-one per cent. upon the
income of the nation! The monarchical nations of Europe,

in the absence of any system of general disarmament, must of necessity be prepared for emergencies from a military point of view; but the Republic-of the United States of America is in an exceptionally fortunate position; and can, so far as foreign enemies are concerned, considerably reduce even her present light armaments, should the people desire it, and invest the money thus saved in internal and external improvements such as the Three Americas Railway, or a Ship Canal through the Isthmus of Nicaragua or Tehuantepec. Eighteen or twenty millions of dollars per annum seems a considerable sum for America to pay for her navy in a period of profound peace; and were only a portion of that sum expended in opening up the immense resources of Central and South America, the commercial interests of the country could not fail to be greatly benefitted thereby. Thoughts such as these, based upon the study of political economy and sound financial reform, will induce us the more readily to embrace a scheme having for its main object the general good, and will have the effect of slackening the purse-strings and enlisting the aid of all who take a genuine interest in the welfare of any portion of the New World.

Little need here be said upon the subject of the financial arrangements necessary to be effected in connection with this mammoth concern. No doubt they will be carried out by the competent gentlemen who may be honored with seats among the Board of Directors, with all the care and forethought which former experience may enable them to concentrate upon the object of their laudable ambition. A grand Syndicate of Bankers and other large capitalists, thoroughly versed in monetary affairs and the application of capital to the requirements of large corporations, would form a suitable Committee of Finance. Such a body of honorable and influential men would, of course, be absolutely necessary in order to inspire public confidence in the perfect legitimacy and *bona fides* of the undertaking.

In rough figures, it is estimated that the line,—so far at least as the Company would feel justified in carrying it for the present,—may be built for three hundred millions of dollars; but the actual amount of capital required for construction and equipment cannot, of course, be even approximately ascertained, until accurate surveys shall have been made, and the capabilities of the districts adjacent to the line shall have been taken into account. Whatever the total cost of construction may be, however, the railway will open up vast agricultural and timbered areas hitherto untouched by axe or plough; the products of which will be the means of realizing good dividends to shareholders and landowners.

It is not at all improbable that the stock of the Three Americas Railway may yet become as favorite an investment in this country as Consols are in England, should the Government of the United States, while granting the Syndicate all the rights, powers and privileges usually accorded to such companies, retain the right in common with the other specifically interested Republics, of controlling, within reasonable limits, the rates, tolls and charges levied by the Company upon all passengers and freight. The government might guarantee the payment of interest on the bonds for a certain number of years, reserving the privilege of transporting provisions, troops and munitions of war, and imposing certain restrictions against the carriage of the same for any nation or faction at war with the United States.

The construction of the Canada Pacific Railway will be prosecuted with all the speed and energy that capital and talent can command. The Canadian Government has made the most liberal concessions in land and money to the powerful corporation engaged to complete and work this line; but the western territories through which it will pass cannot be compared in fertility to those vast southern tracts through which the locomotives of the Three Americas Railway will run; and moreover that portion of the Canada Pacific running across British Columbia will include some very costly sections.

The Government of the United States might appoint a Commission to report upon the merits and practicability of the proposed Three Americas Railway; such Commission to include men of the best engineering and diplomatic talent to be found in America or elsewhere, and whose report might be based upon a preliminary survey of the whole route at the earliest moment practicable. It is calculated that the liberal grants of land expected from the various American Congresses, together with handsome bonuses from other contributing governments, (also American, but not so immediately concerned,) in the shape of money, or its equivalent in labor, provisions or materials,—such as hardwood for ties, and other timber for the construction of stations and rolling-stock,—would be amply sufficient to build the road.

For Canada, it is believed that the Grand Longitudinal Railway will be a decided benefit; as, for many years, she will be occupied in building her Pacific Road, and will greatly need one running north and south to connect with those which will soon radiate in all directions throughout the Northwest Territories. It is greatly to be hoped that no feelings of jealousy may be allowed to interfere with the natural pride and harmony which all the dwellers on the two continents of America should experience in the advancement of industrial science and the success of this unrivaled undertaking.

The estimated cost of construction may appear enormous to those unaccustomed to large figures; but the benefits will, in all probability, be proportionate to the cost; and it is easy to spend large sums in ways quite unproductive in a pecuniary sense.   For instance, the British Government expended no less than one hundred millions of dollars as compensation to slaveholders in the West Indies for the freedom of 770,000 slaves; and many more millions subsequently in the suppression of the slave trade on the coasts of Africa. That was a noble expenditure certainly, and one worthy of the nation; but were a similar amount expended on a gigantic railway passing through the midst of a large series of ignorant and benighted populations, a road which, when completed, would bring light and liberty to scores of millions of human beings, at present confined within their own limited surroundings, the benefits would far exceed the granting of mere liberty to hordes of slavishly inclined negroes.

Branch roads will, of course, be constructed from time to time, either by the company or by the co-operating governments, as circumstances may dictate.   Thus, in the course of time, the whole vast domain of the two American continents will be woven together by iron bands in a perfect network of railways.   It is a question whether the different co-adjuting governments should be expected to pay *pro rata*, according to population, or on the basis of the assessed value of their respective lands, which will vary greatly, according to the nature of the soil, location, and other circumstances.   Such questions, however, are precisely those which are to be discussed by the gentlemen selected to represent diplomatically, or under special commission, the interests of their respective countries.

As regards the location of the line, no actual survey having yet taken place, nor any detailed plan of operations agreed upon, the proposed route is now only to be suggested as approximate. In general terms it may be stated that it will run,—as nearly as the physical nature of the country will permit,—along the line of the one hundredth

degree of west longitude, reckoned from Greenwich, as regards North America; taking a middle course through Central and South America, following the sinuosities of the
mountain ranges, and diverging either to the east or to the
west in order to avoid formidable natural obstructions.
Starting from the northern terminus of the railway, say, at
its junction with the Canada Pacific, on or near the fiftieth
degree of north latitude, it is proposed, when the prospects
give warrant for doing so, to construct two branches, one of
which will run in a northeasterly direction, toward the southwest corner of Hudson Bay, and the other diverging north-
westerly, to a point on the distant shore of Alaska, crossing
the headwaters of the great rivers on its way.

The Nelson River, which runs from Lake Winnipeg into
Hudson Bay, has been utilized as a means of commuication
with the interior since the establishment of the Hudson Bay
Trading Company; and it is very hopefully regarded, by
the settlers of the Northwest, as a transporting medium for
the immense surplus of agricultural produce which will
shortly be seeking the most available outlet to salt water.
It is probable, however, that the Nelson River will be unequal to the accommodation of so large a traffic, inasmuch
as the safe navigation of Hudson Bay is, according to some
navigators, limited to a few weeks in midsummer. Even
with steamers, the eccentric movements of ice-floes would,
during the night-time especially, be attended with considerable danger; and shippers would be saddled with a proportionately high rate of insurance. Other and safer commercial channels must therefore be discovered, in order to
convey the produce of the fertile plains of Manitoba, either
directly to the ocean, southward, or by railway and the great
lakes to eastern markets.

The great inland sea called Hudson Bay, is about 1,200
miles in length, and has hitherto been regarded almost as a

mare incognitum. One or two charts have been made of its coasts and bearings, but none are considered reliable; and its many intricacies have been comparatively unknown to navigators beyond those in the service of the Hudson Bay Company. Should the contemplated railway from Winnepeg to Hudson Bay (184 miles) be built, the line would afford excellent facilities for the transportation seaward of the produce of the Great Northwest; but should it be true that the only safe and practicable navigation of the Bay is confined to the month of August, or a week or two more or less, immense quantities of produce must either be shut out entirely from shipment, or seek some other route o the Lakes. The wonderful development of the Great Northwest during the last half decade, will, as a natural consequence, largely augment its exporting powers and necessitate the introduction of means adequate to accommodate such increasing traffic, the prospects for which were never so good as they are at present.

Going southward, and crossing the Saskatchewan and other rivers, we come to Lakes Manitoba and Winnipeg,—which empty their waters into the Nelson River,—and a cluster of smaller lakes contiguous thereto. These convenient waterstretches, being largely utilized by the adjoining districts for the conveyance of their grain, will serve as auxiliaries to any trunk line offering the combined advantages of cheap and rapid transit eastward, by tapping connecting lines having termini either at Duluth or some other point on Lake Superior. The traffic in agricultural produce, together with that in coal, iron, and other minerals, which are known to exist in abundance, and which, for the greater portion of the year, would be debarred from any other available outlet to eastern ports, or Great Britain, would, it is estimated, be simply enormous. There can be no doubt that it would sorely tax the strength and resources of any but a really

wealthy and first-class railway corporation to provide the
necessary rolling-stock and other appliances for the successful carrying on of the enterprise, and for the accommoda·
tion of the immense business which would thereby be developed. In the winter season, when navigation on Lake Superior is closed, and the eastern railroads are blocked up
with snow, produce can be carried by rail to the Gulf ports,
if this should be found desirable.

It is as yet problematical whether the snows in the northern latitudes will impede the traffic to any considerable extent. The general opinion is that it will not do so; and
that any suspension would be but partial and temporary;
for it is well known that in Manitoba, and other portions of
the Northwest, the snowfall is, for a given area, considerably less than on the peninsula of Ontario. There are exceptional years there, as elsewhere; but should it be conceded that the traffic might be so hindered, there would, on
the opening of the Spring trade, be a tremendous rush of
accumulated goods flowing down the Longitudinal Line, like
an impetuous torrent whose pent-up waters have burst their
frozen bounds to find their level in the lakes and seas below.
From these semi-hyperborean regions, vast quantities of
fresh fish, packed in ice, salt fish, fish oils, seal and walrus
skins, and ivory, together with bales of valuable furs, will
always seek the safest and speediest route to market.

The acreage of land under wheat in the Northwest, will,
in a few years, should the conditions for freightage be favorable, yield quantities almost beyond belief, and quite sufficient to supply all the requirements of Europe in ordinary
seasons. At the present time the United States alone grows
ten times more wheat than Great Britain; and the wheat-
area of the former is continually increasing. To meet this
growing traffic, the Canadian government has recently expended a sum of three hundred thousand dollars, in the en-

14

largement of canals, which were previously unequal to the increasing trade; and it is now expected that, ere many months, vessels of very large tonnage will be enabled to utilize them in passing from Chicago or Duluth to the ocean direct. In Minnesota alone there are about 3,000,000 of acres under wheat this year; being an increase of more than 190,000 acres over last year's acreage. There are immense wheat-fields in the regions north of the fifty-fifth degree of latitude; for it is well known that the isothermal line deflects considerably to the northward after passing to the westward of the center of the continent.

The intention of the promoters of the Three Americas Railway is, in this case at least, to prevent the possibility of such expensive contingencies as alterations and enlargements; by providing at the outset a double-track railway of the hardest steel, and a roadway so compact, so substantially built, and so liberally equipped, as to be capable of accommodating at once the largest possible quantities of goods and passengers; a road, in fact, which will redound to the credit of the builders, and remain for all time, an enduring monument to the remarkable energy and ability of the age. Continuing their journey southward, the powerful locomotives of the Three Americas Railway Company, merrily drawing their mighty loads, soon leave the rich and extensive territories of Canada behind them, and enter the wide domain of the Stars and Stripes, traversing, in their triumphant course, the teeming valleys of the Missouri, the Platte, and the Arkansas, receiving and delivering their plethoric cargoes on the way. These products are destined to find their way, either by land or water, to the Gulf of Mexico, through the cities of St. Louis, Chicago and Detroit, or to Baltimore, New York, and other more distant markets on the Atlantic seaboard.

Crossing the great American rivers, and keeping as nearly

as possible along the track of the one hundredth degree of longitude, the Ironhorse now scampers at its highest speed across the open prairies, as if revelling in the sense of absolute freedom and an unlimited field in which to display his prowess and endurance. Here, among the bright flowers and luxuriànt grasses that clothe the Texan plains as with a verdant mantle, he gallops resolutely forward; startling the silly sheep and cattle that roam in countless thousands over those immeasurable pastures which may always be confidently depended on to supply the markets of the world with the primest beef and mutton.

The cattle trade of Texas, with the Northern and Eastern markets, is assuming gigantic proportions, which, by a little extra care and attention, may still be indefinitely extended. It only requires, for its more profitable development, the introduction of better blood into the native herds, to enable the ranchmen to raise a class of cattle better suited, not only to our home requirements but also to the markets of Great Britain and the Continent of Europe. The consumption of meat in France is greatly in excess of what is raised in that country, which is sufficiently obvious when we learn that, within four months, the French imported eighty-seven thousand head of horned cattle, five hundred and seventy-five thousand sheep, and ninety-five thousand pigs. Most of the cattle were imported from Spain and Italy, which countries, however, cannot supply it so cheaply as it can be laid down from this side of the Atlantic, even after freight, insurance, and all other charges are deducted. There is therefore a prospect of establishing an almost unlimited trade in beef and cattle with that particular country, in addition to the markets of Great Britain; provided that railway companies and steamship owners will supply still greater facilities for the comfortable transportation of live stock, combined with economy and celerity.

Continuing our course through the plains of Texas, we shall shortly arrive in the neighborhood of the historic and beautiful city of Mexico, with its broad and regular streets, its handsome churches and numerous convents, its fine avenues of trees, and its crystal fountains. Alas, poor Mexico! Torn and bleeding from the effects of frequent invasions and inward commotions, what torrents of blood have been shed by thy noblest sons since thy soil was first desecrated by the ruffian hordes that accompanied the cruel and unprincipled Cortez! Here we may properly indulge in a few painful reminiscences of the unparalleled treachery practiced upon the generous Montezuma and his faithful Aztecs, by the greedy and heartless invaders. The proficiency of that interesting people in the finest mechanical arts, the wonderful accuracy of their chronological computations, their exquisite skill as lapidaries and goldsmiths, and their use of hieroglyphics, tinges them with a very striking resemblance to the ancient Egyptians. We may give rein to our imagination, and contrast the chronic condition of revolution in which that unfortunate country, together with those of Central and South America, have been struggling ever since the Spanish invasion, with the state of comparative peace and prosperity which they are likely to enjoy under the fresh impetus and favorable auspices of freedom and international intercourse by means of the contemplated railway. Such intercourse will, I venture to predict, eventually be of infinitely greater value to them than the ransom of Atahualpa, or the silver mines of Potosi, when happiness, security and commercial prosperity are the pleasing results of the enterprise.

The originators of this noble project hasten to lay it before the public even in its present inchoate condition; confident that the general information respecting it, gathered from various sources, at very great cost and trouble, will

prove sufficiently interesting and instructive to enlist substantial aid in the attainment of an object so manifestly necessary and desirable. What line of action the Congress
of the United States may see fit to adopt, we cannot tell;
but some considerable time must yet necessarily elapse ere
the sterling merits of the project can be fully investigated
and understood. It is certain, however, that Mr. Helper's
valuable suggestions will erelong meet with the courtesy
and consideration they deserve. In this progressive age,
the "rest and be thankful" theory is becoming quite obso-
lete. The world moves on, and we must naturally keep
pace with it. Time and material space are far too valuable
to be left unutilized; and yet, in our inconsistency, we are
endeavoring to annihilate both.

Some easy-going and conservative people experience un-
disguised alarm when any new theories or propositions above
mediocrity are started. The projectors and promoters are
denounced as hare-brained visionaries and little better than
lunatics; when, in fact, their minds are perhaps traveling in
a clearer and more exalted sphere of intellectual sublimity,
and amid the very noblest and grandest conceptions. Such
men, however, if sometimes misunderstood, are the world's
greatest benefactors, and the pioneers of knowledge and
civilization. It was ever thus, when great and original doctrines were first promulgated, or thoughts suggested out of
the common groove. Time is required for reflection ere the
minds of the masses can grasp the idea, and their mental
standard be raised sufficiently to enable them to understand
and appreciate what more astute intellects can encompass
at a glance. When the great engineer Stephenson first asserted that he could run his locomotive at the rate of twenty
miles an hour between Liverpool and Manchester, the idea
was scouted as preposterous, and when Galileo insisted that
the earth moved in its regular orbit round the sun, he was

laden with reproaches and cast into a dungeon. We might quote innumerable instances of similar ignorance, bigotry and incredulity; but the above must suffice. Who would have ventured to declare, half a century ago, that a message could travel all round the earth in the course of an hour or two? or that the Electric Light could illuminate the troubled waters of the ocean within a radius of forty miles?

It is an established fact, recognized by all, that, as part and parcel of man's destiny, each generation, as it floats onward upon the waves of Time, must be content to assume the duties and responsibilities imposed upon it by the inexorable demands of progress, and resolutely take in hand whatever those improving circumstances may render necessary of accomplishment. The Three Americas Railway is a case in point; and is one of those mighty necessities which have been gradually gaining force and energy until it can no longer be restrained. It is destined to fill up a vast social void, and to supply a want long sorely felt by the residents of the New World.

The assumption of somewhat novel functions or increasing obligations, when such are intimately connected with the furtherance of an especially useful and popular scheme, is not what any government having proper regard to the individual and collective advancement of the people, would seek to avoid; and it is clearly manifest that, in every unusually important movement,—no matter what labor or expense its advocacy may involve,—that of the United States has always been prominently to the front as the faithful reflex of the spontaneous energy and generosity of the people. A system of swift and regular communication with the more distant portions of the two continents of America, which, connecting their farthest extremities, shall pass along the center of their entire length, will be instrumental in instilling life and activity, and in developing the latent resources of those magnificent territories, in which lassitude and stagnation are the present prevailing features.

The introduction of so great an industrial phenomenon into the midst of vast countries, which, for lack of such beneficent agencies, are comparatively valueless, will tend to arouse the dormant energies of the peoples, and stimulate salutary enterprises and industrious habits in all directions. It will certainly be recognized as the most efficient means of actively promoting education and refinement along its entire course, together with the *savoir faire* (skillful and successful management) of more practical and disciplined nations; quickening the commercial instinct, and establishing the most agreeable relations between numerous peoples at present virtually isolated from each other.

The inventive genius, alike original and aggressive, of the Americans, will be found equal to the demands for its exercise in any emergency; and their natural readiness to embark in enterprises offering sufficient scope for their ideality, constructive talents and exemplary perseverance, augurs well for the complete success of any undertaking, however formidable, which the people and government may deem worthy of popular recognition and support. No doubt need therefore be entertained that a prodigious work, like the one now under consideration, involving to a great extent the national credit and prestige, and possessing within itself such attractive elements of promise, will, if judiciously undertaken, be permitted to lack the means necessary for its speedy and vigorous prosecution to completion. We have only to estimate, calmly and thoughtfully, the extent of the benefits which its early consummation must scatter broadcast throughout the land; its intrinsic importance; and the healthy improvements, in a moral and commercial sense, to which its various social ramifications

may lead, to be convinced at once of its practical utility.
The immense amount of labor involved in the work, the
dangers and triumphs, and the satisfactory solution of knotty
engineering problems, will only tend to stimulate ambition
and act as incentives to increased exertion, with an unyielding determination to succeed.   Such at least I assume will
be the leading characteristics of those who join the noble
army of workers in this exceptionally grand undertaking.

  - Difficult indeed would it be to overestimate the many
genial and elevating influences which so great a civilizing
power is capable of exercising over the welfare and destinies of the inhabitants of Central and South America;
bringing them within easy distance in regard to time and
into closer fellowship with one another; strengthening the
ties of friendship, based upon mutual interests; and introducing among them the glorious revelations of the Gospel
of Progress.   For many centuries, the animosity between
England and her Gallic neighbors was both marked and enduring; but, for the last thirty years, their interests having
been more closely identified through the medium of commercial treaties and improved travelling facilities, that unhappy feeling of hostility has been eclipsed by others of increasing respect and consideration.   In like manner, by a
frequent interchange of courtesies between North Americans
and their intelligent Mexican and other Spanish American
neighbors, the remembrance of all former antagonisms will
be effaced, and even the bitter feelings of aboriginal Mexicans against the descendants of their Spanish oppressors,
will be toned down and finally obliterated in presence of the
urbanity and dignified civility of those of their countrymen
through whose veins flow the chivalrous blood of Iberia.
Under the depressing yoke of bigotry and intolerance, long
might the teeming soil of Central and South America, rich
in all the elements of fertility, have remained undisturbed,

through the apathy of a scattered and illiterate peasantry; but the proposed railway will remedy all these paralyzing influences, and supply a want profoundly felt and urgently demanded by the more intelligent among both the white and the mixed races in Spanish America.

Free intercourse between the different peoples of the world, is becoming a necessity almost as indispensable as the air we breathe; and it is everywhere sought for with the greatest avidity. The railway mania is not yet at its height; and hundreds of lines will still have to be constructed ere the world will be satisfied. Mr. Helper may be accepted as a reliable authority in regard to the sentiments of the peoples of South America in that respect; he having resided for several years in different sections of the country, during which time he twice crossed the continent, on muleback, and the Isthmus three times. He also visited Peru, Bolivia, Chili, the Argentine Republic, Uraguay and Brazil. Mr. Helper is a man of great energy and perseverance; large-minded and patriotic; and, being naturally straight-forward himself, he abominates everything approaching to chicanery in others. In a book recently published by him, in which he relates many of his Andean experiences, I could not help admiring the steady and persistent courage with which, single-handed, and for the space of ten or twelve years, he prosecuted the claims of two of his clients (Mrs. Helen M. Fiedler, and Joseph H. Colton,) against the Brazilian and the Bolivian governments respectively; claims which were pronounced by the highest legal authorities of his own country, and even by those of the nationalities in question, to be most fair and equitable; and yet, notwithstanding all this, by dint of the most vexatious delays, combined with the grossest quibblings and prevarications, the claim against Bolivia was only partially satisfied; while that against Brazil was finally, by Brazil herself, altogether repudiated! The

ministers who were in office when Mr. Helper was urging
his claim against the Brazilian government, may, ere this,
have been superseded. It is necessary, however, to the ultimate and perfect success of the project, that the railway
should have the enthusiastic support of that country. The
present Emperor of Brazil, is, by all accounts, an enlightened and painstaking ruler; and the whole nation must not
be condemned on account of the questionable policy of a
short-sighted ministry. In the course of time, the Brazilians
themselves will recognize the necessity of dealing fairly
and squarely with their best customers. They will also
probably soon establish a republican form of government,
as being more in accordance with the progressive tendencies
of the age.

The world was created by One, for the benefit of all.
Ancient exclusiveness is rapidly giving place to intelligent
appreciation and friendly rivalry between the several nations
of the earth. The cheering rays of Light and Liberty are
gradually dawning in heathen countries; and Civilization
is spreading her sheltering wings over benighted zones.
The news of the day is flashed, with the rapidity of lightning, to earth's remotest corners; and the hearts of
friends, separated from us by immense distances of land
and ocean, can beat in unison with our own; throbbing, almost at the same time, with pleasurable emotions, or con-
vulsed with horror at the same heartrending recitals of
accidents and death. Inasmuch as steam and electricity
have been so largely instrumental in revolutionizing trade,
and in opening up new channels of industry with countries
the most remote, there is no reason why Americans should
not concentrate their energies and utilize them by establishing profitable business relations nearer home. We have no
occasion now-a-days to travel to Cathay in order to procure
luxuries wherewith to gratify our appetites or æsthetic

predilections; as from our own brace of big and beautiful continents we can procure every article, useful or luxurious, necessary to mankind.

The Three Americas Railway will become a most powerful auxiliary toward the promotion of universal peace, where only anarchy and bloodshed have hitherto prevailed; and in blending and consolidating the conflicting aims and interests of the different Republics and other States through which its active and life-giving Iron Angels may pass. By its agency, Americans will enjoy the advantages of easy access at all points to the oceans which surround their native land; and wherever the steam engine and its concomitant blessings are introduced, population will increase, the peaceful and mechanical arts be encouraged, and the boundless benefits of improved social, political and commercial relations between many sister nations be scattered throughout the length and breadth of the land. Hitherto the conditions of society in Central America and the other Spanish American Republics have been thoroughly disorganized; a chronic state of internecine warfare having prevailed ever since the repulsion of the Spaniards from the country; but perhaps the resistless attractions of an ever-increasing commerce with their northern neighbors, may become sufficiently absorbing to change the current of their thoughts, and demand and receive henceforth their exclusive attention. The example of systematic industry, gradually introduced from the north, may possibly neutralize and overcome entirely that warlike restlessness at the far south, which foments perpetual discord and keeps the people in a chaotic state of poverty and insecurity. When the cursed emissaries of War enter the gates of a city, the genius of Commerce at once flies over the ramparts; and it is by no means easy to induce its return. The constant repetition of so terrible a scourge as war, is even worse than the plague

itself in reducing men and nations to a condition of utter
inability and despair.

Among the great natural divisions of the North American Continent, in latitude and configuration, there are certain belts of land better adapted to the growth of wheat,
some to stock raising, and others to mixed husbandry, such
as the growing of fruit, cotton, tobacco and maize. So
likewise, on the continent of South America, the natural divisions and climatic ranges regulate the capabilities of the
soil. Free access to all these various belts is the great desideratum; and a Central Longitudinal Railway, from which
branches can be easily constructed as required, will well supply it. A Grand Trunk Railway from north to south, along
the middle of the South American continent will become
the nucleus of prosperity to all the inhabitants, and the
central pivot upon which their social and industrial interests
will revolve.

Simultaneously with the indefinite expansion and improvement of existing conditions of trade, the inestimable boon
of safe, speedy and cheap communication with distant markets will be attained. Enterprise will follow in the track of
the locomotive; cities will multiply along the line and its
different branches in all directions; immigration will be induced; and trade and capital will flow in new and unex-
pected channels. Only let the genius of prospective gain
just beckon to the world with tempting finger, and we know
—for we have seen—the results. Speculations which could
not have been conducted on a limited scale, will, under the
influence of energy and capital, be largely and enthusiastic-
ally promoted. The precious metals do not usually lie upon
the surface of the ground for any casual idler to pick up;
but they require shafts to be sunk, tunnels to be bored, and
waters to be drained, ere the richest lodes can be reached.

Only let the way be opened for the unrestricted interchange of merchandise, and the space will be speedily occupied by a host of eager merchants and traders. Remove all burdensome restraints upon trade, and it will constantly increase. Wherever business is to be fostered, thither will capital flow, as surely as water seeks and finds its own level; and of this physical fact Americans are perfectly cognizant. The powerful stimulus which the opening of the great Longitudinal Railway will create, in developing the adjoining territories for agricultural purposes, must yield abundant employment to millions of human beings at present living in a state of comparative inaction and want. Young and vigorous communities would spring up, and the citizens would be benefitted in a thousand ways. Wealth and commercial activity would be substituted for apathy and distress. Cheap supplies of foreign goods could be obtained with regularity and dispatch; and the volume of trade being greatly enlarged, all parties to the contract would be more than compensated for any aid in the way of grants and subsidies furnished by their respective governments. Lands now next to worthless, would attract attention as safe and encouraging investments, and the owners thereof, whether governments or private individuals, would reap a harvest of rich results by their enhanced value. Past experience proves, however, that, in order to achieve such results, the lands contiguous to the line should be promptly brought into the market, instead of being locked up for speculative purposes; and profits, in the form of dividends, should be rather dependent upon the legitimate working of the line, and upon the amount of public support extended to it, than upon longer deferred advantages in the shape of future enhancement in the value of adjacent lands. This railway is not to be likened to those which, running through inhospitable latitudes and wild regions, would have to be worked at a positive annual loss. It is the extreme fecundity of the soil and the geniality of the climate, along the greater portion of the route, that form its most attractive features. The locking up of more than a tenth part of the railway lands for speculative purposes, could not fail to be detrimental to the interests of the shareholders, by retarding settlement and consequent immediate profit.

It is a matter well worthy of consideration, by all likely to be earnestly interested in the railway, whether the best results might not be obtained, were special arrangements made between the several co-operating governments and the United States, for a species of Zollverein, or international tariff, designed with the object of promoting the repeal of all those tedious formalities and restrictions with which commerce is at present crippled; and by facilitating, in every possible manner, the free and expeditious interchange of commodities in trade. A few reforms in that direction would tend to increase business a hundred fold, to the advantage of all concerned; for it is a well-known commercial axiom, that consumption will increase in proportion to the facilities offered for the reduction in the price of an article, and for the general extension of trade. Backed by the general exchequers and by the hearty support of the peoples, with liberal bonuses from governments and municipalities, and grants of large and valuable bodies of land contiguous to the road, the prospect is most encouraging that the Three Americas Railway will soon become an accomplished fact, as a grand junction, or a great metallic backbone, into which all the present and future transcontinental railway systems will be joined, like so many iron ribs radiating in all directions.

In a Customs Union between the several Republics and other States, it surely would not be impossible to form combinations equitable alike to the smaller and to the larger members of the federation. This question of tariffs is, however, one which might be entirely left for future consideration, or delegated to a committee of mercantile representatives, selected according to population, or in any other manner which may be deemed more expedient. By a reduction of the present American tariff, or better still, perhaps, by its complete abolition, new channels of trade with Spanish America, with the West Indies, with China, and with all the Eastern markets, might be struck; from which American manufactures are now practically excluded. The present questionable fiscal policy of the United States precludes her from successful competition with other countries in the way of shipping; and, to a certain extent, on land also. If her manufactured fabrics are exported to Central or South America, she must barter for native merchandise in exchange; which produce, in consequence of the duties which would be levied on its introduction into the United States, is much of it shut out, and sent away direct to the markets of Europe. Were it not for that suicidal "protective" policy, the United States, with all the facilities the country enjoys in regard to the supply of raw material, might soon become the largest manufacturing country in the world.

A very liberal policy should be adopted by the Three Americas Railway Company, in order to induce the settlement of a suitable class of immigrants along the line ; and inasmuch as it would be impossible for them to devote the same amount of hard labor to the cultivation of their farms and plantations in tropical latitudes, as they would of necessity have to expend upon them here, Nature is there sufficiently generous and prolific to yield her treasures with but little human aid. All that is needful, in order to render her subservient to the will of man, and to produce several crops in a year, of many kinds of fruits, roots, and grasses, is systematic industry and an enlightened spirit of enterprise.

The Three Americas Railway should be undertaken less with the object of creating a grand monopoly, and of enriching at once those whose pecuniary interests may be embarked in it, than as a grand international work, which, while profitable to the shareholders, shall redound to the credit of the American Republics for all time.   American railway companies understand perfectly the science—for it already amounts to that—of setting a small fish in order to catch a large one, and of speculating in future material development.   The present expenditure of a few thousands of dollars, in establishing settlements along their lines, is wisely regarded as trifling compared with the immense revenues to be derived within a few years, in the shape of taxes and land sales and traffic from rapidly-increasing cities, with their thousands of busy inhabitants.

According to the *Railway Age*, of the 29th of July last, 1,790 miles of rails were laid in the United States, on sixty-seven roads, during the first half of the present year; construction in progress on one hundred and ten roads, a total length of 8,000 miles; while one hundred and ten roads, aggregating 10,850 miles, were projected; making a grand total of two hundred and eighty-seven roads, of 20,640 miles.   At such a wonderful rate of progress, it would not take long, if work be simultaneously commenced all along the line, to complete the Three Americas Railway.   Many of the new lines referred to above will run through new territory, while others are intended as feeders, or continuations of roads already in operation.

Emigration, on account of many disturbing causes in Europe, is increasing at an enormous rate; and emigration to a country in all respects willing and prepared to welcome it, implies great prosperity; while uncommon prosperity necessarily demands new railroads.   The era of railways, even upon the continent of North America, is probably yet in its infancy; and in the course of a few years more, the whole expanse of territory between the Atlantic and Pacific, will require an additional supply. No less than four separate trunk lines are now being pushed across Dakota Terrirory alone in the direction of the Pacific; and hundreds of engineers and surveyors are engaged in running lines across Montana, Wyoming, Idaho, Oregon, and Washington Territory. These transcontinental lines may be regarded as the commencement of the woof of the great iron network of railways destined to overspread this vast continent; and a grand trunk line, running north and south, is imperatively demanded as warp to bind together and strengthen the whole ingenious fabric, and to render it enduring and serviceable forever.

The best interests of the United States would no doubt be promoted, were the government to consent to assume the entire construction and control of this splendid International Highway; or, failing that, to give such guarantees and assistance as could not fail to inspire the fullest confidence on the part of intending investors. A Government Commission could be appointed, from time to time, to report the progress of the work, both from an engineering and financial point of view, and also, with the object of checking any movement not originally contemplated, or any steps in the direction of unjustifiable expenditure; but whether the responsibilities of this colossal undertaking be wholly or only partially assumed by the government, Mr. Helper would probably be ready to assist them to the best of his ability; perfectly content in the proud consciousness of having originated and actively assisted in promoting a work of such incalculable importance, not only to all of his own countrymen, but also to the world at large; a work pregnant with present blessings, and one which future generations will not fail to approve and applaud.

15

In the successful prosecution of this unique work, and for the most perfect development of the magnificent domain which its construction will bring into useful prominence, it is unnecessary to say that the greatest energy and stability of purpose must be consistently maintained, in order to complete the road within the time prescribed, and so as to have it in good running service by the time that the Great American International Jubilee is proposed to take place in St. Louis. Ignorance and bigotry combined can, as we know, raise up hideous bugbears and interpose innumerable barriers to success; but the national spirit must overcome these, and tolerate, in this case, no such word as failure. The diplomatic elements necessary in the negotiations with the different Republics and other States, must so thoroughly lubricate and disintegrate all difficulties as to cause them to fall away and disappear one after another, as if by the mere force of gravitation. Should Brazil prove difficult to deal with, she must by all reasonable arguments, be brought to understand that the strength-gathering tide of improvements will wait for neither governments nor individuals after a certain stage of intelligence shall be reached; and that the evident tendency of the political instincts of Central and South America, is irresistably toward universal republicanism; which, instead of the fratricidal dissensions and wars now devastating those countries may, at no very distant day,—and for the good of all,—at least go so far as to assume the title and the functions of the United States of South America.

In apportioning the assessments as to the bonuses to be paid by the different co-operating republics, in aid of the Three Americas Railway, resources, position and prospective benefits must all be taken into account. Some may prefer to contribute lands alone; some to pay a certain proportion of the subsidy in cash; while others, suffering un-

der a scarcity of circulating medium, but rich in natural productions, may wish to give an equivalent either in labor or
materials. For instance, Lignum Vitæ and other hard woods
could be supplied for constructive purposes, such as ties and
sleepers, and other timber for building stations and warehouses, or for the manufacture of rolling-stock. In localities apparently unfitted for either agriculture or pasturage,
there may lie, nevertheless, within the rocky bosom of
mother earth, vast hoards of wealth, for which valuable
mining privileges might be secured. Not many months
ago, gold mines of surpassing richness were said to have
been discovered at the village of Las Placitas, thirty miles
from the town of Santa Fé, in Mexico; the ore, when es-
sayed, yielding, in some instances, at the marvelous rate of
$6,000 to the ton.

When both parties to a lawful agreement are actuated by
fair and honest motives, there need be little difficulty in
effecting an amicable arrangement. The more enlightened
among our Spanish American brethren are now clamoring
for the very means it is here proposed to supply them. It
is reported that the people of Manaos, a town of 8,000 inhabitants, situated on the Rio Negro, near its junction with
the Amazon, are very desirous of establishing a direct trade
with the United States, and are willing to grant a subsidy of
$3,500 a trip for a steam service. Their import duties are
at present six per cent., and the export duties three per cent.
less at Manaos than at Para. This arrangement was made
especially to encourage foreign commerce. The people who
reside along the banks of the great South American watercourses, are evidently alive to their interests in this direction. An irregular line of British steamers is already established between Bolivia and the United States, by way of
Para; and there is said to be an excellent opportunity to
establish a regular line from some port on this northern
continent to the valley of the Amazon.

A triple combination of ignorance and bigotry and superstition may be among the most serious obstacles which the
United States Commissioners may have to encounter during
their negotiations; and perhaps also a very perceptible
tinge of jealousy on the part of Brazil, of the acknowledged
and undeniable superiority of the commercial, mechanical
and manufacturing resources of North America, and of her
republican powers and proclivities.   Mexico will probably
accept any fair proposals with alacrity; being sufficiently
alive to the advantages of reciprocal trade, closer relations
and rapid intercourse with her enterprising northern neighbors.   As for Bolivia, Chili, Peru and the Argentine Republic, one would naturally think that any mighty agent calculated, as the Three Americas Railway is, to promote peace
and prosperity, ought to be received with open arms.   Without this railway, these countries are more likely than ever to
continue but too indefinitely their revolutionary wars of
extermination.

With an abundant supply of labor, and aided by all the
powerful appliances which modern ingenuity has invented
for blasting and piercing rocks of adamant, the construction
of the greater portion of the line will come within the range of
ordinary contractors ; while skillful engineers will surmount
the more formidable obstacles as they arise.   Should the
different contracts be let in continuous sections, and each
section be utilized as soon as completed, a great saving
would result, and a sort of preliminary traffic be established,
the profits of which would lesson by so much the general
cost of construction.

As to the entire practicability of his stupendous scheme,
Mr. Helper's faith therein is absolute and unbounded.   Personal inspection of a large portion of the proposed route,
and frequent consultations with eminent engineers and other
scientific authorities, upon the subject, have only tended to

strengthen his conviction that the Three Americas Railway will erelong become an established fact. He is a firm be-' liever that the spirit and well-directed energy of his country-men will be equal to any emergency, and that their ability, supplemented by the engrossing nature of the work and the ingenious machinery of modern railroad engineering, will be a power sufficiently strong to overcome any difficulties not absolutely insurmountable, which may present them-selves during the formation of this colossus of roads.

An old-time author of many moral and economic max-ims recommends the indolent and the faint-hearted to take one of the most insignificant of God's creatures as their type and model. " Go the ant, thou sluggard," says Solo-mon, " consider her ways, and be wise." This ancient Hebrew injunction is equally applicable to all modern na-tions and individuals. Many a valuable lesson of self-de-pendence and industry may be derived from watching the systematic movements of that little insect. Was not the heroic patriot Bruce stimulated to grander efforts in behalf of his beloved country, by observing, in the midst of the semi-darkness of his dungeon, the repeated failures and -ultimate success of a persevering little spider ? The move-ments of these insects are the results of an impulsive in-stinct, almost approaching to reason ; and although we may not choose to imitate their wonderful tactics to the letter, we can at least admire them, and recognize therein their special adaptability to the ends for which they were created. Man, however, possesses this great advantage over the mere insect, in that his knowledge assists him in providing powerful engines to do his work ; hence he considers the little ant's roundabout proceedings as rather old-fashioned and tedious. He glories in going right through obstruc-tions ; not hesitating to pierce the solid barriers imposed by Nature, and to blow into ten thousand atoms any impediment which may oppose his passage toward the sphere of his ambition. He delights also in bridging over gullies and ravines, rivers and other watercourses, wherever they may dispute his progress.

The construction of railroads is a science which has apparantly almost reached perfection in regard to labor-saving machinery; and it now resolves itself simply into a question of time and money. The engineering difficulties of the present transcontinental lines to the Pacific were rather exaggerated perhaps in the first instance; and they speedily vanished before the power of intellect and the persistent attacks of a whole army of picks and shovels, in combination with their valuable auxiliaries, gunpowder and other explosives. By means of the improved steam-scoops, trucks can be laden expeditiously, and a moderate-sized mountain shovelled away in a comparatively short space of time. Greater wonders will yet come. Together with economy in construction, there will be economy in working, if it be true that, by means of a few gallons of naptha— costing a mere trifle—and a litle water, a pressure of 125 pounds of steam to the square ihch can be obtained, and a small train run therewith a dozen miles or so, at a fair speed. As to the actual difficulties to be encountered in the prosecution of the great work contemplated, only experts, who have surveyed the route, are competent to speak. All that others can well do is to draw their own conclusions from the character and configuration of the various countries already explored. Physical difficulties there must be, more or less; steep gradients in some places, which, however, are more than compensated for by immense tracts of level plains and table lands. There are rivers to be bridged, embankments to raise, and several tunnels to be excavated; but of course this latter, most expensive item in railway construction, will be resorted to only when unavoidable. There is, though, no likelihood of as great obstructions occurring as have been already conquered in the case of the Gothard, the Mont Cenis and the Hoosac tunnels, with less powerful machinery, and with greatly inferior means to those which could now be procurable.

We must not be deterred by the magnitude of the undertaking, in these wonderful days of enterprise and scientific attainments. We have considered the salutary lessons presented by the ant and the spider. We may now look in another direction, and applaud the exemplary patience of the Dutch in their persevering efforts to reclaim from the watery dominions of Neptune the lands at present covered by the Zuyder Zee; a work which they have been assiduously prosecuting for years, by the aid of numerous steam pumps and windmills. Such land, when reclaimed, their indefatigable industry will speedily convert into green fields and blooming gardens, or into a thriving city, like Amsterdam, or Rotterdam. The patient Hollanders, possessing plenty of perseverance, but little land, are determined to procure an addition to their happy little commonwealth, by honesty and legitimate means. They detest the idea of spoliation and murder; and their conquests are peaceful ones, —over the elements and over themselves. This is another instance of how great ends may be accomplished by faithfully carrying out the details of a grand idea. If man cannot literally remove mountains, he does not allow them materially to interfere with his advancement. Even the great Mont Blanc, in Switzerland, will no longer be allowed to rest in peaceful inertia, but must be pierced at the base, in order to meet the exacting requirements of this age of progress. The very Poles themselves are not altogether free from the curiosity and the courageous encroachments of science. Commander Cheyne's ambition now appears to be to plant the ensign of his country upon the northernmost point of

the Earth's axis ; and as he cannot accomplish his object
by either sailing, sleighing, blasting or tunneling, he proposes to fly thither with a tandem of connected balloons!

The question of gauge for the proposed railway, is an
important one to consider. A broad-gauge would seem to
be desirable, for many reasons, for a line of such unusual
length, to be adapted to heavy traffic; but as connections
will, in time, be made with many cross-lines, some uniform
gauge must necessarily be adopted. Practical railway men
will be the best judges as to what should be done in this regard to meet the requirements of a first-class road.

It would doubtless be a grand political consummation,
were all the Republics and other States of South America
harmoniously united into one great federation, instead of
being, as now, constantly engaged in senseless and sanguinary internecine strifes. There can be little social improvement or commercial prosperity in any country in which life
and property are not safe. For the sake of peace and good
government, the smaller nationalities should submit to be
amalgamated with the larger ones, as, with prudence, was
recently done by the smaller principalities in Germany. The
other day a vessel arrived in New York from Rosario, in the
Argentine Republic *en route* for the Canary Islands, whither
the passengers were bound, in search of the longed-for
peace and quietness denied them at home. They might
have been supremely happy on the borders of the River
Plate, with its fertile plains and enjoyable climate, were it
not for the frequent recurrence there of wars and revolutions. Besides being enriched with grain and fruits in
abundance, the Argentine Republic can boast of possessing
nearly eighty millions of sheep, in addition to cattle innumerable and immense droves of horses.

At the present time, and under existing circumstances, a
journey throughout the length of the two continents of

America would, by reason of its attendant perils and serious inconveniences, be only practicable for the hardier sort of adventurers. The time also and the expense involved in so arduous an undertaking would greatly detract from its popularity with travellers. It is hoped, however, and believed, that our proposed Longitudinal Line will offer unequaled facilities to the travelling public, for making extended journeys, north and south, east and west, to the Atlantic and to the Pacific, and throughout the immense length and breadth of both of these beautiful and bountiful continents; than which, with their varied and romantic scenery, nothing terrestrial can be found more interesting and instructive. We may confidently predict that vast multitudes from Europe and elsewhere, will take advantage of the inducements it will offer, to make the Grand American Tour, which will soon become indispensable to all who are fond of traveling for its own sake.

Partly owing to the density of some of the forests and the inadequate means of locomotion, and partly on account of the venomous and ferocious animals inhabiting those countries, scientific explorations in Central and South America, have been few and far between. One or two of the most prominent naturalists have, however, given us some intensely interesting accounts of the flora, the fauna, and the matchless vegetable productions of those tropical latitudes; but much undoubtedly remains to be done in that direction, when increased means of communication shall have opened the way. This very desirable result the Three Americas Railway will also accomplish. It is, in all truth, a great and glorious enterprise, which, fraught with the richest blessings to humanity, may be regarded as the Keystone of the Arch of American Unity. It may also be confidently regarded as affording bases for the most practical methods of binding together the whole fabric of Western-World society, with its

various peoples, climates and languages, in community of
sentiment, and in one grand, indissoluble and harmonious
whole.

There are thousands of Americans, to whose practical
knowledge and native ingenuity and daring, a scheme of the
magnitude and importance of the one now under consideration,—so fertile in adventure, so promising in good results, and so rich in all those intellectual prizes and honorable distinctions which are very dear to the professional
spirit,—will present irresistible attractions. It must naturally commend itself very strongly to young men of talent
and enterprise, who are ambitious to enrol their names upon
the register of their country's achievements; while those
who are their seniors in age and experience, and who have
already acquired fame and reputation in their respective
professions, will not be averse to adding additional laurels
to those already won.   There are, moreover, many thousands whose enthusiasm, with regard to anything permanently
good and great, will be easily awakened; and, in the present instance, they will undoubtedly be prompted to identify
themselves with the practical propositions and interests of
this most extensive international and intercontinental operation, and to lend their influence and capital toward the
furtherance of an object so preëminently useful and patriotic.

Men are not easily deterred now-a-days from battling
with the forces of Nature; nor are they wanting in the
courage and perseverance necessary to prosecute vigorously, works, however difficult and costly, upon which they
have once firmly set their minds, and which the ever-
exacting laws of progress seem imperatively to demand.
Even the depths of the ocean are not proof against their
strange and unwelcome encroachments; these submarine
regions are invaded at will by divers   hideous helmets,

and by metallic cables trailing in all directions,—the wonderful creatures of man's invention, and the practical illustration of his irrepressible energy and genius. The earth itself is, figuratively speaking, bridled and engirdled by an electric band; and by man's controlling hand all that takes place upon her surface is duly and speedily recorded. Commercial exchanges pass safely and currently beneath the stormy billows; while messages of peace on the one hand, and hostility on the other, flash constantly to and fro. The suppressed whisper of sorrow or suspense can be heard afar; while the joyous echoes of affection speed on lightning pinions through the realms of space; and,—like the spirits of the departed,—greet distant friends in earth's remotest corners. Structures of iron and steel, the most beautiful and elegant, resembling in their graceful outlines the fairy meshes of a spider's web, hang suspended, as if by enchantment, over giddy heights and roaring cataracts; whilst the mightiest rivers themselves are confidently spanned by noble arches and metallic tubes.

Another engineering work, of really extraordinary proportions has lately been completed. The great Gothard, between Italy and Switzerland, has been successfully tunnelled. Mont Blanc will soon have its rocky bowels torn to fragments by the explosive blast, and its solitude invaded, day and night, by the passing trains. Not content with their great achievement from Cairo to Suez, the French government have granted many millions of francs toward the building or a railroad across the formidable Desert of Sahara, and a canal is also to be cut which will connect the Bay of Biscay with the Mediterranean through French territory. This canal, in connection with that across the Isthmus of Suez, will further shorten the passage of steamers to India, by many days, avoiding much dangerous navigation round Cape Finisterre. Such an important saving of time and expense is a great object in these days of swift transit and keen competition ; and the world is evidently ripe for still greater improvements in this direction.   Another remarkable instance of the scientific enterprise of the day, and of indefatigable perseverance under difficulties, is to be found in the working of the Comstock lodes in Nevada, at a depth of three thousand feet below the surface ; and also in the working of the mines at Silver Islet, which lie beneath the waters of Lake Superior.   A far mightier effort than either of these will be represented, by the successful completion of a Longitudinal Double-Track Steel Railway, traversing a region extending over more than one hundred and ten degrees of latitude, with its various peoples, climes and scenery, between Alaska and Cape Horn.

Let us now return to the route which this railway is likely to enrich and enliven with its propitious influences. We had reached the historic city of Mexico ; and the Ironhorse was rushing along with breathless energy in the direction of the Isthmus of Tehuantepec. Thence the line would trend in a southeasterly direction, having regard to the sinuosities of the broken mountain ranges, toward the Isthmus of Panama ; drawing support from the peninsula of Yucatan,—famous for its gallant stand against the invading Spaniards, —from the Bays of Campeachy and Honduras, from the neighborhood of Vera Cruz, on the Gulf, and from Acapulco, Guatemala, and other important places on the western coast ;—support in the shape of large supplies of most valuable tropical produce ; such as mahogany and a variety of dyewoods, cochineal, cocoa, and luscious fruits *ad libitum* ; in addition to the precious metals, rich scarlet cloths and gold embroideries.   It will then continue its interesting course between the great logwood country of Nicaragua, on the one side, and the celebrated coffee and cocoa plantations on the other, to its junction with the present Trans-

Isthmian Railway on the banks of the river Chagres ; from which connections at once can be made for Aspinwall and Panama.

We have thus travelled, on the wings of imagination, over the greater portion of the northern half of the Western Hemisphere ; but however encouraging and profitable such an excursion may have been so far, in the way of assumed support to the railway and of convenience to the travelling public, a yet fairer prospect is still in store for us, by extending our grand civilizing track of steel right through the heart of the vast continent of South America. Here we have the advantage of a virgin soil of surpassing richness, capable of producing several crops in a year, without the aid of any sort of artificial or foreign fertilizer, and with a minimum of manual labor ;—a territory, nearly 4,600 miles in length by 3,200 miles as its extreme width, and embracing an area of 7,000,000 of square miles. In these expanded regions are to be found almost impenetrable forests, in a state of primitive wildness and grandeur; boundless plains, or llanos, covered with mantels of the richest grasses, and studded with gorgeous flowers ; and perfumed groves of spices, alternated with plantations of bananas, guavas, cocoanuts, lemons, oranges, olives and almonds.

Noble mountains, towering heavenward, stand like giant guardians over the scene, and contain within their rocky bosoms more wealth than all the glittering treasures of Golconda. Diamonds, rubies, sapphires, emeralds, and gold and silver are there in abundance. In this terrestrial Paradise there is ample scope for the skill of the painter, the energy of the merchant, the zeal of the naturalist, and the numerous and profitable industries of the husbandman, in their different spheres and callings. Millions of acres of this most valuable territory are capable of being reclaimed from their present wild and tangled growth ; and millions of

men and women may be withdrawn from the paralizing influences of ignorance and superstition, to occupy them and
develop their resources.   Here is a country whose mineral
and vegetable productions are among the most valuable in
the world, and which when overreached through the agency
of steam, cannot long remain neglected.   This lovely territory, which the grasping but courageous Spaniards shed
their blood in torrents to obtain, they were ultimately compelled to surrender.

South America is so rich and capable as to be able to
maintain surpassingly profitable commercial relations with
other countries for centuries to come, on the strength of her
raw materials alone ; for her soil is practically inexhaustible
in the warmer latitudes ; where its volcanic origin, combined
with the constantly recurring deposits of decaying vegetable
matter, keep up a continuous supply of the elements of fertility.   The great desideratum is a large infusion of an energetic white population among the present indolent mixed
races of Spanish and Indian blood, and free intercourse
with the rest of the world.   Soon or late this must happen ;
and railways, more than any other agency, will contribute to
hasten that eminently desirable result.   In Bolivia and the
Argentine Republic there exist immense plains, capable of
producing grain and of raising stock in the greatest abundance ; also, in many portions of them, cotton, tobacco,
sugar, olives, dates, figs, lemons, nectarines, grapes, and
other excellent fruits, and are, besides, where not liable to
be flooded, especially adapted to the growth of maize and
millet.

Leaving the Isthmus of Panama, and passing along
down toward the southern end of the Darien Gulf, the railway will probably trend in a southeasterly direction, following the course of the Magdalena River to Santa Fé de Bogotá ; drawing large quantities of sugar and other tropical

produce from the Republics of Venezuela and Ecuador; and then, crossing three large rivers, the Orinoco, the Rio Negro, and the Amazon,—those mighty arterial drains that intersect the country in all directions,—continue southward along the valley of the Paraguay, in about the 57th meridian west, to the city of Asuncion, the capital of Paraguay, situated at the confluence of the rivers Paraguay and Pilcomayo. From thence, the line would probably run through the Argentine Provinces of Corrientes and Entre Rios, (between the rivers,) and then cross the river Parana, after which it would soon find its way to the cities of Santa Fé and Rosario.

From the northern portions of Columbia, Ecuador, Venezuela, and the Guianas, (British, Dutch, and French,) there would probably soon be a superabundant support for a good trunk railroad, and plenty of freights for steamers on the rivers besides. All descriptions of valuable produce will be forthcoming from these teeming regions of the torrid zone, toward the western borders of Brazil. Much of this produce, being of a more or less perishable nature, would be liable to damage by carriage on shipboard; and for such produce a railway would be most essential. Coffee, sugar, cocoa, dyes, choice drugs, and cotton, in addition to a great variety of delicate and delicious fruits, are among the staple exports of these tropical latitudes. Venezuela comprises an immense plain to the east of the Andes, and is capable of being made very productive. The above-mentioned countries are mostly well watered, and not subject to the protracted drouths which are experienced in higher latitudes. Cumana, Caracas, and Maracaibo, are the chief seaports of Venezuela ; Panama, Aspinwall, Santa Marta, and Cartagena, of Columbia; and Quito, and Guayaquil, of Ecuador. The mountains, being volcanic, earthquakes are of frequent occurrence in these localities.

It is not, however, so much with the coast line, as with the interior of South America, that our proposed railway will have to deal; for it is there where its value will be most appreciated and its great utility demonstrated, by opening up to life' and commercial activity, vast regions at present abandoned to tapirs and monkeys. Let us reflect for a moment, upon the encouraging prospect which our new and grand road would open out, if fairly and heartily participated in by the immense empire of Brazil; with its boundless natural resources, superb climate, and its amazing extent of upward of 3,000,000 of square miles of territory. This broad domain, in which the climatic zones range from the torrid to the temperate, is capable of producing everything necessary to the wants of mankind; and it contains within itself perhaps greater natural riches, in proportion to its area, than any other country in the world. It has the inestimable advantages of a coast-line extending about 3,600 miles north and south; along which the chief shipping ports are Rio de Janeiro, Pernambuco, Bahia, Maranham, Paraiba, and Pará, with Rio Grande do Sul, and lastly, Ceará to the northward. To these ports does the produce of the interior slowly and laboriously find its way; partly by means of rivers, the navigation of which is often impeded, but mostly over the roughest and almost impassable roads, on the backs of mules and oxen. Much waste, damage and loss are therefore inevitably incurred by the way.

The inhabitants of the provinces farthest removed from the sea are consequently among the poorest and most thriftless; and it is no wonder that they are discouraged, when no means exist for carrying their produce to market, should they raise any for sale, and there are no business centers to stimulate them to increased exertion. But, by the wonderful interposition of steam, the desired ends will be ac-

complished.   Those extensive and valuable tracts will erelong be metamorphosed into productive gardens and plantations, by tens of thousands of willing hands, eager to assist in their further development.   Within the boundaries of
the Brazilian empire flourish what we may denominate the
chiefs of the woody world, represented by gigantic trees.
One may also meet there many of the brightest and most
beautiful natural objects, and some, it must be admitted,
that are exceedingly repulsive and deadly.   When, in the
year 1808, the ports of Brazil were first thrown open to foreign commerce, trade and civilization were at a very low
ebb ; but consecutive improvements, social and commercial,
were the immediate consequences of free and unrestricted
intercourse with other nations.   When, therefore, we consider the extent of the country and the extraordinary capabilities of the soil, we are furnished with good and sufficient
reasons for endeavoring to establish regular and swift communication with the interior of Brazil and other South
American countries, by means of a well-equipped railroad.

The Three Americas Railway Company will doubtless
offer every inducement to the Brazilian government to assist
them in a scheme so likely to prove beneficial in the highest
degree to each and every contracting party.   Among the
mountains of the Brazilian Cordilleras, is a rich mining district, in which are found gold, diamonds, the topaz, rubies,
emeralds, and other precious stones.   The diamond-fields
extend about fifty miles in length by twenty-five in breadth.
To these mines, in which large numbers of men are regularly employed by the government, constant supplies of
clothing and provisions must be sent ; and the greater the
regularity of supplies, the greater will be the development
of treasures.   By nature, Brazil is preëminently a wealthy
country; but good roads, free intercourse, the removal of
vexatious restrictions on trade, an absence of petty jeal-

16

ousies, and the encouragement of a suitable class of immi
grants, are imperatively necessary in order to raise that
country to a high state of civilization and prosperity.

Dom Pedro the Second is, by all accounts, a well-meaning man, of exemplary industry, and also of genuine solicitude for the good government of his subjects; but it is
quite possible that his enlightened views may frequently be
overruled by a bigoted and short-sighted ministry. As a
constitutional sovereign, as an experienced traveler, and as
a diligent student and observer, he has acquired a thorough
insight into the different social and political systems of government now extant in North America and Europe; and is
hardly the man to allow small considerations and petty jealousies to warp his matured judgment, nor deprive his country of those great and permanent privileges which the
more enlightened of his subjects earnestly seek to obtain.

Brazil is, for the most part, well watered; and the climate,
on the higher lands, is most delightful. In addition to a
large amount of grain, the country yields many valuable
dyes, turning woods, lignum vitæ, ebony, cedar, satin, and
tulip woods, boxwood, fustic, rosewood, and mahogany;
also cotton, tobacco, sugar, coffee, cocoa, spices, indigo, tapioca, rice, rubber, and fruits, and drugs in great variety.
Brazil furnishes, in fact, the most generally valuable and
miscellaneous assortment of exports to be found in any
country on the face of the globe,—so especially as regards
natural productions. Hitherto the more costly and deli-
cately flavored articles have had to perform a most tedious
and circuitous pilgrimage to the coast, entailing very considerable expense and delay; while, from distant points inland, whence water-carriage is not available, there is no inducement to grow much in excess of the actual requirements of the inhabitants on the spot. Cheap facilities for
transport are therefore the great want of the people in the

interior; and when such facilities are supplied, the production will increase a thousandfold. This lack of good roads and quick transit fully accounts for the prevailing inactivity in all the back settlements of Brazil; but that deplorable condition of things will be as surely remedied, when the interior of the country shall be rendered accessible to the vivifying influences of the Three Americas Railway, as its revenues were benefited after its ports were thrown open to the commerce of the world.

The consumption of coffee is increasing so enormously that, forming as it does, an important factor in the exports of Brazil, the question of a supply which shall keep pace with the demand for that exhilarating berry, is one of great moment. Its cultivation is at present confined almost exclusively to Brazil, Mexico, Costa Rica, Venezuela, Java, Sumatra, Ceylon, and a few of the West Indian islands; but Brazil alone exported, during the past season, no less than 273,000 tons. These figures are wonderfully suggestive and attractive to those who contemplate entering into the business of coffee-planting, or of purchasing lands on which it may be grown, in close proximity to a leading railway, and with a view to future cultivation. Capital and labor will do all that is requisite, when the means of transport are provided, to double the present production of coffee-plantations.

As the population along the whole line will be its chief support, every possible encouragement should be extended to settlers, of whatever nationality. The constant feeding of the road, at the different way-stations, would perhaps pay better dividends than unfair discrimination in favor of wealthy firms, and through freights at greatly reduced figures. The company might offer such guarantees and inducements to the better class of immigrants as would attract them to settle on their lands and permanently improve them.

There is no natural reason why tea should not be largely grown in South America, as in that country there are many localities exactly adapted to its growth. The native Paraguay tea, which is much used as a beverage, can be greatly improved. Ready markets for every description of produce will be found at the different stations along the line, whither merchants will hasten to purchase them, and who will absorb all that may be offered. Hence, all the more costly and delicate commodities, such as drugs, spices, groceries, and the less perishable kinds of fruits, would reach their destination in the primest condition, without being subjected to the detriorating influences of defective ventilation, or possible contact with sea-water. Of such goods there will be a constant supply for shipment, so long as the railway freights are not actually prohibitive. Another argument in favor of transportation by rail is that, besides the improved condition in which goods would be received, the time saved in transit would be equivalent to a considerable saving of interest on the capital invested in the purchase. There would also be a proportionate reduction in rates of insurance over those by water.

The Three Americas Railway, as an incomparable pioneer line, will traverse territories hitherto unexplored; but which, under its stimulating influence and the introduction of the more economical labor appliances of the day, will soon be greatly improved, and become tributary to it in the form of flourishing farms and prosperous settlements. These cheering evidences of diligence and thrift will soon transform the appearance of the country; while towns and villages, scattered along the entire route, will attest the service of the locomotive and form attractive *nuclei* for the commercial and industrial activity of their respective districts. Instead of continuing to groan under the selfish extortion of the cruel and bigoted blacks and half-breeds, the

continent of South America will,. in a short time, be enlivened with enterprising and peaceful citizens from all
parts of the world, in pursuit of honorable business or
pleasure, which will be beneficial to the whole country.

History is said often to repeat itself; and lost arts are
sometimes recovered. Who knows whether the arts and
sciences in which the original inhabitants of portions of
South America so greatly excelled, but which were lost
during their repeated struggles with the Spaniards and
the introduction of foreign blood into their country, may
not be revived under fairer auspices, after the lapse of
centuries, through friendly intercourse with the outside
world? A mere suggestion, or a comparison of methods,
might enable the natives to discover the clue, even as we
ourselves sometimes recover a long-lost thread of thought,
through some trifling accident. It would be no great
stretch of the imagination to picture, in the beginning of the
next century, thriving cities and important industries established all along the Longitudinal Line which we are now
sketching; where, in fact, millions of happy mortals will be
found enjoying the blessings and amenities of life in their
own way; having at their command all the conveniencies
and elegancies which so largely contribute to the pleasures
of existence.

During the long continuance of Spanish rule in Central
and South America, the invaders exercised their characteristic jealousy and exclusiveness in regard to commercial and
political intercourse with foreign nations. Monopolies and
the most unreasonable restrictions were maintained. Forced
labor was exacted from the people; and the unfortunate natives were compelled to toil in the mines to gratify the selfish cupidity of their invading despoilers. How different
will it be in the near future? How changed the conditions,
when, with peace and contentment predominant throughout

the land, their descendants will be enabled, by means of the
intervention of steam, to enjoy fully the fruits of their labors, and to sit in absolute quietness and security under the
shades of their own vines and fig trees.

In describing the probable course of the railway, we had
reached the cities of Santa Fé and Rosario, on the Parana
river, a little to the north of the latitude of Valparaiso.
Thence we must go southward, through the Argentine Republic, to the borders of the southern Rio Negro.   The capabilities of the almost immeasurable Argentine plains,
called pampas, for both cattle-raising and agriculture, are
enormous.   The vast flocks of sheep and herds of horses
and horned cattle that can be raised on the succulent grasses
of those extensive pampas are every day becoming more
and more valuable; as, with reference to fresh meats, the
refrigerating processes now in use permit of the dressed car-
casses being carried from the antipodes in the hottest
weather without detriment.   There is excellent room also
for an important industry in the manufacture of glue and
superphosphates, from the holocausts of bones and accu-
mulations of hoofs and horns and damaged hides, which lie
drying and bleaching on the praries in all directions.   These
articles of commerce would find a ready and profitable market in North America.   Grain and flour, together with hundreds of thousands of tons of copper ore, sulphur and nitrate of soda, will also be regularly and pressingly forthcoming to swell the traffic on our railway, from the vast
areas of fertile lands and mineral districts on the east side
of the Andean range.   On or near the Atlantic coast, we
find the thriving seaports of Montevideo and Maldonado,
in Uruguay, and Buenos Ayres and Ensenada, on the Rio
de la Plata; whence a most important export business, in
wool, hides, horns, hoofs, hair, jerked beef, tongues, bones,
and tallow,—all the produce of the neighboring Pampas,—

is carried on; in addition to large exports of cereals and cereal products.

There need really be no jealousy on the part of any one of the various republics through whose territory our modern and model highway will pass; for the immense benefits in prospect are too apparent, and cannot be otherwise than reciprocal. The government of the United States and the representatives of the Longitudinal Railway, will doubtless be prepared to make the most equitable and satisfactory arrangements for successfully carrying out this famous project. Everything should be done in perfect harmony with the feelings and interests of all the respective governments as relatively equal co-partners in an unparalleled and mutually international undertaking.

Guano from the coasts of Peru and Patagonia, may possibly continue to be carried, as heretofore, more cheaply and conveniently by water; but, even under the most favorable circumstances, a voyage round Cape Horn is both costly and tedious. The articles which chiefly compose the mineral wealth of the eastern slope of the Andean chain,—the gold, the silver, the copper, the quicksilver, the nitrate, and the sulphur, will doubtless, to a great extent, pass over the Longitudinal Line, on their way to their ultimate destination. Hitherto we have been speaking of only a few of the principal exports of Central and South America; but we must bear in mind that their imports of manufactured products, in exchange, will be on an enormous scale. In these days of increasing production and keen competition, it behooves America to cast about for an ever-enlarging field of absorption for her manufactures, her ingenious mechanical appliances, and her thousand and one articles of luxury and utility, which are now among the indispensables of life in all of our more civilized communities. These numerous articles need only to be fairly introduced abroad in order to be well appreciated; and the demand for the same will increase in exact proportion to the facilities afforded for obtaining them. Even the uncouth and unsophisticated Araucanians, and also those giant inhabitants of the wilds of Patagonia, may erelong be reckoned upon by us as regular customers; and it is by no means improbable that they will eventually re- gard the little comforts of their northern brethren as quite essential to the enjoyment of their own existence. These things may, in time, be considered as great a boon to them as was the manufacture of cheap calicoes to the working classes of our own country, or as was ever the introduction of coffee, tea, or tobacco to any portion of the human family. The factory, the telegraph and the printing press, as valuable auxiliaries to civilization, will supplement, to great advantage, the introduction of our great railway; and these will lead, by sure and certain gradations, to the attain- ment of a higher and purer tone of moral development in South America; alike beneficial to the natives and to the foreigners.

For centuries the quarrelsome and dissentious elements have had control of the beautiful countries of Spanish America; and the soil there has been desecrated by violence and blood. From generation to generation the inhabitants have been in a state of chronic revolution. At best, we have been able to discover only brief intervals of cessation from hostilities, and but little inclination on the part of the people to engage in peaceful pursuits. Even the Argen- tine Republic, one of the most orderly and prosperous of the South American commonwealths, has but recently been in a state of chaotic confusion, and is still in arms; while the Chilians and the Peruvians are, at this very time, making every effort—and at a fearful cost of life and treasure—to exterminate each other, by sea and by land. What these peoples seem to require, in order to avoid and prevent these ceaseless and self-destroying strifes, is a spirit of patriotism for their country *as a whole*, instead of indulging in local and sanguinary squabbles, which, crippling their resources and stifling all enterprise, drain off the inhabitants; too much, indeed, on the principle of the fatuity of the drunkard, who encompasses his own ruin by the constant gratification of his fatal passion. Sterling and absorbing interests appear to be necessary, in order to engage earnestly the attention of these people upon other objects, and in a more honorable direction,—certain substantial attractions in the shape of energy-creating and wealth-yielding commercial undertakings, which will wean them from their besetting weaknesses, and divert them from their thriftless habits of restlessness and discontent, begotten of indolence and aggravated by want.

When the cruel and unprincipled Pizarro first took possession of the golden sands of Peru, and rewarded the hospitality of the generous Incas with unblushing treachery and abuse, there were in that country evidences of wealth, talent and refinement truly remarkable; not only in the aspect and manners of the people themselves, but also in respect of their laws, their public works and their habitations. The government of Peru, before the advent of Europeans, was indeed a paternal one. The people were universally industrious and thrifty; living together in a state of almost Arcadian simplicity and happiness; while the country generally was eminently prosperous, yielding everything necessary to satisfy the moderate wants of its inhabitants. Implicit obedience to the ruling power was exacted; idleness in any form was not permitted; neither were any sick or enfeebled Peruvians allowed to languish for want of the common necessaries of life. The climate and the soil were all-sufficient, under proper industrial conditions, (including extensive systems of irrigation,) to supply the usual require-

ments of the people; yet they lacked one or two elements
which would have rendered their lot even happier; they
stood in need of absolute personal freedom and the facilities for speedy and distant travel.

As in Palestine so in Peru, if the people would obtain the
best results from their rich and volcanic soil. It became
necessary, in the prolonged absence of rain, to expend a
very ccnsiderable amount of labor in irrigating the fields, by
diverting the mountain torrents from their natural course,
and leading them to the thirsty plains, by means of numerous and massive aqueducts of stone. Nor were these
stupendous achievements the only enduring memorials of
the industry of that interesting nation. Contemporaneously
with the building of these myriads of elevated and meander-
ing water-ways, they erected palaces and temples of the
most unique and beautiful workmanship; leveled the tops
of hills into gardens; and hewed terraces, for agricultural
purposes, upon the rock-formed slopes of almost inaccessible mountains.

The seaports along the shores of the Pacific may continue
in undiminished prosperity; and the fine harbors of Valparaiso, Callao, Guayaquil and Panama may still bristle with
the masts of foreign ships; yet there will be plenty of support for a grand Longitudinal Railway on the eastern side of
the Andes; and branch lines will, soon or late, have to be
built to connect the same with Lima, Santiago, and other
west-Andean cities. Another impending crisis is near at
hand. The irrepressible Ironhorse will speedily eclipse
the stubborn mule and the weakly llama, the present
national beasts of burden, and will far excel them in docility,
obedience and service. What has been said of Peru, applies equally, or with but little modification, to its southern
neighbor, Chili. The war element, though slightly self-
disciplined, is ever in the ascendant there; and since the

declaration of the independence of Chili, in 1820, there have been almost incessant conflicts or quarrels between that country and Peru and Bolivia.

When the brave Bolivar first aroused the enthusiasm of his compatriots, and urged them to throw off the hated yoke of Spain, he instilled into their bosoms so great an amount of martial ardor, that it is apparently now inherent in all their descendants. Nevertheless, they do devote a considerable share of their time to spasmodic industry; and there is a large amount of business transacted through the ports of Antofogasta, Coquimbo and Talcahuano, which are fine commercial towns, enjoying much prosperity, but liable, like other localities along the coast, to frequent earthquakes. The very limited portion of the soil of Chili that comes within the influence of even occasional rain, is exceedingly fruitful; and the climate and scenery are delightful. In the deep valleys, fertilized by the melting snows from the mountains, magnificent crops can be raised; and much grain and flour and other breadstuffs are annually exported. The copper mines of Chili are very rich; and her vast stores of other mineral wealth are but in the infancy of their development. Chili and Peru are countries illustrating strange physical contrasts and extremes of temperature. For instance, the coast-deserts are exceedingly hot and sandy; while the mountain ranges are covered with perpetual snow. There is the boiling volcano, and here the ice-crowned summit;—everlasting winter above and incessant tropical summer below.

Even when the Three Americas Railway shall have reached the distant Strait of Magellan, commercial instinct and its best material representative, the enterprising merchant, will straightway follow up the attractive band of steel to its uttermost limits. Among the bleak and forbidding mountains of that Ultima Thule of civilization, lie vast

quantities of metallic treasure securely hidden in its rocky
bed, and only awaiting development by the hand of man;
while myriads of oleaginous monsters play in shoals around
its frowning coasts, furnishing ample supplies of oil and
whalebone, blubber, skins and ivory.   There is also to be
found, on the islands of those far-southern waters, guano of
excellent quality, to replenish our exhausted soils, and sufficient in quantity to freight whole fleets of ships.

The coming railway must not be regarded in the light of
a mere speculative undertaking, but as a stern national necessity.   It is a superb work, the successful inauguration of
which should awaken feelings of unbounded hope and pride
in every American breast.   By means of this it will be possible to make the journey from the northern to the southern
terminus of the line, in as many days as it will require
weeks—if not months—to go by water; and with infinitely
more comfort and satisfaction.   The saving of time alone
on this journey, together with its far greater safety, and the
enlivening interest which it cannot fail to awaken, will be
important factors in our calculations for either pleasure or
profit; and especially so to the majority of our active and
hard-pressed business men of to-day.   The multitudinous
array and miscellaneous character of the merchandise constantly streaming along this great commercial channel, will
form a most lively and attractive picture of international
traffic, ebbing and flowing with all the regularity of the
tides; and will doubly demonstrate the practical utility of
that mighty work.

The scenery in Central and South America is, in many
places, grand, exqui ite and romantic; and Nature there
appears on a larger and much more magnificent scale than
in most of the countries of Europe.   There are immense .
rivers, wonderful caverns, and stupendous mountains, whose
hoary heads are forever buried in fleecy clouds; immeasur-

able plains and tablelands thousands of feet above the level of the sea; roaring cataracts and eruptive volcanos, which belch forth their sulphurous vapors and lava with an awful display of subterranean force. Then there are frightful precipices overhanging the gloomiest gorges; and also some of the fairest and softest landscapes and rustic pictures of which the world can boast; where, in the green and smiling valleys, dotted by cheerful farm-buildings, well-tilled fields and blooming gardens, the sheep and cattle are feeding beside the sparkling streams in perfect quietness and peace. South America can also boast of astonishingly luxuriant forests, containing some of the largest specimens of animal and vegetable life; the most valuable timber, the brightest flowers and the richest minerals; the rankest poisons, and birds and butterflies of the most gorgeous plumage; some of the grandest representatives of the brute creation; and not a few of the most loathsome reptiles on the face of the earth. It is, in short, a country of boundless resources, and of rare contrasts on a grand and colossal scale. It is pre-eminently worthy of at least one visit, and of very careful study by all observant students of Nature.

With the means, comforts and appliances which modern science can command, a journey throughout the entire length of the two American continents, upon this greatest and best of all the world's highways, could be made with unexampled safety and expedition; and it certainly could not fail to be in the highest degree entertaining and instructive. What indeeed could be found more conducive to a vigorous recreation of both body and mind, or more gratifying to a really æsthetic taste, than the delightful privilege of traveling in well-appointed cars, in which every comfort and luxury for an extended tour would be provided, and witnessing from the open windows the ever-changing panorama, and the features, dresses, occupa-

tions and peculiarities of the people we pass by the way ?
It is quite probable that the valuable lessons in geology,
natural history, and the *savoir vivre* (genteel manners) of
society, which a young student might pick up, during a long
journey of this character, (stopping over occasionally, for a
day or two, at places especially worthy of examination,)
would be more than an equivalent for the money expended,
and add no little to the general knowledge which older passengers might possess.   Practical lessons these would be,
from Nature's charming volume ; imparted after her own
interesting and attractive fashion, and in a manner far more
acceptable to the minds of her students than when obtained
only through the dry and unsatisfactory medium of books.

On the way, in addition to the ever-varying scenery, at
one time grand and bordering on the sublime, and at another calm and peaceful, we may have many opportunities
for studying the formation of the rocks and the strange
tricks of the denizens of the forest and the lagoon, in their
own habitat.   We may recognize the terrible alligator, bask-
ing in the sun on the reedy banks of some stagnant pool,
and looking more like an inanimate log than a thing of life ;
the bald-headed and carrion-eating vulture, perched upon
his solitary rock, after having gorged himself with his un-
savory meal ; the patient llamas, tripping along with their
burdens, in single file, upon the very edges of the precipice ;
the ferocious puma, springing upon his prey ; and perchance
the great anaconda, strangling a deer or a kid for his sup-
per.   There are the agile and chattering monkeys, springing
from tree to tree, in the height of apparent enjoyment,
startling the gay-plumaged parrots and other birds, which
fly away to hide themselves within the more solemn recesses
of the forest, in which the deep silence is occasionally broken by the roar of the prowling panther, or the loud and
harsh screams of macaws and cockatoos.   Directing our

view upward toward the loftiest mountain peaks, we may distinguish with the naked eye, the great condor of the Andean world, like a tiny speck against the clear, blue sky, watching his quarry,—a graceful vicuna, perhaps, or a young alpaca, as it skips, innocent and unsuspecting, from rock to rock beneath that eagle-like and unavoidable glance. Amid all these scenes, when the snow-capped summits of yonder mountains are tinged with the warm glow of the departing sun, and the almost fathomless precipices along their rugged slopes are cast in deepest shadow, ere the first sweet herald of the night lights her twinkling lamp in the broad bosom of the firmament, few pictures on earth can compare with the one before us for grandeur, sublimity and peace.

How largely and how frequently, since their first invasion of these beautiful lands, has the Spanish exchequer been replenished from their South American possessions! How greatly have Chili, Peru, Mexico, and the Isthmus, contributed, from time to time, to the rapacious maw of the Iberian cormorant! What countless treasures yet lie hidden within the rocky fastnesses of that great Andean chain, only waiting for man's persevering industry, to satisfy his most sanguine expectations! How vast may be the accumulation of riches locked up within the adamantine breast of the giant Aconcagua alone, which raises its majestic head full 24,000 feet above the level of the sea! The very thought is bewildering. There are doubtless many other Potosis and Bonanzas yet undiscovered, which are destined to eclipse in fame and richness those already known. Capital, enterprise, and the facilities for transporting men, materials and powerful mining machinery, are now absolutely necessary to prosecute with greater energy the development of those inexhaustible mines.

There are many other important interests which a substantial railway, suitable for heavy mineral traffic, would sub-

serve.   Coal might be carried in large quantities direct from
the mines to depots established at Aspinwall. and Panama
respectively, for the use of the additional lines of steamers
which the increasing trade of the country would consequently demand.   Immense values in coin and treasure
would necessarily circulate to and fro, and seek the safest
and speediest route to their destination.   Goods from North
America, intended for shipment to any portion of South
America, could, in order to lessen the cost of freight, (if
time be no object,) be sent by steamer to Aspinwall, and
thence by the cars southward.   To the inhabitants of the
low-lying and unhealthy districts around the gulfs and bays
of Mexico, Honduras, Campeachy, and the Caribbean Sea,
a railway would prove an inestimable blessing by enabling
them to transfer themselves swiftly from their swampy and
fever-ridden surroundings near the coast, to the refreshing
altitudes of the table-lands.   It would also be a decided
benefit during the seasons when hurricanes prevail, and
when all shipping is exposed to infinite danger and delay.
As has already been remarked, the delightful plateaus, or
table-lands, yield grain and fruit in abundance, in addition
to valuable timber, such as oak, pine and cypress.   Here,
as elsewhere, all lands contiguous to the main or branch
lines of railway will respond to the increasing activity resulting from their establishment, and will add their quota of
support to the same.   Thus the Three Americas Railway
will prove itself a vehicle of prosperity to many districts at
present either isolated or ignored.

Mexico is among the most prolific in natural resources of
any portion of America; and few countries are blessed with
a finer climate than that on her elevated lands, or with
greater fertilility of soil, which, it may be stated, is more
than ordinarily volcanic.   The plateau of Anahuac is about
fifteen hundred miles in length, and some of the highest

mountains on the northern continent of America are found there. The city of Mexico itself stands 7,471 feet above the level of the sea. The table-lands of Mexico are a peculiar feature of that country, rising in step-like gradations until they reach a point midway between the two oceans, and then descending in a similar manner to the other side.

A word now about the Isthmus of Panama,—that little neck of land which unites the two large continents of America. How lovely is it in its wealth of waving foliage, choice fruits, and other tropical productions! How beautiful is Nature in all her forms as here represented! The Spaniards might well have called this narrow belt of land a Valparaiso,—a "Valley of Paradise;" and it would well have merited the designation. But the climate is rather unhealthy in portions of it, near the low-lying lands; and this greatly militates against its settlement by Europeans. During the construction of the present Trans-Isthmian Railway, coolie labor was procured at a high rate of wages; but the mortality from miasmatic and other causes was something fearful. Riches may be acquired in this region; but the risk, here and there, amounts almost to repulsion. What dazzling treasures of pearls and gold and silver fascinated the greedy eyes of Balboa and his unprincipled crew, when they first visited Darien and the adjacent shores!

The Three Americas Railway will itself, in the course of time, be regarded as a perfect Paradise for tourists; and a trip, from one end of our double continent to the other,—when traveling can be accomplished with so much comfort and celerity,—will be a treat to be looked forward to by millions. Such an exceedingly interesting journey, so full of incident and pleasure, combined with constant instruction, would amply repay, and more than repay, all travelers having time and money at their command. To the sporting

17

world, in all its branches, it offers rare opportunities for excellent shooting and fishing.   Whether one would hunt for either large game or small, in the forests, on the mountains, or upon the plains, the country presents irresistible attractions.   For artists and naturalists, students of Nature and philosophers, there is the fullest scope for the indulgence of their several gifts and predilections.   Lovers of the marvelous in nature will find, in the mighty rivers that intersect the country, in the gigantic mountains and the fierce volcanoes, in the dense forests and interminable plains, and in the unique appliances and different social characteristics of the various peoples of every clime, who inhabit this western hemisphere, sufficient to excite their admiration and tax their wondering powers to the utmost extent.

The lofty mountains of Mexico, scarcely less heaven-kissing than those of the Andean range, will also come in for a share of particular attention, and will be frequently visited by members of the different Alpine Clubs.   Surely there are not many climbers, but there are some who am-bition would carry them higher than 25,000 feet above the ocean's level; but such a grand height as that America can supply for their especial delectation.   Nature's most earnest students will not be content to rush at the highest speed through rocky pass or fertile plain ; nor will they be satisfied with a mere superficial examination of her particularly attractive features.   They will remain over at the different stations, to seek for new specimens, botanical or entomological, to decipher her indelible characters on the everlasting rocks, and to study well those wonderful registers whose records extend backward for thousands and thousands of years.

The opening up of direct water communication by means of a Ship Canal through either the Isthmus of Darien or that of Tehuantepec, would greatly tend to increase the trade of the United States with China, Japan, and the numerous islands of the Pacific. The latter route would be most attractive to North Americans on account of its situation; and as we may assume that the Darien Canal will be cut, if cut at all, by a French company, the choice, for people of our own continent, would seem to lie exclusively between the Nicaraguan route and that of Tehuantepec. The former isthmus is 173 miles across, and the latter 181 miles; and this latter possesses superior climatic advantages over the more southern ones. It has also the advantage of greater proximity to the southern and eastern ports of the United States. If Lakes Nicaragua and Leon and the rivers San Juan and Tipitapa could be fully and freely utilized, there would be only about a dozen miles of excavation between the latter river and the Pacific; but, all things considered, there are weighty reasons why the Tehuantepec canal should be preferred by North Americans. It is nearer to the mainland, healthier, and the cost of construction—should the water-stretches on the Nicaraguan route not be utilized—would be no greater. The trade of all the Gulf ports will undoubtedly increase very rapidly soon after their vessels shall find it possible to pass uninterruptedly through that great tide-level and interoceanic canal. It will be well to abandon every sentiment of undue sectionalism and centralization, in the interest of the whole country; so that all the ports along the American seaboard may be benefited equitably, if not equally, from the ramifications of its commerce. New Orleans, as the outlying port of the Mississippi, and the other ports on the Gulf, are especially worthy of national encouragement; for they have hitherto certainly made the most of any advantages they possessed; and as for St. Louis, Chicago, Cincinnati and the other large cities on the great rivers and lakes, it is confidently asserted that they are already capable of taking care of their own interests without extraneous aid.

It is evident that the manufacturing interests in the South and West are becoming very important; many cotton and woolen factories having been recently established; which, on account of cheaper raw materials, cheaper labor, and the considerable saving in carriage, can compete quite successfully with the northern mills. All these indications of substantial prosperity will be greatly improved and strengthened in time by the construction of the Three Americas Railway, and a free Ship Canal across the Isthmus of Tehuantepec,—or that of Nicaragua. By means of the canal, the trade of the United States with China, Japan, Australia and the Maylay Archipelago, from which countries such enormous quantities of tea, coffee, spices, and other costly produce are received, will assume increasing proportions.

Let us glance again at some of the territories, and the conditions of soil and climate, on the western shores of South America. In the eastern portions of Peru and Bolivia, cotton and sugar are largely cultivated; while wheat, maize and other cereals are also grown in rich abundance; besides a vast profusion of oranges, lemons, figs, grapes, nectarines, and other luscious fruits. To the east of Bolivia are extensive plains,—well adapted by nature for cither stock-raising or agriculture,—which run as far as the Argentine Republic, and thence to the Atlantic Ocean. The forests east of the Andes also furnish the justly celebrated cinchona bark, together with ebony, cedar, mahogany and other valuable woods. Among the mountains themselves immense mines of mineral wealth could be successfully worked for centuries without any perceptible diminution of their value.

The extensive plains lying between the larger South American rivers, the Amazon, the Orinoco, the Rio Negro, the Madeira, and their tributaries, are mostly composed of a rich alluvial soil, capable—where not liable to be flooded—

of producing the finest cereal crops in the world. These plains are more valuable than the gold mines themselves. In so vast a region, there is necessarily a considerable diversity of climate; but the general geography of the country exercises a greater influence in that respect than mere difference in latitude. The climate on the table-lands, elevated, for the most part, several thousand feet above the level of the sea, is temperate and healthy, and is remarkably well adapted to the growth of wheat; while the temperature of the low-lying districts and bottom lands is better suited to tropical and semi-tropical products. Taking that part of the continent, as a whole, it is a most valuable territory, which, as has already been stated, with a minimum of labor bestowed upon it, will yield a maximum of profit. This produce will find its way partly by water, and partly by land, to the great Longitudinal Line and the various branches which will be constructed, from time to time, to connect with it. It is a land which, in more energetic hands, will literally flow with milk and honey, and in all respects be ready to pay a willing tribute to the earliest cultivators. It is believed that, independently of all other produce, grain enough could be raised in those valleys to exceed the exports of California and Australia combined. On marshy lands and river bottoms, unsuited to the cultivation of wheat or maize, a very superior quality of rice, equal to that of the finest Carolina, can be largely and profitably grown; while on the drier lands, favored with frequent showers, or capable of irrigation, the best coffee, sugar and cotton can be raised in the greatest abundance.

It will be a grand and interesting metamorphosis, when the comparatively feeble and dilatory movements of the mule and the ox, as beasts of burden, shall be substituted by the strength and irrepressible energy of the Ironhorse; and when toilsome drudgery over rough and almost impassable roads shall be exchanged for the smooth and expedi-

tious track of shining steel.   Over such a road the locomotive, man's willing and untiring servant, will yet speed like
lightning through the greater portion of one hundred and
twenty degrees of latitude!   When the first news shall be
flashed along the far-extending wires, that the first sod of
the proposed railway has been cut, or the first shot fired on
the commencement of the most formidable tunnel, there
will be universal rejoicing throughout the land; but when
the exultant scream of the steam engine shall be heard
throughout the whole extent of the line, announcing to the
world the perfect triumph of man's labor and engineering
skill over the innumerable obstacles which have beset his
path during the whole process of the construction of this
ever-memorable work, it will be an event never to be forgotten, as a glorious consummation of energy and enterprise of which all who have in any way contributed to that
success may feel justly and honorably proud.   Moreover,
when the many prospective advantages to be reaped by the
world at large, and by the people of these two continents
in particular, by the successful completion of this railway,
shall be better understood and appreciated, as a work that
will bind together in sentiment and interest all the different
peoples of this Western Hemisphere, the extent of the benefits
in view will appear almost bewildering in their multiplicity and
grandeur.   Rivers of good results are likely to flow with resistless force from the introduction of this great developing and civilizing medium, which will irrigate the land with
perennial blessings, instead of the torrents of human blood
which have so long deluged its fruitful soil.

If the French people, whose government is always so
ready to foster and further great enterprises, think it worth
their while to spend hundreds of millions of francs in constructing a railway across the barren desert of Sahara, what
prosperity may we not reasonably expect from the completion of a scheme by which the moral, social and political

standard of at least a dozen populous nations, inhabiting two of the most fertile continents on the earth, will be permanently elevated and improved? In the course of a few years, perhaps, this startling Three Americas Railway project, which to certain feeble and irresolute minds may now appear impracticable, will be brought tó a glorious and successful issue, and will rightly be regarded as indispensable to the comfort and well-being of society; even as the electric telegraph, and the present transcontinental railroad systems are so considered to-day. The lands reclaimed through its instrumentality will be a net gain and acquisition to the districts to which they belong, and will far more than compensate for any aid granted to the undertaking.

That the respective municipalities and national governments interested in this superlative scheme will be willing, so soon as they clearly understand its aim and objects, to endorse it heartily, and to grant to it liberal subsidies in the shape of lands, money, labor, and materials, is, in view of the many inducements offered, altogether probable. The advantages are patent to every thoughtful mind; and it is sincerely to be hoped that the diplomatic representatives who may be appointed by the different Republics and other States, to negotiate upon the subject, will fully and promptly recognize the momentousness of their mission. Only the most stolid ignorance, or the grossest indifference and bigotry, can be proof against the powerful and trenchant arguments which may be readily and copiously adduced in support of a scheme which will eventually confer immeasurable material benefits upon all who are willing to participate in them. Jealousy, or groundless fear, may possibly delay the adhesion of some for a time; but wiser counsels will surely prevail in the end.

In return for the cession of territory and other helpful and necessary grants, certain equitable privileges may be conceded respectively to the several coöperating and contributing Republics and other States, as may be agreed upon by a majority of the delegates to an American International Railway Congress, or other body of commissioners, to be assembled so soon as all the preliminaries shall have been arranged. The stipulations might contain clauses to the effect that the contracting nationalities bind themselves, conjointly and separately, to guarantee the integrity of the railway itself, and also a certain space or strip of land on either side thereof, as civilly neutral territory forever, free from military occupation or encroachment, should war unfortunately break out between two or more of the contracting powers, or between revolutionary cliques or parties in any one of the concurring and coadjutant commonwealths. Any nation or faction violating these provisions should be at once regarded and treated as the common enemy of all the other signatories to the stipulations.

It is a difficult matter to restrain one's enthusiasm in writing upon a subject of such paramount importance and absorbing interest as Spanish America now presents in connection with this Three Americas Railway project, which, if it shall be carried out successfully, is destined, more than any other physical or moral agency, to revolutionize for good the existing state of things on two continents, to promote the development and expansion of their unexampled natural resources, and to assert the commercial and industrial supremacy of the United States. May this colossal undertaking, which promises such an abundant harvest of perpetual benefits and blessings to the three Americas and their scores of millions of inhabitants,—an undertaking so noble in its aims, so grand in its scope, and so worthy of the highest appreciation of the enlightened peoples who compose a mighty and invincible sisterhood of Republics, be earnestly and consistently supported, and ably and energetically prosecuted to a full and triumphant completion.

FROM ZONE TO ZONE.

A First-Prize Poem, on the Three Americas Railway, projected by Hinton Rowan Helper, of St. Louis, Missouri.

BY FRANK DEYEAUX CARPENTER,

(United States Engineer, Washington, District of Columbia.)

When any great design thou dost intend,
Think on the means, the manner, and the end.
—*Sir John Denham.*

FROM ZONE TO ZONE.

I.

As once, with tiny hands,
The pygmies bound the giant of the fable,
So men have bound the earth with iron bands
Of railway track and lines of ocean cable,
Which link us to the far Levantine lands.

The world is ours at last,
And captive to the hand and brain of science;
No more its unknown wastes and oceans vast
Shall daunt the traveler with their defiance,
As in the fearful, unprogressive past.

Now, in captivity,
How small it seems, how shrunken and diminished;
How changed from the expanse which Ptolemy
And Strabo left upon their maps unfinished,
And bounded only by the boundless sea.

Then the horizon lay
Around them like a curtain never lifted;
    The ruddy sunset sky and waters gray
Inclosed the realms to which the daylight drifted,
    And what was out beyond, no man could say.

What was beyond the West?
The people asked, but found no certain answer.
    What was beyond the ocean's convex crest
None knew except the poet and romancer,
    Who saw in dreams the Islands of the Blest,

And Islands Fortunate,
Which held the cities and the Fields Elysian;
    For then the broad earth could accommodate
The heaven and hell of priests' and poets' vision,
    Which we to-day on other spheres locate.

II.

With all these things unknown,
Can we but scorn the boastful Alexander,
    Who longed for other worlds to call his own,
Yet dared not leave the shores of his own land, or
    On other continents build up his throne?

O better, braver he,
The thoughtful Genoese, who, all undaunted,
    Sailed out upon the trackless Western Sea,
And, from that space by mythic people haunted,
    Redeemed this land which is our legacy.

What though he broke the spell
Of legend strange and beautiful tradition;
    No fiction of the fancy could excel
The wonders he discovered on his mission,—
    The riches of the country where we dwell.

What though the myths are fled;
The truth is yet more wondrous than the fable,
    And better than the Islands of the Dead
Are these Americas, where all are able
    To earn and eat in peace their daily bread.

    The home and social tie,
The wise provision for the coming morrow,
    Are better than the tents of those who lie
In happy dreams, but wake to bitter sorrow,
    With want and wretchedness to greet the eye.

    Utopia's great plan
Is more than realized in our completeness,
    For through Utopia no railway ran;
No steamship sailed its seas in strength and fleetness;
    No telegraph embraced it in its span.

    Our poorest citizen
Is richer than the chief of savage Indians,
    And richer than the kings of Europe when,
For chariots, the royal Merovingians
    Rode forth in ox-carts with their councilmen.

    By ship and railway car,
In comfort such as kings of old might covet,
    We journey, swift as birds of passage are,
Across the ocean and the land above it,
    And learn this great world's glories, near and far.

    Then who shall dare profess
To think that we are daily retrograding,
    And call our enterprise mere restlessness;
We profit more than lose by this abrading;
    Our lives are lengthened though our years be less.

III.

The railway is a tie
From State to State, and Nation unto Nation;
　　It breaks their barriers down, which were so high;
It cures the selfishness of isolation;
　　It turns the enemy to an ally.

　　Its rapid wheels ne'er find
Repose, but run through night and day unceasing,
　　While post-boys halt and stages lag behind,
And travelers perish in the winter's freezing,
　　Or in the desert, far from human kind.

　　It brings the absent one
To join the circle, once again united;
　　It brings the school-boy when his year is done;
It brings the guest, by wedding-bells invited;
　　It brings the mourner, when life's sands are run.

　　We are possessed of things
Of pleasure and of use we never thought of
　　In those old days when we were ruled by kings,—
Those old days, comfortless, when men knew naught of
　　The varied freight the railway carriage brings.

　　The richly laden car
Bears us the latest book and daily journal;
　　Dear words from friends who live in lands afar;
Sweet fruits from climates which are ever vernal;
　　Bright stuffs from cities where the merchants are.

　　And cityward once more
Comes with the corn and meat of Western prairies;
　　Coal from the mine's black depths, and precious ore;
The golden products of a thousand dairies;
　　And autumn's harvest from the farmer's store.

So go the ways of trade,
And merchant and producer, each is richer;
    For, by the railway's swift and certain aid,
He finds himself endowed with blessings which are
    Brought to his door and on his threshold laid.

IV.

Now from the east to west,
And westward round unto the east returning,
    Apparently in eager, fruitless quest
Of that bright land where sunset fires are burning,
    The railways circumscribe the earth's broad breast.

Still, as in days of yore,
The path of commerce runs with the equator;
    As if the merchants, all the wide world o'er,
Yet imitate the daring navigator
    Who first sailed west in search of India's shore.

At last our empire's course
Has found a limit by the wide Pacific;
    To farther go would be to reach the source
Of humankind, now crowded and prolific,
    From which we seek already a divorce.

And yet it seems unknown
That in the South lie our best fields for barter;
    The trader's route should be from zone to zone,
And to some far and yet untrodden quarter,
    Where other wares are made and fruits are grown.

·Where glows the Southern Cross
There is a new world for the Anglo-Saxon,
    Whose treasures, vast and varied, run to loss
Until the Northman's auburn hair and flaxen
    Shall mingle with the Spaniard's raven gloss.

Where flows the lost Xingu,
Through regions which the foot of white invader
　　Has never touched, are savage people who
Have waited long for some intrepid trader
　　To take their gold and leave his goods in lieu.

　　The Amazonian plain
Is wild as in the days of Orellana;
　　Its forests yield their products, but in vain
Are cocoa, caoutchouc, orange, and banana,
　　If none are there to gather and to gain.

　　To that new land must go
Our Progress by the western ocean thwarted;
　　Already it is heard in Mexico,
With noise of mines in mountains silver-hearted,
　　And stamps of quartz-mills in the vales below.

　　Brave men of enterpise,
It is for you to guide this march and lead it.
　　Go build your railroad, and there will arise
New cities to support it and to need it;
　　Along the railway riches crystallize.

V.

　　From Oregon to Maine,
From Maine far southward to the shores of Texas
　　The railways interlink and form a chain;
The chains are interlinked in one great plexus,
　　Which stops, however, on the Texan plain.

　　Are we so timid, then,
As not to dare to leave our territory?
　　And are we children of those mighty men
Who crossed the seas and won eternal glory,
　　As pioneers with plough and sword and pen?

The nations all await
Our coming, with their portals opened freely;
　　They are Republics, each our sister State,
And down the world, from Mexico to Chili,
　　The railway's mutual commerce should pulsate.

　　The route is found with ease;
As though by Nature's kind coöperation
　　The Isthmus is a dike between the seas,
And road-bed ready built for occupation
　　By whatsoever band of men shall please.

　　Now lost and waste it stands,
The heritage of bravos who retain it;
　　O haste the day when sturdy Northern hands
Shall conquer this wild region and shall chain it,
　　And civilize it with the railway's bands.

　　With traffic's pulse replete,
The Isthmus then shall rouse to useful living,
　　And tremble with the tread of busy feet;
For commerce is a nation's blood, life-giving,
　　And here the trade of all the world shall meet.

　　Beneath this railway's span
Shall lie, some day, the great canal, whose function
　　Shall be to speed our ships on to Japan,
And make this spot the most important junction
　　And greatest cross-roads ever known to man.

VI.

　　Is this too rash a scheme?
Few plans are rash in these progressive eras.
　　A life-time back, and who would dare to deem
Pacific Railways other than chimeras?
　　Yet the results have far surpassed the dream.

It may seem very far,
But distances have changed since by-gone ages;
    The daily journeys of our fathers are
Accomplished now in easy hourly stages,
    All through the magic of the railway car.

    As miles are told to-day,
Along the level railway designated,
    We would be near to South America:
But now, though joined, yet are we isolated;
    She is our neighbor, yet so far away.

    Our ships which thither sail
Make voyages irregular, uncertain;
    Their trips are tardy and of slight avail.
Sometimes the tempest's dark and dreadful curtain
    Enfolds them, and they perish in the gale;

    Sometimes, in sultry bays,
The sailors, one by one, die of the fever;
    Sometimes, upon the ocean's broad highways,
The ship, becalmed, feels all the breezes leave her
    To rock in idleness for many days.

    Discouraged, in despair,
Our captains turn their barques to better uses,
    Abandoning this field of barter, where
Old Europe gains the trade our country loses,
    Because our railway has not entered there.

    All Europe's marts combine
To heap their wharves with traffic's box and barrel.
    The fields of France contribute food and wine;
The looms of England furnish their apparel;
    While our own trade and industries decline.

VII.

From where St. Louis lies,—
Some day to be metropolis and center
    Of this the fairest land beneath the skies,—
Our railway, like an artery, shall enter
    The hearts of other nations with its prize'

Of foreign freight and thought,
New truths to take the place of superstition,
    Ideas on the tide of travel brought,
Inventions made to better man's condition,
    And wisdom by the sage and statesman taught.

We are Republics all,
In one long series, side by side extended ;
    Apostles of new faiths political
Which our forefathers published and defended
    In battle-smoke and legislative hall.

Since it is therefore meet
That we should be in brotherhood united,
    The railway forms a union more complete
Than treaties by diplomatists indited
    In words of subtle meaning and deceit.

The railway will bring peace
To countries long accustomed to disorders,
    Which then will find in commerce a release
From foreign wars which devastate their borders,
    And from internal strifes will find surcease.

Their citizens will gain
At last a rest from fratricidal clamors,
    And hear, instead, prosperity's refrain,—
The farmer's whistle and the smithy's hammers,
    And sound of lowing cattle on the plain.

The engine's shrill halloo,
As faithfully it comes upon its mission,
    Will tell the flight of time in accents true,
And teach the use of promptness and precision
    To all the country that it passes through.

The engine's heavy tread
Shall press the ruins of the Incas' Palace,
    Where art and artist both alike lie dead;
And roll above the fallen Teocallis
    By Aztecs built in ages that have fled.

Lands of these ancient folk
Shall live again, through traffic's channels nourished.
    Their sons shall throw off priestcraft's hood and cloak,
And they shall flourish as of old they flourished
    Before they felt the Spaniard's heavy yoke.

VIII.

To this great thoroughfare
Shall flow, upon a thousand tributaries,—
    To meet and mingle and be traded there,—
The products of the pampas and the prairies,
    And those which Orinoco forests bear.

The road which Meiggs designed
Shall be continued o'er the Cordillera,
    Beyond whose walls Bolivia is confined;
While, through the jungles of the dark Madeira,
    A second outlet to the east shall wind.

Through lofty mountain pass,
Through hidden groves of mango and anana,
    Shall come commodities of every class.
The rhubarb, jalap, ginger, and cinchona,
    Whose harvests graceful Indian girls amass;

The coffee of Brazil;
The precious woods and useful which are found there;
The healing herbs which benefit the ill;
The undeveloped riches which abound there
In valleys that are undiscovered still;

The tea of Paraguay,—
Their forest tea, which few abroad have tasted;
The ruddy cochineal, the saffron dye,
The essences and gums which now are wasted
Because no one to gather them is nigh;

The spices rich and rare,
The pepper and the clove of the Guianas;
The nuts and fruit which are decaying there
Upon the lordly palm and low ananas,
Whose fragrant apples scent the summer air;

The cotton and the cane;
The mandioca, tonka, and vanilla;
The nitrates which the nations strive to gain;
The coats of the alpaca and chinchilla;—
All these shall freight the future railway train.

IX.

By snowy mountain side
And plains o'ershadowed by the peaks Andean,
Within whose molten hearts great treasures hide,
From Chili northward to the Caribbean,
The garnered wealth of trade shall swiftly ride,

And meet, along the way,
The loads of merchandise we send in payment,
Extending southward in a rich array.
Our mills shall weave them fabrics for their raiment;
Our stores supply their markets every day.

Our cunning hands shall fill
Their homes with things of comfort, use, and splendor,
    With works of art and scientific skill.
Our farms shall give their grain to the fazenda;
    Our shops shall furnish axe and plough and drill.

Our furnace-fires shall make
The busy nights' horizon red and rosy
    While shaping new machinery for their sake.
Our pumps shall drain the mines of old Potosi;
    Our boats shall sail on Titicaca's lake.

Their engine-wheels shall run
On tracks of steel and iron from our forges.
    By mills of ours their grinding shall be done;
Our spans shall bridge their mountain streams and gorges,
    When once the railway joins us, twain in one.

X.

These benefits are few
Of those to come from the transfer and movement
    Of men of ours to stock these lands anew,—
Of men with zeal to aid the world's improvement,
    With brain to plan great works, and will to do.

Our civil engineers
Shall tunnel through their mountains' rocky layers,
    And build their aqueducts, their docks, and piers;
Their country shall be mapped by our surveyors,
    And settled by our hardy pioneers.

Soon will our West be filled,
Soon must our surplus people, by the million,
    Seek elsewhere for a place to plough and build;
Then they shall find, upon the plains Brazilian,
    A farm for each, untaken and untilled.

The city's crowded throng,
The laborer, the clerk, and the mechanic,
    Shall there find refuge from a master's wrong,
In homes secure from poverty and panic,
    In lands where summer lasts the life-time long.

    For how can hunger harm
Where Nature's choicest fruits are ever growing ?
    There are both food and shelter in the palm;
And, with the softest breezes ever blowing,
    What need is there of fuel to be warm ?

    And there in winter-time,
By fragrant ways along the leafy Isthmus,
    The invalid shall seek a milder clime,
And find it where the showy Flower of Christmas
    Is blooming while our fields are white with rime.

    Or, where the llanos rise
In terraced plains, from sea to summit, giving
    All climates that the zones of earth comprise,
A morning ride will change one's place of living
    From tropic shores to realms of snow and ice.

XI,

    Of all things that are sure,
The railway must be built there, soon or later.
    Our ships are slow, and, prison-like, immure
Their passengers becalmed on the Equator,
    In sickness which the land alone can cure.

    Why then this long delay ?
Is it to count the cost and linger o'er it ?
    And know ye not the railroad paves the way
Of its advance, and smooths the ground before it
    With profits that are earned from day to day ?

Who build to Mexico
Will find there, in her mines and merchants' coffers,
    Repayment of the cost they undergo,
And means to traverse lands beyond, whose offers
    Invite them to the hemisphere below.

All honor then be paid
To those, the brave, sagacious, and clear-sighted,
    Whose hands shall be the first to sink the spade
In this great labor, which shall be requited
    In riches gathered in the paths of trade.

XII.

And honor hundredfold
To him who gives this work his life's endeavor,
    With zeal unstained by sordid greed of gold.
His name shall stand in history forever,
    With Humboldt, Eads and Lesseps there enrolled.

It is such men as he,
The daring thinkers and the earnest actors
    Who build new roads and search the unknown sea,
That are the world's best friends and benefactors,
    Outranking diplomatesand soldiery.

What matter though he hear
The pedant's protest and the fool's derision,
    The scoff of shallow minds and faint hearts' fear;
Such doubts are vain to darken the prevision
    Of one who sees the future, far and clear.

No thought nor care for gain,
No foolish wish for glory's gilded letter,
    Have bought these efforts of his heart and brain;
But only that the world may be the better
    For one who has not spent his life in vain.

So may the railway run
That he may live to hear this message given
    To all the waiting nations 'neath the sun:
'The golden spike which marks the end is driven;
    The Three Americas are joined in one."

STATISTICS OF SPANISH AMERICA.

NATURE knows no pause in progress and development; she attaches her anathema on all inaction.—*Goethe.*

DIVISIONS, AREA AND POPULATION OF SPANISH AMERICA.

Names, Area, and Population, respectively, of the fifteen Republics of Spanish America, in 1880.

COUNTRIES.	AREA.	POPULATION.
Mexico, - - - - - -	761,603	9,466,209
Guatemala, - - - - -	44,800	1,342,868
Honduras, - - - - -	58,168	396,660
Salvador, - - - - - -	7,500	447,221
Nicaragua, - - - - -	58,206	361,479
Costa Rica, - - - - -	21,495	328,384
Columbia, - - - - -	467,220	2,904,823
Venezuela, - - - - -	401,580	1,883,446
Ecuador, - - - - - -	248,577	1,038,563
Peru, - - - - - - -	512,682	2,893,676
Bolivia, - - - - - -	496,241	1,827,809
Chili, - - - - - - -	338,870	2,211,345
Paraguay, - - - - -	71,223	644,148
Uruguay, - - - - -	68,792	537,601
Argentina, * - - - - -	1,556,629	3,136,932.
Totals, - - - - -	5,113,586	29 421,164
Brazil - - - - - -	3,140,202	11,360,448
Guiana, (all) - - - - -	163,413	378,926
United States, - - - -	3,603,884	50,152,866

* The Argentine Republic, including Patagonia and the Gran Chaco.

COMMERCE OF SPANISH AMERICA.

Value of the Exports and Imports of the fifteen Spanish American Republics, respectively, in 1880.

COUNTRIES.	Total value of Exports.	Total value of Imports.
Mexico, - - - - - - -	$ 38,411,93:	$ 36,854,663
Guatemala, - - - - - -	5,162,426	4,726,484
Honduras, - - - - - -	1,404,379	1,385,738
Salvador, - - - - - -	3,993,267	2,672,399
Nicarauga, - - - - - -	1,867,108	1,943,244
Costa Rica, - - - - -	6,740,877	4,983.337
Columbia, - - - - - -	11,422,338	8,695,123
Venezuela, - - - - -	17,908,682	16,582,707
Ecuador, - - - - - -	5,826,664	3,212,516
Peru,* - - - - - -	69,314,730	37,420,352
Bolivia, - - - - - -	4,268,913	5,880,424
Chili, - - - - - -	44,662,314	39,837,391
Paraguay, - - - - - -	594.147	841,915
Uruguay, - - - - - .. -	18,378,565	15,219,631
Argentina, - - - - - -	48,786,209	43,607,880
Total, - - - - - -	$278,742,551	$223,863,804
Brazil, - - - : - - -	$ 89,473,714	$ 98.396,460
Guiana, (all) - - - - -	18,279,604	12,816.962
United States - - - - -	$ 852,786,053	$ 760,989,154

* Including exportations of guano and nitrate of soda from Peruvian territory—by. Peru and Chili.

UNITED STATES TRADE WITH SPANISH AMERICA.

Value of Exports to, and Imports from, the United States, by the fifteen Spanish American Republics, respectively, in 1880; not embracing any amount of the precious metals, in any case, but limited exclusively to merchandise.

COUNTRIES.	Exports to the United States.	Imports from the United States.
Mexico,	$ 5,864,648	$ 6,793,586
Guatemala,	590,314	422,789
Honduras,	327,266	284,808
Salvador,	428,783	313,262
Nicaragua,	234,607	147,129
Costa Rica,	842,171	321,616
Columbia,	6,487,269	5,870,418
Venezuela,	4,993,860	3,363,833
Ecuador,	481,212	229,665
Peru,	1,916,839	1,411,547
Bolivia,	274,968	139,822
Chili,	766,307	1,607,498
Paraguay,	94,526	46,912
Uruguay,	1,829,493	1,038,924
Argentina,	3,780,502	2,382,346
Totals,	$28,912,765	$24,374.155
Brazil,	$ 51,388,610	$ 8,291,817
Guiana, (all)	2,267,898	2,041,737

By reference to the foregoing statistics, it will be observed that our importations from Brazil alone, amount to about seventeen million dollars more than our exportations to all the countries of Spanish and Portuguese America! To this ominous balance of trade against us, (principally for coffee) in the strengthening of an imperial and slavery-sustaining power—like the portentous balance of trade against us (chiefly for sugar from Cuba) in support of monarchical and bondage-enforcing Spain—it behooves us to give immediate and earnest attention. Our entire patronage for the two great luxuries mentioned above, should be transferred, at the earliest possible period, to the free and republican nationalities of Mexico and Central and South America; yet there is now no prospect of our ever being able to make such an eminently desirable, and necessary transfer, except by means of the projected Three Americas Railway.　　　　H. R. H.

REVENUES, EXPENDITURES AND PUBLIC DEBTS
OF SPANISH AMERICA.

Revenue, Expenditure, and Public Debt, of the fifteen Spanish American Republics, respectively, in 1880.

COUNTRIES.	Revenue.	Expenditure.	Public Debt.
Mexico,	$ 21,270,000	$ 23,845,000	*$386.492,000
Guatemala,	5,626,000	5,344,000	4,328,000
Honduras,	558,000	533,000	36,743,000
Salvador,	1,420,000	1,906,000	1,319,000
Nicaragua,	2,715,000	2,880,000	3,874,000
Costa Rica,	4,202,000	4,492,000	12,623,000
Columbia,	6,846,000	7 781,000	16,718,000
Venezuela,	7,248,000	6,830,000	67,122.000
Ecuador,	2,809,000	4,117,000	23,867,000
Peru,	23,408,000	30,390,000	242,388,000
Bolivia,	4,821,000	6,184,000	30,454,000
Chili,	21,796,000	27,643,000	86,916,000
Paraguay,	418,000	476,000	† 234,638,000
Uruguay,	11,735,000	10,841,000	48,227,000
Argentina,	22,448,000	23,716,000	62.414,000
Totals.	$137.320,000	$156,978,000	1,258.123,000
Brazil,	$ 54,128.000	$ 73,847,000	$ 408,216,000
Guiana, (all)	2,326,000	2,197,000	11,572,000
U'ted States	$ 333,526,611	$ 267,642,958	$2,120,415,379

*Much the greater part of this Mexican debt, having been due to England, France and Spain, has been repudiated, because of the atrocious attempt of those European Powers, during the reign and under the machinations of the charlatan Napoleon III, and while we ourselves were in the most stressful period of our civil war in the United States—and therefore but imperfectly able to assert and maintain our position on the Monroe doctrine—to impose on Mexico, under the odious adventurer, Maximilian, of Austria, a monarchical form of government.

†Paraguay was but recently involved in this overwhelming debt, principally through the vaulting ambition and folly of her military monster, Lopez, in the disastrous war which, for five years, from April, 1865, to March, 1870, he waged at once against his three antagonists, the Argentine Republic, Uruguay and Brazil.

RAILROADS AND TELEGRAPHS IN SPANISH AMERICA.

Miles of Railroads and Telegraphs completed and in operation in the fifteen Spanish American Republics, respectively, in 1880.

COUNTRIES.	Miles of Railroads.	Miles of Lines of Telegraphic Wires.
Mexico,	863	8,670
Guatemala,	122	1,268
Honduras,	58	696
Salvador,	26	320
Nicarauga,	—	287
Costa Rica,	84	398
Columbia,	112	2,143
Venezuela,	78	466
Ecuador,	67	278
Peru,	1,803	2,240
Bolivia,	34	488
Chili,	1,116	4,633
Paraguay,	45	127
Uruguay,	261	776
Argentina,	1,829	4,741
Total,	6,498	27.731
Brazil,	1,794	4,462
Guiana, (all)	23	189
United States	92,628	109,220
British America,	7,487	14,346
Insular America,	1,039	4,206
Europe,	104,313	269,717
Asia,*	11,104	38,218
Africa,†	2,876	13,920
Oceania.§	4.912	34.380

*Chiefly within British India.
†Principally within Egypt, Algeria and Cape Colony.
§Mostly within Australia and New Zealand.

BRAZIL'S PERFIDIOUS FORFEIT-
URE OF FRIENDLY REGARD.

IN a free government there is much clamor, with little suffering ; in a
despotic country there is little complaint, but much suffering.—*Carnot*.

SHOW me a people whose transactions are dishonest, and I will
show you a people whose religion is a sham.—*Carlyle*.

PARTICULARLY on account of the odious evils of monarchy and slavery in Brazil, and also on account of the inde-
scribable depressions and abasements caused there by the
vile priesthood of the Romish religion, the exact position of
that nationality in relation to the projected Three Americas
Railway had long been with me a matter of serious and in-
decisive consideration, until early in the year 1876, when
Mrs. Helen M. Fiedler, a worthy and widowed citizen of the
United States, offered to me the management of her clearly
rightful claim against the government of the Emperor Dom
Pedro II. After familiarizing myself with the very obvious
facts and merits of that reclamation (the details of which
have recently been published in a separate volume and presented to the Congress of the United States, which has been
formally memorialized upon the subject,) I immediately predetermined that, so far at least as I was concerned, the Empire of Brazil should stand or fall by its own future action
toward my injured and unredressed client. More than once
Brazil had already officially proceeded in the case, with the
grossest subterfuge and injustice ; and she has since perpetrated the unpardonable wrong of reaffirming and defend-

ing the whole course of her transparently unlawful and immoral conduct.   Hedged about with a monarchical form of government absolutely anomalous and out of place in America, Brazil has taken her position ; I have taken mine ; we shall see which will stand the firmer and the longer under the invisible equities and destinies which control nations and individuals.

It has been more than once intimated, if not positively asserted, that it is an exeedingly difficult task for even the blandest and best-intentioned philanthropist to bless certain needy but idiosyncratic individuals.   How much more difficult it has been for me, not being a philanthropist of any sort, but only an average sort of man, of common sense and common justice, to bless Brazil by well-meant correspondence and interviews with her Emperor Dom Pedro II and the head of his Home Ministry, the history of the Fiedler claim will plainly attest.   My own judgment, whatever may be believed of any other man's, is fallible, and my thoughts may not be perfectly well founded in this case ; but it is my candid opinion, nevertheless, that Brazil, as an Empire, has irretrievably lost the opportunity of earning and securing the choicest blessing ever yet placed within her reach ; and it may now behoove her, amid the confusion of her great guilt, to avoid, if she can, a blessing's antithesis. It may be, though, and it is by no means improbable, that, as a sort of final issue of this affair, the loss of the Empire will prove the gain of the Republic,—the Republic of Brazil ; and if so, both happenings will ultimately afford occasion for the most profound and prolonged rejoicing among all right-thinking and well-acting Americans, whether of South America, of Central America, or of North America. Meanwhile, let the railway of railways be built with such wholesome deflection to the west of the western boundaries of the Empire of Brazil, that all the Spanish-speaking Re-

publics of America, following the example of the United
States, shall respectively and speedily become rich, populous and powerful; and then, if not before, the broad valley of the Amazon, and other misgoverned lands adjoining,
may be easily reclaimed from the rickety and ruinous rule
of royalty.   Placidly, contentedly, confidently is the Fiedler
claim held in abeyance.   If not paid in one way, it being
just and legal, it must be paid in another.   Twice, thrice,
ever so many times, has this valid and equitable reclamation
been rejected by the Brazilian Empire; it is now preparing
to await, if necessary, the action of the Brazilian Republic.

Other and abler artists than the projector of the Three
Americas Railway have drawn the truest and most striking
pictures of Brazil; and some of Brazil's delineations of
herself present conspicuously the features of easily recog-
nizable portraiture.   Several of the paintings thus alluded
to, though they appear only in words, are exhibited upon a
score or more of the following pages; and if studied well,
they will be found full of meaning for all those, whether natives or foreigners, who may have occasion to acquire a
more adequate knowledge of the country.   In reference to
Brazil's so-called religion, the Catholic, the projector aforesaid is quite willing to have everything which he himself
has written upon the subject, accounted as of no importance whatever, though it is all strictly true; but, as a Protestant of Protestants, he protests against the folly and
wrong of ignoring the wisdom of Thomas Jefferson, Thomas
Ewbank, Wm. H. Seward, Prof. John Fiske, Jean Baptiste
Say, Adam Smith, John Stuart Mill, John William Draper,
Godfrey Higgins, Herbert Spencer and others, herein
quoted, whose deep erudition entitles them to the profound
respect of all fair-minded men.

The questions of ecclesiasticism and jesuitry as they exist in Spanish and Portuguese America,—but more especi-

ally as they exist in the latter,—are rapidly assuming such
portentous dimensions that it is impossible to overlook them
in any well-considered views which may be advanced for
the betterment of those naturally magnificent portions of
the New World.   It is no more meet that Mussulmanism
should be suppressed in Turkey, that Mormonism should be
crushed out of Utah, and that Voodooism should be done
away with in Ashantee, than that both Catholicism and
Monarchy should be at once and forever extirpated from
Brazil.   A still wider, an almost world-wide, range of view
might be taken of these questions pertaining to the progress-
retarding and State-destroying tendencies of Catholicism.
It would be an easy matter to point to Poland, to Hungary,
to Ireland, to Italy, to Spain, to Portugal, and to lift the
veil from the enervation and poverty and famine and beggary and desolation which everywhere result from the fatal
superstitions and tyrannies which, soon or late, Catholicism
invariably inflicts upon every community of its dupes.

While it is true that the Empire of Brazil has fewer
political revolutions than any of the Republics of South
or Central America, it is equally true that her apparent
peace is not peace in fact, not the peace of a healthy and
energetic organism, but only an anæsthetic pathway to decay and death.   In proportion to its size, its age and its
opportunities, there is not a Republic under the sun that is
not far more prosperous and progressive than the sable and
sluggish Empire of Brazil.   The foremost and most powerful countries to-day are Protestant countries ; and if the
Protestant countries themselves were still more protestant,
more rational and more liberal, they would be still further
advanced in all matters and things essential to the well-
being of mankind.   It is only the Protestant countries which
are, in a pefect sense, truth-telling and honor-observing
countries, industrious and thrifty conntries, educated and

scientific countries, inventive and enterprising countries, banking and money-lending countries, like the United States of America, Great Britain, Germany, Holland, Sweden and Switzerland;—and latterly, as she is fortunately becoming both Republican and Protestant, France, brave and beautiful France, whose master-minds, for the last two hundred years at least, have been actively and effectively antagonistic to the preposterous pretentions of popery.

H. R. H.

MR. HELPER TO THE EMPEROR DOM PEDRO II.

[As written and held in readiness for submission to His Imperial Majesty's judgment, but never read nor delivered nor sent to him, for the reason that His Imperial Majesty and his unworthy Ministers of State were not pleased to comply with the conditions of justice, which the writer had distinctly made in many previous communications respecting the Fiedler Claim against Brazil.—*H. R. H.*]

RIO DE JANIERO, October 12, 1877.

TO HIS IMPERIAL MAJESTY DOM PEDRO II,

Emperor of Brazil:

SIRE: Coming now, in this manner, concordantly with my letter of yesterday, to an explanation of the nature of my subordinate and confidential business here, in connection with the Fiedler claim against Brazil, I have the honor to venture the remark, that, if I am not laboring under the spell of an egregious error of judgment, your Majesty will hardly fail to recognize at once the unequalled magnitude and importance of the enterprise to which I have already alluded, in several previous communications, when I inform you that it looks to nothing less than the construction, within thirteen or fourteen years from to-day, of a double-track railway, of first-class materials and workmanship, from the

19

southwestern part of Canada, or from southern Manitoba, or from the western shores of Hudson Bay, to that particular part of Southern Patagonia bounded or divided by the Strait of Magellan,—right down along or near the longitudinal centers of North and Central and South America, with lateral lines leading to the capitals of all the nationalities through which the main trunk will pass. At a later period, perhaps, yet probably not later than two or three generations hence, extensions may, for the profit and well-being of all concerned, be made northwestwardly through British America and Alaska to Behring Strait, and southwardly through Tierra del Fuego to Beagle Channel, and possibly beyond, even to Cape Horn.

Animated as she is by the liberal spirit of the most enlightened statesmanship of modern times, Brazil, I am fully persuaded, will look with none the less but rather the more favor on this project, because it aims at the improvement and elevation of other nations as well as herself. Brazil will be benefitted and advanced, and in no way injured, by a degree of welfare on the part of her sister States corresponding with her own prosperity; and as with Brazil, in this respect, so also with all the other Commonwealths, a dozen or more, which are to be leagued and linked and locked together in inviolable unity, comity and reciprocity, as the happy recipients, during all the ages to come, of the brilliant honors and advantages which will accrue to them from ownership in, and connection with, the largest and best railroad on the face of the earth; a skillfully constructed railroad, of steel and other superior substances, and of double-track width and facility, which, lying midway between the two great oceans of the world, will grandly and conspicuously utilize and enrich the length, yes, and breadth as well as length, of two continents to a distance, in length alone, of nearly or quite eight thousand miles! If the uniquely outstretching and far-extending intercontinental railway thus contemplated should ever be constructed all the way from Behring Strait to Cape Horn, or from a particular point to a specified locality in proximity to those widely-separated places respectively, following the deflections suggested in the last foregoing paragraph, then the entire length of the road will be not less than ten thousand miles!

Besides the almost incalculable advantages of a material nature which this road, with its great Brazilian branch, will bring to the vast dominions of your Majesty, to Brazil will also belong the honor of having been the place where the idea of building it originated; for my first thought on the subject (whilst writhing under the tortures of a terrible attack of seasickness, during a three days' tempest, sixty miles or so off the coast of Brazil, in the very latitude of Rio de Janeiro, in November, 1866, I being then in the course of my first return from the Argentine Republc to the United States,) was only suggestive of a road from Rio de Janeiro to New York; and from that thought, good as it was in itself, but less feasible, has been gradually evolved the immensely larger and better scheme here partly presented.

It is but reasonable to hope and believe that, directly and indirectly, by an adequately elongated straightforwardness of the main stem, and by a judicious deflection of its branches, the railway thus projected is to become a general diffuser of peace, prosperity and plenty throughout most of the larger and better portions of the New World. Yet, in the very nature of things, Brazil in South America, and the United States in North America, will probably be greater gainers by the road (though not, it may be supposed, in proportion to territory,) than any other two countries. It is believed, moreover, that by the general and dextrous use of certain of the latest and best inventions in the art of rail-road-building, the vast system of railways here contemplated can be constructed at less cost per mile (on the average, and in comparison of conditions of Nature and quantities and qualities of performance,) than any similar work that has ever yet been done in any part of South America.

This, then, thus briefly, is the most significant part of the outline of the enterprise which, with all due deference, I have the honor to submit for the consideration of your Majesty; and for the consummation of which, including the eastern and western branches of the main road, the enormous sum of three hundred millions of dollars, more or less, will probably be required; every dollar of which amount can, I think, at the proper time, and under proper guarantees of interest,—at a rate not exceeding six per cent. per annum, proportionately divisible in its obligations among all the nations to be benefitted by the road,—be easily raised in the United States.

Only there are certain somewhat voluminous, and as yet incomplete details (such as showing specifically how the several States of South and Central America and Mexico may, respectively in one or two or more ways, for their own advantage, bear a fair ratio of the burden of the undertaking,) concerning which I do not deem it necessary to venture a definite or written opinion at this time. A fitter time, not more than two or three years hence, (nearly eleven years already have I silently studied these problems,) will, I trust, afford me the occasion to present, in a well-digested and practical form, all the details to which I have here and elsewhere referred.

Meanwhile, in order that I may be free and able to work out these details in the best possible manner,—a task by no means simple, nor exempt from either labor or expense,—I only ask that your Majesty will be good enough to do now, or cause to be done, what it is but right that Brazil should do in any event, even though she should be found to be wholly disregardful of the gigantic scheme here submitted for her betterment, and for making all American interests mutually convergent and helpful to each other; and that is to command, or at least recommend, speedy justice to my client.

Let the Fiedler claim be paid.   It is a just claim, already of nearly ten years' standing, and might certainly, with all propriety, have been paid long before this time.   The entire sum due on this claim, with interest, at six per cent. per annum, from the date of Chevalier Fleury's advice to Mr. Fiedler to abandon the voyage, December 18, 1867, up to the 18th instant, October 18, 1877, amounts to only $31,-800; and this, too, to a citizen of the United States, a country which bought from Brazil, last year coffee and other South American products of the value of nearly $46,000,-000; while Brazil bought from the United States, during the same time, North American products of the value of but little more than $7,000,000.   So that with a mere fraction, so to speak, of the enormous balance of trade against us, as between the United States and herself, Brazil can easily pay off this obligation.

For Brazil's sake, for the claimant's sake, and, above all, for the sake of justice itself, cause this ten years' claim to be paid within the next two months, (why not within the next two weeks?) and I can then promise at least a fair possibility, radient with the roseate hues of probability, that your Majesty may, on a certain Saturday morning, not more than fourteen years hence, take a special train from Rio de Janeiro, and arrive in New York, amid demonstrations of the most hearty welcome, in the afternoon or evening of the following Saturday, if not sooner.   Besides, your fare and other general accommodations, all along the route, shall be quite as good as those obtainable in any of the better sort

of hotels ; and in thus making an overland pleasure excursion from the greatest city in South America to the greatest
city in North America, your Majesty will, in 1891, a little
earlier or a little later, unlike your Majesty in 1876, avoid a
long voyage, seasickness, storms at sea, and all the other
discomforts and perils incident to ocean travel.

It is intended that the numerous sections of the unmatched and unmatchable intercontinental railway here proposed, shall be so equally and perfectly finished and inter-
locked, into a single line of vast longitudinal stretch, as to
constitute, in this nineteenth century, and in all the centuries
to come, one of the most palpable and imperishable proofs
of the superiority of North American and South American
and Central American energy, ingenuity, enterprise, integrity, honor and achievement ; and while no part of the road
itself, the tunnels, the bridges, or the viaducts, no part of
the rolling-stock, or other property or appurtenances of the
road, must be other than first-class in all respects, yet everything, including the obtaining from Governments of the necessary charters and franchises, must be done with such exact rectitude and economy, that, from the beginning to the
end of the work, not so much as one dollar shall be use-
lessly, extravagantly or corruptly expended.

Another very important condition which it is desirable
shall be well understood and established in relation to this
road of roads, is that a strip of territory of reasonable
width, on both sides of the main stem, shall be declared
and forever maintained as neutral ground to all belligerents ;
that the road itself shall never be interrupted in its regular
schedules of daily working, nor used in any manner whatever for facilitating military movements, or for other purposes of war ; and that any nation or faction daring to
violate this signally benificent compact of peace and improvement, shall at once become the common enemy of all

the other parties to the agreement, and be punished accordingly.

Superior lines of telegraph along the entire length of all the roads here projected, are held in view as collateral improvements which it will be well to construct simultaneously with the roads themselves ; so that, in this way, correspondence may be greatly facilitated, business promoted, and the invincibly powerful and widespread family of American nationalities, occupying all the territory between the Arctic Regions and Cape Horn, and harmoniously allied with each other in the industrial development and enlightening march of peaceful and prosperpous and progressive civilization, may be respectively heard from, in accents of sisterly greeting and fraternal emulation, every morning at the breakfasttable.

Under the existing condition of things, the one great desideratum of Brazil, at this particular time, is the development of her exhaustless internal resources; and these resources she can develop only by enlarging her facilities for internal communication.   Whilst heretofore Brazil has laudably and liberally encouraged the growth and extension of her interests without, that is to say, her interests on water, yet it seems to me that she has, meanwhile, given too little attention to her interests within, that is to say, her interests on land.   The grand and mighty railway, with its many connections, which I now propose for Brazil, will act upon her much the same as the heart, the seat and center of life, acts upon the human organism; by channels of radiation in every direction, it will vigorously dispense its vitalizing forces to the very extremities of the Empire, and help very obviously and largely to impart prosperity and happiness to millions upon millions of grateful souls.   In short, the road will be of immense usefulness and profit to Brazil, a benefit to every other nationality in South America, and an advantage, without exception, to all the States and other Common-wealths of North America. How high the privilege, how great the honor, and how certain and glorious the gain, to be engaged, as Brazil may now engage herself (at the cost of only an act of justice in another matter of comparative in-significance,) in the joint inception and furtherance of a work so vast and so good ; a work which, when completed, will conduce to the marvelous and ever-increasing welfare of nearly half the world ! In the course of my letter to your Majesty, in Paris, France, five months ago, I said, in allu-sion to this great railway scheme, that, if successfully carried out, it would, in time, as I believed, give back to Brazil at least one hundred dollars for every dollar which she will pay me on the Fiedler claim. Your Majesty or any other just-minded and clear-sighted personage, may now decide whether, if, in that opinion, I had used the ten times greater numeral *thousand*, instead of " hundred," I would not have been much nearer to the prospective and probable facts. Not only will the great Empire of your Majesty, by the con-summation of this enterprise, gain very largely in trade and money, but it will also, at the same time, gain immensely in white immigration, which is the only sort of immigration that can henceforth be decently or respectably useful to Brazil or to any other country,—and in general improve-ments ; so that, in this way, the Fiedler affair, which at first might seem to have been a minor misfortune, may at last prove to be one of the greatest possible blessings to Brazil. So may it prove !

I have the honor to be, most respectfully,

Your Majesty's obedient servant,

H. R. HELPER.

MR. HELPER TO MR. COLTON.

[A LETTER containing incidental suggestions looking to the down'all
of the Brazilian Empire, and an enlargement respectively of the areas
of several, or all, of the adjoining Republics. Meanwhile, let the
Three Americas Railway be built, wholly independent of Brazil, and
let the Republics of the Pacific coast, with the consent and co-operation of all the other South American Republics, give formal notice to
Brazil that she must, by or before a specified date, republicanize herself from within, or be republicanized from without.   Otherwise,
Brazil not gracefully yielding assent to the indispensable governmental
rectification so outlined, and failing to comply with the wholesome ad-
monitions so given, let the great family of neighboring democracies,
consisting of Venezuela, Columbia, Ecuador, Peru, Bolivia, Paraguay,
Uraguay, Chili, and the Argentine Republic, take immediate steps for
the extension eastward of their respective territories,—as may be jointly
and definitely agreed upon,—if not all the way to the Atlantic ocean,
at least to the fiftieth degree of longitude west of Greenwich, corresponding to the twenty-seventh meridian east from Washington.]

ST. LOUIS, Mo., *December 6, 1880.*
JOSEPH H. COLTON, ESQ., *New York City,*

DEAR SIR: In addition to the aggregate of balances actually and obviously due to you from the governments of
Bolivia and Peru, on account of the maps which you en-
graved and published for the former, in the year 1858, the
amount of damages which should be rightfully adjudged to
you, is a question of grave consideration and uncertain
issue.   On the simplest principles of justice and equity,—
could such principles be practically summoned to your aid
in this case,—you should receive, in a suit for damages
alone, at least ten thousand dollars, and I doubt very
much whether twenty thousand would fully indemnify you
for all the losses you have sustained on account of the numerous acts of bad faith and diplomatic despoliation so long
and so persistently waged against you by the governments
of both Bolivia and Peru.   This I say, in all sincerity and
frankness, with reference only to yourself.   As regards my
own personality, as your attorney, I will be equally candid in

assuring you that I would not again engage to undergo the same amount of mental labor and vexation and physical suffering and peril which, on sea and land, amid marsh and mountain, and beneath extremes of heat and cold, I have already endured in the prosecution of this claim, during the last ten years, for every cent of the round sum of fifty thousand dollars.

Notwithstanding the exact truth of all these statements, I have, even aside from the profound consciousness of sacrifices and hardships undergone by myself, a very special and important reason for requesting that you will—if you will—kindly yet conditionally consent to forego, entirely and forever, the presentation of any claim whatever for damages, and content yourself, if it be possible for you to do so, with claiming henceforth only the total amount of balances at once demonstrably due to you. The aggregate of these balances is a principal of $7,757.94 in silver; the larger item of which, $6,631.60, with interest thereon at the rate of six per cent. per annum, from September 9, 1878, represents the expenses of litigation and other necessary proceedings in Lima, during a period of more than six months to induce the government of Peru to honor its formally and legally and justly accepted draft to my order, in your behalf, for $19,609.40 in silver, drawn upon it by the government of Bolivia, on the 12th of October, 1876, and due at Lima on the 1st of March, 1878, but which was not paid until the 9th of September of the same year; and the smaller item of which sum total still due to you, is $1,126.34, with interest thereon at six per cent. per annum from October 13, 1876; this latter item of indebtedness having arisen from the failure of Peru to pay Bolivia's draft upon her, though it also had been previously and regularly accepted in your favor, for $10,794.27 in silver, due June 30, 1876, but not honored until the 13th of October following, when the value of the

Peruvian paper currency with which the draft was finally met, had so greatly depreciated that you received in New York the sum of 1,126.34 less than you would have received, if your instalment-draft from Bolivia, in this particular case. —unconditionally accepted as it was by Peru,—had been honored at maturity.

Under all these circumstances, therefore, my request is, that you will now give your consent for further and final proceedings against Peru, and against her only, considering yourself as having finished with Bolivia, for the sum of $7,757,94 in silver, with interest thereon as mentioned above. The particular reason why I would earnestly ask of you this special favor,—though I fear it is asking too much,—is because I have it in contemplation soon to present to Peru, Bolivia, and all the other independent nations of Spanish America, an application for certain elaborate charters, which will be indispensable to the complete success of my proposed Three Americas Railway; wherefore I am very anxious to avoid every matter or question which, however legitimate and equitable in itself, might yet be the occasion of serious displeasure.

The building of the unparalleled railway thus projected would, I am quite sure, be to both Peru and Bolivia, and also to most of the other Spanish American Republics— certainly to all those through which the road would pass—a benefit, a blessing, such as has never yet been achieved by any one of them; and, casting from myself everything like unwelcome remembrances and ill-feelings, I am, with an impartial view to the permanent welfare of both Peru and Bolivia, and all the other Republics of the Western Hemisphere, especially desirous to advance the undertaking as rapidly as possible in every proper manner.

With the aid of one or more of their neighboring Andean nationalities, Peru and Bolivia may yet achieve, even within the comparatively few remaining years of the present century, the resplendent glory of extending the free and enlightened principles of republican institutions eastward to the very shores of the Atlantic, and all along the coast thereof, and interiorly, from French Guiana to Uruguay; and not themselves be compelled to submit to the baneful and execrable power that threatens to enthrall them under the galling yoke of a monarchical despotism now secretly and insidiously struggling to establish itself all the way westward from beyond the Rivers Paraguay and Guapore to the Pacific Ocean. On this weighty subject,—a subject of infinitely greater political importance to South America than it has ever yet been thought to be by any considerable number of our own people, a subject affecting in fact the very foundations of our own system of government,—I shall have more to say hereafter. Meanwhile, I would respectfully suggest the propriety of you yourself writing to the Hon. Secretary of State at Washington, requesting him to instruct our Minister at Lima to make a firm but polite demand on the Peruvian Government, as a finality in your behalf (you conditionally relinquishing all claims for damages,) for the sum of $7,757.94 in silver, so plainly and justly due to you, with interest, as stated above.

A clear and brief restatement by yourself of your great grievances in this regard,—you having now ·reached the honored age of more than eighty years,—would, I doubt not, be certain to receive from Secretary Evarts, at the proper time, such wise and earnest consideration and action as any new adduction of the facts, whether by yourself or by your attorney, would·so manifestly deserve. Possibly he may advise comparative forbearance in the matter until after the close of the unfortunate war now being waged between Peru and Bolivia on the one side, and Chili on the other; and his opinion or advice on this or any other subject may be well worthy of deferential acceptance by either you or myself. Of course Congress itself may be appealed to again, should you deem it fit to carry the case directly back into that potent body of national worthies; but it would, as I think, be more prudent first to seek redress, as patiently as possible, through our Department of State at Washington.

I remain, dear Sir,—venerable octogenarian as you are,—
Yours, very truly,

H. R. HELPER.

EWBANK'S LIFE IN BRAZIL.

One of the best books on Brazil is entitled " *Sketches of Life in Brazil*," by the versatile and distinguished Thomas Ewbank, President Fillmore's Commissioner of Patents, who also had the honor—and it was certainly a very high honor—to be the founder of the American Ethnological Society. The most candid and correct criticism which has yet appeared of this book speaks of it in these words:

" To those who wish to know how deep human nature can sink in moral degradation and the extreme limit of monarchial imbecility, we recommend a careful reading of Ewbank's ' Brazil,' whose details of hopeless superstition, general ignorance, and political demoralizations have no equal."

In the course of his excellent work, which, in order to be duly appreciated, should be read as a whole, Mr. Ewbank says:

" Romanism, as it exists in Brazil and South America generally, is a barrier to progress, compared with which other obstacles are small; and there are native statesmen alive to the fact; but incorporated as it is with the habits and thoughts of the people; transfused, as it were, through their very bones and marrow, unless some Kempis or Fénélon, Luther, or Ronge, arise to purify it, generations must pass before the scales drop from their eyes, and they become mentally free. * * * To preach against Romanism in Brazil is as much treason against the State as attempting to introduce the republican form of government, but the greatest of obstacles would probably be found in the reverence paid to the Virgin. Mary of Nazareth is the great goddess of Romanists. Her deification was no chance matter, but the deliberate adoption of a principle, which was too closely interwoven with the habits, thoughts, and feelings of ancient nations to be at once torn away. The most refined and the most illiterate of the heathen were steeped in Polytheism. Every system of worship had its goddesses as well as gods, the one being held as essential as the other. It was deemed the dictate of reason that females should have feminine divinities, to whom they could prefer petitions peculiar to themselves, and such as they could not be induced to make known to male deities, and here was found a prime hinderance to the reception of Christianity. We can imagine how the high-minded Lucretias and Virginias of Athens and Rome would be shocked at the proposition to transfer their petitions in the most delicate matters from the mother of the gods to one whom they could at first only view as a Jewish bachelor. A Madonna was therefore held necessary by the early fathers of the Church, in order to overcome the scruples of the sex, and she was realized in the exaltation of Mary. Moreover, in making her ' Queen of Heaven,' the way was opened to associate with her other ladies celestial, and to rival in that feature the court of Jove.

" Brazil is poor in population, and must be till she adopt a comprehensive and liberal system of immigration; but this is dreaded on account of the leveling spirit of the age, and a fear that both the church and the throne would be endangered.   No subject is more involved in uncertainty than the census.   Official accounts, it is alleged, are often based on imperfect data, and not seldom on mere assumptions. As respects certain portions of the inhabitants, it is considered discreet in the authorities to say little; thus no reliable comparison of the numbers of whites and free colored are given, on account of the alleged overwhelming proportion of the latter.   In the maritime cities and provinces the mixture of blood is obvious, but in the interior the preponderance of color is awful (I use the words of a native.) In the city of Tejuco, the most thriving one in Minas and of the interior of Brazll, are only five pure white families among twelve thousand inhabitants."

BRAZIL'S HATRED OF DEMOCRACIES AND REPUBLICS.

Overwhelming evidences of the intense hatred which Brazil cherishes against all democratic and republican forms of government, especially in America, and also of her insidious efforts to weaken and destroy them, may be found in the secret instructions given to tbe Marquis Amaro, whom, at Rio de Janeiro, April 21, 1830, the Emperor Dom Pedro I commissioned to proceed to Europe as his special Embassador in direct opposition to the supremely excellent institutions and tendencies of liberty and self-government throughout the New World.   The following extracts from those secret Brazilian instructions to her monarchy-extolling Embassador, the Marquis Amaro, are copied and translated from the *Archivo Americano* in the Public Library at Montevideo:

" Your Excellency will endeavor to demonstrate to the Sovereigns who may take part in this negotiation, that the only efficacious means for the pacification and constitution of the old Spanish colonies is that of establishing constitutional or representative Monarchies in the different States which are independent. * * * In treating of the founding of representative Monarchies, and only in that case, your Excellency will manifest the expediency of considering the rising national pride of the new American States. Already separate and independent of each other, Mexico, Columbia, Peru, Chili, Bolivia, and the Argentine Provinces, may constitute so many distinct and separate Monarchies. * * * With regards to Uruguay, which does not form a part of the Argentine territory, which was incorporated with Brazil, and cannot exist in a state of independence, your Excellency will opportunely and frankly endeavor to prove the necessity of again incorporating it with the Brazilian Empire. It is the only side on which Brazil is vulnerable. It is difficult, if not impossible, to prevent acts of hostility, and to put down the outrages of malefactors on either side of the frontiers. It forms the natural boundary of this Empire, and would be the means of preventing future causes of disputes between Brazil and the more Southern States. In case England and France should oppose its reannexation to Brazil, your Excellency will insist, for reasons of political expediency, which are obvious and weighty, that if Uruguay is to remain independent, it should be constituted into a duchy or principality, so as in no manner to form part of the Argentine Monarchy.

" In the choice of Princes for the thrones of the new Monarchies, and if it should be necessary to bring them from Europe, your Excellency, will not hesitate to give your vote in favor of such members of the august family of Bourbon as may be disposed to repair to America. Those Princes, besides the prestige in their favor as descendants of, or nearly connected with, the dynasty which for so many years reigned over the States in question, offer, through their relationship and friendship with so many Sovereigns, a solid guarantee for the tranquillity and consolidation of the new Monarchies. In the event of any young Princes being selected, as for example the second son of the Duke of Orleans, or of any other having sons, it will be expedient, and His Imperial Majesty desires, that your Excellency should immediately propose a marriage, or promise of marriage, between them and the Princesses of Brazil.   *   *   *

" Your Excellency may engage and promise that His Imperial Majesty will employ every means of persuasion and counsel on his part in order to pacify the new States, and, with a view to the projected establishment of representative Monarchies, binds himself immediately to open and cultivate relations of intimate friendship with the new Monarchs. Having had the glory of founding and maintaining almost alone the first constitutional Monarchy in the New World, His Majesty the Emperor wishes to see his noble example imitated, and those principles of government which he has adopted made general in all South America. *   *   * If your Excellency should deem it absolutely necessary to make some promise of assistance, His Imperial Majesty will not hesitate to bind himself to defend and aid the Monarchical representative government which may be established in the Argentine Provinces, by a sufficient naval force stationed in the Rio de la Plata, and with the land forces which he maintains on the southern frontier of the Empire."

20

JEFFERSON'S VIEWS CONCERNING SOUTH AMERICA.

[Postulates for Brazilian Statesmen.]

As the versatile and unrivaled Shakespeare is the most quotable of all poets, so the profound and incomparable Jefferson is the most quotable of all statesmen. Though he could lay no claims to a possession of the wonderful powers of oratory, and was wholly free from pretensions in that regard, having, it is said, never made a speech in the whole course of his extraordinarily prominent and influential career in the public service, yet his writings, upon almost every question of governmental affairs, are undoubtedly the soundest and clearest that can be found anywhere within the vast compass of political literature, whether ancient, mediæval or modern. Nor was it alone in statesmanship that the Sage of Monticello excelled. He was a scientist, a philosopher, an oracle. Twenty-six years the senior of the erudite Humboldt, much friendly and learned correspondence, on a great variety of subjects, was carried on between these two intellectual giants of a past generation. At the age of eighty-three, Jefferson died in 1826; at the age of ninety Humboldt died in 1859. Acknowledging receipt of one of Humboldt's books, a complimentary present from the author, Jefferson took occasion, under date of July 13, 1817, to speak of the hopeful revolutions then going on throughout South and Central America against the monarchical sway and mastery so persistently asserted by the crown of Spain. In that letter, as in all others on the same topic,—for he wrote many,—he gave emphatic expression to his apprehension that priestcraft, as practiced by the narrowminded and fanatical followers of the Romish religion, was then, and for a long while would probably continue to be, the most formidable obstacle in the way to full freedom and true reformation and progress in Spanish America.   Said he:

* * * "The physical and geographical information which you have given us of Spanish America, a country hitherto a sort of sealed book to us, has come exactly in time to guide our understandings in the great political revolutions now bringing it into prominence on the stage of the world.   The issue of its struggles, as they respect Spain, is no longer a matter of doubt.   As it respects their own well-ordered liberty, peace and happiness, we cannot yet be quite so certain.*   Whether the blinds of bigotry, the shackles of the priesthood, and the fascinating glare of rank and wealth, will give fair play to the common sense of the mass of the people, so far as to qualify them for self-government, is what we do not know at this time.   Possibly our hopes and wishes may be stronger than our expectations.   The first principle of republicanism is, that the *lex-majoris partis* is the fundamental law of every society of individuals of equal rights; to consider the will of the society enounced by the majority of a single vote, as sacred as if unanimous, is the first of all lessons in importance, yet the last which is thoroughly learned.   This law once disregarded, no other remains but that of force, which ends necessarily in military despotism.   The history of the French revolution is conclusive as to these facts; and it is to be hoped that the minds of our brethren of Spanish America may be sufficiently enlarged and firm to see that their fate depends on their sacred observance of the primary rules and indispensable requirements of the republican system of self-government.   * * *   In our own America, we are turning to public improvements.   Schools, roads, and canals, are everywhere either in operation or contemplation.   The most gigantic undertaking yet proposed is that of the State of

New York, for draining the waters of Lake Erie into the Hudson River. The distance is three hundred and fifty-three miles, and the height to be surmounted is six hundred and sixty-one feet. While the expense of opening the canal will be very great, the effect of cutting and operating it will be incalculably powerful in advancing the Atlantic States. Internal navigation by steamboats is rapidly spreading through all the States; and that by sails and oars will erelong be looked back to as among the curiosities of antiquity." * * *

Acknowledging with renewed expressions of gratitude that the great German traveler and author had but recently given to the world the fullest and best general information then extant in relation to South and Central America, Jefferson, in the course of a letter to Humboldt, written at Monticello, under date of April 14, 1811, said:

* * * "Your very valuable and magnificent works on Spanish America give us a knowledge of that country more accurate than, as I believe, we possess of Europe, the seat of the science of a thousand years. They come out, too, at a moment when the various larger divisions of that country are beginning to be interesting to the whole world. Those divisions are now becoming the scenes of important political revolutions, and will soon take their stations as integral members of the great family of nations. All are now in insurrection. In several, the Independents are already triumphant, and before the lapse of many years they will undoubtedly be so in all. What kind of government will they establish? How much liberty can they bear without intoxication? Are their chiefs sufficiently enlightened to form a well-guarded government, and their people brave and vigilant enough to watch their chiefs? All these questions you can answer better than any other. They will probably copy our outlines of confederation and elective

government, and abolish distinctions of rank ; but will they
not, nevertheless, bow their necks to their priests, and persevere in intolerantism ?"   *   *   *

Again, writing to Humboldt, under date of December 6,
1813, Jefferson threw out, even at that early day, several
capital hints for the promulgation of the Monroe doctrine,
which, however, was not formally promulgated until about
ten years afterward.   Said he:

*   *   *   "That the Spanish Americans will succeed in
separating themselves from all dependence on Europe I
have no doubt ; but in what kind of government their revolutions will end I am not so certain.   History furnishes me
no example of a priest-ridden people maintaining a free
civil government.   This marks the lowest grade of ignorance of which their civil as well as religious leaders will
always avail themselves for their own purposes.   *   *   *
The different castes among the inhabitants of Spanish America, their mutual hatreds and jealousies, their profound
ignorance and bigotry, will be played off by cunning leaders, and each be made the instrument of enslaving the
others.   *   *   *   But whatever governments they may
establish, they will be *American* governments, no longer to
be involved in the never-ceasing broils of Europe.   The
E. ropean nations constitute a separate division of the;
globe ; their localities make them part of a distinct system
they have a set of interests of their own in which it is our
business never to engage ourselves.   America has a hemisphere to itself.   It must have its separate system of interests, which must not be subordinated to those of Europe.
The insulated state in which nature has placed the American continent, should so far avail it that no spark of war
kindled in the other quarters of the globe should be wafted
across the wide oceans which separate us from them.   And
it will be so.   In fifty years more the United States alone

will contain nearly fifty millions of inhabitants; and fifty years are soon gone over. The peace of 1763 is just within that period. I was then twenty years old, and of course remember well all the transactions of the war preceding it. You will probably live to see the epoch now equally ahead of us; and the numbers which will then be spread over the other parts of the American hemisphere, catching long before that the principles of our portion of it, and concurring with us in the maintenance of the same system. You perceive how readily we run into ages beyond the grave; even those of us to whom that grave is already opening its quiet bosom. I am anticipating events of which you will be the bearer to me in the Elysian Fields fifty years hence." * *

Again, under date of February 4, 1816, in further elucidation of the principles of the Monroe doctrine,—this time writing to Monroe himself, who was then, though President-Elect, still Secretary of State under President Madison,—Jefferson says:

* * * "The ground you have taken with Spain is sound in every part. It is the true ground, especially as to all those countries which Spain claims as her dependencies in the Western Hemisphere. Every kindness which can be shown to the South and Central Americans, every friendly office and aid within the limits of the law of nations, I would cheerfully extend to them, without any fear whatever of Spanish displeasure. For this indeed would only be a re-assertion of our own independence. * * * So long as those portions of America are dependent, Spain, from her jealousy, is our natural enemy, and will always be in either open or secret hostility to us. Those countries, too, in war, would be a powerful weight in her scale, and, in peace, totally shut to us. Interest, then, on the whole, would wish their independence, and justice makes the wish a duty. They have a right to be free, and we a right to aid them, as a strong

man has a right to assist a weak one assailed by a robber or a murderer."

SEWARD'S INQUIRY TOUCHING PRIEST-RIDDEN COUNTRIES.

[An inquiry which affects Brazil as a priest-propped monarchy, tenaciously wedded to the unseemly and sinister ways of its Lusitanian mother.]

In his *Travels Around the World*, Wm. H. Seward is on record as having asked the following question:

"Why have Portugal, Spain, and France, failed to retain the foreign dominions they founded, while the United States, Great Britain, and the Netherlands, continually acquire new territories, instead of losing those already secured? The reasons must be found in a difference in the characters and genius of the nations. Portugal colonized only with merchants and priests, and sought to monopolize the products of her colonies. Spain colonized only with soldiers and priests, and practiced restriction, monopoly, and extortion; while Great Britain, Holland and the United States, send out, for colonists, agriculturists, mechanics, miners and laborers; and, when they cannot do this, they introduce cultivation, mining, and the mechanical arts among the conquered people. France conquers, not for the development and improvement of the country subdued, or to increase her own wealth and power, but chiefly for the glory of the conquest. To compare great things with small, France conquers, as the sportsman kills, only to show his skill as a marksman."

JEAN-BAPTISTE SAY AGAINST PRIESTCRAFT.

[Thoughts for Brazil to ponder.]

In his *Political Economy*, Jean-Baptiste Say says, and says well:

" The saints and madonnas of superstitious nations, the splendid pageantry and richly decorated idols of worship, give life to no agricultural or manufacturing enterprise. The riches of the fane and the time lost in adoration would really purchase the blessings that barren prayers can never extort from the objects of idolatry. * * * In countries of rude culture it is not an uncommon practice to consign certain civil functions, such as the registry of births, marriages and deaths, to the ecclesiastical body, whose emoluments, arising from their clerical duties, might be supposed to enable them to execute these without pay. But there is always danger in confiding the execution of civil duties to a class of men who pretend to a commission from a still higher than a national authority. * * * Many times, during several of the centuries last past, the papal priesthood, in different countries, refused to execute their duties to the State, in spite of all that their respective governments could do ; on the pretence that it was better to obey the divine command as conveyed by the voice of the Pope, than yield obedience to any human requirement ! * * * So too will the Mussulman incur certain destruction in defense of the Sultan and his faith, when, in fact, neither the one nor the other is worth defending. But political and religious prejudice will sooner or later fall to the ground, and leave mankind to seek for some more reasonable object of devotion. * * * All travelers agree that Protestant countries are better educated, and richer and more prosperous, than Catholic countries ; and the reasons are the prevalence in the former of far greater freedom and cheerfulness, and the consequent incentives to new industries, the development of new and elevated desires, and an almost unlimited power of producing multifarious things, useful and beautiful, which now contribute so largely to the general convenience and welfare of our species. * * * Ignorance is the inseparable concomitant of that slavery of custom which stands in the way of all improvement; it is ignorance which imputes to a supernatural cause the ravages of an epidemic disease, which might perhaps be easily prevented or eradicated, and makes so many of our fellow-creatures recur to superstitious observances, when a proper precaution, or the application of a natural remedy, may be all that is required to secure good health."

ADAM SMITH ON CHURCH AND STATE.

[Facts which Brazil, and all other superstitious States with State religions, should treasure up in their minds.]

In his *Wealth of Nations*, Adam Smith writes as follows:

" The revenue of every established church, such parts of it excepted as may arise from particular lands, is a branch, it ought to be observed, of the general revenue of the State, which is thus diverted to a purpose very different from the defence of the State. The tithe, for example, is a real land-tax, which puts it out of the power of the proprietors of land to contribute so largely towards the defence of the State as they otherwise might be able to do. * * * The more of this fund that is given to the church, the less, it is evident, can be spared to the State. It may be laid down as a certain maxim, that, all other things being supposed equal, the richer the church, the poorer must necessarily be, either the government on the one hand, or the people on the other; and, in all cases, the less able must the State be to defend itself. In several Protestant countries, particularly in all the Protestant cantons of Switzerland, the revenue which anciently belonged to the Roman Catholic church, the tithes and church lands, has been found a fund sufficient to defray, with little or no addition, all the other expenses of the State. The magistrates of the powerful canton of Berne, in particular, have accumulated out of the savings from this fund a very large sum, supposed to amount to several millions, part of which is deposited in a public treasure, and part is placed at interest in what are called the public funds of the different indebted nations of Europe ; chiefly in those of France and Great Britain. * * * In the colonies of Spain and Portugal, and also of France, ecclesiastical government is extremely oppressive. Tithes take place in all of them, and are levied with the utmost rigor. All of them besides are oppressed with a numerous race of mendicant friars, whose beggary being not only licensed, but consecrated by religion, is a most grievous tax upon the poor people, who are most carefully taught that it is a duty to give, and a very great sin to refuse them their charity. Over and above all this, the clergy are, in all of them, the greatest engrossers of land."

HERBERT SPENCER ON RATIONAL EDUCATION.

[An elementary lesson for Brazil to learn.]

In his work on *Education*, Herbert Spencer says:
" When men received their creed and its interpretations from an infallible authority deigning no explanations, it was

natural that the teaching of children should be purely dogmatic. While 'believe and ask no questions' was the maxim of the Catholic church, it was also the maxim of the secular schools. Conversely, now that Protestantism has gained for adults a right of private judgment and established the practice of appealing to reason, there is harmony in the change that has made juvenile instruction a process of exposition addressed to the understanding."

CAPT. CODMAN'S OBSERVATIONS IN BRAZIL.

In his work entitled *Ten Months in Brazil*, Capt. John Codman says:

"We had seen the Roman Catholic religion in all parts of the world, and frequently observed how it was modified or intensified to suit national exigencies. We had seen it in Rome, where the headquarters of its ceremonies are admitted to be the headquarters of its abuses; but nowhere, excepting perhaps in Spain, is it so much like child's play as in Brazil. Elsewhere, sensible and educated men comply with some of its unimportant observances, from habit or from interested motives; but here, the most potent, grave and reverend seigniors 'assist' with pious decorum at the wax-doll exhibitions and performances of miracles. On these occasions not a smile is seen, except on the face of a foreigner, or in the sly twinkle of a priest's eye. The morals of the clergy are such as would be considered depraved in any other country than this. It is true that the priests almost universally keep their mistresses, that they seduce many fair penitents, and are allowed all sorts of intimacies with married ladies, about which the husbands are not much concerned; for the Brazilians revel in such beastly impurities, that little priestly sins like these may be regarded as quite venial.

" The custom-house in Rio de Janeiro is closed on all holidays and saints' days ; and there are holidays many, and of saints' days an unknown number, which is continually increasing.   By and bye, when there come to be more than three hundred and sixty-five of them in the calender, the days must be divided, one saint taking the morning and another the evening.   As it is now, the festival-days occupy only about half the time.   On these days no business is done.   *   *   *   There is no true idea of system or order among the Brazilians; at least this is so in public affairs. The post-office is quite as badly administered as the custom-house.   There is no certainty whatever that your letters will be dispatched, or that your correspondence from home will ever reach you.   There is a possibility of suc-cess, and that is all.   Bushels of letters are scattered about in the post-office of Rio de Janeiro.   You are invited to enter and help yourself ; and it may readily be supposed that in this way some people find the letters of others if they cannot find any of their own.

" It does not seem that the Brazilians can compete with the Anglo-Saxons, or with that pure Latin race from which they claim to have originated, and from which they have degenerated.   *   *   *   All the endeavors of miscegen-acionists have proved failures.   No people has attempted the experiment more recklessly than the Brazilians. Wherever their ancestors, the Portuguese, have gone, this has been their character.   Thus, in India and in China, they have brought the human race down to a level scarcely a step above the orang-outang.   In those regions the name of ' Pariah Portugues ' signifies all that is low, vile, and beastly.   Will Brazil rise from her present condition to be a fit member of the great family of nations, or will she sink lower and lower, until she reaches the very lowest depths of degradation ?   Some years ago, when a census was to be taken in Brazil, it was proposed to divide the classes of the community, and to enumerate separately the white, black, and mixed.   The Brazilians themselves laughed at the imbecile who wasted his ink in the suggestion. Mixed! There is black blood everywhere; compounded over and over again, like an apothecary's preparation.   African blood runs freely through the best mansions, as well as in the lowest gutters, and Indian blood swells the general current.   There is no distinction between white and black, or any of the intermediate colors, which can act as a bar to social intercourse or political advancement.   * * * The greatest pest in Brazil is amalgamation—the mixing of two bloods which the Almighty never intended to course in one current."

RABELAIS ON MONKS.

[A species of idlers and parasites obnoxiously superabundant in Brazil.]

In his *Pantagruel*, Francois Rabelais says:

" If you will but observe how an ape in a family is constantly mocked and teased, you may easily understand how monks are always shunned by worthier men, both young and old. The ape protects not the house as does the dog; he pulls not the plow as does the ox; he yields neither meat nor wool as does the sheep;—in like manner the monk. He works not as does the farmer: he defends not the country as does the patriot; he cures not the sick as does the physician; he neither teaches as does the schoolmaster, nor preaches as does the evangelist; he imports not commodities and things necessary for the commonwealth as does the merchant. Therefore it is that, by all men of merit, monks are hooted at and abhorred."

GALLENGA ON THE SOUTH AMERICAN HIERARCHS.

[Applicable, in the widest possible sense, to the ecclesiastics of Brazil.]

A. Gallenga, a recent traveler, of rare powers of observation and description, speaking particularly of Roman Catholic priestcraft in Chili and Peru,—though, as is well known, its sway is much more complete and pernicious in Brazil than anywhere else in South America,—says:

"Tnere is no doubt that the cowled or tonsured man is still the 'lord of all' in this country; and, with the women under his control, he may well afford to set the sneers of sceptic men and the enactments of the civil law at defiance. The best houses and gardens in dull provincial towns are the houses of religious fraternities. Even where the church is shabby the priest is fat. He wears the finest cloth, smokes the best perfumed cigarettes, and struts about with an arrogant domineering look, as of one as sure of the fee-simple of this world as of the next. The clergy of Chili may be more dangerous to its liberties, and more fatal to its social progress, than the slovenly, greasy, and scandalous priests of Peru, of whom the Pontifical Nuncio at Lima, speaking on the subject to a foreign diplomatist, a Protestant, declared that he would never have believed that so brutified and profligate a set of ministers of the altar could exist in any Christian country. Whereupon the foreign Minister said, 'Dear me! I suppose every priest in Lima keeps a mistress?' 'Ah!' sighed the sleek Monsignore, 'If they would but be satisfied with one a piece.'"

Through the superstitious folly and fanaticism of an extremely absurd ceremonial of the Catholic religion, in Santiago, the capital of Chili, on the 8th of December, 1863, was witnessed one of the most appalling and fatal horrors that ever happened in church or theater or other structure. On that occasion, while the nominally bachelor-priests were celebrating, around the altar of what they did not blush to call the Church of the Holy Matrix, the feast of what they were not ashamed to designate as the Immaculate Conception, at least *sixteen hundred* of the wealthiest and most fashionable women in the city, mostly young ladies, who had neither the sense nor the self-respect to hold themselves aloof from such an idolatrous gathering, were burned to death; the capacious church itself, with almost all its worshippers, having been consumed by fire, in consequence of the ignition of the immense profusion of frippery and finery with which the ridiculous images had been bedecked.

H. R. H.

GODFREY HIGGINS AGAINST THEOCRATIC GOVERNMENT.

[Recommended for the careful consideration of the actual theocracy, the nominal monarchy, of Brazil.]

In his brilliant *History of the Celtic Druids*, Godfrey Higgins, Fellow of the Society of Antiquaries, says:

"Of all the evils which escaped from Pandora's box, the institution of priesthoods was the worst. Priests have been the curse of the world. If we admit the merits of many of those of our own time to be as preëminent above those of all others as the *esprit de corps* of the most self-contented individual of the order may incite him to consider them, great as I am willing to allow the merits of many individuals to

be, I cannot concede that they form exceptions strong
enough to destroy the general nature of the rule. Look at
China, the festival of Juggernaut, the Crusades, the Massacre of St. Bartholomew, of the Mexicans, and of the Peruvians; the fires of the Inquisition, of Mary, of Cranmer, of
Calvin, and of the Druids. Look at Turkey; look at Ireland; look at Spain; in short, look everywhere; and you
will find the priests reeking with greed and with gore. They
have converted, and are converting, populous and happy
nations into deserts, and have transformed our beautiful
world into a slaughter-house drenched with tears and with
blood."

——————

PROF. FISKE'S OPPOSITION TO RELIGIOUS UNITY.

[A philosophy worthy of the fullest acceptation by Brazil, and by all
other countries.]

In a late number of *The North American Review*, Prof.
John Fiske says:

"The ecclesiastical idea, as it is promulgated in the
church of Rome, demands religious unity. Bigotry and fanaticism, as they manifest themselves in the Catholic priesthood, require that all men should think exactly alike about
questions which, among scholars and philosophers of the
deepest learning, are confessedly unfathomable by the human mind. Measured by the quantity of suffering it has
entailed, as well by the wholesale disregard of moral rectitude it has involved, the history of the attempt to enforce
religious unity, is, no doubt, the blackest of all the black
chapters in the awful career of mankind upon the earth.
Yet the object for which all this agony has been inflicted,

and all this villainy perpetrated, is an utterly worthless object, when considered with reference to the true conditions of life in a civilized society. .Not only is it not desirable that all the members of a community should hold the same opinions about religious matters, but it is far better that they should not hold the same opinions.   To the old-fashioned Frenchman's sneer about the newly-developed Americans, who have twenty religions and only one sauce, I should answer, By all means let us have twenty religions, even if we can have but one sauce.   In comparison with the inscrutable realities which religion postulates, our most elaborate attempts at theology are so feeble that it is not likely that any given set of opinions can represent more than the tiniest segment of essential truth."

JOHN STUART MILL ON SEMI-PAGAN CATHOLICISM.

[A species of Catholicism which is much more than half, almost entirely, paganish in Brazil.]

In his very able work on *Liberty*, John Stuart Mill, one of the most learned and industrious of modern philosophers, who has enriched the world with an almost inexhaustible fund of great thoughts, says:

"What is called Christian, but should rather be termed theological, morality, was not the work of Christ or the Apostles, but is of much later origin, having been gradually built up by the Roman Catholic church of the first five centuries, and though not implicitly adopted by moderns and Protestants, has been much less modified by them than might have been expected. * * * "The dictum that truth always triumphs over persecution, is one of those pleasant

21

falsehoods which men repeat after one another till they pass
into commonplaces, but which all experience refutes.
History teems with instances of truth put down by persecu-
tions.   If not suppressed forever, it may be thrown back for
centuries.   To speak only of religious opinions;—the Reformation broke out at least twenty times before Luther,
and was put down.   Arnold of Bresica was put down.   Fra
Dolcino was put down.   Savonarola was put down.   The
Albigeois were put down.   The Vaudois were put down.
The Lollards were put down.   The Hussites were put down.
Even after the era of Luther, wherever persecution was per-
sisted in, it was successful.   In Italy, Spain, Flanders, the
Austrian empire, Protestantism was rooted out; and, most
likely, would have been so in England, had Queen Mary
(Bloody Mary) lived, or Queen Elizabeth died.

    *   *   *   " Mankind can hardly be too often reminded
that there was once a man named Socrates, between whom
and the legal authorities and public opinion of his time,
there took place a memorable collision.   Born in an age
and country abounding in individual greatness, this man
has been handed down to us by those who best knew both
him and the age, as the most virtuous man in it; while *we*
know him as, the head and prototype of all subsequent
teachers of virtue, the source equally of the lofty inspiration
of Plato and the judicious utilitarianism of Aristotle, the
two headsprings of ethical as of all other philosophy.   This
acknowledged master of all the eminent thinkers who have
since lived—whose fame, still growing after more than two
thousand years, all but outweighs the whole remainder of
the names which make his native city illustrious—was put
to death by his countrymen, after a judicial conviction, for
alleged impiety and immorality.   Impiety, in denying the
gods recognized by the State; indeed his accusers gravely
asserted that he believed in no gods at all.   Immorality, in

being, by his instructions, a teacher of false doctrines. Of these charges the tribunal, there is every ground for believing, honestly found him guilty, and condemned the man who probably of all then born had deserved best of mankind, to be put to death as a criminal.

* * * " The peculiar evil of silencing the expression of an opinion is, that it is robbing the human race ; posterity as well as the existing generation ; those who dissent from the opinion, still more than those who hold it. If the opinion is right, they are deprived of the opportunity of exchanging error for truth ; if wrong, they lose, what is almost as great a benefit, the clearer perception and livelier impression of truth, produced by its collision with error. * * * No one can be a great thinker who does not recognize, that as a thinker it is his first duty to follow his intellect to whatever conclusions it may lead. * * * It often happens that the universal belief of one age of mankind—a belief from which no one *was*, nor without an extraordinary effort of genius and courage, *could* at that time be free—becomes to a subsequent age so palpable an absurdity, that the only difficulty then is to imagine how such a thing can ever have appeared credible. * * * It is as certain that many opinions, now general, will be rejected by future ages, as it is that many, once general, have already been rejected by the present."

DR. DRAPER'S CONFLICT WITH CATHOLIC CANT.

[A scientific morsel recommended as possessing the properties of a peculiarly wholesome kind of pabulum for Brazil's ritualistic and otherwise irrational mind.]

In his latest great work—*The Conflict Between Religion and Science*,—published only a few years ago, Dr. John

William Draper, a much wiser and better man, a far more profound philosopher, than any pope or prelate or priest, of any period, past or present, says :

" When the old mythological religion of Europe broke down under the weight of its own inconsistencies, neither the Roman Emperors nor the philosophers of those times did anything adequate for the guidance of public opinion. They left religious affairs to take their chance, and accordingly those affairs fell into the hands of ignorant and infuriated ecclesiastics, parasites, eunuchs, and slaves. * * * A few years ago, it was the polite and therefore the proper course to abstain from all allusion to this controversy, and to keep it as far as possible in the background.   The tranquillity of society depends so much on the stability of its religious convictions, that no one can be justified in wantonly disturbing them.   But faith is in its nature unchangeable, stationary ; Science is in its nature progressive ; and eventually a divergence between them, impossible to conceal, must take place. * * *   In a matter so solemn as that of religion, all men, whose temporal interests are not involved in existing institutions, earnestly desire to find the truth.   They seek information as to the subjects in dispute, and as to the conduct of the disputants.   The history of Science is not a mere record of isolated discoveries ; it is a narrative of the conflict of two contending powers, the expansive force of the human intellect on one side, and the compression arising from traditionary faith and human interests on the other.   Science has never sought to ally herself to civil power.   She has never attempted to throw odium or inflict social ruin on any human being.   She has never subjected any one to mental torment, physical torture, least of all to death, for the purpose of upholding or promoting her ideas.   She presents herself unstained by cruelties and crimes.   But in the Vatican—we have only to

recall the Inquisition and the Massacre of the Huguenots
—the hands that are now uplifted in appeals to the Most
Merciful are crimsoned.   They have been steeped in blood.
*   *   *   " That a crisis is impending is shown by the
present independent and half-disdainful attitude of the great
powers toward the papacy.   *   *   *   Will modern civilization consent to abandon the career of advancement which
has given it so much power and happiness?   Will it consent to retrace its steps to the semi-barbarian ignorance and
superstition of the middle ages?   Will it submit to the dic-
tation of a power which, claiming divine authority, can present no authentic credentials of its assumptions; a power
which kept Europe in a stagnant condition for many centuries, ferociously suppressing by the stake and the sword
every attempt at progress ; a power that is founded in a cloud
of mysteries; that sets itself above reason and common-
sense ; that loudly proclaims the hatred it entertains against
liberty of thought and freedom in civil institutions; that
professes its intention of repressing the one and destroying
the other whenever it can find the opportunity; that denounces as most pernicious and insane the opinion that liberty of conscience and of worship is the right of every man;
that protests against that right being promulgated and asserted by law in every well-governed State ; that contemptuously repudiates the principle that the will of the people,
manifested by public opinion or by other means, shall constitute law; that refuses to every man the privilege of exercising his own opinion in matters of religion, but holds that
it is simply his duty to believe what he is told by the church,
and to obey her commands ; that will not permit any temporal government to define the rights and prescribe the limits
to the authority of the church; that declares it not only may
but will resort to force to discipline disobedient individuals ;
that invades the sanctity of private life, by making, at the

confessional, the wife and daughters and servants of one suspected, spies and informers against him; that tries him without an accuser, and by torture makes him bear witness against himself; that denies the right of parents to educate their children outside of its own church, and insists that to it alone belongs the supervision of domestic life and the control of marriages and divorces; that denounces ' the impudence ' of those who presume to subordinate the authority of the church to the civil authority, or who advocate the separation of the church from the State; that absolutely repudiates all toleration, and affirms that the Catholic religion is entitled to be held as the only religion in every country, to the exclusion of all other modes of worship; that requires all laws standing in the way of its interests to be repealed, and, if that be refused, orders all its followers to disobey them.

" Conscious that it can work no miracle to serve itself, this power does not hesitate to disturb society by its intrigues against governments, and seeks to accomplish its ends by alliances with despotism. Claims such as these mean a revolt against modern civilization, an intention of destroying it, no matter at what social cost. To submit to them without resistance, men must be slaves indeed ! Yet no one need be in any serious doubt as to the final issue of the coming conflict. Whatever is resting on fiction and fraud will be overthrown. Institutions that organize impostures and spread delusions must show what right they have to exist. Faith must render an account of herself to Reason. Miracles and other Mysteries must give place to Facts. Religion must relinquish that imperious, that domineering position which she has so long maintained against Science. There must be absolute freedom of thought. Silly and superstitious ecclesiastics must learn to keep themselves within the domain they have chosen, and cease to tyrannize over the philosopher, who, feeling well assured of his own strength and the purity of his motives, will bear such interference no longer."

DILLON'S DESCRIPTION OF CATHOLICISM IN MEXICO.

[Being, at the same time, a substantially true statement of what Catholicism is in Brazil; only it is, in fact, in the latter country, a religion of a still more heathenish type.]

In one of his recent highly interesting and instructive letters from the City of Mexico, Mr. John A. Dillon, of St. Louis, an associate editor and special correspondent of the *Globe-Democrat*, says:

"I had a hard struggle to understand the present situation of the religious question in Mexico; but I think I have solved the difficulty at last. There are two classes here, the upper and lower—no middle class—and I am satisfied that the upper classes have lost their religion, and that the lower classes never had any. The conclusion would be that there is no religion in Mexico; but this would be a mistake. There are the women, and the women here, as everywhere, are religious. * * * The women cling to the faith of centuries; they may be seen regular in attendance at early mass on week days, and at high mass and vespers on Sundays; and they throng the confessionals on Saturdays. But in Mexico women do not count. They do not influence society, for there is none; nor literature, for there is none; nor politics, for they are not allowed to bewilder their minds with the affairs of State; they are allowed to be religious, because if they do not have their faith to guide their minds they would get into mischief; their sphere is the family, and they teach religion to the children, which the girls retain, but which the boys ostentatiously get rid of at the proper age.

" I have said that the upper classes, meaning thereby the men of the upper classes, have lost their religion, and the statement is strictly true. The revolt against religion, or rather against the power and authority of the hierarchy, was the principle underlying the whole long bloody struggle from 1824 to 1855. It found an apostle finally, a Luther and a Henry, united in Benito Juarez; it conquered in the constitution of 1857; it was so complete in its mastery that when Maximillian came, dull as he was, he did not dare to attempt a restoration of the old order, and if Mexico has finally found peace, and if its annals are monotonous, it is because among the small class who really control the strength of the country and rule it, there is almost unanimity in the sentiment, not only that church and State must be separate, but that the only church which Mexico has ever known is incompatible with the existence of the only State which Mexico can accept. Nominally the men are still Catholics, but those who accept the creed of the church are perhaps more bitter than the infidels in resisting the pretensions of all ecclesiastics, and the tone of Government and the law, of the press, and of all forms of discussion, is a deep-seated, unrelenting, unexpugnable hostility to that church which ruled and ruined Mexico, which kept the country poor and the people ignorant, and which fought so persistently against the only progress by which Mexico could ever hope to hold up her head in the family of decent nations.

" Until a comparatively recent date the church in Mexico was a greedy, ignorant, sordid and licentious church; the most hideous mockery of religion seen on earth since the preaching of the gospel. It started badly with wholesale baptisms of the Indians who accepted, and with wholesale slaughters of the Indians who resisted it. It allied itself with slavery, and the curse it brought upon the hovels of the conquered race came back to roost among the gilded

domes of its temples.   The monks who, in the sixteenth
century, boasted of baptizing five thousand and ten thousand idolaters in a day, were represented in the nineteenth
century by swarms of greedy, ignorant and licentious parasites, who had sunk to the level of their degraded flocks.
They lived in open concubinage, and held their own bastards
at the baptismal font; they sold indulgences, and they sold
masses, levied protective duties on matrimony, and divided
death's harvest with an avarice more cruel than death's
sentence.   The Aztec religion was perhaps not an admirable one, but it was a thousand times better than the religion
which revolted the senses of decent men a quarter of a century ago.   Some of its features still survive; sometimes its
baleful ashes flicker into a glare of the old flame, as in Que-
retaro a month ago, when the mob stoned the Protestant
chapel and drove the missionaries to Mexico for safety; or
in Apezaco, a fortnight ago, when Lenten zeal inspired the
murder of a missionary named Monroy.

" The rites and orgies which were practiced in the name
of religion are hardly credible outside of Africa; but there is
no resisting the testimony which proves their recent reality.
The law against open-air religion is stringent and is generally enforced; but some of the customs which have been
banished from Mexico survive to worry us in New Mexico.
Good Friday is a very bad Friday among the penitents, who
abuse the freedom of our laws to scourge themselves and
to renew the bloody procession of Calvary. · Before the Reform stopped it, such scourging was a part of the religion
of Mexico.   At every shrine and in every parish and village
the devotion of the faithful was stimulated by a ritualistic
repetition of the Passion.   Christ in the person of a living
peon was scourged and buffeted, and crowned with thorns;
he dragged the cross amid stripes and blows, and did not
earn his pay unless he hung on the cross; Judas was hired to

let the faithful spit on him; he was hung in a hundred thousand life-size effigies of paper which were burnt, but inasmuch as each effigy was lurid with fireworks, the spirit of the performance was rather pyrotechnic than devotional. At Christmas the sacred mystery of the incarnation was represented by a life-size effigy of the pregnant Virgin which was placed on the altar; then the divine infant was taken out from under her petticoat. This was the religion which Mexico enjoyed only twenty-five years ago. Is it not kinder to say that she had no religion?"

BLACKFORD'S BURNING ATTESTATION AGAINST BRAZIL.

Albert L. Blackford, long a resident of Brazil, makes the following condensed statement of facts, which every well-informed traveler in that country can readily confirm as but too true in all respects:

" Romanism was inherited by Brazil from Portugal, the mother-country. It has held almost undisputed sway in Brazil for over three centuries. It is but fair, therefore, to infer that the system has brought forth its legitimate fruits in that great and beautiful land. The moral results have been graphically described by Paul of Tarsus in the last twelve verses of his Epistle to the Romans. Not one word of that tremendous indictment need be changed in relation to Brazil; and doubtless the same thing is true in relation to all other countries wherein Romanism prevails as a State religion."

Reference has already been made to the extraordinary and scandalous lechery of the Brazilian clergy, which—here as elsewhere—is doubtless attributable, in great part, to the unspeakable and measureless villainies of the confessional. During several months' residence at Rio de Janeiro, in 1877, I was one day shown the house of one of three well-known mistresses of a certain priest, by whom it was said she had already been the mother of five children.   Each of his other (known) mistresses also had children by him. Many of the wealthy and fashionable people here have in their houses an oratory,—an apartment decorated with one or more of their so-called saints, and dedicated especially to family worship.   A favorite priest, who not unfrequently becomes a sort of supreme pet and demigod of the family, is selected and hired, often at an exorbitant salary, to offici-ate an hour or so, in this oratory, every day ; more particu-larly for the edification and moral training of the mother and daughters and small boys ; all of whom, in early life, are taught to advance and kiss the celebrant's hand, both when he arrives and when he departs.   In one of these cases, an elder son, a young man,—who himself related to me his experiences,—became so irreverent that he imposed upon himself the task of ascertaining some of the other haunts of his mother's and sisters' spiritual guide, who, in the course of a somewhat prolonged investigation, was traced to no less than six mistresses, most of whom had bastards by him.   It is only in words, and not in practices, that the adherents of the Romish religion in Brazil are op-posed to the principal article in the creed of Mormonism.

Neither the civil nor the ecclesiastical authorities ever take any notice whatever of any of these illicit and dis-graceful relations, notwithstanding the fact that they are matters of general and incontestable notoriety in the com-munity.   Without doubt the proper place for these profli-gate priests would be the penitentiary, at hard labor for a term of years; but they are left absolutely undisturbed in the performance of their " sacred " functions. Excepting the practical sustainers of the liquor traffic, on the one hand, and the gamblers and counterfeiters and forgers, on the other, there is probably no class of men in Brazil who are such conscienceless and indiscriminate despoilers of female chastity as the Roman Catholic clergy. Though the flagitious conduct here animadverted upon is not characteristic of all the Catholic priests in Brazil and in other sections of South America, yet it is truly indicative of the character of a large majority of them. From the lay natives, with few exceptions, a slight shrug of the shoulders and a subdued smile were almost the only responses I received to my expression of surprise at the silent toleration of so many glaring evidences of licentiousness and bastardy among the clergy; an extent of toleration which, inexplicably enough, seemed to amount to a species of general acquiescence. The common opinion, so far as I could understand it, was that, regardless of anything that may have happened, these were still holy men, who had only betrayed an ordinary weakness of human nature, and that it was best to say little or nothing on the subject, and to take no positive action in the matter, as any legal or other formal proceedings would, in all probability, only result in bringing upon their precious religion and the church a far more indelible stain. Where such vitiated sentiments and vile practices prevail throughout a nation—as they now prevail throughout Brazil—it is of course only a question of time when they will be followed by the utter demoralization and disruption of society. Obviously unbalanced and in imminent danger of being at once dashed to atoms amid its crumbling foundations, the whole empire of Brazil is to-day quivering on the very verge of a vast and unvoidable abyss.

Is it prudent—or, propounding a more manly and important question—is it right, for me, as the projector of the

Three Americas Railway, to antagonize, in this most unmistakable and uncompromising manner, the Catholic
church throughout Spanish and Portuguese America? I am
already aware that certain amiable and well-meaning gentlemen, who are staunch friends of the proposed Longitudinal Line, but who are, nevertheless,—if they will pardon
me for saying so,—somewhat deficient in fullness of fore-
cast and courage, are beginning to worry their souls with the
apprehension that I may weaken and cripple my own
scheme.   At this very time, the eleventh hour preceding the
publication of these papers, a highly esteemed correspondent, more than a thousand miles distant, has volunteered
to write to me in these words: "No one can detest Roman
Catholicism, as it prevails in South and Central America,
more than I do.   It is there, as I have seen it myself, overflowing with the grossest superstition and corruption.   But
I fear it might not be wise for you to assail it just now."
Shall I be so blunt as to repeat to my friend—I having already notified him in effect—that this is my affair, and not
his?

In the year 1871–72, when I first crossed the continent of
South America, and when I passed longitudinally along a
long section of the Andes, I found the priests and their fel-
low-fanatics, at Cordova, in the Argentine Republic, ar-
rayed in riotous hostility to the Wheelwright Railroad, then
in course of construction; from the track of which they
threw the engines and tore up the rails, and otherwise made
every possible effort to prevent the Ironhorse from entering
their city; because, as they alleged, it would bring in her-
etics and infidels, who would compass the destruction of
their "holy" religion!   During a period of nearly two weeks,
these ignorant and turbulent bigots kept all the forces of
the railroad completely in abeyance; but finally the authorities of the national government interposed very decisively

in behalf of justice and common sense, and the road was soon afterward built into Cordova, and provided with a station in lively proximity to the dingy, dilapidated and century-saddened old cathedral.

Not one of the railroads or other public improvements in Spanish or Portuguese America owes its existence, in any degree whatever, to clerical encouragement; on the contrary, from first to last, everything of the kind has, of necessity, and only by invincible perseverance, been accomplished in direct opposition to the depressive and pernicious influence of the priests. But there is now a glowing prospect that brighter days will soon dawn. Throughout Central and South America, there are, to-day, two great parties, nearly equally divided numerically; the Liberal party, the party of truth, honor, virtue, republicanism, and progress; and the Catholic party, the party of dissimulation, intrigue, vice, monarchy, and retrogression. As if by a natural and irresistible influence, I have been led to take my stand with the Liberal party; and with it I am determined to struggle, in the body and in the spirit, until that worthiest of all parties in the countries of the far south, shall have achieved permanently a splendid and perfect victory. Despite the senseless counteraction of the priests and their deluded satellites, the conjoint framers and fosterers of military and ecclesiastical despotisms, the Three Americas Railway must and will be built; and, as I am well assured, its completion will be unanimously and heartily hailed by the better classes of Sanish Americans themselves, as the precursor of the final triumph of true liberty and civilization throughout the southern continent of the Western Hemisphere.

H. R. H.

COMMERCIAL VIEWS OFFICIAL-LY EXPRESSED.

ENTERPRISES fraught with world-wide benefits.—*I. Taylor.*

NATURE seems to have taken a particular care to disseminate her blessings among the different regions of the world, with an eye to mutual intercourse and traffic among mankind, in order that the natives of the several parts of the globe might have a kind of dependence upon one another, and be united together by their common interests.—*Addison.*

PRESIDENT HAYES,
(Ohio.)

EXTRACT from the Message of President Hayes, under date of December 17, 1878, communicating, in answer to a Senate resolution, of the 5th of the same month, information concerning postal and commercial intercourse between the United States and the various countries of Spanish America:

" In answer to the resolution of the Senate of the 5th instant, requesting the transmission to the Senate of ' any information which may have been received by the departments ' concerning postal and commercial intercourse between the United States and South American countries, together with any recommendations desirable to be submitted or measures to be adopted for facilitating and improving such intercourse,' I transmit herewith reports from the Secretary of State and the Postmaster-General with accompanying papers.

" The external commerce of the United States has for many years been the subject of solicitude, because of the

351

outward drain of the precious metals it has caused. For fully twenty years previous to 1877 the shipment of gold was constant and heavy, so heavy during the entire period of the suspension of specie payments as to preclude the hope of resumption safely during its continuance. In 1876, however, vigorous efforts were made by enterprising citizens of the country, and have since been continued, to extend our general commerce with foreign lands, especially in manufactured articles, and these efforts have been attended with very marked success.

" The importation of manufactured goods was at the same time reduced in an equal degree, and the result has been an extraordinary reversal of the conditions so long prevailing, and a complete cessation of the outward drain of gold. The official statement of the values represented in foreign commerce will show the unprecedented magnitude to which the movement has attained, and the protection thus secured to the public interests at the time when commercial security has become indispensable.

" The agencies through which this change has been effected must be maintained and strengthened if the future is to be made secure. A return to excessive imports, or to a material decline in export trade, would render possible a return to the former condition of adverse balances, with the inevitable outward drain of gold as a necessary consequence. Every element of aid to the introduction of the products of our soil and manufactures into new markets should be made available. At present such is the favor in which many of the products of the United States are held, that they obtain a remunerative distribution, notwithstanding positive differences of cost resulting from our defective shipping, and the imperfection of our arrangements in every respect, in comparison with those of our competitors, for conducting trade with foreign markets."

SECRETARY EVARTS.

(New York.)

The Hon. Wm. M. Evarts, our learned and distinguishea late Secretary of State, in his extraordinarily lengthy and important communication, covering no less than one hundred and eighty-eight finely printed pages in pamphlet form, addressed to the Hon. Samuel J. Randall, Speaker of the House of Representatives, under date of May 1, 1880, very ably epitomizes and exhibits the commerce of the whole world, and shows distinctly the share of the United States in the same,—saying:

" Europe has girdled South America with steamships, and thereby swept the trade of our continent from under our very eyes. * * * By reference to that portion of this letter which enters into details concerning our trade with Mexico, Central and South America, the reasons which have contributed to the diversion of so large a portion of the commerce of America to Europe will be fully noted; the principal reason being the magnificent commercial marine of Europe. Added to this, and only subsidiary thereto, are the long-established European branch houses at every port and point where commerce might hope to find profitable lodgment. Outside of these advantages all else is in our favor. Our products are recognized in many markets as superior, in most cases, to those of Europe; and the feelings of the peoples and governments are for closer relations with the United States. But until we inaugurate and perfect a system of steam communication equal to that of England or France, and give the different countries the many other trade facilities which are now afforded them by Europe, we should not expect that mere sentiment or natural preferences can offset positive and profitable trade advantages. * * *

"All consular reports from South America agree that the lack of direct American steam communication between the several countries and the United States is the chief drawback to the introduction and development of our trade therewith. According to the report of Consul Russell, at Montevideo, there are fourteen lines of steamships running between Europe and the River Plate. The aggregate number of vessels of these lines entering the port of Montevideo is 26 monthly. *　*　*

"While the reports, herewith, from our consuls in Mexico are highly interesting as showing the condition of trade, as well as the many hinderances thereto, in the several districts, they do not enable me to give the necessary statistics concerning the total foreign trade of the country; even the report by Consul-General Strother, which is otherwise full and comprehensive, fails in this regard. The failure to supply this information, however, does not reflect upon our consuls, but is due wholly to the peculiar condition of affairs surrounding the Mexican customs, the central government, even, not being able, it would appear, to give the desired information. As I remarked in last year's Commercial Relations, the impossibility of securing definite information concerning the foreign trade of Mexico opened up a broad field of speculation to imaginative statisticians concerning importations into the country, some prominent individuals going so far as to assert that the imports into Mexico from Europe alone amounted to $70,000,000 annually. Without having any reliable Mexican data at hand, upon which to base a statement concerning the import trade of that country, this department possessed sufficient European official returns to lead to the belief that such assertions were wild exaggerations, calculated to mislead our manufacturers and exporters who were trading, or who might be inclined to open up trade, with the sister republic. *　*

" In the article of cotton manufactures, in which we so much excel, our sales in Central America are scarcely one-fortieth those of England. A further aid to the development of our trade with Central America is the certainty of our ships being always sure of return cargoes therefrom, the exports of those States, coffee, indigo, fine woods, rubber, and cochineal, &c., being always sure of finding a profitable market in the United States. The principal cause of the predominance of European trade in Central America is direct steam communication. A line of British steamers runs from London to Aspinwall, and thence, skirting the Central American coast, around Yucatan, makes Vera Cruz its terminus; thus sweeping off the entire trade of Central America on the Atlantic, and of the Gulf of Mexico. * * *

" With all due respect for the opinions of many of our consuls as to the great advantages which foreign merchants are supposed to possess over American merchants in reaching and controlling the markets of South America—such advantages as technical education, business apprenticeship, personal application, &c., &c.—and without, in any manner, reflecting upon the abilities of the business men of other nations, whose systems and ways may be often studied with profit by our merchants, it is not too much to say that in all the qualities which enter into commercial success—intelligence, aptness, comprehension, audacity, persuasiveness, and most direct application of means to reach the ends in view—the American merchant stands on a par with the merchant of any other nation; and as far as our products and manufactures are concerned, with the exception of a few of our manufactures not yet fully developed, their superiority is recognized in the various markets. * * *

" It would seem as if the Argentine Republic were following in the progressive footsteps of the United States more successfully than any other of the South American Republics —for they all seek to follow the example of the United States, even though they do not all succeed in their laudable ambition. As this feeling of admiration for our institutions and people has a deeper significance than even that which its complimentary application suggests—a feeling of political and commercial affiliation with us—it must be the sincere wish of the American people to note the broadest fulfillment of the aspirations of the government and people of the Argentine Republic. * * * Not a single steamer entered at or cleared from the Argentine Republic during the year 1878 from or to the United States, nor did a single steamer in the fleet of 1,590 carry the American flag. Among the many reasons which might be given in accounting for the meagerness of our trade with the Argentine Republic this single reason would outweigh all others. * * * Of the dozen principal articles of import into Brazil the sales of England are as twenty to one of ours; and the total trade of England with Brazil is nearly four times the total trade of the United States therewith. * * *

" American manufactures have grown into favor everywhere, and have won the highest recognition for strength, grace, and durability. This immediate and general recognition of the superior qualities of American manufacturers is a victory in itself pregnant with future profit. All our consular reports agree in this one respect, that American cottons, American tools and agricultural machinery, and all the fine manufactures which enter into the advanced utilities of the day, especially in their happy combination of the useful and the beautiful, are recognized as superior to all others. * * * We have advanced in manufactures, as in agriculture, until we are being forced outward by the irresistible pressure of our internal development, and we find it easier to meet and overcome opposition in the various foreign markets than to cry halt to progress at home. Strong hopes were entertained by the older manufacturing nations that American enthusiasm would give way before the many vexations and losses incident to the introduction of our trade in the various countries. It was expected that we, who were accustomed to immediate successes, would grow tired of canvassing the slow-moving and slow-accepting peoples who have grown up in fixed and conservative principles, and retire from the field in disgust. They now begin to see that the enthusiasm of the American exporter is as fixed as the conservatism of the Old World, and that this enthusiasm is accompanied by a spirit of patient persuasiveness which is hard to resist.   *   *   *

" British trade being universal,—it being almost safe to say that where England has no trade there is none,—and British and American trade being homogeneous to a large extent, I have dwelt more upon British trade comparisons than even upon the French, for it seems to me that wherever the British merchant has found a market the American merchant can also find one. In reading this letter, as well as in reading the principal consular reports herewith, the lack of an American steam marine will be found to be a continued theme of regret. Indeed, it may be said that there are only two things necessary to the enlargement of our trade to universal proportions, viz: American steamships, and American depots or warehouses in the principal foreign marts of the world. While we must trust to foreign ships to carry our exports, and to foreign agents to introduce our manufactures and products into the several markets, often in direct conflict with their own interests, our best efforts can only result in comparative success.   *   *   *

" Great efforts are being made, and will doubtless continue to be made,—as witness the reports from our consul-general in China—to convince us that our manufactures are *too good*, and, consequently, too dear, for the various peoples, and that until we manufacture inferior goods we cannot hope to compete with the other countries in the several markets. While the wisdom of lowering the prices of our various manufactures must be apparent to all, the moment we surrender our fair name by deteriorating the quality of our goods, that moment we descend from the high vantage ground which we have acquired by honest manufactures, to the level of the recognized manufacturers of inferior goods, where we will be surely and justly beaten. ' There is only room for American manufactures at the top,' and having attained to that position we should not lightly surrender the same by any allurements of immediate profit.

     * * * " The causes which operate against American trade with Africa and with South and Central America,—the want of steam communication and of representative American commercial houses,—apply in a still more emphatic manner to our trade with Asia. Our flag is scarcely ever seen in many important ports, and American goods are unknown in some of the principal marts. Relying upon foreign merchants for the introduction of our goods into the several markets, often in opposition to their own interests, our exporters and manufacturers must always expect unsatisfactory results, such as those reported from Ceylon, which are good illustrations of the evils which flow from the very uncommercial principle of relying upon others to do that which should be done by ourselves. * * * We must win our way by superiority alone,—superiority in business, in manufactures, and in all the subsidiary factors which go to build up a perfect commerce. But our manufacturers and exporters possess all the necessary elements to enable them to win the most brilliant success in this branch of our foreign trade. Happily this is so, for while the European merchant is di-

rected and aided to reach the foreign markets in many essential ways,—for that which is the life of all countries, commerce, appeals to those governments for favorable legislation as a first duty,—the American merchant must inaugurate, introduce, and develop the foreign commerce of his country as though it were wholly a personal speculation in which the nation at large had no interest. * * * Let there be wisdom in our strength, and open, upright dealing in all our transactions with the world, and our advantages shall grow so much apace as to preclude any successful competition from any source whatever."

MINISTER BAKER.

[Venezuela.]

The Hon. Jehu Baker, our Minister to Venezuela, writing from Caracas, under date of October 12, 1878, to Secretary Evarts, says:

" I desire to draw your serious attention and that of the administration to the subject of this communication, thinking, as I do, that it may be found to involve a matter of grave moment to the future commercial interests of the United States.

" 1. In view of the geographical position of our country in reference to the countries bordering on the Gulf of Mexico, the Caribbean Sea, and the Spanish Main, it is apparent that the United States should be dominant in the foreign commerce of these countries, and that our trade with them should be greatly extended.

" 2. There appear to be three great natural lines of communication between the United States and the countries indicated:

" *1st*. From Boston, New York, Philadelphia and Baltimore, by the way of St. Thomas.

" *2d*. From New Orleans, Galveston, and Mobile, by a route passing west of Cuba, and not a great way from Grand Cayman.

" *3d*. From our Pacific ports by way of the Isthmus, and thence east along the Spanish. Main, and not a great way from Curaçoa.   Thus, each of the three great seaboards of our country, the East, the South, and the West, seems to be placed in natural relation with the countries alluded to by a line of its own.

" 3. In order to carry on and develop the extended scheme of commerce which is here hinted at, it appears to me that certain commercial organs are needed, which we are now totally without, namely, naval stations and commercial depots on the respective routes.   It seems to me that we should have one such station and depot for each of the lines pointed out.   For the first, Saint Thomas appears to be strongly indicated.   For the second, my present knowledge admits no other suggestion than that of the bare geographical position and small size of Grand Cayman. For the third, Curaçoa might be well worth looking at.

" 4. In view of our home policy, it appears to me that these stations and depots should consist of small islands with good ports, so small and so appointed as to admit of no population large enough to disturb our home system.   I attach the last degree of importance to this condition, and would far sooner have our commerce undeveloped than bring in political power from the West Indies.   Owing to the climate and other conditions, such power would necessarily be too unhomogeneous to be safe.   We should seek stations and depots which will serve simply as naval and commercial organs, and which can never expand into political forces.

" 5. What I have said respecting our relation to the commerce of the countries bordering on the Gulf of Mexico, the Caribbean Sea, and the Spanish Main, and the usefulness of naval stations and commercial depots in relation thereto, is equally applicable to our relation and trade with the West Indies. It appears to me that possession of some such stations and depots as I have supposed would greatly facilitate and strengthen our trade with those islands.

" 6. What I have said respecting the usefulness of some such stations and depots is in like manner applicable to our trade with Brazil, Uraguay, and the Argentine Republic. Our commerce with these countries must find its way to and from the United States by all three of the great routes alluded to; and it seems apparent that it would be greatly accommodated and aided by suitable naval stations and commercial depots situated on the routes which it traverses.

" 7. The suggestions I am making look to the improvement of our commerce upon a scale commensurate with the West Indies and all the countries that border upon the north and the east of South America. As matters are at present, in reference to this great area of trade, the United States appears to me to be an immense commercial force without suitable organs to work with. If we can do so consistently with our internal policy, it strikes me that we should conform to that law of all vital and all social development, by which the growing organism supplies itself with special organs for the employment and application of its force. Naval stations and commercial depots, such as I have supposed, appear to me to be the special organs that are needed, in order fitly to wield and develop our commerce upon the extensive scale which I have pointed out.

" 8. Not alone the present industrial production and trade-capacity of the countries in question should be looked at. In my judgment, the future will bring a great increase of both. The production and trade of Brazil is certainly increasing apace ; and as for the various republics —Venezuela and the rest, and the communities of some of the great West India Islands—they are, in my opinion, passing through a transition period of internal agitation, to be followed by a more stable social order, and-a consequent large increase of population, industry and trade. I suspect that the prospective importance of this trade in the aggregate—excepting that of Brazil—is far from being duly appreciated in the United States.

" 9. Aside from the direct commercial advantages which would seemingly attend the possession of such stations and depots as I have suggested, it appears to me that certain highly important indirect results would follow: *1st*. The facilities for the protection of our commerce would be greatly increased. *2d*. The prestige of the United States— which I fear is not now what it should be in these regions— would also be greatly increased. *3d*. The legitimate influence of the United States would become potential—which can hardly be claimed for it at present—in the way of discouraging disorder and promoting order over a wide industrial region, thus fostering the production of the material of commerce, while benefitting various communities. As an element of a just foreign policy, this last consideration appears to me of much moment. I presume it may be fairly said that the United States is, more than any other great nation, interested in the political success of the Spanish American republics. By the possession of such footholds of naval and commercial power as I have indicated, she would be in a far better position to exercise a legitimate friendly influence in favor of order, and to become, in a much better sense than at present, the head of the great family of republics upon the Western Hemisphere.

" 10. I presume that such stations and depots as I have

supposed might now be acquired at a cost of a few millions of dollars; and, taking a strictly economical view of the case, and saying nothing of the higher considerations of national standing and influence to which I have alluded, I suspect that the increase of our commerce and the consequent increase of our revenue, the enlarged demand for our products, and the extension of our marine employment, would make it a capital investment.

"11. For reasons which I need here only allude to,— connected with the rivalry incident to that great industrial development which is going on in Europe as well as in the United States,—I suspect that the acquisition of suitable naval stations and commercial depots may become more difficult in the not distant future than at present."

MINISTER DICHMAN.

[United States of Columbia.]

Under date of October 17, 1878, the Hon. Earnest Dichman, our Minister to the United States of Columbia, (which, among the excessively numerous family of South American nationalities, was formerly called New Granada,) writing from Bogota to Secretary Evarts, says:

"It is difficult to understand the differences between the two political parties, except that in an indefinite way the Conservatives are supposed to be identified with, and the Liberals opposed to, the Catholic church; otherwise the most careful inquiries fail to elicit any difference of principles in the administration of the government. The presidential term being so short, only two years, agitations for the succession are always in order, and pervade all the state elections, the doctrine of state rights being firmly established here to an extent which the most violent supporter of the doctrine in the United States would not dream of. The Conservatives being disorganized, although numerically very strong, the next presidential contest will be between the two wings of the Liberal party; but as the issues are merely personal, it would require an intimate acquaintance with the Columbian statesmen (of whom there are a great many,) to form an opinion as to the chances of success of either side. The administration of General Trujillo appears to be deservedly very popular on account of his unquestioned honesty, the purity of his motives, his success as a general, and good conduct during the late war. It is hoped, principally owing to General Trujillo's personal influence, that the next election will pass off without an attempt at a revolution, in which case no political disturbances are anticipated for some time to come, and the country will have an opportunity to recuperate from the wounds inflicted by the late civil war, from the effects of which it is yet suffering.

"The relations between Columbia and foreign countries appear to be friendly; but, aside from the question of treaty stipulations, it seems to me that the government of the United States has a greater interest in this republic than any other foreign government can have. The proximity to our country and the similarity of institutions give us the advantage of a political sentiment in our favor which cannot exist for any other nation, and which a wise policy will foster and strengthen; for out of it will come an increased intercourse between the two countries and corresponding commercial advantages. * * * In many respects the commerce of this country offers a very inviting field to the American merchant and manufacturer. Owing to the conditions of the climate, a competition in the way of manufactured goods need never be apprehended; the country requires everything manufactured in the United States, and can offer in exchange a variety of tropical productions which we need. Owing to the disturbed political condition of the country, and the falling off in the yield of quinia bark and tobacco, the foreign trade of Columbia has declined considerably within the last two years, but the cultivation of coffee, the production of many textile fabrics, materials for paper stock, and the development of the mineral wealth can hardly be said to have commenced. American goods, notably dry-goods and hardware, have already gained quite a foothold for themselves in the markets of Columbia, the superior excellence of the goods, at the same prices of the foreign article, being readily conceded; while the trade in supplying the coast States, in fact the entire Magdalen Valley, with flour, soap, vegetables, and candles, has assumed no inconsiderable dimensions.

"Among the chief difficulties in the way of commerce with the United States are the well-established connections with Europe and the habit of trading there; also the want of knowledge on the part of our exporters in selecting, preparing, and packing goods for this market. The people in this country are used to certain patterns, sizes, and quantities in piece-goods; and as all the transportation has to be done by mules, the packages have to be so arranged as to load easily and not exceed a certain weight. * * *

"While I do not wish to express an opinion in favor of what is commonly know as a subsidy for steamships, yet I am satisfied that if the Government of the United States would pay a liberal sum for the carrying of the mail at frequent and regular intervals, particularly to the port of New Orleans, I have reason to believe that a proportionate amount of money could be obtained from this government. I suggest New Orleans on account of its proximity, and because an opportunity would be afforded to our Southern railroads to transfer to the United States the passenger and freight traffic which now exists between this country and Europe by sea. In this way the time between this country and Europe could be shortened, and a part of the sea voyage avoided; but the principal advantage to the United States would be in the fact that in passing through the United States the Columbian merchant would find it impossible not to become interested in our commercial and manufacturing centers, and our merchants would have an opportunity of becoming acquainted and establishing personal relations with the commercial men of this country. Nor can the advantages arising from the establishment of frequent and regular mail-communication be overestimated in increasing the commerce between the two countries. In these days of steam, the post-office is the great auxiliary of commerce. Samples sent with each changing fashion bring to the consumer the stores and factories of merchants and manufacturers; and the market-price sent by mail brings to the door of every one the markets of the world. * * *

"Not only would regular and frequent communications increase the direct exchange of commodities, but there is another advantage which would accrue; namely, the continuation of public improvements, which, with a better acquaintance between the people of the two countries, would naturally fall into the hands of our people. The crying want of this country is roads—common roads and railroads—and nobody is better qualified to build them than the American engineers and contractors who have gained their experience from building and constructing the railroad sytem of the United States.

"Another matter of importance, if not directly in a commercial point of view, yet of some consequence as affecting the future political and commercial relations between the two countries, is the number of students who go to Europe

every year from this country for the purpose of being educated.   By bringing the advantages of our educational
institutions to the notice of the people of this country, much
can be done to have these students sent to the United
States; for there, after all, is the country where, by daily observation and contact, the students from this country can
learn how a great people can govern itself under republican
institutions without the constant fear of political disturbances.

" Considering the limited means at the command of the
government of Columbia, much is being done for the cause
or education ; and in my conversations with the superintendent of public instruction I have impressed him with the
advantages of sending to the United States for teachers in
the normal schools; and I am well assured that if it should
be desirable to employ foreign teachers, they would be selected from the United States.   There is a great desire here
to know more about the workings of our government, and
nowhere can this be taught better than in the schools of our
country."

CONSUL McLEAN.

[Ecuador.]

Alexander McLean, late United States Consul at Guayaquil, Ecuador, in a very thoughtful and perspicuous communication, addressed to Secretary Evarts, at Washington,
in special reference to the imperfection of our postal arrangements and facilities with the Spanish American countries, says :

" The basis of a successful foreign trade is a prompt and
reliable mail, and our mail is anything but prompt and reliable.   Of the Ecuadorian mail, it is only necessary to say

that the mercantile community send their letters in the sacks of the British Consul here for safety. Even the mail for the United States is sent in his care to the British Consul at Panama; each merchant inclosing his letters for the States in a large cover addressed to the United States Consul at Panama, and bearing the British stamp. Eighteen cents per half ounce must be prepaid at the British Consulate, which is the postage to Panama only. United States postage stamps are not procurable here, and the letters are forwarded from Panama without being prepaid."

———

MINISTER OSBORN.

[Chili.]

Speaking especially of the superiority of American manufactures, the Hon. Thomas A. Osborn, our Minister to Chili, writing from Santiago, under date of November 2, 1877, to Secretary Evarts, says:

"In the September number of *Harper's Monthly* appeared an article entitled, "The American laborer as seen by Europeans," which attracted my attention and seemed to me worthy of reproduction here. I have therefore secured a faithful translation thereof, and had it published in the *Ferrocarril,* the leading daily paper of Chili. The purpose of the writer of the article evidently was to direct attention to the great superiority of some of our American manufactures over those of Europe; and I cannot but feel that he succeeded in a marked degree. In my judgment a proper dissemination of correct information in regard to the manufactures of the United States among the people of South and Central America would result in great benefit to our country. The commerce of Chili has been almost totally absorbed by Europeans, and the people are comparatively ignorant of the advantages which they would derive from a direct trade with the United States. To present the facts before them, and have them understand that very many of the articles which they consume are manufactured in the United States and transported twenty-five · hundred miles to Europe, and thence nearly ten thousand miles from there to this country, should, it seems to me, be the work of our government. By bringing the facts to the attention of the people and showing them that these same goods can be brought here direct from our country with half this distance of transportation, the way to a revival of our trade with Spanish America will be greatly simplified. I respectfully . suggest to the Secretary of State that it would be good policy, in my opinion, to cause to be translated into Spanish and forwarded to the various diplomatic and consular representatives of the government in South America, short articles of this character, with a view of having them republished in the country to which they are sent."

Again, Mr. Osborn, writing to Secretary Evarts, under date of October 24, 1878, says:

" The importers of Chili are nearly all foreigners, and confined principally to the English and Germans. They have their home connections ; and it can hardly be expected, therefore, that they should encourage the building up of a competing commerce. American dealers in Chili are exceedingly scarce ; and such trade as we have here is absolutely forced upon the European merchants by reason of the demand for our goods. The attention of the public is being directed to the' superiority of our manufactures, and the desire for an improvement in our commercial relations is becoming quite general; but if our business men would reap the full benefit of this, they must establish commercial houses in Chili, and place their goods here in competition with the importations from Europe."

23

MINISTER OSBORN.

[Argentine Republic.]

The Hon. Thomas O. Osborn, our Minister to the Argentine Republic, writing from Buenos Ayres under date of November 18, 1877, to Secretary Evarts, says:

"No steam vessels arrive at the port of Buenos Ayres direct from any part of the United States, and no vessels of that class leave this port, or the river La Plata, direct for any port in the United States, except an occasional vessel of a single line, carrying the British flag, and that at irregular periods, and which returns to this port by way of Europe; hence this uncertain means of communication can do little or nothing in the way of fostering or enlarging the trade between the river La Plata and the United States. On the other hand, direct and rapid communication is at present, and has been for a long time, maintained between the Argentine States and Europe by eleven different lines of steamships, of which five are British, four are French, one German, and one Italian. These steamships carry passengers, not only those whose destination is Europe, but those who desire to go to the United States, and also articles of commerce for the latter which are required to be delivered as promptly as possible on orders. Our merchant-fleet in the river La Plata, comparatively small, is wholly under canvas, and while it may be able to do all the carrying demanded, yet the arrivals and departures of vessels of that character are uncertain, and are not calculated, in this age of speed and improvements, to inspire merchants with confidence. * * * With the exception of lumber, kerosene, tobacco, and some agricultural implements, and a few other specialties, which are strictly of American growth or manufacture, and cannot be obtained elsewhere, little or nothing is imported thence. I am informed that from the United States thousands of tons of cheese, butter, beef and pork are annually exported to England, and none to the river La Plata; nevertheless, all these articles are received here from England, and, although of American origin, are sold as English products. American cotton goods, deservedly famed for their excellent quality and low cost, are, notwithstanding these advantages, rarely or never seen in this market; while of English manufactures of similar styles, large quantities are imported and meet with ready and profitable sales. So, too, refined sugar and Carolina rice were formerly among the principal imports to this country from the United States; now the chief supplies of sugar are drawn from France, Germany, and Holland, while most of the rice is received from Italy."

MINISTER STEVENS.

[Uruguay.]

The Hon. John L. Stevens, late United States Minister to Uruguay and Paraguay, and now Minister from the United States to Sweden and Norway, in one of his recent dispatches to Secretary Evarts, says:

" Countries with which we are not connected by continuous steam lines, with which our rivals in manufactures and trade have unbroken steam connection, can deal with us and we with them only at marked disadvantage. This fact is strikingly apparent as to the present condition and necessities of our trade with South America, with all parts of which England has continuous lines of steamers, while the United States have not. The strongly *protective policy* of England as to her manufactures is obvious to all who have given attention to the subject. The vast sums which her government has expended in subsidizing her continuous steam lines, in maintaining her colonial policy, her Eastern policy, her Indian domination, her expensive activity in China, her watchful regard for the new islands of the seas— all this vast expenditure that her manufactures and shipping may grow and be maintained, is as distinctive and positive a protection as English patriotism and statesmanship can devise. At least a partial imitation of this kind of national encouragement and protection of American productions and manufactures, which has so much aided in the distribution of English, German, French, and Belgian productions, might not be unwise. The vast annual products of the United States should be allowed to a large degree to go to their foreign consumers without passing through too many foreign hands and undergoing the expense of too many transshipments and intermediary commissions."

MINISTER HILLIARD.

[Brazil.]

The Hon. Henry W. Hilliard, our Minister to Brazil, writing from Rio de Janeiro, under date of November 6, 1877, to Secretary Evarts, says :

"Upon my arrival here, I felt it to be my duty to inform myself in regard to the state of what may be called American interests in this country. My attention was attracted to the remarkable fact that, while the United States take so large a proportion of the coffee of Brazil, the great bulk of the trade of this country is controlled by England. We furnish the money which the people of this country use in purchasing their supplies from other countries; and much the larger proportion is imported from England. I shall at some time state the figures which represent this state of trade. Some of our products are actually sent from the United States to England, sold there, and then reshipped to the ports of Brazil in the steamships of Great Britain, where they are sold in the market at a great advance upon the original prices. The want of the facilities for rapid transit between the principal ports of the United States and those of Brazil must, of course, subject us to great disadvantage in our commercial intercourse with this country. * * * It is a remarkable fact that, while there is not a single line of direct communication by steamship between the ports of the United States and those of Brazil, other countries have established lines which are in full and, I believe, successful operation. The Liverpool and Pacific Mail Steamship Company sends two steamers per month. The Royal Mail Line sends steamships which sail from Southampton twice a month. There are three lines of steamships from France, —one from Havre, one from Bordeaux, and one from Marseilles,—sailing each semi-monthly. There is a line from Hamburg, and another from Bremen. There is also a line from Genoa. It is impossible to overlook the importance of a line of steamships between the ports of the United States, for example New York and New Orleans, and this port, touching at other ports of Brazil."

Again, Mr. Hilliard writing to Secretary Evarts, under date of May 23, 1878, says:

" It is very important that we should acquire the control of the commerce of Brazil. English capital is largely invested here ; it is a rich field, with a great future, and we ought to be willing to spend money to open it to the people of the United States. Even if the immediate results should not be satisfactory in a pecuniary sense, we should persevere and make the country from which we receive such large importations the market for the products of the labor and skill of our people."

SENATOR WINDOM.

[Minnesota.]

In the course of his very able speech, on *Isthmus Ship-Canals*, in the Senate of the United States, February 28, 1881, the Hon. William Windom, now Secretary of the Treasury, said:

" I do not hesitate to declare that I am in favor of wise and judicious expenditures to develop our magnificent resources, expand our foreign trade, and restore our lost ocean commerce. * * * If we deny to the rest of the world the right to break down this isthmian barrier between the two great oceans, we must be prepared to remove it our-selves. It does not comport with our honor or our national traditions to stand stubbornly blocking the world's progress. Our mission is to lead, not to obstruct. * * * It may be said that no other nation shall be permitted to control this isthmian highway. That sounds well. It is brave talk ;• but I repeat that in this last quarter of the nineteenth century we cannot afford to stand in the way of the world's progress, refusing to open this highway of commerce our-selves, or to permit any other nation to do it. Have we counted the possible cost of enforcing such a dog-in-the-manger policy? * * * The time has come when this barrier is about to be removed. The wonder is that it has been permitted to remain so long. If we do not remove it somebody else will. It is now too late to discuss the ques-tion as to whether there shall be a ship-transit-way across the Isthmus. The necessities of commerce as well as the spirit of progress have decreed it; and powerful as we may

be, we cannot resist that decree.   Already a company has
been organized, in France, for the purpose of constructing
a tide-level canal at Panama, and subscriptions amounting
to $60,000,000 have been obtained, a large part of which
has already been paid in, and another payment is about to
be made. * * *

" When we declare to the nations of Europe that we will
not consent to their control or interference with an isthmian
highway, we must also be prepared to declare that we are
ready to strike down this barrier ourselves and give to the
commerce of the world those facilities which it demands
and to which it is entitled.   Then, and then only, will we
speak with a voice potential and in a way to command the
attention of the nations of the earth.   Inasmuch, then, as a
transit-way must and will be constructed, either under foreign auspices or those of our own Government, it will at
once be conceded that such transit should be located at that
point on the Isthmus which offers the greatest advantages to
our own country.   The value of Tehuantepec as a commercial highway has always been recognized by our Government.   In 1847, during the negotiations for the treaty of
Guadalupe Hidalgo, the United States Commissioner was
authorized to offer Mexico $15,000,000 for the right of way
across the Isthmus ; but Mexico was precluded from accepting the offer, by reason of the existence of a previous
grant.   For half a century or more, many of our far-seeing
statesmen have looked with longing eyes upon this natural
and most.desirable pathway of commerce.   It will be apparent, by a glance at the map, that Tehuantepec is, in
every sense, the American route ; but I desire to indicate
briefly some of its peculiar and specific advantages to our
own country over all other routes :

" First. It is much shorter and hence will afford cheaper
transportation.

"Second. It will require far less time and money for its construction, and hence will afford much earlier relief, and cheaper transit.

"Third. It will be peculiarly adapted to the use of sailing-vessels.

"Fourth. For the above reasons, and others, it will prove a far better and more effectual regulation of railway charges.

"Fifth. Its military advantages are incomparably superior to those of any other route.

"Sixth. It will establish intimate commercial relations between the United States and Mexico, while the other routes would not.

"Seventh. It will prove the most effectual method of rebuilding our commercial marine, and restoring our lost supremacy on the ocean."

SPEAKER RANDALL.

[Pennsylvania.]

The Hon. Samuel J. Randall, Speaker of the House of Representatives, in the course of a letter which he addressed to the citizens of Galveston, Texas, under date of May 25, 1877, gave expression to the ideas and language of an enlightened American statesman in these words :

"The time has come, in my opinion, when the policy of the government should be to enlarge our trade relations with Mexico and with the Central and South American republics. It is well for us to study the statistics of the trade between these countries and the markets of the world, from which we find that the people of the United States are not receiving a due share of the commerce of the countries I have named. We need more favorable commercial relations and more comprehensive trade connections with other nations. Let me cite a few figures to prove the truthfulness of my assertion. The public documents show the foreign commerce of the countries lying south of the United States on the American continent to be about $520,000,000. Our share of this amount is about $112,000,000, of which only about $37,000,000, is transported in American vessels and under the American flag. Such a statement should at once arouse our people from their lethargy. The war stimulated the manufacturing facilities of the North enormously, and only by the adoption of such a policy can we keep up the activity of our manufacturing districts and secure a market for our productions. It is a discredit to our enlightenment that we, as a people, stand quietly by and do not make sufficient endeavor to increase our meager share of this important trade. When the extended policy to which I have referred is inaugurated, as it must and will be, then will your city, your State, and the entire coast of the Gulf, receive the advantages which nature has bespoken for them."

CONGRESSMAN KING.

[Louisiana.]

Extracts from the speech of Hon. J. Floyd King, of Louisiana, in the House of Representatives, at Washington, June 1, 1880, on the importance of improving the navigation of the Mississippi River:

* * * "Probably never before in the history of this country has Congress had before it so many important commercial questions. The bills and resolutions in which they are presented for our consideration reflect public sentiment,

which is unusually alive to all that will enlarge our internal
and foreign commerce, and thereby stimulate greater material development and business prosperity. There are at
present awaiting our action the report of the Mississippi
River Commission, various bills relative to an interoceanic
ship-canal, the report of the Army Engineers relative to a
ship-canal across Florida, several resolutions seeking new
commercial treaties, resolutions aiming at the development
of Spanish American trade, a bill providing for the appointment of a commission to revise the tariff laws, several bills
providing for an extension of our merchant marine, and
many others which I might enumerate of the same general
nature. Some of these are so very important that a delay
in their passage for even one session of Congress is a loss
to the country of millions of dollars. *   *   *

"This work of improving the navigation of the Mississippi River is as broad and national as are the great agricultural interests which have contributed more than all else
combined to the development of the United States, until
she ranks as the chief granary of the world. The national
importance of this industry will also be appreciated when
we reflect that the value of one year's grain crop in the
United States is equal to that of all the gold which the
mines of California have yielded since their first discovery,
in 1848, to the present hour.   .

*   *   * "Great Britain has more than enough of our
carrying trade at present, and it will be a discredit to our
business capacity to remain inactive until she has completed
new transportation lines to tap the grain-fields of the Mississippi Valley and deflect the course of shipments away
from our seaports. *   *   * Throughout the country there
is a demand for new foreign markets. In looking over the
field, I find a most astonishing, and I may justly add, dis-
graceful, neglect of commerce with the neighboring Amer-

ican countries, at the south, toward whose doors the Mississippi is constantly flowing.   Of the total trade of those nations and islands, which now amounts to nearly one thousand million dollars annually, the Mississippi Valley controls, directly, less than one per cent.   With a portion of them, namely: Hayti, San Domingo, Porto Rico, the French West Indies, the Dutch West Indies, the Danish West Indies, the Argentine Republic, Chili, Peru, Bolivia, Ecuador, Paraguay and Uruguay, she has no percentage of direct trade. * * * With an unobstructed river, it is possible for us to wrest from England, Germany and France this enriching Spanish American trade, which they now monopolize.   Each year's delay in our control of the same is a serious and unnecessary loss to the business of the whole country."

CONGRESSMAN COLE.

[Missouri.]

In the course of his very able speech on our commercial relations with Mexico and other Spanish American Republics, delivered in the House of Representatives, February 14, 1879, the Hon. Nathan Cole, of Saint Louis, Missouri, said:

" The United States to-day stand first among nations in commercial opportunities.   The outside world observes them and comments on our possibilities in terms of unqualified praise.   A former prime minister of England, Gladstone,* prophesies that we will in the future probably wrest from them, commercial supremacy.   At the opening of Parliament, in December, the present premier, Lord Beacons-

*Again Prime Minister, in 1881.

field, expressed substantially the same sentiment, when he said : ' Enterprise in America reacts on that of England. I look forward with much confidence to the influence of American industry and enterprise shortly producing more favorable results than we can now estimate.' Lord Derby recently paid us a similar compliment. The question arises, do we see ourselves as others do ? Do we see and appreciate our brilliant opportunities ? I fear not, and that politics still retain the throne while material interests play a minor part. But there are many present indications that the order will soon be reversed, placing business before politics. Our distinguished Secretary of State, Mr. Evarts, has more than once pointed out to the people of this country as a desirable policy for the future ' full ' foreign trade. In a recent after-dinner speech in New York he said :

" ' Sometimes statesmen have had no resources, after the dissensions of civil war were composed, but to find some new energy, and some new excitement, that would unite the discordant elements and impulses in an advance upon a foreign enemy ; but this great and enlightened people know that it is better worth their while to make an advance upon the commerce of the world.'

" Mr. Evarts himself set the example by making such an advance more than a year and a half ago when he sent instructions to our consuls and other official representatives of the United States throughout the civilized world, to examine and report how we could best extend our trade. It devolves upon us to give this new commercial departure every possible support. We, who are sent here to serve the people, have material as well as political interests to guard. We will fail in our duty if we leave obstacles in the way of commercial progress. We should rather be the pathfinders of commerce in advance of the people, and see that all avenues of trade are kept open for their unrestrained use and profit.   It is my privilege to represent in this House one of the districts of the commercial metropolis of the Mississippi Valley, a city with whose interests I have all my life been identified.   Looking from that stand-point, I see south and southwest of the great valley the Spanish American nations, which constitute a new, open, and all-important field for the exports of our surplus products and manufactures.   I believe that to be a favorite field of the State Department which would make a specialty of American commerce and build up a continental policy.

"All the Republics of Spanish America have in the past depended chiefly upon Great Britain, France, Germany, and Holland for the supply of their varied demands.   But they are to-day seeking more intimate commercial relations with us ; and blind indeed will we be to our own interests if we repel their friendly advances.   Of these nations the first in order of distance, natural resources, and demand for the arts of our civilization to help develop their wealth, is Mexico.   She should, then, first receive our consideration ; self-interest requires it.   Unless we soon occupy more foreign fields, the fallacious cry of overproduction will necessarily gain many converts.   It is claimed that overproduction has thrown upon our hands millions of dollars in wares which cannot be disposed of, and that the products of the farm yield a return so small that the producer is discouraged ; while the manufacturer stores away his surplus product for a future market, closes his mills and furnaces entirely, or runs them upon half or one-third time.   But I maintain that the proper term is underconsumption.   Just so long as there is upon the face of the earth a human being unshod, unclothed, or unfed, a farm without implements, a mine in need of machinery, a State without railways, it is idle to talk of overproduction.   We should continue to produce and manufacture until the whole world is supplied with the necessities and conveniences of life."

EIGHTEEN ADDITIONAL PAPERS
FROM THE PROJECTOR.*

MAN can effect no great matter by his personal strength but as he acts in society and in conjunction with others.—*South.*

CIVILIZATION is a constant warfare of man against Nature.—*Seward.*

TO A COMMITTEE OF AMERICAN SENATORS.

RIO DE JANEIRO, BRAZIL, *December 1, 1877.*
TO THE HONORABLE THE SENATE COMMITTEE
ON FOREIGN AFFAIRS, *Washington.*

GENTLEMEN: About to undertake a second fatiguing and perilous journey, on mule-back, across the continent of South America, from the Atlantic to the Pacific, I respectfully request that, in the event of my death within the next two years,—only in which event my brother, Mr. Hanson Pinkney Helper, at Davidson College, North Carolina, will forward to you this communication,—you may be pleased to give special attention to the subject explained in the accompanying papers.

It has been frequently remarked, and quite as truthfully as frequently, that every country in Europe which, for any considerable period, has ever yet enjoyed anything like a monopoly of the trade with India, has thereby greatly enriched itself. By the consummation of the gigantic inter-

*For still eighteen other papers from the Projector, (three dozen in all,) yet counting the five tables of statistics as only one paper, see pages 3–30, 33–35, 38–43, 125, 208, 296–317, 319, 322, 335, 346–350.

continental railway scheme proposed in the annexed communication, (addressed to the Emperor of Brazil, but never
sent nor shown to him, for the reason that he has manifested no disposition to comply with the only conditions,
fair and simple as they were, on which I could prudently
explain the matter,) the United States may soon be made
the peerlessly powerful and self-protective recipient in perpetuity of the untold and inexhaustible riches of no less
than three Indias,—the India of all South America, the
India of all Central America, and the India of all Mexico.
That is to say, all the separate and distinct countries in the
New World south of the United States, and north as well as
south, including moreover every State and Territory of the
American Union itself, may thus reciprocally, for their own
advancement and for our advancement, for their own
aggrandizement and for our aggrandizement, be at once and
forever rendered plentifully and peacefully and prosperously
tributary to the Republic of Republics.

Under the regular and rightful operation of the vast system of railways here projected, we can, in the course of the
next fifteen or twenty years, take permanently from Europe,
as, by virtue of our geographical position and contiguity,
and in consideration of our superior energy and skill, we
ought to take, the immense trade and the profits of trade of
the greater part of the southern hemisphere. At the same
time, and by the same means, we shall become much more
generally and genially and thriftily identified with that adjoining but as yet comparatively undeveloped and uninhab-
ited hyperborean region, British America, which we find
delineated as forming such a marvelously extensive portion of our own continent.

Gentlemen of the Committee: I honestly believe that if
you will kindly and actively and successfully carry out this
enterprise, in all the breadth and fullness of detail suggested

by me, and with such important improvements in plans and principles as you yourselves will doubtless be able to introduce, you will thereby do for your own country, and for all the other countries of the New World, one of the very greatest services upon which you can possibly bring to bear the benign and far-reaching influences of your wisdom and patriotism. For my inception of this grand and prospectively glorious enterprise, I expect no remuneration whatever, other than that which I now find, and shall always find, within the recesses of my own breast; only I profoundly hope and trust that you will cause the work to be done in a manner every way worthy of American statesmanship, American honor, American interests, and, above all, American unity and nationality.

I remain, gentlemen, most respectfully,

Your fellow-citizen abroad,

H. R. HELPER.

———

TO SECRETARY THOMPSON.

SOUTH AND CENTRAL AMERICAN TRADE WITH THE UNITED STATES.

[From the *South Pacific Times*, Callao, Peru.]

Our enterprising and progressive neighbors of North America, always having an eye to new avenues of business, seem to have fixed their attention upon both the Atlantic and Pacific coasts of South America, with a zeal and thoroughness especially characteristic of the citizens of the Model Republic. The grand and colossal achievements of the United States in agriculture, stock-raising, mining, railway construction and other material industries, as also in new inventions and discoveries, in science, in literature, and in the fine arts, are now patent to all the world; and what those States are yet destined to accomplish in manufactures and commerce, will probably soon surprise, and may possibly astonish, their friendly rivals on the other side of the Atlantic.

In the intelligence brought by the steamer of last week, not the least significant item is the assurance, all the way from the Palace of the Universal Exhibition in Paris, that " The United States will get a large proportion of the grand prizes and gold medals."

We have recently published several communications advocating closer commercial intercourse between the two continents, and now we place before onr readers a lengthy letter on the subject from Mr. Hinton Rowan Helper, an American author and traveler, who became famous, just before the war of the great rebellion in the United States, for the peculiar and forcible combination of anti-negro and anti-slavery views advanced in his work entitled *The Impending Crisis of the South*. Mr. Helper, we learn, has twice crossed the continent of South America, by dfferent routes, and he appears to have been a careful observer of many things. His letter, as will be seen, is addressed to the Hon. Mr. Thompson, a member of the Cabinet of President Hayes ; and the points he makes in connection with the navy of his country, and what he says in favor of New Orleans and the proposed ship-canal across the Isthmus of Darien, will doubtless be read and pondered with lively interest.

LIMA, PERU, February 22, 1878.

HON. RICHARD W. THOMPSON,
Secretary of the Navy, Washington.

SIR : Though far away from home, and yet but little beyond the middle of a long journey by sea and land still before me, so much pleased am I with both the letter and spirit of your Annual Report to the President in December last, which, however, I have only now been able to obtain and read, that I beg the privilege of specifying at least two or three of the passages which have impressed me as being filled with suggestions of the very greatest importance to our future national welfare. Especially do I refer to those passages wherein you hint, and well and wisely hint, at the necessity for a better adjustment of relationship and interaction between our Navy of Force and our Navy of Freight ; between our men-of-war and our fleet of unarmed vessels engaged in the merchant service. In this regard, as it seems to me, our one great need at this time is more clip-

pers and crafts for commerce, and fewer frigates for fighting;
more useful industry and trade and traffic, and less wasteful
indolence and extravagance and ostentation.

Only a few days have elapsed since my arrival here from
Brazil and the Argentine Republic, on the east side of South
America; I having, for the second time, (first in 1871–72,
and now again in 1877–78,) come overland, across the Continent, most of the way on mule-back, with servant and
sumpter-mules, carrying my bed and baggage, and often
water and provisions with me. During these two trips over
the Pampas and over the Andes, over the Llanos and over
the Cordilleras, by different routes, the first through the upper provinces of the Argentine Republic, through Bolivia
and Peru, and the second in almost a straight line westwardly from Buenos Ayres, near the River Plate and the
Atlantic Ocean, to Valparaiso on the Pacific coast, I have
been everywhere kindly received and welcomed, not because
I was Mr. Helper, but because I was an American citizen,
a plain and simple child of the Great Republic. Yet it
always grieved me exceedingly, and was particularly offen-
sive to my sense of the fitness of things, to find almost
everything in the way of foreign merchandise, throughout
the length and breadth of my routes of travel, of European
manufacture.

At different ports along the Atlantic and Pacific coasts, in
many cities of the plains, in various towns on the mountain
slopes, on the apex of Potosi, and on the tops of other
Andean peaks higher than Mount Hood, I have gone into
stores and warehouses, and looked around in vain, utterly in
vain, for one single article of American manufacture. From
the little pin with which the lady fastens her beau-catching
ribbons, to the grand piano with which she enlivens and en-
chants the hearts of all her household; from the tiniest
thread and tack and tool needed in the mechanic arts, to

the largest plows and harrows and other agricultural implements and machines required for use on the farm—all these
and other things, the wares and fabrics and light groceries
and delicacies in common demand, the drugs and chemi-
cals sold by the apothecary, the fermented and malt and
spirituous liquors in the wine saloon, the stationery and fancy
góods in the bookstore, the furniture in the parlor, and the
utensils in the kitchen, are with very rare exceptions of English, French, German, Spanish or Italian manufacture.   And
what makes the matter still more unsatisfactory and vexatious to the North American, and more expensive and otherwise disadvantageous to the South American, is that these
articles are, as a general rule, inferior, both in material and
make, to the corresponding articles of American manufacture.   In form, in style, in finish, most articles of American
manufacture are really far superior to the corresponding
European articles, which are generally ill-proportioned,
heavy, and clumsy.   Yet the American articles, so much
more elegant, so much better adapted to the special uses
for which they are intended, might be sold here with fair
profits, at even less prices than the purchasers now have to
pay for those they obtain from the old country.   It is, perhaps, not too much to say that our improvements over the
handcraft of the Old World have only been in thoughtful
harmony and keeping with our improvements over the anti-
quated and absurd systems of government and religion
which still hamper and oppress all the peoples of the Eastern Hemisphere.

Now arises the question, What methods ought we to pursue for the mutual advantage of the inhabitants of both
North and South America, in order to introduce successfully, and as soon as possible, our manufactures into this
great and constantly increasing field of demand and consumption ?   That is the important question.   How and

when shall we begin ? We ought to have begun long ago.
Duty alike to ourselves and to our neighbors ought to have
prompted us to governmental effort in this undertaking at
least as early as the middle of the present century. Delay
has already largely cost us, and is still more largely costing
us, prestige and profit and power. We should go to work
at once, and in solemn earnest, determined to succeed,
even to the extent of making up in some degree for the long
time already lost. Not another day should be allowed to
elapse unimproved. From our Navy Department, directly
and actively, or indirectly and passively, as it seems to me,
should issue the first necessary and practical impulse. Our
people, right meaning and trustful, but more or less short-
sighted, like other people, and not knowing perfectly well
their own interests in all respects, are willing to pay eighteen
millions of dollars per annum for the expense of a navy.
That is more, much more, in my opinion, than we ought to
spend for a navy in times of peace. Thirty eight first-rate
war ships for service at sea, and the same number of well
constructed cutters for river and harbor service—one of each
class for each State and State capital in our Union, and so
named respectively—would, as I think, constitute all the
floating force we require in ordinary periods ; and the entire
cost of such a force, being once provided, ought certainly
not to exceed ten millions per annum. Does not this sug
gestion present an opportunity for judicious retrenchment
and reform ? —and can you not put it into practice, and
thereby save to the country annually eight millions of dollars ? And then, because of your having thus lightened the
burdens of our patriotic taxpayers in the sum of eight millions a year, may you not, in the further interest of those
same taxpayers, (for eventually it will be very greatly in
their interest), induce Congress to grant a subsidy of two
millions or more a year for the establishment and perma-

nent maintenance of a line, a large line, a long line, of first-class steamers, to run from New Orleans, twice a month or oftener, to all the ports of Mexico and Central and South America, both on the Atlantic and Pacific coasts?

Do that, Mr. Secretary of the Navy, do it at once, do it bravely, do it successfully, and you will thereby readily solve one of the most important problems to which you yourself have alluded in your admirable report. In the interest of the industrious and dextrous labor of our country, you will have found fields of almost illimitable dimensions, and of ever-increasing demand, for our surplus products and manu-factures; and in that finding you will have proved yourself, beyond all doubt, the most useful and profitable Secretary of the Navy we have ever yet had.

Under proper guarantees, and with a potent governmen-tal voice in the management of the affairs of the company, a subsidy—considering the old and strong and tenacious hold which Europe already has on the trade of this conti-nent—a subsidy of at least two millions a year should be granted for a term, to start with, of not less than fifteen years, or until a ship canal shall be cut through Nicaragua, or across Tehuantepec, or Darien; but for every million thus spent, from two to five millions ought to be gained, and under an energetic and prudent administration of the busi-ness of the company, that much, or more, probably would be gained as an accretion to the general wealth of the country. Here, however, it may be proper for me to assure you, as I do with all sincerity and truth, that, so far from being myself pecuniarily interested in any enterprise of this sort, I have never had a business word with any one upon the subject. In this respect I really have no more at stake nor in prospect than yourself, or President Hayes, or any other gentleman who is wholly disconnected from mercantile pur-suits. It is only because, having two eyes, and having seen so repeatedly and extensively, during my two crossings of this continent, the great requirements and opportunities of American commerce in the Southern Hemisphere, that I have given myself the liberty of addressing you in this manner.

Another point.   You will have observed that I have mentioned New Orleans as the port in the United States from which our ships under governmental patronage should sail to Mexico and Central and South America, and to which they should return with their cargoes of far-south products. All the maps and lands and winds and waters of the New World, not less obviously than animated common sense, are equally emphatic in suggesting New Orleans as the only convenient and proper port, the only natural and auspicious port, for the concentration of our trade with these many vast countries, every one of which lies south of the mouth of the Mississippi River.   Besides, for pleasure-seekers and other passengers, and also for the mails and for freight from all these southern climes, New Orleans is, by sea, from twelve to fifteen hundred miles nearer than any one of the great cities of the North.   Moreover, by going directly to New Orleans, and thence by railroad or by steamboat to other places, as may be desirable, both time and pleasant changes of situation will be gained, and the ever-stormy and fatal regions of Cape Hatteras, that howling and harmful headland of horrors, the Carolina haunt of Charybdis and Scylla, will be shunned.   Furthemore, the climate of all our Northern cities, as I am well aware from the woeful experience of several personal friends, on various occasions, is much too rigorous, much too perilous, for visitors and other passengers from the tropics in the winter season; especially is it so for those who may have been born and reared within the tropics; and they will prudently, for their lives' sake, remain away from our country altogether, rather than enter it on the Atlantic coast north of Pamlico Sound, between November and March inclusive.

It is alike due to the Great West, the South, the North, and the East—it is preëminently due to the United States as a whole—that the marvelously favorable geographical position of New Orleans for the concentration in North America of our trade with the Southern Hemisphere, should be at once recognized and acted upon with good faith, and with unyielding vigor and perseverance. Being so far behind as we are now in the matter of this commercial and manufacturing outlook, any further failure on our part to avail ourselves of the wonderful facilities which Nature so freely and conspicuously offers us, would only be a most culpable continuance of the stupid and discreditable indifference which we, as a contiguous nation of nearly fifty millions of inhabitants, have thus far strangely manifested toward South and Central America. The large commercial cities of the North have now, and will always retain, the trade of the greater part of the Northern Hemisphere, and much also of the Southern; but our government should not favor those cities exclusively, and, as if both blind and deaf to the unmistakable indications of Nature, neglect all the cities of the West and South; for there is much danger that such favor on the one side, and neglect on the other, carried to excess, might render the country topheavy and unsteady.

The remarkable wisdom and liberality of little England (only a fraction larger than North Carolina, and considerably less than Missouri,) in dividing her commercial favors between London, Liverpool, Bristol, Hull, Southampton, and many of her other ports, in divers sections of her coast —not to speak of Swansea or Cardiff in Wales, of Dublin or Cork in Ireland, or of Glasgow or Dundee in Scotland— may very well serve as an excellent example, and as a policy

of great prudence, eminently fit and profitable for us to follow.   That is the way for nationalities to be truly national
within themselves, and not sectional.   Cincinnati, Indian-
apolis, Chicago, Saint Louis, Louisville, Minneapolis, Kansas City, Omaha, and many other great and growing cities
of the West, can find a cheap outlet and lucrative market
for the immense surplus products of their manufactories and
slaughter-houses and granaries and tanneries and brewer-
ies, only through the mouth of the Mississippi river, near
which, at New Orleans, an extraordinary amount of exchanges and transshipments will always need to be made.
. The sooner we accept the simple truths of these facts in nature, the sooner we establish a line of first-class ocean
steamers to run regularly all along both coasts of Mexico
and Central and South America, and the sooner we cut, or
aid in cutting, a commodious ship canal through Tehuantepec, or Nicaragua, or across the Isthmus of Darien, the
sooner we will become in reality the grand and glorious Republic of which our wisest and best statesmen have often
dreamed, and dreamed longingly, with their eyes wide open.
                    Yours, very respectfully,
                            H. R. HELPER.

                    ―――――――

EXTRACTS FROM THE PROJECTOR'S WORK EN-
TITLED "ODDMENTS OF ANDEAN
DIPLOMACY."

* * *   These problems are submitted to the public as
a special contribution to the general stock of ideas which,
auspiciously for the future of the whole Western Hemisphere,
are now beginning to actuate the higher and better portions
of the peoples of the three Americas, North, Central, and
South, who have already come to be affected by a yearning

and unyielding desire for an early and permanent establishment of closer commercial and companionable relations
with each other. During more than a dozen years,—
counting back from to-day,—while constantly and successfully exercising the utmost care never to say anything in
positive explanation of the subject until now, I have been
deeply and anxiously impressed with the conviction that the
one thing most needed to secure in perpetuity an uncommonly high degree of well-being for the inhabitants of all
the countries of the New World, is a longitudinal midland
double-track steel railway from a point far north in North
America to a point far south in South America; it being important, as I think, though not superlatively important, that
the line of the road should, in most latitudes, be as nearly
as possible equidistant between the Atlantic and Pacific
oceans.   This is a consideration, however, which may very
rightly be influenced and modified by the physical features
and characteristics of particular tracts of country through
which able engineers will make all necessary surveys and
examinations, preparatory to the final selection and location
of the route.

Since November, 1866, scarcely one of my wakeful hours
has been free from thoughts on the subject of this road; and
yet, to a mind of mere mediocrity like my own, the unmeas-
ured dimensions, the curious complications, and the diverse
difficulties of the problem, are so formidable and overwhelming, that I am still involved in serious doubt as to the steps
which might perhaps be most prudently taken in certain directions.   In this dilemma, before attempting to proceed
any further with the enterprise on my own account, I have
deemed it proper to call to my aid, as will more specifically
appear on subsequent pages, the superior wisdom of five of
my probably unknown fellow-men, no matter in what part of
the universal Republic of Letters they may reside; for whose

written facts, arguments, suggestions and sentiments at large,
prosaic and poetic, in support and improvement of the plans
of the project here presented, I have already had the pleasure of making provision to pay in cash an aggregate of five
thousand dollars ; a much too meagre sum, which I should
most willingly increase twofold at least, so it might be more
in harmony with the unequaled greatness and grandeur of
the undertaking, but for my financial inability to act herein
commensurately with my desires.   It is believed, though,
that the friendly competitors,—and more especially the successful ones, respectively,—in this literary contest, controlled
by a courteous and freehearted spirit of emulation, will be
influenced quite as much by the impulses of patriotism, and
by the honorable ambition to achieve an intellectual triumph,
as by any mere pecuniary consideration.

In addition to the five thousand dollars thus given in
lump, I have, with an eye and purpose principally devoted
to the prosecution of this design, already expended considerably more than a like sum in the long courses of my
two crossings and other trying and tiresome traversings of
the continent of South America.   As a mere matter of fact,
therefore, I may here very properly speak of an actual expenditure, by myself alone, thus far, of from eleven to
twelve thousand dollars, as representing to that extent the
illimitable degree of hope and confidence which I repose in
this grand scheme.   Moreover, in this connection, it may
not be amiss for me to state, that, down to the present time,
I have finished no less than five trips to and from South
America since the spring of 1851, when I first went there.
That was a trifle more than twenty-eight years ago, and was
only a few months after I had attained my majority.

The multifarious and ever-enduring benefits which this
road will bring about, on a scale almost inconceivably extensive, will themselves but constantly increase and expand the

vast sphere of their own inherent usefulness, and, whether as active or passive sources for good, will forever foster and develop the very weightiest and loftiest interests of mankind, material, mental and moral, sanitary, sacred and sublime. For the perfect unfoldment and preservation of these transcendent interests, there will be a wide and always widening and invariable demand for a much higher order of intelligence than one may ever find emanating from the peurile understanding of little boys, or from the feminine intellectuality of underteen girls; the proper performance of these mighty tasks, alike noble and ennobling, will require nothing less than the virile thought and mature judgment, the robust and rectifying wisdom, of full-grown men.

Every State in South and Central America and Mexico is now sorely afflicted with at least half a dozen overpowering evils, separate or in combination, and yet another even more sweepingly and perniciously overpowering afflicts Brazil. These various deadly drawbacks may be grouped and catalogued in the following order:

1. A largely preponderating, idle, vicious and worthless population of negroes, Indians and bi-colored hybrids.

2. The complete, intolerant and fanatical sway of Roman Catholicism, which, when seen and felt and known, as I have seen and felt and known it, on no less than four continents and divers islands of the oceans, but more particularly in South America, where its maleficent mastery is yet unopposed and undisputed, and where, on the right hand and on the left, before and behind, it brazenly unvails itself in all its naked deformity and dishonor and shamelessness, may very justly be regarded as the meanest and most irrational religion ever recognized by any race of white men, Mormonism and Mohammedanism only excepted.

3. General apathy and improgressiveness, and the very common and calamitous neglect of agricultural, mechanical,

manufacturing, and other highly important industrial pursuits, coupled with an almost universal contempt and disdain of every sort of manual labor.

4. Among the masses of the people, unlettered stupidity,
excessive thrumming and twanging on the guitar, attuning
and tinkletankling on the tambourine, maudlin singing,
senseless and vulgar dancing, fortune-telling, lotteries,
gambling, bull-fighting, intemperance, licentiousness, social
and political depravity, brutal violence, and cruelties and
crimes of every class.

5. On the part of a very small but extraordinarily influential minority of the inhabitants, arrogant and aristocratic
absolutism, in conjunction with oligarchal and military despotism; and also the outbreak of such frequent, unnecessary and sanguinary revolutions as bring deep and indelible
reproach on the true principles of republican institutions.

6. Disregard of the sacredness of individual and official
engagements, both verbal and written, and the most scandalous incompetence and malfeasance in public office.

7. Throughout the vast valley of the Amazon, a glamour-
glazed, hollow-hearted, meretricious and obstructive monarchy, which, despite all imperial and splenetic denials of
the truth, is still banefully black and brown and beggarly
with Africans, Indians, mulattoes and other menial and mon-
strous mongrels; and balefully base and besotted and bar-
barous with chattel slavery, rigidly and brutally enforced
under the thin gauze of delusive laws ostensibly framed for
emancipation.

In the direct and indirect influences which will be gradually exerted by the New World Longitudinal Railway herein
proposed, every one of the ponderous and portentous evils
thus listed and held up to public reprobation, will be mitigated and lessened; and at least a few of them, it is confidently believed, will be eventually and utterly destroyed.   It

is true, unfortunately true, that our own country is not entirely free from all the evils thus inveighed against in Spanish and Portuguese America. On the contrary, it must be admitted that many of these evils are indisputably of more than sufficient rifeness and enormity in certain localities not far from us, as, for instance, in such Catholic-cursed cities as New York and Cincinnati, where, with the plottings and prayers and other peculiar practices of the priests, and with the apparent approbation of the prelates and the primates and the popes, power is deliberately placed in the hands of such detestable miscreants as Tweed, Purcell, Sweeney, Barnard, Walsh, Morrissey and Reilly, and in such wretched and despicable negro or semi-negro States as Mississippi, South Carolina and Louisiana, as also in portions of Tennessee, where that high and saving degree of moral sense which is always inseparable from honor-affecting rights and obligations, is only half perfect, because the population is only half white. But with us as a nation, such gross immoralities are only spasmodic and exceptional; whereas in all South and Central America and Mexico, as indeed in all Catholic countries, as also in all non-Caucasian countries, they are both regular and general.

But why, if the standard of integrity among the peoples of this vast southerly region of the Western World is no higher than I have here depicted it, why do I advocate the construction of the longest and the costliest and best railway ever yet devised, expressly as a means and for the purpose of cultivating more amicable and intimate relations with them ? Because without the road it is not likely that there will ever be much amendment; and even the little that may be reasonably expected, will be at best only one-sided and slow; but with the road, the opportunities and prospects for mutual improvement will soon become absolutely boundless and interminable. The dwellers in those countries have

millions of square miles of fertile lands and precious metals
and tropical forests and fruits, and other sources of inexhaustible wealth, the true values of all of which we shall
help them to develop, in a cheerful spirit of ready amenabil-
ity to the great commercial law of demand and supply ; and,
on the other hand, we shall sell to them, at handsomely remunerative profits to ourselves, tens of thousands of car-
loads of our surplus manufactures and other merchantable
products, which, while fitly affording them all promised gratification, will constantly create within them a craving for still
newer and better things, and will thereby, for the first time
in their lives, awaken within them the exquisite delights of
self-regulated and rightful unrest, activity and achievement.

Journeys of both vocation and recreation southward will
be made by countless numbers of our own people at particular seasons; and similar journeys by corresponding numbers of their people will be made northward at certain other
seasons ; whilst at all times there will be a merry stir and
noisy bustle of regular and abundant business. A continuous rush of trade and travel each way, occupying both tracks
day and night throughout the year, may be taken into account with quite as much certainty as we may depend on the
rising and setting of the sun, or the ebbing and flowing of
the tide. At first, as happy results of our uninterrupted and
general intercourse with each other, they will be rendered
richer in mind and morals, and we shall be rendered
richer in money and manners; for it is but frank to state the
fact, that the genteel and educated classes of the Spanish
Americans,—of course I mean those of them only who are
purely white,—are the peers, if not the paragons, of the po-
litest and highest-toned people in the world. They are,
besides, possessed of the cardinal virtues in as full degree
and practice as the most moral-reputed portion of mankind.
By association with this superior class, whose comparative

smallness of number is almost the only bad thing about them,—a class, by the way, which, as I have often noticed, one never finds at church, for the very good reason that there is no church among them in any respect worthy of their devotional presence or attention,—we, as well as they, shall be gainers from the very start; and so, each will soon become and forever remain toward the other a respectful and sincere and equal friend, a well-wishing and reciprocal and perfect helper.

This is the class of eminently able and good men in South and Central America and Mexico, which, though numerically weak, yet, being intellectually and morally strong, will most earnestly and efficiently co-operate with us in building the road, and also in effecting every necessary change and reform in other matters. Even now it is possible for them to be of very great service to us; and it may, as I doubt not it will, soon be possible for us to be of corresponding service to them. With much manly and patriotic solicitude for the future welfare of their respective countries, they are now crying aloud to us for help in the strenuous efforts they are making to attain for themselves and for their posterity a civilization less akin to the twelfth century, and more in harmony with the nineteenth. If we do not help them in the sagacious manner suggested by the exigencies of the situation, which ultimately will cost us nothing, but in the end prove of profuse and perpetual advantage to us as well as to themselves, we shall, by such refusal of expedient and friendly assistance, deserve to be roundly censured and even execrated by the enlightened judgment of all mankind. Helping them, in conformity with their very reasonable and right request, we shall thereby but simply do our duties to our neighbors and to ourselves; not helping them, we shall be recreant to one of the plainest and brightest duties that ever devolved on a mighty people; a remarkably peculiar and attractive duty, fragrant with dignity and honor for all who engage in it, and dazzlingly lustrous with the fascinating qualities of legitimate self-interest.

Notwithstanding the astounding prevalence of wrong-doing and wickedness in high and low places throughout all the States of South and Central America, yet in every one of those commonwealths there are tens of thousands of well-informed and upright men,—white men in fact and anti-Catholics at heart,—with whom it will be just as safe to do business as with the very best men in our own or any other country. The more generally and intimately we become acquainted with this conspicuously honorable and excellent class of Spanish Americans, the better we shall like them, and, in all things, the better will it be for both them and us. It is this class whose numbers and powers we must, by extending to them the right hand of good-fellowship, help to increase to such an extent that, in due course of time, they will be enabled to supplant entirely the cumbersomely and worthlessly base and black and brown elements in the vile-visaged and deleterious forms of human rubbish around them. Moreover, it is this very class to whom we must now look for several of the necessary charters and franchises, for the requisite guarantees of interest on capital, and for other proper pledges of practical coöperation, which will make it possible for us soon to evolve into one of the grandest realities of the nineteenth century the idea of a New World Longitudinal Double-Track Steel Railway. So soon as we shall be favored with the vital and indispensable assistance which it is believed the intelligent and enterprising Spanish Americans will promptly render in the premises, let us all go to work at once, and build the road without permitting any one of ourselves to indulge too leisurely a day's absence from labor until we shall have consummated an undertaking so indubitably essential to the high and perfect civilization of the three Americas.

TO VARIOUS UNITED STATES CONSULS, RE-SPECTIVELY, IN SPANISH AMERICA.

St. Louis, Mo., *January 1, 1881.*

Dear Sir: You will confer on me a special obligation, which I shall hope to have an opportunity to discharge in reciprocity, some day, if you will be so kindly laborious and accommodating as to favor me, at your earliest convenience with laconic replies to the following ten brief inquiries:

1. How many miles of Railroads, completed and open for traffic and travel, were there in ——, on the last day of December, 1880?

2. How many miles of finished lines of Telegraphs were in operation within the limits of ——, on the last day of December, 1880?

3. What was the total value of all the Exports from ——, during the year 1880? In this case, as in all others where sums of money are involved, please give the amount in dollars of our own currency.

4. What was the total value of all the Imports into ——, during the year 1880?

5. What was the entire value of all the Exports from —— to the United States of America, during the year 1880?

6. What was the entire value of all the Imports into —— from the United States of America, during the year 1880?

7. Leaving frigates, gun-boats, and other men-of-war altogether out of consideration, what was the whole number of tons of Shipping actually engaged or engagable in commerce, whether propelled by steam or by sail, under the flag of ——, at the close of the year 1880?

8. What was the gross Revenue of ——, during the year 1880?

25

9. What was the gross Expenditure of ——, during the year 1880?

10. What was the whole amount of the Public Debt of ——, at the close of the year 1880?

Hoping to have the pleasure of hearing from you as soon as you may find it possible and convenient to answer the several foregoing questions, which I have propounded with no small degree of diffidence and hesitation, and authorizing you to impose on me, at any time, a task of equal or greater magnitude,

  I have the honor to be, very respectfully,
    Your obedient servant,
         H. R. HELPER.

TO MR. CANONGE.

        St. Louis, *October 11, 1880.*
L. Placide Canonge, Esq., *New Orleans.*

Dear Sir: In my letter to you, two or three days ago, I should have suggested, had I then thought of it, that, in the event of your volunteering to say something, however brief, in advocacy of my projected railway through the three Americas, it may perhaps be well worth while to defend my recognition of the power of the poet in helping to arouse the necessary earnestness and enthusiasm to undertake and carry forward to completion an enterprise of such unequaled magnitude and importance. I say this, because several persons of rather sordid views, if not of a decidedly grovellling disposition, while approving my offer of prizes for essays in prose, have presumed to speak almost contemptuously of my offer of prizes for essays in poetry. What, inquire they—in the narrowness and stolidity of their conceptions—what has poetry to do with such a very material

work as the building of a great international and intercontinental railway?

Might I not fitly inquire of them in turn, What has poetry
not had to do with the foundations and careers and histo-
ries of all the famous nationalities around the Mediterranean
Sea, especially the principal commonwealths and dependencies of ancient Greece and Rome, whose wars and religions
and romances and mythologies are so imperishably em-
balmed among the strangest curiosities of literature? Ask
Homer, Hesiod, Æschylus, Sophocles, Euripides, Anac-
reon, Simonides, Pindar, Aristophanes, Menander, Varro,
Virgil, Horace, Ovid, and Lucretius. What has poetry not
had to do with the theocratic aspirations and restless wan-
dering and wordly immortality of the Hebrews of both ancient and modern times? Ask Job, David, Solomon,
Isaiah, Jeremiah, Ezekiel, and a dozen or so of other Jewish poets of less potency of expression. Who can treasure
up within himself an adequate knowledge of the past or
present glories of Italy, or of Spain, or of Portugal, without
first imprinting upon his mind the names and sayings of
Dante, Petrarch, Ariosto, Tasso, Lope de Vega, Calderon,
Zorrilla, and Camœns? How deplorably incompact and
incomplete would be the almost perfect civilization which
has been attained by beautiful and lovely France, by strong
and manly Germany, and by colony-planting and savage-
subduing and light-dispensing Great Britain, but for the in-
spiriting and ennobling languages respectively, according to
nationality, of Corneille, Racine, Moliére, Lamartine, Hugo,
Goethe, Schiller, Uhland, Heine, Klopstock, Spenser,
Shakspeare, Milton, Byron, Scott, Burns, Wordsworth,
Southey, and Tennyson? Nor, considering the comparative
juvenility of her motherhood, has America—soon to become
a sure and steady beacon-light for guidance to the general
welfare of mankind throughout the whole earth—been less

fruitful in evolving brilliant meteors of intellectual power in
the persons of Poe, Bryant, Emerson, Lowell, Longfellow,
Whittier, Whitman, Pike, Hayne, Lanier, and (last though
not least) Canonge.

No, indeed, never yet has any nation achieved greatness
on a scale of undeniable permanence and grandeur, that
did not first give birth to genius-endowed poets and other
writers, whose impressive words of counsel and encouragement, followed by prudent and energetic action, led to the
very results so obviously worthy of universal admiration and
praise. Neither Upper Guinea nor Lower Guinea has ever
yet produced a poet; nor has Soudan, nor Senegambia, nor
any other part of Negroland. Nor will nor can any one of
the countries of Equatorial Africa ever be able to boast of
so precious a product as a poet, a poet in any manner entitled to the designation, until, by way of opening a path
for the ingress of civilization, the negro himself shall there
cease to be a pernicious encumberer of the soil; giving
place, as soon or late he must and will give place, not by his
own volition, but in spite of his ever-barbarous resistance,
to his white superiors of Caucasian bravery and blood and
brain.

The Feejee Islands, too, and all other countries of similar
savagery, are, and always have been, as poetless as Hades
or Tophet, or Tartarus. Only in regions fit to be and destined to become the abodes of the blessed, like the Gardens
of the Hesperides, the Elysian Fields, and other bright and
blissful lands occupied exclusively by white people, may
genuine poets ever be found in the free and full exercise of
their functions. Prehistoric America, inhabited solely by Indians, not one of whom have ever learned to lisp a language
of lyrical lore, was literally good for nothing until Columbus, on his voyage of discovery, being himself only
the emanation of a poetic idea, came with his comrades and

followers, and transformed the dull and unserviceable prose of boundless forests into the lively and utilitarian poetry of numberless fields of grain, and orchards of fruit, and homesteads of plenty, and parks of pleasure, and joy-yielding villages and towns and cities, all harmonious and musical with the echoes of peaceful and prosperous industry.

In moments of relaxation from regular vocations, all the builders, proprietors and patrons of the Three Americas Railway, whether resting under the shade of the pine, the oak or the palm, or in whatever other position or circumstance they may seek restoration from physical fatigue, will, I trust, be afforded at least an opportunity, if so discreetly inclined, to avail themselves of more rational pastimes than they can ever possibly find in grogshops or other low dens of demoralization. Believing that it is alike the privilege and the duty of the poet to teach them—just as it is his privilege and duty to teach all others of his race—I should wish them to learn from him that every blow they strike with pick or spade, or other implement, in effective furtherance of the projected international and intercontinental highway, is, directly or indirectly, only a vigorous expression of poetic impulse; and that the truest poetry, the poetry of the future, like its handmaid, the music of the future, is to be tested, and exemplified and perpetually established in its power to relieve all well-meant and worthy work from the character of mere drudgery, and in its beneficent office of elevating every rightly designed effort into a highly honorable and healthy diversion.

What better service can the world possibly receive from any human being than a few lessons—even though those lessons should consist respectively of only a small number of lines—from the poet on this very subject? How incomparably pleasant and advantageous all such lessons might eventually prove to every navvy and to every other employé, aye, and to every passenger and friend of the Three Americas Railway! Well conceived and well expressed, such lessons might indeed, for all true men and women, without ever interfering in the least with their appointed hours for manual labor, serve forever as most delightful and profitable pastimes. No longer a dreaded task approached with reluctance, labor intelligently planned and pursued would thus, in most cases, become everywhere an avocation of hilarity, melody and song, and should be invariably and promptly accounted to the credit of every person so engaged in its performance. At the same time, all adults not diligently employed in some legitimate and useful occupation should be unvaryingly regarded with the most castigatory disapprobation and disdain.

These views disclose some of the general reasons, in themselves sufficient, why I was pleased to set apart fifteen hundred dollars for two short essays in poetry, as well as thirty-five hundred dollars for three moderately lengthy essays in prose; but there is also a special reason, a weighty and all-sufficient reason, why I considered it proper to do precisely as I did; and this paramount reason—not to be now stated with assured propriety—I hope to have the pleasure of explaining to yourself and others a year or so hence.

In conclusion, let me assure you that, should your charming Muse not now be graciously disposed to inspire you to pen the few poetic lines which you have so generously suggested in further laudation and advocacy of the proposed Three Americas Railway, you may, I think, well excuse her, and demand of her nothing more upon this subject; for she has already kindly moved you to indite, in the praise of the project, several stirring letters in prose, which are themselves fuller of true poetry than most of the stanzas framed by other bards.

Yours, very truly,

H. R. HELPER.

TO MAJ. HILDER.

ST. LOUIS, *January 10, 1881.*

MAJ. FRANK FREDERICK HILDER, *St. Louis.*

DEAR SIR : For complimentary distribution to well-proved friends and coadjutors, I have at my bestowal five beautifully wrought crowns of laurel; of all of which the largest and finest best befits your own brow.   Receive it, Sir, and wear it with all the unaffected grace and honor so becoming to one of your superior intellectual endowments.

Possibly you may not be distinguished by any playful pseudonym in politics, nor any solemn *sobriquet* in religion, nor any noble *nom de plume* in literature; yet I am tempted to apply to you, though somewhat egotistically and by way of compliment to myself, the auxiliary appellation of Fellow-Helper.   So, how do you do, my dear fellow, as the winner of the first prize, amounting to thirteen hundred dollars, offered by me, last year, for the best prose essay in advocacy of my projected Three Americas Railway?

Evidently you have been holding converse with the American Eagle, the emblem of our liberties, the guardian of our laws, the promoter of our progress; and it is but reasonable that you should feel proud of the gratifying results of your privileged consultations with that mighty bird. Yet your pecuniary gain on this occasion is very insignificant, a mere *bagatelle,* in comparison with the formally awarded honor to you of having achieved the highest and most admirable success in presenting to the world what is intended to be an ever-improving and all-benefitting enterprise, whose agencies for good, if established in accordance with well-settled desires and purposes, will eventually outstretch themselves to the very extremities of both continents of the Western Hemisphere.

If Alexander were now alive, or Cæsar, or Napoleon, or any of the other red-handed manslayers,—I came very near saying monsters,—whose names blacken and befoul the pages of history, yet I should not be disposed to press the palm of any one of them half so cordially—if thereto disposed at all—as I should like to grasp your own. Accept my thanks, my congratulations, and also my heartfelt wishes for your health, happiness and long life.

Yours earnestly,

H. R. HELPER.

TO COL. BEELEN.

St. Louis, January 10, 1881.

Col. Frederick Anthony Beelen,

Cortlandt-on-the-Hudson, New York.

Dear Sir: By means of your uncommon talents and industry you have earned, and you will receive, both honor and reward. The second prize, amounting to twelve hundred dollars, offered by me for the best prose essay that could be obtained for that sum, on the subject of my special proposition for a longitudinal double-track steel railway through North and Central and South America, has been adjudged to you; and I take the liberty—as it certainly gives me great pleasure—to congratulate you on the success and distinction which you have thus achieved.

The money which you have received in this regard is not much; it is only a trifle in comparison with the inexpressibly preponderating importance of the undertaking which induced you, amid other praiseworthy considerations, to work for it. May I indulge the hope that, in the future, as well as in the present, you will kindly avail of every favorable opportunity to speak a good word in furtherance of the idea and purpose of constructing, at the earliest practicable period, a Three Americas Railway? I know of no manner in which any American, whether he be a North American, a Central American, or a South American, of rightly-trained heart and well-balanced mind, may better spend his time, his labor, or his money. All work done in this behalf, wherever it may be executed, if it shall only be prudently performed under proper combination and direction, will evince on the part of all those engaged in it, sagacity and patriotism of the very highest order.

' Yours sanguinely,

H. R. HELPER.

TO MR. ARCHER.

St. Louis, January 10, 1881.

WILLIAM WHARTON ARCHER, ESQ., *Richmond, Virginia.*

DEAR SIR: Smile complacently, but do not laugh aloud; stand erect; walk in a straight line; sit with composure and dignity; salute your friends with respectful and pleasing observations; enliven others and be enlivened yourself with social chat; partake of a palatable repast, with no stronger liquid than coffee, tea, or chocolate; sleep soundly; and to-morrow morning arise joyfully with the sun, as, in all his dazzling effulgence and glory, he mounts up majestically from the eastern horizon. Yes, be amiable, be cheerful, be happy,—as I dare say it is your custom to be, —and accept these little word-tokens as evidences of my sincere regards and congratulations.

To yourself has been awarded, by the Three Americas Railway Committee, the third prize, amounting to one thousand dollars, offered by me more than twelve months ago, for the best prose essay that could be obtained for that sum, in support of my proposition to build an unparalleled and first-class railway, running north and south, through all the Americas. The proposition was and is preëminently worthy of the very ablest efforts which you or any other man of genius and learning could or can possibly exert in its advancement; and, thanks to Heaven, I am, at this hour, far more fully assured than ever before, that the incomparable undertaking thus projected will soon be accomplished in such a well-devised and excellent manner as to properly unify, protect and augment, for all time to come, the highest and best interests of the good peoples of sixteen republics.

Yours perseveringly,

H. R. HELPER.

———

TO MR. CARPENTER.

St. Louis, *January 12, 1881.*

Frank DeYeaux Carpenter, Esq., *Washington, D. C.*

Dear Sir: Greet your Muse with the very perfection of manly address and admiration; frankly acknowledge your gratitude to her for favors already received; salute her with new pledges of devotion; bestow upon her ample evidences of the sincerity of your vows, by ardently kissing her hands, —her cheeks also, if she will permit you,—and thank Jove and Apollo and all the Grecian gods of grace and gallantry for sacred friendships and delights still possible to mortal man.

Why? Because—prominently successful bard that you have proved yourself to be—because, through the brilliant inspiration of that same Minerva-like Muse, you have achieved the honor and the profit of winning the first prize, amounting to one thousand dollars, offered by me for the best poem promotive of my published proposition for a Three Americas Railway; a proposition, as it really seems to me, full of poetry, full of prose, full of peace, prophetic of plenty, and overflowing with practicable promises for the permanent prosperity and progress of half the world.

In greeting you as a worthy coadjutor in this great enterprise, I would also offer to you a renewal of a friendship which was begun, years ago, in the far-off Southern Hemisphere, where you, as well as I, have seen and felt the disadvantages of a commercial isolation, and the need of an intercontinental railway, such as I have projected. Here and at this time I may not dwell especially upon the incalculable benefits which will almost certainly result from the construction of the proposed railway.

Although the highest flights of the imagination, on the one hand, and the most sober and methodical labor, on the other, would do but scant justice to the possibilities of the theme, yet I am irresistibly impelled to congratulate you upon the threads of practicality and common sense which you have so skillfully woven through your verses. Your warmest admirers will probably be found among the higher and better classes of men of business.

In the development of a new world, like ours, there is no time to waste in vain conceits and mere excursions of the fancy. The homely arts of peace, as I foresaw, and as you have proved, are not necessarily without their poetic side. The progress of a civilization is not less grand than the formidable advance of an ocean wave, or the outburst of a dreadful storm. Certainly, as yet at least, there seems to be no good reason why we Americans should go with Milton into Heaven, or follow Dante to his Inferno, while we have so much unexplored territory of our own. As our pioneers have taken the wild horses of the plains, and subdued them to the routine of daily labor, so should the winged steeds of our ambitious writers be called down from the clouds, and broken to the harness of useful pursuits.

The wedding of poetry to prose is not entirely without precedent. It has become almost proverbial that the dream of one age is the science of the next. Other able engineers, besides yourself, have not disdained to handle the lighter pen of metrical construction; and other distinguished poets have taken delight in contributing efficiently and largely to the world's material improvement. Michael Angelo and Leonardo da Vinci were poets as well as builders; and Saint Pierre's engineering studies and practice did not prevent him from writing his charming story of *Paul and Virginia*. On the other hand,—as an instance of the poet turning his attention to engineering—Goethe shows us his later *Faust* building dikes and draining pestilential marshes to provide comfortable homes for his people; and the present Poet Laureate of England "saw the heavens fill with commerce, and argosies of magic sails." The proposed Three Americas Railway may seem rather prosaic to some people, and decidedly visionary to others; but it is not quite so unpoetical as the reclamation of a swamp, and by no means so improbable as the aërial routes of commerce suggested by Tennyson.

With pleasure and satisfaction, I remain,

Yours musingly,

H. R. HELPER.

TO MR. DEEKENS.

St. Louis, *January 11, 1881.*

Francis Augustus Deekens, Esq.,

Norwich, Ontario, Canada.

Dear Sir; Pat your Pegasus on the shoulders; run your kindly-combing fingers through his mane; and give him an extra feed, even to repletion; for, with his proud steps and lively prancings around the picturesque prominences of Parnassus, and amidst the pleasant groves and peaceful pastures of Arcadia, he has safely carried you to, and placed you in possession of, the second prize, amounting to five hundred dollars, offered by me, more than a year ago, for the best poem attainable for that sum, in advocacy of my proposed Three Americas Railway; an enterprise which, even in its present inchoate condition, is, I am strongly inclined to affirm, a subject for one of the grandest poems ever yet extracted from the empyrean regions of thought.

Yours merrily,

H. R. HELPER.

TO SECRETARY EVARTS.

St. Louis, *December 22, 1880.*

Hon. Wm. M. Evarts, *Secretary of State, Washington.*

Dear Sir: I have the honor to acknowledge my very pleasant obligation to you for No. 2 of the *Reports from the Consuls of the United States*, which came to hand last evening. This is the third of a series of the most suggestive and valuable commercial documents ever issued from any department of our government. The two *Reports* are unusually interesting and valuable companion volumes to your recent very able abstract of *The Commerce of the World*, which I have read very carefully from beginning to end. * * * For myself, South and Central America and Mexico constitute a vastly more than ample field for my imperfect thoughts and labors. Through these Spanish American countries, intimately connecting them with our own Republic, I desire to encourage, in every possible and prudent manner, the early construction of an all-supplying and all-surpassing intercontinental railway, which, in my humble

judgment, may be ma.. the means of securing to us, at no
very distant day, from two-thirds to four-fifths of all the foreign trade and travel of those expanding and improving
commonwealths.

As you yourself are well aware, by far the greater part of
the foreign trade of Spanish America is now transacted with
Europe ; and I fear we shall never be able to compete successfully for our national share of it, that is to say, almost
the whole of it, by merely buffeting and bobbing about for
it over the two billowy and doubtful realms of old Neptune.
Than this same foam-forming Poseidon, with his briny beard
and uplifted trident, a mightier and better god, and one of
far more friendly disposition toward us, is the incomparable
Jupiter, a preëminently terrestrial deity, of immeasurable
domains, who yet manifests no special inclination to tax
himself, in our behalf, with the duty of exercising guardian-
ship over any ventures launched upon the wavy deep.
* * * What I am particularly desirous of accomplishing
by my scheme of an international and intercontinental railway, is to secure for the United States, for all time, the bulk
of the foreign trade and travel of ..lexico and Central and
South America. With this projected railway completed and
in operation, our nation would probably never suffer any
material commercial disadvantage in competition with European rivals because of the cutting of an Isthmian ship-
canal, at whatever place, across Central America ; for, availing of the extraordinary facilities offered by the railway,
most of the foreign trade and travel of all Spanish America
would, it may be safely assumed, naturally and inevitably
come to us, despite all the ships and shipping interests in
the world. * * * Therefore, as I firmly believe, the
proposed Three Americas Railway is what is now especially
needed, as an indispensable factor, in a proper adjustment
of our commercial and economic relations with thirty odd

millions of Spanish-speaking peoples on the southern continent of the New World.

I am, Sir, with great respect,

Your obedient servant,

H. R. HELPER.

TO SECRETARY EVARTS.

ST. LOUIS, *December 27, 1879.*

HON. WM. M. EVARTS, *Secretary of State, Washington.*

DEAR SIR: I have the honor to request that you may be pleased to receive, in much the same way as if it had been originally addressed to yourself, the following copy of a letter which I have just written to His Excellency President Hayes; the communication being one which has for its principal object, the presentation of such suggestions as may lead to a better solution of the problem of the commercial, social and political relationships which ought soon to exist between the United States and Mexico and all the countries of Central and South America.

I have the honor to be, most respectfully,

Your obedient servant,

H. R. HELPER.

TO PRESIDENT HAYES.

ST. LOUIS, *December 27, 1879.*

TO HIS EXCELLENCY THE HON. RUTHERFORD B. HAYES,

President of the United States.

DEAR SIR: By the Adams Express Company, I have this day taken the liberty of sending to you, and also, separately, to each member of your Cabinet, (except the Hon. Secretary of State, who has already been served in this manner,)

a copy of my " Oddments of Andean Diplomacy," wherein,
among other matters, I have dared to suggest the practicability, advisability and indispensability of a vast longitudinal
double-track steel railway through the three Americas.
Closely connected with the colossal enterprise thus projected,
are many exceedingly delicate and important considerations,
which, however, may not reasonably be expected to receive
adequate attention at once, nor even very soon ; but, in behalf of the herculean undertaking itself, and the various
momentous issues which it contemplates, I beg leave to request that you and all the members of your able and distinguished Cabinet, may be pleased to take cognizance of the
subject now, and revert to it, from time to time, as opportunity may offer, until it shall be convenient for you yourself
and them to perceive the weighty and diversified merits
which, as it really seems to me, are embraced within the
scheme, not only for ourselves as a nation, but also for all
the other republican and democratic nationalities south of us.

I have the honor to be, most respectfully,

Your Excellency's obedient servant,

H. R. HELPER.

TO CONSUL CAHILL.

St. Louis, *April 5, 1881*

Hon. John F. Cahill, *Consul for Mexico.*

Dear Sir : Herewith I have the honor to inclose to you
a copy of a communication which I addressed to His Excellency the Secretary of State for Mexico, on the 27th of
last January, in relation to the projected Three Americas
Railway ; the particular communication thus dispatched to
you being the last of a series which has already been mailed
by me directly to Mexico, during the last eighteen months,

on this very same subject.   At this time I beg the privilege of repeating to you, and through you to the Honorable Secretary of State aforesaid, the special information and request therein contained.   With this letter I also take the liberty of transmitting to you, for your examination, the five excellent essays, in manuscript, which I have recently received in support of the proposed international and inter-continental improvement.   Unforeseen and unavoidable delays have thus far prevented the publication of these papers ; but they will all be placed in the hands of the printers, a few days hence, and will soon be issued in one volume ;' three copies of which will be sent to you; one for yourself, one for the Mexican Minister at Washington, and the other for his Excellency the Secretary of State for Mexico.   At or about the same time, other copies of the work will be dispatched to the Secretaries of State, respectively, of all the Spanish American Republics, and also to their Ministers at Washington.

I have the honor to be, very respectfully,

Your obedient servant,

H. R. HELPER.

TO THE MEXICAN GOVERNMENT.

St. Louis, Mo., November 1, 1879.

To the Honorable the Secretary of State
for the Republic of Mexico.'

Distinguished Sir: Inclosed herewith your Excellency will find in print the title-page of my "Oddments of Andean Diplomacy," a forthcoming book, wherein, nothwithstanding my self-conscious inadequacy of ability in the premises, I have cursorily advocated the early construction of a longitudinal double-track steel railway through North and Central and

26

South America.   For the further advancement of the vast and incalculably important international and intercontinental highway thus projected, I have, as is amply explained in the book itself, given five thousand dollars in gold for five of the most powerful and persuasive essays that can be obtained collaterally and coincidently with my own disquisition.

With a view of avoiding all confusion and all clashing of plan or procedure in this colossal undertaking, I have the honor to request that your Excellency's government may be pleased to abstain from granting to mere novices or speculators, or to other unmeritorious persons, any charter, franchise, privilege, or guarantee, which might delay or hinder in any manner the progress of the enterprise as it is outlined in the aforementioned publication.   Almost immediately after its issue from the press, I shall have the pleasure of transmitting a copy of the book to your Excellency, either through the hands of your distinguished Minister at Washington, or by means of the courtesy and kindness of your Consul at New York.

I confidently hope to enlist in this gigantic scheme many of the ablest and best financiers in America ; that is to say, a sufficient number of them to commence and complete the work by or before the 14th day of October, 1892 ; and to this unparalleled and momentous endeavor, looking impartially to the development of the most vital and precious interests of all the countries through which the road will pass, I earnestly bespeak, for my associates and myself, the enlightened and friendly coöperation of all patriotic and progressive Mexicans.

I have the honor to be, most respectfully,

Your Excellency's obedient servant,

H. R. HELPER.

Communications similar to the foregoing letter, and of exactly corresponding purport, were addressed, at the same time to the Secretaries of State respectively of all the Spanish American Republics, as follows :

1.	México,	8.	Venezuela,
2.	Guatemala,	9.	Ecuador,
3.	Honduras,	10.	Peru,
4.	Salvador,	11.	Bolivia,
5.	Nicaragua,	12.	Paraguay,
6.	Costa Rica,	13.	Uraguay,
7.	Columbia,	14.	Chili,

15.   Argentine Republic.

What preliminary action, in furtherance of the proposed Three Americas Railway, has been taken in the great Anglo-American Republic—the United States of America—is sufficiently well known.   Every reply thus far received, whether official, semi-official, or·unofficial, is favorable ; and I am fully persuaded that the constant application to the undertaking of an abundance of good hard sense and good hard work, will erelong lead to the most reciprocal and extensive development of human welfare that the world has ever witnessed.

H. R. H.

TO THE MEXICAN GOVERNMENT.

St. Louis, Mo., June 5, 1880.

To the Honorable the Secretary of State
for the Republic of Mexico.

Distinguished Sir : Early in the month of November last I had the honor of communicating to your Excellency information of the fact of my having projected a longitudinal double-track steel railway through North· and Central and South America.   After a brief explanation of the steps then taken by myself, in the hope and effort to secure proper attention to the subject, and desiring to avoid all dangerous complications and delays, I took the liberty to request—and would now respectfully and earnestly repeat the request—that your Excellency's Government may be pleased to refrain from compromising itself with any other party or parties whomsoever, in any manner whatever, in this vast international and intercontinental enterprise, which is sincerely intended to promote, as equally as possible, the highest and best interests of all concerned.

Permit me now to invite your Excellency's serious consideration of the various views which are presented in the SECOND PART of the inclosed pamplet entitled THIRTEEN PAPERS, relating to the magnitude and importance of this unrivaled undertaking. The five essays for the writing of which I have made provision, and which several essays in the aggregate will, I dare say, adequately elucidate all of the more difficult points of this complex proposition, are to come into my hands on or soon after the first day of next December, and will all be published, a few months afterward, in one volume; a copy of which I shall have the pleasure of addressing to your Excellency.

I have the honor to be, very respectfully,

Your Excellency's obedient servant,

H. R. HELPER.

<hr>

TO THE MEXICAN GOVERNMENT.

ST. LOUIS, MO., *September 7, 1880.*

TO THE HONORABLE THE SECRETARY OF STATE
FOR THE REPUBLIC OF MEXICO.

DISTINGUISHED SIR: Your Excellency's attention is respectfully invited to the annexed printed communication, signed by myself, and clipped from a late issue of *El*

Comercio del Valle, of this city, in relation to my projected Three Americas Longitudinal Railway. Requesting the privilege of now reiterating to your Excellency the substance of my two previous letters on this subject, the first bearing date of November 1, 1879, and the second under date of June 5, 1880, permit me to remark, as a simple matter of fact, that neither the government of the United States, nor any other government, nor any company, nor even individual, has as yet any sort of authority or copartnership or connection with me in this affair. It is earnestly hoped, however, and confidently believed, that both times and circumstances will soon be so well developed in support of the enterprise as to bring about such general and effective cooperation as may be indispensable to success.

Meanwhile, if, without officially obligating or compromising yourself, you can give some assurance of Mexico's friendly disposition in an undertaking so largely American, so entirely republican, so wholly peaceful and civilizing, so immeasurably utilitarian and progressive, and withal so perfectly well-meaning, in every respect, toward the peoples of all the countries through which the road is designed to run, such assurance from your Excellency may help very materially to lay more firmly the foundations of success in my own country, where, as it seems to me, it is first necessary to make a good beginning.

Several of the governments of Central and South America have already favored me with very encouraging expressions in commendation of the unequaled international and intercontinental highway thus proposed; but up to the present time I have not been honored with so much as even one word from Mexico. May I indulge the hope that such an honor is yet in reserve for me?

I remain, with great respect,

Your Excellency's obedient servant,

H. R. HELPER.

TO THE MEXICAN GOVERNMENT.

St. Louis, Mo., *January 27, 1881.*
To the Honorable the Secretary of State
FOR THE REPUBLIC OF MEXICO.

Distinguished Sir: I have the honor to express the hope that your Excellency may be pleased to read and ponder at least so much of the foregoing circular-letter as is occupied in presenting in print the Report of the Three Americas Railway Committee. In connection with the several previous communications which I have had the honor of addressing to your Excellency upon this same subject, permit me now to remark further, that, as I sincerely believe, the Republic of Mexico will, in all probability, greatly promote its highest and best interests, national and international, by rigidly refraining from granting any charter, or other positive right or privilege, that would, in any manner, operate as a bar or hindrance to favorable action, at the proper time, in this particular case. Please continue absolutely uncompromised in this respect until July or August of the present year, or possibly until a few months later, when I and others associated with me will, I feel confident, be ready to submit for your approbation the most comprehensive, prudent and practicable plans that have ever yet been devised for assuredly adequate and mutually advantageous intercommunication between all the Republics of the New World.

    With great respect, I am, Sir,
                Your Excellency's obedient servant,
                            H. R. HELPER.

THIRTY MISCELLANEOUS COMMUNICATIONS TO THE PROJECTOR.*

An idea, like a ghost, (according to the common notion of ghost,) must be spoken to a little before it will explain itself.—*Dickens.*

There is nothing in the world really beneficial that does not lie within the reach of a thoroughly informed mind and a well-directed pursuit.—*Burke.*

Not one of the writers of the following letters is in the least responsible for any statement or sentiment contained in any part of this book beyond the limits of his own communication. Exclusively with the projector of the Three Americas Railway himself rests all the responsibility for the existence of the chapter or section headed *Brazil's Perfidious Forfeiture of Friendly Regard;* but to the extent that that section deals with the indescribably revolting and calamitous evils of Catholicism in South and Central America, —in Brazil especially,—the honor and the responsibility therefor are quite equally and complacently divided between Adam Smith, Herbert Spencer, John Stuart Mill, Godfrey Higgins, Jean Baptiste Say, Francois Rabelais, Thomas Jefferson, Thomas Ewbank, William H. Seward, John Fiske, John William Draper, John A. Dillon, and (filling out the complement of a baker's dozen,) the humble owner of the three initials hereunto subscribed.

H. R. H.

---

*But for the lack of space, many other relevant, instructive and admirable letters, similar to the thirty here introduced, would also appear in print in this volume.

FROM PRESIDENT HAYES.

EXECUTIVE MANSION,
WASHINGTON, *January* 4, 1880.

HINTON R. HELPER, ESQ., *St. Louis, Mo.*

DEAR SIR: I am in receipt by express of your volume entitled *Oddments of Andean Diplomacy,* and have to thank you for it. In compliance with the suggestion of your letter, the subject of the work, in so far as it relates to your projected Three Americas Railway, will receive such attention as its importance demands, and as circumstances may enable me to give.

Sincerely,

R. B. HAYES.

— —

FROM THE GOVERNMENT OF GUATEMALA.

[Translation.]

NATIONAL PALACE,
GUATEMALA, *December* 3, 1879.

HINTON ROWAN HELPER, ESQ., *St. Louis, Mo.*

DEAR SIR: I have received the esteemed communication which you have been so kind as to send to me, under date of November 1, 1879, in relation to the construction of an international and intercontinental railway; in the realization of which you hope to receive the recognition and aid of the Governments of both North and South America.

Your project being extremely flattering and congenial to the Government of this Republic, you may count upon its efficient coöperation, so soon as the scheme shall take proper shape and begin to be put into practice.

It is not quite possible, however, to assure you that none

of the companies, to whom concessions have already been granted in this country, will not themselves object, fearing that the realization of your enterprise may be disadvantageous to their own interests.

Hoping soon to receive the interesting publication you have promised to send to me, and thus thanking you for it beforehand,

I remain, dear sir, yours very truly,
MANUEL HERRERA.

FROM THE GOVERNMENT OF GUATEMALA.

[Translation.]

DEPARTMENT OF STATE,
GUATEMALA, February 19, 1881.

HINTON R. HELPER, ESQ., *St. Louis, Mo.*

DEAR SIR: I have received your note of the 27th of last month, inclosing the documents in relation to the proposed Three Americas Railway. Your note and the said documents, having been translated into Spanish, have been passed to the Department of Public Works, in order that that Department may be enabled to determine what may best be done in the premises. Whatever that Department shall resolve upon will be duly communicated to you.

I remain, your obedient servant,
L. MONTUFAR.

FROM EX-GOVERNOR AGUIRRE OF HONDURAS.

[Translation.]

With all the sincerity of my heart, I offer my humble co-operation to Mr. Helper, in the furtherance of his grand scheme for an international and intercontinental American railway; trusting that the undertaking may be pushed to a consummated fact in the history of the wonders of the nineteenth century.   To the realization of this magnificent project I consecrate all my vows, my labors and my ardent hopes.

JOSÉ M. AGUIRRE.

Dec. 22, 1879.

FROM THE GOVERNMENT OF SALVADOR.

[Translation.]

DEPARTMENT OF STATE,
SAN SALVADOR, Jan. 14, 1880.

HINTON ROWAN HELPER, ESQ., *St. Louis, Missouri.*

DEAR SIR: I have received your polite communication, under date of the 1st of last November, in which you announce the probable early publication of your new book, entitled " Oddments of Andean Diplomacy," which, as you inform me, treats in part of the advisability of the early construction of a great longitudinal railway, which will embrace North and Central and South America.   I am looking with much interest for the copy of the work which you have promised to send to me; and I believe that, in all probability, if your unparalleled project should attain to the requisite point of realization, San Salvador will be found to be quite free from all compromises.   Please accept, Sir, the assurances of my especial consideration.

MANUEL T. MORALES.

FROM THE GOVERNMENT OF SALVADOR.

[Translation.]

DEPARTMENT OF STATE,
SAN SALVADOR, *February* 22, 1881.

HINTON R. HELPER, ESQ., *St. Louis, Mo.*

DEAR SIR: Your circular-letter under date of the 27th ultimo, in which you indicate your desire that this Government will abstain from granting concessions, and from giving privileges, to any longitudinal railroad undertaking, until you shall have presented the plans of your projected Three Americas Railway, has been received.   It affords me pleasure to be able to assure you that your wishes in this regard will be borne in mind.

Your obedient servant,
T. GALLEGOS.

FROM THE GOVERNMENT OF NICARAGUA.

[Translation.]

DEPARTMENT OF STATE, REPUBLIC OF NICARAGUA,
MANAGUA, *October* 14, 1880.

HINTON R. HELPER, ESQ., *St. Louis, Mo.*

DEAR SIR: In reply to your esteemed communication of the 7th ultimo, I take pleasure in manifesting to you the good dispositions of the Government of Nicaragua toward your proposition for the construction of a longitudinal railway through the three Americas; assenting as does the Republic to the measure of the possibility of the realization of this vastly important enterprise, which you are now advocating and promoting with so much earnestness.

I remain, sir,

Your obedient servant,
CANDANE.

FROM THE GOVERNMENT OF COSTA RICA.

[Translation.]

DEPARTMENT OF STATE, REPUBLIC OF COSTA RICA,
SAN JOSÉ, *January* 29, 1880.
HINTON ROWAN HELPER, ESQ., *St. Louis, Mo.*

DEAR SIR: Your courteous communication of the 1st of November last, relative to a prodigious railway undertaking, the realization of which would doubtless prove most efficacious to the prosperity of all the Americas, whose vast and numerous countries the unrivaled international and intercontinental railroad proposed by you would unite, was both satisfactory and pleasing.

The government of this Republic is now actually constructing, with praiseworthy energy and determination, an interoceanic railroad from Port Limon, on the Atlantic, to Puntarenas, on the Pacific; but this does not, in any manner whatever, prevent Costa Rica from accepting with enthusiasm, and giving its moral support to, the gigantic enterprise here mentioned, so long as there appears to be a fair probability of carrying it out successfully; and, fortunately, the government of Costa Rica has not yet contracted, nor will it contract, any obligations or compromises which would embarass your action in this affair.

We have not yet received in this office the copy of the work which you say you had sent, or would send, to Consul-General José M. Muñoz, for transmission to this government; but I hope and trust it will soon come to hand; when it shall be read and pondered in this country, with all the interest and earnestness which your colossal project inspires.

It now only remains for me to express my very sincere thanks for the promised copy of the book; and thus having done so, I avail myself, dear Sir, of this opportunity to offer to you the fullest assurances of my esteem and of my most distinguished consideration.

JOSÉ MARIA CASTRO.

FROM THE GOVERNMENT OF COLUMBIA.

[Translation.]

DEPARTMENT OF STATE,
BOGOTÁ, COLUMBIA, *June* 5, 1880.

MR. HINTON ROWAN HELPER, *St. Louis, Misssouri.*

DEAR SIR: This dispatch will reach you in acknowledgment of the receipt of your letter of the first of last November. I have carefully considered the views you advance in advocating the construction of a longitudinal railway through North and South America, from Hudson Bay to the Strait of Magellan. The project is indeed stupendous and majestic; and you may confidently rely on the coöperation of the United States of Columbia, so soon as the enterprise shall be so far organized and developed as to render such coöperation possible with a fair prospect of the ability to further the undertaking to completion.

I am, dear Sir,

Your obedient servant,

LOUIS CARLOS RICO.

FROM THE GOVERNMENT OF PARAGUAY.

[Translation.]

DEPARTMENT OF STATE,
ASUNCION, PARAGUAY, *December* 10, 1880.

HINTON R. HELPER, ESQ., *St. Louis, Missouri.*

DEAR SIR: In reply to your polite letter of the 7th of September, it is proper for me to apprise you of the fact that the Government of Paraguay is animated with the best dispositions in favor of the projected railway through North and Central and South America.   On this account it is therefore a pleasure to me to offer to you the assurances of my most distinguished consideration.

I remain, Sir,

Your very attentive servant,

JOSÉ A. DECOUR.

FROM MAJOR HILDER.

St. Louis, *January* 14, 1881.

HINTON R. HELPER, ESQ.,

DEAR SIR: I have received your kind letter, congratulating me on having been awarded the first prize for my Essay on the Three Americas Railway.   For the kindly sentiments you express, I feel sincerely grateful.   As a matter of course, I am much gratified at finding that the Committee have selected my paper as worthy of the first place among so many competitors; but I do not, by any means, arrogate to myself all the credit.   The enterprise is so grand in its conception, and the results to be attained so important and extensive, that the brain must be dull indeed that would not be incited to put forth its best efforts after having given the subject the consideration necessary to fully grasp the magnitude and sublimity of the theme.   The builder who erects the stately edifice may be worthy of praise for excellent work within his own sphere; but the enduring glory of the achievement must be with the architect who conceived the idea in all its symmetry and beauty.   I would myself rather be the projector of the Three Americas Railway, the author of *The Impending Crisis of the South*, and, from your anti-slavery standpoint, occupy your position on the questions of

the various races of mankind and educated suffrage, than
be President of the United States. With the warmest
wishes for the most complete success of your great project,
I remain,

Faithfully yours,

FRANK F. HILDER.

———

FROM COL. BEELEN.

CORTLANDT-ON-THE-HUDSON,
NEW YORK, January 15, 1881.

HINTON R. HELPER, ESQ., *St. Louis, Mo.*

DEAR SIR: Yesterday's mail brought to me your letter
of the 11th inst., and also, separately, a communication from
the·Committee, inclosing a check for one thousand two hundred dollars, for the second prize-essay on your projected
Three Americas Railway. The receipt of these valuable
papers—valuable in more senses than one—was, as you
may well suppose, extremely gratifying to me. In fact, I
am more than grateful for the very kind, if too flattering,
letter in which you so happily inform me of my success.
That I did not secure the first prize brings with it the satisfactory thought that a more fortunate advocate of your colossal scheme has adduced stronger and more convincing
arguments in its favor.

Yet I beg the privilege of contending that no one can
rightfully take precedence of me as a fervent well-wisher of
the enterprise. My profound interest in the undertaking
impelled me, by degrees, to devote to my essay a great deal
of study; much more indeed, than, in the first place, I had
ever dreamed it would require. Step by step I found myself led on; and step by step I learned how practicable, how
advantageous, and how remunerative, the Three Americas

Railway will prove. If all your special coadjutors have labored as earnestly as I have, and as much *con amore*, the greatest work of the century will soon be well started on its way toward completion. The essay finished, approved by the Committee, and now in your possession, material enough still remains on my desk for a volume of very considerable dimensions.

My thanks are also due to you for your kind thoughtfulness in sending to me Col. Fisher's letter, written from Pullay, near Ligua, in Chili. Colonel F. is an intimate friend of the substantial and estimable Hemenways of Boston; and his opinions are generally well founded. His views, as expressed in the letter before me, are essentially correct. A man who thinks always likes to hear from sensible people a corroboration of the soundness of his own spoken or published impressions; and, in this sense, I have enjoyed vastly the perusal of Col. Fisher's letter. The able and excellent gentleman whom he alludes to, as a possible President of Chili, at no distant day, merits all the eulogies bestowed upon him. In Chili, fortunately, as in the United States, there is now no lack of worthy men to fill, with honor to themselves, and with advantage to the public, the highest offices which have been established in the economy of their affairs.

Trusting that you will never hesitate a moment to advise me of any additional service which I—though myself not at once perceiving the opportunity—may yet be able to render in furthering the proposed Three Americas Railway, I remain,

.Yours faithfully,

FRED'K A. BEELEN.

FROM MR. ARCHER.

RICHMOND, VA., *January* 14, 1881.
HINTON R. HELPER, ESQ., *St. Louis, Mo.*

DEAR SIR : Your kind letter, bringing your congratulations on my success in obtaining the third prize for an essay on your projected Three Americas Railway, has been received. Accept my warmest thanks, and be assured that I am deeply and pleasurably affected by your appreciation of my effort. You may imagine my own gratification at succeeding in being thus recognized and honored as one of the effective advocates of your magnificent scheme.

While the delay of the Committee, because of the great amount of work before it, must have proved more or less vexatious to all those immediately interested in the results of its deliberations, yet I am strongly inclined to believe that the postponement was fortunate for the undertaking itself, inasmuch as the Committee's action will reach the country at the very time when the question of the rival Isthmian routes for a ship-canal is coming forward so prominently. I maintain that neither a ship-canal nor a ship-railroad, across Central America, can be seriously compared in importance, so far as the United States and other American nationalities are concerned, with our proposed Three Americas Railway. Yet there is in each scheme much of splendid promise, and much of absolute certainty of good. Nor is there the least ground for justifiable opposition of the one as against the other. Each aims at the enlargement and betterment of every distinctive American interest ; but their respective missions are widely different ; one will deal continuously and forever with two continents, and the other with two oceans.

During the progress of the discussions of the rival advan-

27

tages of Darien, Nicaragua and Tehuantepec, the indispensability of a fuller development of Central and South America, and the impossibility of our ever conveniently reaching
those countries otherwise than by means of your projected
railway, must become more and more apparent.   Such discussions will only whet the appetite of all the peoples of the
three Americas for an early and adequate consideration of
the Longitudinal Line.   Therefore, as it seems to me, we
are favored with a very auspicious outlook; and, with the
able and distinguished Chairman of your Committee in
Congress,—nominated and elected more than a year since
his acceptance of service on the Committee,—we shall
probably have little or no difficulty in soon getting the subject fairly before that most learned and potent American
legislature, and securing therefrom such enlightened and
honorable action as will, in due time, and for the enduring
welfare of all the Americas, result in the construction of the
grandest international highway upon the earth.

Very truly yours,

W. W. ARCHER.

FROM MR. CARPENTER.

WASHINGTON, *January* 11, 1881.

HINTON R. HELPER, ESQ., *St. Louis, Missouri.*

DEAR SIR: A thousand thanks for the interesting and valuable information which this morning's mail brought to me,—
and yet a thousand more thanks for the knowledge that my
poem, *From Zone to Zone,* in advocacy of your projected Three Americas Railway, gives satisfaction and
pleasure to your own worthy self.   It is but seldom indeed
that an unprofessional poet becomes at once the recipient of
so much good fortune as I have thus realized; and you

may rest assured that both the honor and the emolument are duly appreciated. I sincerely hope and trust that the sequel may show that the decision of your committee, in this case,—as in fact in every other case,—was wisely made, and that what I have written may render good service in helping to arouse proper attention to the great international improvement with which, through your generous instrumentality, I am now beginning to feel myself fully identified.

The public mind, as I believe, will soon be quite ready for a thorough and practical consideration of the merits of your projected Three Americas Railway,—an excellent name, by the way, for an excellent undertaking. Even now our most enterprising merchants and capitalists heartily concur in the opinion that the American railroad system cannot be too speedily extended into Mexico; and, among statesmen, so sound an authority as Ex-Secretary Thompson is already in the field prophesying for us early railway connection with the Isthmus of Darien. Of course I need not assure you—you feeling already fully assured—that if we go to Panama, we shall not stop there, but will push still farther southward until we reach the austral confines of the Argentine Republic.

Very truly yours,

FRANK D. Y. CARPENTER.

FROM MR. DEEKENS.

NORWICH, ONTARIO, CANADA, *January* 14, 1881.
HINTON R. HELPER, ESQ., *St. Louis, Mo.*

DEAR SIR: My acknowledgments are due to you for your letter of the 11th instant. It is with a fair—but not full—degree of satisfaction that I have learned that my poem has

been the subject of an award of merit at the hands of the
Three Americas Railway Committee, from whom I have received a cheque for five hundred dollars; that being the
amount offered by you for the second best effort in poetry.
I certainly expected that my prose essay would obtain a
prize and a good place.   One of our highly educated scholars here, who perused it prior to my submission of it for
competition, seemed to be strongly impressed with the conviction that it was almost certain to find acceptance with the
Committee.   Of ample measure, my essay touched upon
almost every imaginable subject (except the details of engineering) in connection with the scheme; and I flattered
myself—perhaps too unreservedly—that I had succeeded in
elaborating and fortifying your own views in such manner
and degree as to be especially clear and convincing.   In
behalf of the enterprise itself, I heartily congratulate you,
therefore, if you have received from the Committee three
better papers than mine; for in that case you have undoubtedly secured a series of very able and effective documents, wherewith it will not be a difficult task to influence
public opinion in the right direction.   All the papers which
may be published in this connection will be very closely
scrutinized by parties especially interested in the undertaking.

   Of your own kindness and impartiality, through the whole
of this trying business, I am myself perfectly satisfied; and
I am glad that an end has come at last to the arduous labors of the Committee.   I suppose it not unlikely that you
will, for " extra work and over time," have to regale the
Committee with a champagne dinner!   After reading two
of your publications, your book entitled *Oddments of Andean Diplomacy*, and your pamphlet entitled *Thirteen Papers*, I seemed intuitively to know the projector of the Three
Americas Railway; and our subsequent correspondence
through the post has only confirmed that impression.   Your

suggestions of the advisability of making the Longitudinal
Line a purely governmental work,—a grand continental and
intercôntinental improvement of national and international
concern,—have interested me very much; and I am curious
to see what the other successful writers have to say, if they
say anything, on this particular feature of your project. If
the dozen or more great governments which will be so directly and largely benefitted by the Three Americas Railway should not be able to harmonize upon proper bases for
building it, then private enterprise must come to the rescue,
in order to carry out the colossal scheme.

Faithfully yours,
F. A. DEEKENS.

FROM PROF. DAVIDSON.

NEW YORK, February 2, 1881.

HINTON R. HELPER, ESQ.,

DEAR SIR: Your circular-letter on the Three Americas
Railway, announcing the result of the prize-essay contest,
came duly; and I am really very glad to see this other important step so successfully taken. May you go on con-
quering and to conquer. You are to become—let me assume the rôle of the Pythoness—you are to become the
Colossus of Roads; eventually to bestride the tri-American
lands, like riding three horses at once. Systematic and
business-like as are your proceedings, and practical as your
extraordinary propositions are beginning to appear, yet the
scheme, viewed as a whole, is a regular poem in itself. I
did not enter the list of competitors for prizes, mainly for
lack of leisure to perform the requisite labor. But I join
sincerely in rejoicing that the work has been so well done
by others; and trust that—like " the silken cord that binds

two loving hearts "—the steel bands you are now hammer-
ing out to bind together two willing continents may also
prove to be golden. Success to your enterprise and to
yourself!

Faithfully, hoping, believing,

JAS. WOOD DAVIDSON.

MR. PARMER TO MR. ALLEN.

St. Louis, *November* 15, 1879.

Hon. Thomas Allen:

Dear Sir: I have just been perusing Mr. Helper's new
book, entitled " Oddments of Andean Diplomacy," which
is now before me.   Carefully reading the preface and other
important portions of the volume, I have drifted through
the whole work, and have thus endeavored, successfully, I
think, to grasp the leading idea and purpose of its author.
The scope and magnitude of the Three Americas Railway
enterprise was at first a great surprise to me.   With my limited knowledge of railroad building, and without going over
the entire ground, from terminus to terminus, but considering the manifold and measureless interests which will inevitably be developed by the carrying out of such a gigantic
project, I must here express my wonder at the order and
vastness of the conception.

The book itself is simply the materialization and manifest-
ation of a mighty thought. As we clear away from the
author's stupendous·proposition the first crude impressions
of the impossible, reason and facts crowd upon us, and the
feasibility and grandeur of the scheme loom up before us,
distinct and brilliant with the charming graces of a new
evangel. With but very little, if any stretch of the imagination, the practicability of the undertaking confronts us
with the force of a positive demonstration.

It almost takes away one's breath, yet with a sort of ec-
static pleasure, to contemplate the salutary revolutions
this enterprise, when consummated, will produce in the commercial, social and civil progress of the Western Hemisphere. I now not only consider this proposed intercontinental railway possible, but have no hesitation in saying
further, that, in my opinion, it is the grandest thought in the
wide field of trade and civilization that has been evolved
from the mind of man during the present century.

Yours respectfully,

ENRIQUE PARMER.

MR. BARNES TO MR. ALLEN.

BROWNSVILLE, OXFORD COUNTY,
ONTARIO, CANADA, April 3, 1880.

HON. THOMAS ALLEN, *St Louis, Mo.*

DEAR SIR: The longitudinal and intercontinental railway, which has recently been proposed in your city, by a
gentleman whose mind seems to be imbued with a spirit of
enterprise of almost superhuman character, is an undertaking quite unparalleled in the world's history; neither the
Great Wall of China nor the huge Pyramids of Egypt bearing any resemblance to it in point of usefulness. The grandeur of this idea of building a double-track steel railway
from the Arctic to the Antarctic Circle, is coupled with a
sublimity of sentiment that could have had its origin only
within the range of the boundless ambition of American enterprise; but from that ever-overflowing fountain it has issued forth, with a completeness of form and comeliness
which at once challenge and receive the admiration of all
lofty-minded men.

Utility is the first and most important consideration in

the construction of a railway.   Fidelity to this principle requires that the road shall be judiciously located and substantially built.   Even in the building of roads of minor importance, the principle thus mentioned should be strictly ad-
hered to ; but more especially should it be kept in view and
applied in the construction of a work of such incomparable
magnitude as the projected intercontinental American railway, which, when completed, will bind together one hundred
degrees of latitude ; the railway itself running the whole
distance in nearly a straight line ; and which will then, at its
Northern terminus, (say its junction with the Canada Pacific,) form two branches, whose diverging courses will be
more or less transcontinental ; the one extending to the
Southwest corner of Hudson Bay, and the other in a Northwest direction across the headwaters of the great rivers, to
a harbor on the Western shore of Alaska.

By reason of its international and intercontinental character, this far-reaching longitudinal railway will directly
affect many of the commonwealths of the torrid zone, whose
civil, social and educational institutions have not yet been
well developed.   Consequently the people of those commonwealths, with few exceptions, are in a state of almost
constant anarchy and revolution ; their superstition, bigotry,
ignorance and poverty always remaining in a sort of fixed
and fatal quantity.   To all those nations the consummation
of this Herculean railway enterprise would be a most
gracious inheritance ; for it would, though slowly. yet surely,
introduce among them the order-loving and highly enlightened and progressive civilization of the Anglo-Americans.
In this way the so-called Latin nations of the New World
would peacefully and prosperously secure for themselves
and for their posterity what, for their own permanent welfare, they so much require ; namely, liberal and honest and
stable governments, and also more refined and exalted con-

ditions of private life than they have hitherto generally known. Not only to these people in South America, but to our own also in North America, this road would be a perpetual stream of gold, a never-failing river of riches and recreation, with wide-branching trees of knowledge growing luxuriantly on both sides. What a matchlessly grand and glorious enterprise indeed, alike unequaled in either its magnitude or its magnificence!

Where, though, shall be found the best location for this all-reaching and all-serving international highway. The verdict of sound common sense is explicit in demanding the selection of the hundreth parallel of longitude, reckoned from Greenwich, and fixing the Northern terminus in conjunction with the Canada Pacific Railway, on or near the fiftieth degree of latitude in the center of the Swan River Territory. That would be not far from the very heart of the vast region which, in its eminently true signification, is generally denominated the Great Northwest, where, north of the forty-ninth degree of latitude, at least fifteen millions of people can be amply and happily accommodated with not only a healthy climate, but also an arable soil of unsurpassed fertility. There too, to a very great extent, the surface is underlaid with thick veins of coal of as good quality as was ever extracted from the bowels of the earth.

If, at some period in the future, another railroad running still farther northward, should be required, a more favorable point to start from could probably not be found than the interjunction of the Three Americas and the Canada Pacific. The paramount consideration, in connection with the proposed Three Americas Railway, being utility in its most comprehensive sense, it would seem to be a self-evident truth that the hundredth parallel of longitude is, in almost every respect, the best that can be chosen. This fact appears in the bright and persuasive light of demonstration, when we pass in review the entire route and scope of the undertaking. So surveyed, the peerless Three Americas Longitudinal Railway will, at junctions midland between the two great oceans, cross at right angles, and feed profusely, the several transcontinental railroads; and these, in turn, will reciprocally and largely promote the interests of all concerned. In this manner may be reached, with excellent system and advantage, every point of either continent where railway facilities are desirable. As a matter of course, it is only a question of time when, along the grand longitudinal trunk line and all its tributaries, flourishing cities and towns and villages will continuously adorn the plain of vision.

Yours, very respectfully,

THOMAS BARNES.

FROM MR. CARMER.

OLEAN, NEW YORK, January 7, 1880.

HINTON R. HELPER, ESQ., *St. Louis, Mo.*

DEAR SIR: In thus addressing you, I must first request you to pardon the presumption of one whose acquaintance with you has been so brief as mine, but which to me, notwithstanding the space of several intervening years, is yet associated with many pleasant memories. I have recently read in the New York *Evening Post*, a very handsome notice of your grand scheme for constructing a longitudinal railway through the three Americas. You may possibly be somewhat ahead of the times in this heroic undertaking; but the world moves rapidly, and men's minds are fearlessly venturing out into unexplored regions, and forming ideas of unprecedented moment and magnitude. The present is undoubtedly an auspicious period for inviting to your enterprise the attention of that large and influential class of American citizens who prudently combine and adjust within themselves the true principles of business and patriotism.

That the intercontinental railway which you have so perspicuously sketched and proposed, would, by bringing the South and Central American Republics into closer affiliation with our own, be of incalculable benefit to all concerned scarcely admits of even the shadow of a doubt.   *   *   * It is safe to conclude that this road would become a very important factor in extending the diversified blessings of our Anglo-Saxon civilization among the mixed races of Central and South America, and especially in imparting to them a knowledge of the subtle strength that inheres in a law-abiding, educated and popular will, which generally exercises such a potent influence for good over our own rulers, and which, without boasting of the fact, makes our own republic so much more stable and prosperous and powerful than any of theirs.   These are considerations, however, which will probably not command much serious attention from capitalists; as they will be chiefly concerned to know what dividends or rates of interest they will be likely to receive on their respective investments.   Many of the largest and best results which may be reasonably expected to flow eventually from the building of the Three Americas Longitudinal Railway, will flow only as sequences from its successful opening and operation on the simplest bases of business.   *   *   *   When the time for action shall have come, you will, I trust, find many strong men who will put their shoulders to the wheel with you, and work cheerily and diligently onward, until your brightest hopes and expectations, in this most laudable effort, shall be fulfilled.   *   *   *

Sincerely, your friend and well-wisher,

. LEWIS A. CARMER.

FROM THE HON. NATT ATKINSON.

ASHEVILLE, NORTH CAROLINA,
January 12, 1880.

HINTON R. HELPER, ESQ., *St. Louis, Mo.*

DEAR SIR: Most fully and heartily do I approve your magnificent project for building a longitudinal double-track steel railway through North and Central and South America. It is a matter worthy to receive at once the serious consideration of every inhabitant of the Western Hemisphere; and I have no doubt that, so soon as your proposition shall be well understood, it will meet the enthusiastic approbation of all the enlightened minds of both continents. It makes my heart swell with emotions of pride when I contemplate the completion of this matchless undertaking; and by no means the less so when I remember that its forethoughtful originator is a North Carolinian.

May your efforts be crowned with the grand success to which you are so deservedly entitled; and may a proper recognition of the extraordinary merits of your enterprise soon lead to the consummation so devoutly wished. If I were in Congress, and you should come to the National Government for aid in this most ponderous and important international project, I should, if assured of reasonable coöperation on the part of the Central and South American Republics, feel it my duty to vote you and your co-workers a Round Billion, if so large a sum should be found to be necessary, to secure the construction of the road.

Pardon me for suggesting that a copy of your letter to the three trustees of the fund which you have so generously set apart in this behalf, and their reply, should be published in every newspaper in North and South America. All liberal and progressive newspapers would doubtless make room in their columns for both letters, if copies were addressed to them with a polite request to publish. In this way, better than any other that I can think of, the subject would soon come to be generally known and discussed; and it is almost certain that, after a little while, many able men, in both private and public life, would espouse the cause, and advocate it with great warmth and effect. At the earliest convenient and practical period, a well-digested plan of operations should be presented. Yet, in my opinion, the scheme should not be submitted for the consideration and action of any body of legislators, Federal or State, until the peoples of all the countries specifically interested shall have freely interchanged their views upon the more obstinate and perplexing points involved in the undertaking.

Always yours,
NATT ATKINSON.

FROM REV. DR. BOWMAN.

ATLANTA, GEORGIA, *January* 5, 1880.

H. R. HELPER, ESQ., *St. Louis, Mo.*

DEAR SIR: * * * Were it not that my time is so constantly occupied in discharging my ministerial and other imperative duties, I should myself be strongly tempted to try to write something in furtherance of The New World Intercontinental Railway so grandly projected by you. Yet, branching off for a moment to another subject, I dare say it will be gratifying to you to learn that I have a good prospect for success in the cause of Liberal Christianity in this growing city. I am endeavoring to be rightly brave and candid in the propagation of my views, and am much encouraged by the presence of an increasing audience of intelligent and thoughtful people, who have either lost or are fast losing their faith in the old superstitions. I fully concur with you in the sentiment that it is not best for human beings to attempt to be too divine, even in religion. Subjectively, religion undoubtedly has its seat in humanity; objectively, it is of course in God. In its development and manifestations, I now think it more human than I once thought. As for yourself, it is evident that you believe more in humanity than in theology. So do I, and moreover I am firmly of the opinion that Jesus did.

Your colossal railway undertaking is one of unique and preëminent grandeur; and I doubt whether there is another man in America, or elsewhere, who would have thought of it. Perhaps your peculiar relations toward the governments and peoples of South America, both as an official and as a lover, —you having married in the Argentine Republic,—may have served to crystalize this mighty conception for you. I own to the sincere pleasure and enthusiasm with which a perusal of your scheme has filled me, and am hopeful of the ultimate realization of all the grand and advantageous results, commercial, civil and moral, which you seem to have had in view in formulating and proposing the gigantic enterprise.

Faithfully, your friend,

W. C. BOWMAN.

FROM MR. CANONGE.*

[Translation.]

NEW ORLEANS, *December* 18, 1879.
HINTON R. HELPER, ESQ., *St. Louis, Missouri.*

DEAR SIR: * * * Your huge proposition, for a longitudinal railway through the three Americas, is well worthy of our epoch, so rich in unmatched and meritorious audacities, and so fruitful of wonder-works attempted and accomplished. All the things of this life are essentially mutable. If, as is by no means improbable, the pivot of the world should change its present place, and come from the other hemisphere to ours; if some day,—a day near by, perhaps,—the Americas should, in their turn, become the center and standard of all progress and all civilization, your stupendous project of an intercontinental railway, serving them as a vertebral column, will not be one of the least agents of that magnificent consummation. What a superb spectacle that would be, of the giant of this civilization proudly reclining his head on the westerly shore of Hudson

---

*Prof. James Wood Davidson, in his scholarly work entitled "The Living Writers of the South," pronounces Mr. Canonge (a son of the learned and distinguished Judge Canonge, of New Orleans), the most brilliant Franco-American poet and dramatist of the present period; and I have other excellent reasons for believing that his estimate of the abilities of this gifted author of dramatic literature, several of whose tragedies and comedies have been succesfully performed in the theaters of Paris, is wholly correct. The poetic beauty and force of expression so striking in the three letters here given from Mr. Canonge, although his communications, in the process of translation, have lost much of their original merit, show unmistakably that the mortal who wrote them must be a special favorite and companion of more than one of the Muses.

H. R. H.

Bay, and laving his feet in the Strait of Magellan! One more effort, and there he is, grandly stretching himself out to the very perimeters of the two poles!

Always faithfully yours,

L. PLACIDE CANONGE.

———

FROM MR. CANONGE.

[Translation.]

NEW ORLEANS, *April* 23, 1880.

HINTON R. HEPLER, ESQ., *St. Louis, Mo.*

DEAR SIR: * * * I sincerely trust that the lofty conviction and enthusiasm which, for a period of more than thirteen years, have sustained and guided you, will at last conduct you successfully to the great end at which you are aiming. Yes, with all my heart, I hope and believe that, aided by an areopagus of five,—an enlightened quinquevirate whom your munificence calls around you,—and through the coöperation of our own compatriots, and the concurrence of the peoples of Spanish America, where, in the higher ranks of society, as you yourself have remarked, are to be found the brightest intelligencies and the most finished types of natural nobility, you may live to behold the perfect realization of your unrivaled conception of a double-track steel railway, extending itself longitudinally over the three Americas to a distance almost equal to that of either of the two great oceans, which will continuously salute it with their mysterious and eternal echoes.

Well indeed may our own countrymen, and all other friends and promoters of progress, ardently hope that the magnificent dream of your imagination, which seems to have come to you when you were even yet a comparatively young man, will be the crowning and most important achievement of your latter days. The handfuls of grain which you have so lavishly yet prudently scattered among the four winds of the globe, have fallen on fertile soil, and will soon germinate into precious seedlings, from which, in due time, under the benignities of heaven, will be developed a marvelously abundant and glorious harvest.

Your proposition, as you have made it, imparts standing and strength to those other resolute and gigantic schemes in which, so to speäk, are concreted and crystallized the predestined aspirations and intentionalities of mankind, now agitated and oscillating with a spirit of unrest aroused by the consciousness of an unduly lengthening period of imperfect advancement in the world's weal. The most wholesome and necessary demands of our time look to an extension of the area of enlightenment; and instinctive suggestions of changes of location and new homes are beginning to sway vast multitudes of estimable men and women, who, carrying with them, wherever they may go, the best of their native institutions, will be the discreet and honored introducers of improved systems of social and political life.

Pardon me if the profound interest I feel in your colossal undertaking leads me to seem to speak in a somewhat preceptory manner. Possess yourself calmly and in peace and confidence, and continue to be firm and persevering in the very course which you have thus far marked out and pursued. Pay little or no attention to the shallow-brained skeptics, who will only betray their own insignificance by disparaging your splendid project. What they now condemn they will erelong approve and exalt; aye, just so soon as your grand and unique enterprise shall have passed from the domain of the ideal into that of an accomplished fact, they will themselves at once acclaim it more loudly than its unwavering and steadfast friends from the first. Unreason-

28

ing decriers and deniers have always been, and are yet, but too common in every age and country; and we have, unfortunately, no warrant for expecting a very early extinction of the driveling and detractory race to which they belong.

Again, therefore, in this regard, permit me to express the hope that you will actively retain in full force every particle of your original and courageous purpose. Strong in your well-founded faith, strong in your physical manhood, strong in your intellectual organization, move on steadily and triumphantly in this Titanic contest; in which, however, as a means of achieving ultimate and complete success, you will find it necessary to combat most vigorously and unyieldingly, and hand to hand, with Nature itself. Nothing less than a new and brilliant victory for civilization throughout the Western Hemisphere, will be the result of the accomplishment of your object. In furthering the material and mental and moral interests of society, in developing the resources of extensive regions as yet but sparsely settled, in benefiting the populations of two continents by bringing them into more intimate and profitable relations with each other, you will have largely contributed to the general peace and welfare of nearly a score of mighty nationalities; and, among other excellent outcomes of your efforts, you will also have greatly elevated and ennobled manual labor, which, in many localities, is but too stupidly disdained.

Believe and persevere. *In hoc signo vinces.* Many crooked things in the three Americas need to be straightened up. May your proposed railway of railways soon be constructed, and may it always operate as a powerful instrument in the amelioration of every unsound and troublesome condition of affairs within the reach or shadow of its influence. Then indeed may dawn, with universal welcome, the glorious four hundredth anniversary of the 14th of October, 1492; and may it be fitly celebrated by millions and millions of Americans, of every clime and every zone, justly proud of the superior achievements of their own distinctive methods.

Your faithful friend,

L. PLACIDE CANONGE.

FROM MR. CANONGE.

[Translation.]

NEW ORLEANS, *September* 24, 1880.

HINTON R. HELPER, ESQ., *St. Louis, Mo.*

DEAR SIR : To know that a friend steadfastly entertains a kind thought of us every now and then, is always one of the sweetest recollections of the voyage of life; and the delightful impressions produced by such recollections are much more profound, and all the more endearing and enduring, when we are aware that we occasionally occupy a place in the memory of a man of your nature—endowed with both a mind and a heart of the truest qualities. Of this I cannot permit the indulgence of the least doubt, since the charming attentions which you bestow upon me are the palpable and precious proofs that confirm me in the opinion thus formed. Accept my thanks for the circular-letter which I have this moment received from you, accompanied as it is by such affectionate lines in your own hand-writing.

No, dear Sir, I am not worthy of a place at the table which your generous hospitality has spread out with such bountiful liberality. Yet, if I were a master of your admirable English language, I should certainly have made an effort to be honored as one of your guests. I should have been delighted and proud to respond to the reasonable demands of civilization and progress which you have so practically uttered to the world. But, alas! in my ignorance I must content myself with being only a very humble spectator, yet one well pleased, nevertheless, with that splendid banquet of talent, science, and sentiment. From the furtherest precinct of your festive assembly, I here offer in advance a most cordial toast to the five favorite feasters, whose names are so soon to be publicly proclaimed.

Still—and you will kindly pardon this overture—I desire, when the rather pressing cares of my present existence shall give me a little respite, when again I shall be fortunate enough to find a happy hour of comparative quiet, I desire to request of my enfeebled muse a fragment of poetry which may perchance yet be found within me; that is to say, a few stanzas with which to express, as fitly as possible, the admiration I feel for your surpassingly great and grand undertaking. Side by side with your five crowned manuscripts, or in such other convenient relation as you may prefer, I wish modestly to lay a little piece of poetical patchwork, addressed to the projector of the Three Americas Railway. Your friendship, I am sure, will be indulgent to the child—be it never so badly turned out,—considering the good intentions of the father.

Sincerely your friend,

L. PLACIDE CANONGE.

FROM MR. TAYLOR.

KAOLIN, CHESTER COUNTY, PENN.,
12th of 7th month, 1880.

DEAR FRIEND, HINTON R. HELPER, *St. Louis, Mo.*

Excuse my simple mode of addressing thee, as I am a member of the Religious Society of Friends, (sometimes less properly called Quakers,) one of whose general practices is to avoid compliments.   It was with great heartiness, many years ago, that I welcomed the appearance of thy opportune and valuable work against slavery, entitled *The Impending Crisis of the South*.   From my very childhood, I had been a practical advocate of free labor, rigidly abstaining, on principle, from the use of any and all of the products of enforced servitude.   Some years after attaining the age of manhood, moved by the determination to discourage and resist the system of slavery as much as possible, in my own peaceable and humble way, I embarked in the business of manufacturing and selling goods made only of cotton grown by free labor.   I also dealt in a variety of groceries which, in their origin and preparation, were entirely free from the taint of slavery.   My patrons, whose conscientious scruples, like my own, demanded such commodities, lived principally in the Northern States ; but I also had good customers, of the same way of thinking and acting, in Delaware, Maryland, Virginia, and North Carolina. That business I continued, in Philadelphia, during a period of about twenty years, and retired from it only after the abolition of slavery throughout the United States had rendered such a store no longer necessary.   * * *

Thy very kind letter of the 9th instant, in reply to mine of the 6th, was received this morning, and also thy pamphlet entitled *Thirteen Papers*, which I have read with great interest.   All that I had previously seen or known of thy projected Three Americas Railway, was derived from a paragraph of less than thirty lines in *The North American*, of Philadelphia.   By thy permission, I will make one or two well-meant suggestions.   As a matter of course, in order to ascertain the best route, a very careful survey will need to be made by competent engineers.   Several large rivers will require to be bridged ; and it is probable that many tunnels through the mountains will have to be cut.   Economy in construction, combined with excellence and permanence of finish, should be observed ; and, with reference to sources of revenue, the wisest foresight should be constantly and diligently exercised. My own experience, during many years of my life, as a stockholder in several railroads, and as a director in one, has led me to the decided conclusion, that justice to the original investors in the stock, and the most successful working of the whole business, would be better secured by obtaining in advance the requisite amount of subscriptions to the capital stock to complete the road, from one terminus to the other, without incurring the necessity of ever having recourse to loans. If the equipment could also be paid for from the stock-fund, that also would doubtless be desirable. Then, if the revenues should not be sufficient to pay dividends, which is by no means an uncommon occurrence in the more sparsely populated regions of our country, during the first few years of the operation of a railroad, there would be no mortgages to extinguish the title of the stockholders in default of the payment of interest. * * *

Very truly, thy friend,

GEO. W. TAYLOR.

FROM DR. HARRIS.

St. Louis, *July* 28, 1879.

H. R. Helper, Esq.

Dear Sir: I have the honor to acknowledge the receipt of your communication, under date of the 25th instant, in which you invite me to serve as one of a committee of three appointed to award five liberal prizes offered by you for a corresponding number of the best essays on the subject of constructing an International Railway connecting North and South America, and extending from this country to the southern extremity of the continent.

I take pleasure in accepting the trust offered me, not however, from any peculiar sense of fitness for the work, but because of the fact that I recognize the importance of the undertaking, and have full confidence in your ability to arouse public attention to the great issue now before the people of this Republic; namely, to prepare for the great wave of migration now gathering strength, which must spread out laterally to the North and South, after it has peopled our own wilderness to the West. Hitherto we have had sufficient room for expansion, without approaching the borders of other nations. The special function of América, in the history of civilization, seems to make it the theater for the recomposition of European society, and the means of safety from revolutions occasioned by changes of vocation rendered necessary by the constant invention of labor-saving machinery. Our new territories are therefore a matter of great interest to the thickly-settled Eastern sections of this country; but, at the same time, they are of far more interest to the stability and progress of European nations. The periodic waves of migration from Europe, will necessarily increase in size. Closer commercial relations not only follow in the wake of migration, but must, to some extent, precede it, so as to mark out its path and render it possible. In all this, the Railroad is the most important instrumentality. It permits migration to carry with it and preserve the traditions of metropolitan or urban life, when out on the frontier, and thus prevents too abrupt transitions from the old to the new. I look upon your enterprise as well-timed and of central importance to society, whether commercially or philanthropically regarded.

Yours respectfully,

WM. T. HARRIS.

FROM COL. CHURCH.

No. 19 GREAT WINCHESTER STREET,
LONDON, ENGLAND, *December* 31, 1879-
HINTON ROWAN HELPER, ESQ., *St. Louis, Mo.*

DEAR SIR: * * * The enterprise projected and outlined by you is certainly one of huge dimensions; and there
can be no question that the construction of the railway you
propose would be the giant work of the age.   As it appears
to my mind, that railway, completed and in regular operation, would accomplish far more, commercially and politic-
ally, for the whole western world than any scheme of progress
which has ever yet been devised.

Very truly yours,
GEORGE EARL CHURCH.

FROM COL. W. MILNOR ROBERTS.

[Col. Roberts is originally from Pennsylvania. During a period of
two years he gave much valuable assistance to Capt. Eads, in building the great Steel Bridge over the Mississippi River at St. Louis. For
some time afterward he was President of the American Society of Civil
Engineers. He is now Engineer-in-Chief of the Brazilian Empire.]

RIO DE JANEIRO, BRAZIL, March 4, 1881.
HINTON R. HELPER, ESQ., *St. Louis, Missouri.*

DEAR SIR: * * * In relation to the gigantic
scheme you have projected, the Three Americas Railway,
which at first may be viewed by some as rather visionary,
you have properly adopted the very best plan for securing
to it the serious attention of practical men.   Through your
liberality it is quite likely that the enterprise will soon be
presented to the public in several different and effective
ways.   It is an immense theme, an attractive problem, and

cannot be exhaustively studied without bestowing upon it a a great deal of labor and time. When I can command a reasonable amount of leisure from other duties, which I cannot do just now, I may take occasion to present my views at considerable length. In your previous letter to me, I observed a very strong intimation that this grand trunk line should be so located as to avoid Brazil entirely, on account of what you conceive to have been a particularly unjust proceeding on the part of the Brazilian government, against one of your clients, Mrs. Fiedler; but if it should appear t at, geographically and topographically, the proper route for such a line would be through Brazil, and not on the Pacific side of the Andes, nor high up along the eastern slope of the Cordilleras, it might be deemed advisable to lay the track just where Nature calls loudest for it, regardless of all *now-existing* national peculiarities and delinquencies. Slavery, for instance, one of the bases of your hostility, may perhaps be completely abolished in Brazil before the Three Americas Railway, under any ordinary methods of construction, can become an accomplished fact.

I perceive that you are enthusiastic in regard to the future of St. Louis. Thirty years ago I was equally so, and so I am yet. I have seen no reason at all to change the favorable opinion which I then expressed in various published writings and reports, indicating my unbounded faith in its future greatness. I recognize and admit the fact that Chicago has since gone far beyond my anticipations at the time mentioned; but meanwhile St. Louis has steadily advanced on the way to be, as I then prognosticated, the mightiest inland city on the continent. Her rapid growth since 1850, the wonderful development of the grandest valley on the globe, and, recently, the successful deepening of the mouth of the Mississippi River, whereby a navigable channel has been secured for the largest ocean vessels, (a

national improvement effected through the indomitable
energy and perseverance of Capt. James B. Eads, Civil
Engineer,) and the additional works projected for bettering
in general the boating business on the Father of Waters,
all point to St. Lou:s as the grand central entrepot and commercial metropolis of this vast Valley. It will, of course,
require some time to develop fully the effect of the service
of the Eads Jetties upon the commerce of the Mississippi
Valley; but the commercial world is already learning that
the magnificent water-way between St. Louis and the Gulf
of Mexico is destined to be (as I long since predicted,) the
avenue or current of the largest inland trade that has ever
existed upon the earth.   Whatever number of east and west
and north and south railroads may be built, it will yet be.
seen that a very large proportion of the heavy articles of
commerce will be conveyed in barges between St. Louis
and the mouth of the Mississippi.   Independently of this
consideration, however, St. Louis, from her commanding position, must always remain a great railroad center.   The city
of St. Louis is literally founded upon a rock; and the rock
is so advantageously placed, by nature, that, as time pro-
gresses, it will be seen that there can be no formidable rival
to her eventual supremacy.   I am not therefore in the least
surprised at your enthusiasm for the Three Americas Railway
on the one hand, and for the city of St. Louis on the other.

Of late, as I dare say you yourself have noticed, there
has been manifested an unmistakable sort of jealousy on
the part of the New England politicians against the great
Valley of the Mississippi.   Those lynx-eyed politicians are
beginning to fear that they will no longer be able to control
the commerce of this extraordinarily fertile and extensive
region; and, in my opinion, they ought not to control it.
As I have said and written, years ago, the Mississippi Valley should control itself; and I have no doubt it will soon

do so. Moreover, the shaping and the exercising of the policy of our whole Union would, I believe, be much more just and safe in the hands of the voters of the Mississippi Valley than it is ever likely to be in the hands of Eastern capitalists and other Eastern leaders, who have, for eighty or ninety years, almost invariably exhibited their ruling passion of insatiable and unscrupulous greed. It will doubtless be well for our Republic to continue, broadly, in name and in fact, the United States of America, and not suffer itself to be merged or dwarfed into either the reality or the appelation of the United States of New England. As is generally known, many excellent people in the upper portions of the Mississippi Valley are from New England. That is well, very well indeed,—and there is ample room thereabout for millions more of the same worthy and desirable kind of immigrants. Throughout that grandest of earth's valleys there is a most bracing and wholesome atmosphere, which enlarges and liberalizes and purifies the minds of all those who have established homes within its ennobling influence.

Sincerely yours,

W. MILNOR ROBERTS.

FROM THE HON. JOSÉ FRANCISCO LOPEZ.*

[Translation.]

BUENOS AYRES, ARGENTINE REPUBLIC.
February 25, 1880.

HINTON R. HELPER, ESQ., *St. Louis, Mo.*

DEAR SIR: It affords me much pleasure to acknowledge receipt of your letter of the 1st of December, inclosing a

---

*A learned and eminent member of the bar at Buenos Ayres.

H. R. H.

copy of your communication to the Argentine Government, in relation to your proposed Longitudinal Railway from Hudson Bay to the Strait of Magellan. I shall be very happy to comply with your request for my earnest coöperation in this Republic. You are quite right in addressing yourself directly to the Government here, requesting its recognition of the right of priority for your scheme.

The undertaking is one of such colossal magnitude that it may require a very considerable amount of time and labor to convince the various peoples of Spanish America of its feasibility. As regards the energetic and progressive people of your own country, who have already built the longest railroad in the world, running all the way from the Atlantic to the Pacific, and so connecting both great Oceans as the natural arms of the American Republic, they will be less slow in comprehending the immense advantages foreshadowed in your stupendous project. Your nation is rapidly becoming a marvel of success in human affairs. The United States of America have grown up healthfully and robustly in the battle with Nature, bravely grappling and overcoming the most formidable obstacles in all kinds of industries, discoveries and inventions. Herein we clearly perceive the vocation and mission of the American people. They are at once the prophets and the accomplishers of mighty achievements; thus, almost as if by magic, drawing the future into the present, and anticipating the life, wealth and happiness of many centuries in one. Such is the undaunted spirit and the originality of creative power of the Anglo-American race.

The intercontinental unity of America can be realized only by means of the commercial unity of railway arteries pervading its entire superficies. Then will the United States of America furnish the Spanish American continent with living examples of their own industrial methods and thrift; at the same time infusing among us and putting in practice their lofty spirit of civil self-government and national manhood. Thus far the regenerating and invigorating regions of the North have been inaccessible to South America, the latter being entangled and enslaved by her long-established paganism of idolatry for unworthy persons and dead forms, lowered beneath the standard of sound principles, antagonistic to truth and honor, and incompatible with the gentle and harmonious attributes of good society. Personal adulation and hero-worship are the besetting sins of South America; and the ecclesiastical and military idols of our peoples have almost invariably proved to be the desolators of their respective countries. Politics and institutions have been framed and controlled by them with the same degree of facility and selfishness as are manifested by theatrical managers who manipulate machinery and decorations for the performances of an engaged troupe; the audiences—society in general—being but too often mere passive spectators of the farcical scenes of peculation; and themselves afterward entrapped into the ruinous responsibility of defraying all the expenses of a series of the most demoralizing dramas ever enacted. What is needed, as a means of doing away with the terrible evils here complained of, is a closer and more general intercourse of the people of the United States with the Republics of Central and South America. The vastly important desideratum thus apparent will be amply supplied in the Three Americas Railway.

No longer is it admissible for our peoples in Spanish America to drowse away their lives in apathy and indolence, muffled with the mummeries of mere artificial forms, symphonies of patriotism, and constitutional rhetoric. Stagnation will always result in physical or political epidemics of serious if not fatal tendencies. No man, no people, may ever reasonably expect to produce sound fruits in the fields of Nature without first bestowing upon the ground earnest and intelligent preparation.   Good crops of grain will grow only as a reward for man's industrious and judicious tillage of the soil.   When people are idle and indifferent to Right and Truth, they incur at once the imminent danger of intense suffering from two causes,—a deficiency of bread, and an aggravated condition of political servitude.   Thus victimized in great degree through their own foibles and faults, they soon become the slaves of the merest pretenders, and toil and fight and bleed and die, never for the maintenance of an exalted idea, nor for the establishment of a grand principle, but always and only in the immediate interest of designing persons, for whose individual aggrandizement the lives and properties of whole nations are not unfrequently imperiled.   Such is the Alpha and the Omega of a large majority of our South and Central American revolutions. With very few exceptions, and with slight modifications, this is the synthesis of the history and the philosophy of the history of all Spanish America.   The chronic disease is a chronic glamour, a chronic falsity, intermixed with poisonous compounds, masked and concealed under the name of public good in theory, yet never bringing forth anything but public misery in practice.   In several respects, the frame of our system is as wrong as its working.   Too often the management of our affairs of government is intended only to further personal ends; just as if the government itself were a grist-mill belonging entirely to the officials, and to be used by them exclusively for the trituration of their own cereals.

Your own mighty Republic, the United States of America, being already connected by railroads with the northern frontier of Mexico, it is to be expected that the first material work on the Three Americas Railway will be done there. The track will then be laid down through Mexico and the Central American Republics, crossing the Isthmus of Darien, and entering South America through the portals of the United States of 'Columbia.   Thence it will be brought through Ecuador, Peru, and Bolivia, into the Argentine Republic.   Our Congress at Buenos Ayres has already wisely sanctioned the law for the extension of the Argentine Central Railway from Tucuman to the frontier of Jujuy.   This important extension will be completed in the course of a few years; and we shall thereby secure for ourselves a large part of the commerce of Bolivia, and also a liberal and profitable share of trade with several other portions of the interior of our own continent.   The Southern Railway of Buenos Ayres is now completed and in operation as far as Azul, about three hundred miles southward, in the very direction of the Straits of Magellan.

Your deposit of five thousand dollars in gold, with a committee of discernment and discrimination, for five of the best attainable essays on the subject of your projected Three Americas Railway, will doubtless secure for that gigantic undertaking such relevant preliminary investigation and action as will soon eventuate in a perfect corroboration of your own views.   For us in South America, as also for the peoples of Central America and Mexico, the meaning of your enterprise is new life, new interests, closer commercial and social and international intercourse, and more equitable and friendly relations of every nature, all based upon the superexcellent civilities and industries of peace and progress.   Your people will find on our continent a new world of raw material for your manufacturers, a new world of markets for your merchandise, and a new world for the unlimited exercise of the genius of your incomparable inventors, artisans and mechanics.   Believe me,—whole colonies from the United States will be welcomed throughout our southern continent, as the bringers of the benefits and blessings of a race which bears in its blood and spirit the living germs of manly labor and true liberty.

Yours sincerely,

JOSÉ FRANCISCO LOPEZ.

JUDGE ZUVIRIA* TO MR. RODRIGUEZ.

[Translation.]

ROSARIO, ARGENTINE REPUBLIC, *August* 23, 1880.
FRANCISCO RODRIGUEZ, ESQ., *Buenos Ayres.*

MY DEAR SIR : The newspaper containing a description of Mr. Helper's colossal railway project, and for which I sincerely thank you, came to hand in due time ; and just, when I was about to write to you in recognition of his superb conception, so worthy of an American in whose lexicon there seems to be no room for the word Impossible, I had the additional pleasure of receiving your epistolary favor of the 12th instant.

This grand and feasible proposition, set forth in a manner and with the means necessary to secure at once such full and just consideration as will lead to its ultimate realization, is not merely sufficient for the glory of one man, but it is

---

*The writer of this excellent letter, Fenelon Zuviria, was formerly one of the most distinguished members of the Argentine Congress. He is now Judge of the Argentine Federal Court for the Provinces of Santa Fe and Cordova. What Demosthenes was to Greece, what Cicero was to Rome, what Castelar is to Spain,—the greatest orator of his country,—that is what Zuviria is to the Argentine Republic. Clumsy-tongued Americans (like myself,) not sufficiently familiar with the poetic and musical beauty of Spanish pronunciation, will not be apt to utter his name correctly; but they will come very near it if, with a fair degree of liquidness and animation of voice, they will say *Sooveéreeah.*

H. R. H.

moreover quite enough to raise his memory to the height
of the very greatest benefactors of the human race; a glory
serene, limpid, without blood, without pain, and without
tears ; a pure and enviable glory arising only from the largest and best intentions reciprocated in action by half the
world; a glory of the most profound tranquillity and sweet-
ness, which will henceforth be joyously entoned by a thousand millions of benefited and grateful voices.

What, then, remains to be said upon the more immediate
and transcendant results of this gigantic undertaking,—an
undertaking fraught with prosperity and progress for all the
nations of America from this very moment, and likewise for
the whole world hereafter ?   Neither he who conceived the enterprise, nor those who will execute it, will ever be able to
measure either the magnitude or the magnificence of the results which are destined to flow from it ; as, in fact, no one, by
a single effort of the mind, can well comprehend the prodigious importance of substituting on an immense continent
civilization for barbarism; of the orderly and innocent lives
of myriads of enlightened human beings, in place of countless numbers of ferocious savages and wild beasts; o
boundless and abundant fields and harvests of grain, instead
of interminable deserts; of the merry and marvelous and
multifarious music of mills and other manufacturing establishments, in contrast with the idle and ear-offending din of
the insects and other meager-pated and unimprovable denizens of the forest;—yes, and even of life for death !

No hyperbole at all is there in denominating this a tremendous and glorious project ; for such a project it really
is ; signifying in effect the annihilation of distance ; looking
to the accomplishment in a week of the work of a year ;
and increasing and multiplying enormously those vast stores
of wealth, and that particularly precious kind of money, so
universally current among all the industrious and deserving

28

classes in the word Time. This undertaking, successfully carried out, will strongly and inseparably unite, with an iron embrace, all the Americas forever and ever; and under its its increasingly beneficial operations will be gradually consolidated an impregnable series of the freest, the happiest, the wealthiest, the most virtuous, and the most powerful nationalities upon the face of the whole earth.

So runs my candid judgment in regard to this daring and sublime proposition; not with the affectionate enthusiasm of a friend, prone to err, but with the maturity and calmness of severe reflection. I therefore desire to add my humble but sincere voice to the chorus of soul-stirring praises which will be richly merited by the originator of the scheme, and also by those who will advance it and carry it forward to a happy terminaton. The idea has been prudently and auspiciously launched; it is practicable; it threatens no evil, but is overflowing and brilliant with fair promises and prospects of good; and very powerful indeed, if not irresistible, are the impulses toward its perfect development.

. Whatever may be the nature or the extent of the obstacles or opposition to which this unequaled undertaking, as a human work, will inevitably be subjected for a time, yet, as for myself, I do not doubt in the least that it will be eventually crowned with complete success.

The North Americans, not invariably but generally in the right, are much accustomed to the use of a very brief and expressive phrase: Having an opinion and purpose founded on a conviction of the absolute integrity of their motives, they say, Go ahead!—and onward they go, nothing hindering, and no one daring to attempt to prevent their predetermined steps. They have been going ahead for a long time, and are still going ahead; generally, too, in ways and by methods most admirable. Let us Argentines applaud them on every score of well-doing; and may we and all other South Americans soon learn to emulate them, even in their highest and best achievements. By a rigidly moral discipline of our natures, and by a thorough examination of our own incentives, let us, like them, first prove ourselves in the right, and then manfully exert ourselves to rival and even outdo them, if we can, in the noble science and art and skill of going ahead!

Apropos of our North American friend's incomparable conception, I do not deem it out of place to inform you that, during the evening of the very day on which I received your last letter, at a farewell dinner given to the Agent here of the Bank of London, at which complimentary banquet numerous distinguished gentlemen, native and foreign, were present, I had the pleasure—as it chimed in exactly with the purpose—to heartily commend and advocate this sagacious and splendid scheme; thus rendering, in part at least, merited praise to its projector. Nor need it occasion any surprise that this incident of the entertainment was warmly welcomed with demonstrations of enthusiasm and applause. It is proper for me to assure you, however, that the humility of the orator was totally eclipsed by the magnitude and grandeur of the enterprise proposed. At that reunion were several gentlemen who were well acquainted with the projector of the Three Americas Railway, at Buenos Ayres, many years ago, when he was the Consul there for the United States.

Sincerely, your friend and servant,

FENELON ZUVIRIA.

THE END.

INDEX—ALPHABETICAL.

469

www.ingramcontent.com/pod-product-compliance
Lightning Source LLC
Chambersburg PA
CBHW052346110726
47901CB00005B/1381